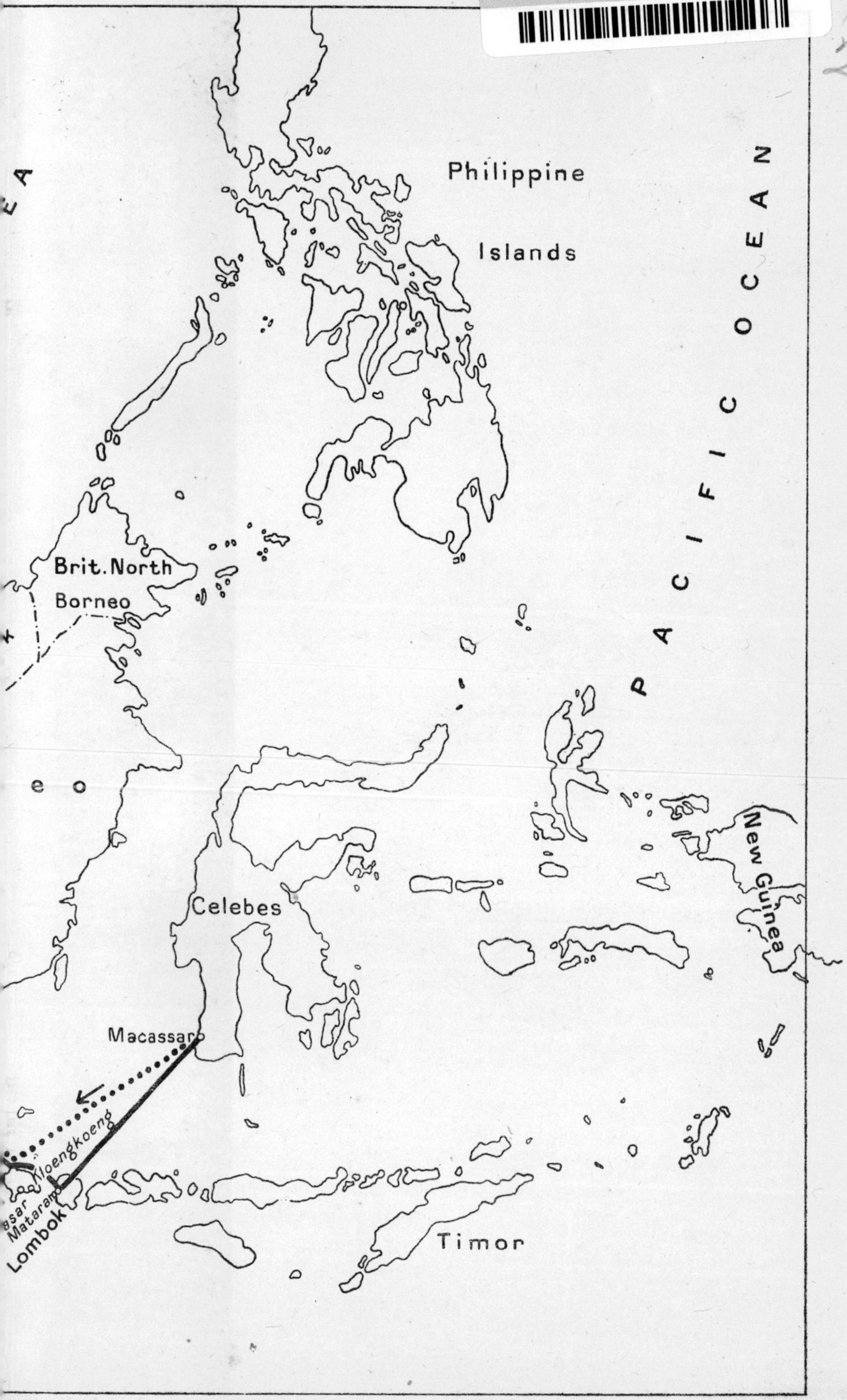

E A
Philippine
Islands
PACIFIC OCEAN
Brit. North
Borneo
e o
Celebes
New Guinea
Macassar
Kloengkoeng
asar
Mataram
Lombok
Timor

RETURN TO
MALAYA

By the same Author

MEMOIRS OF A BRITISH AGENT
RETREAT FROM GLORY

R. H. BRUCE LOCKHART

RETURN TO MALAYA

PUTNAM

---

42 GREAT RUSSELL STREET
LONDON

First Published November 1936

PRINTED IN GREAT BRITAIN BY ROBERT MACLEHOSE AND CO. LTD.
THE UNIVERSITY PRESS, GLASGOW

CONTENTS

"I HAVE *seen so many phantoms defile through the dream of life.*"

BOOK I

TRAVELLER'S HOLIDAY

"IT IS better for mankind to be impressionable than reflective. Nothing humanely great—great, I mean, as affecting a whole mass of lives—has come from reflection."

CHAPTER ONE

THE ISHMAELITES OF this world are sincere and honest people. But they have this defect. More than any other category of mankind they suffer from the sin of self-deception. When they express a desire to turn their back on the rising sun and settle down, they think the desire is genuine. More often than not it is only temporary. They are troubled by the temptations of the wide spaces and by the restlessness of unrealisable dreams. Almost in spite of themselves they are forced to strike their tents and to be off again on the endless road of travel.

In *British Agent* I referred to "that East which I should never see again". When I wrote that line I was sincere. At that time nothing seemed less probable than that I should go back to the East. In 1928 I had exchanged a modest sinecure for a journalist's life with the Beaverbrook Press, because I was engulfed in debt. There seemed little chance of my rising to the surface of freedom again. To me, however, an improbability is a direct incentive to make the improbable not merely probable but certain. Very soon after my arrival in Fleet Street I felt the old restlessness coursing through my veins. Gradually it took the form of a desire to re-visit the scenes of my youth in Malaya.

There was certainly nothing very definite about it. As a boy Pierre Loti, who wanted to be a missionary, was shown a picture of Angkor and knew at once that one day he would visit it. At nine Joseph Conrad put his finger on the then unexplored heart of the map of Africa and saw his future in the Congo. Although I have spent more than twenty-five years of my life in foreign countries, I have never had any premonition about my movements. As far as my restlessness is concerned, travel, I suppose, is in my blood. Unlike the Preacher I have not yet reached the stage when I can say that I have seen everything under the sun and found it vanity.

3

Moreover, a long line of roving ancestors has left me the East as a kind of Galtonian legacy.

Two of my uncles were pioneers of the plantation rubber industry in Malaya. A cousin, a former cavalry officer, went there to die after a long life as a rolling stone. Two cousins are there now, and I have a brother, a colonel in the Indian army, who has spent the best years of his life in Afghanistan and on the North-West frontier.

Some blame, too, for my *Wanderlust* attaches to my father. During the winter Sunday nights of our boyhood in Scotland he used to read to my brother and to me aloud. Sandwiched between *Ivanhoe*, *Quentin Durward*, *Treasure Island*, and *The Pilgrim's Progress* were occasional books of adventure. And of these my favourite was Mayne Reid's *The Castaways*, a tale of shipwreck and adventure in the Malay Archipelago. The book had been given to my father as a prize for geography when he was a boy of twelve at Partick Academy in 1870. I have it still. In one sense it has influenced my life more than any other book. For its account of giant durian trees, of sharks, of men adrift in an open boat on a tropical sea without food and, above all, without water made a lasting impression on my mind.

The impression had active consequences. At the age of twenty-one I turned my back on the "crammer" which was preparing me for the Civil Service examination and went East to Malaya to join my uncles, who foretold fortune and favour in the new plantation rubber industry.

I had spent three years in Malaya. They had been mis-spent years. I had been sent to open up a rubber estate in a Malay district where there were no other white men. I had caused a minor sensation by carrying off Amai, the beautiful ward of the Dato' Klana, the local Malay prince. It had been my first romance. And it had very nearly caused political complications. The Dato', an old friend with whom I had played football, had been hurt. His family, and especially his mother, had been angry, and for some weeks I had been subjected to a persistent pressure. Amai herself had been put in Coventry by her own compatriots. The courage of her race had never failed her, and for some months we had been happy.

Then had come chronic ill-health. The doctors pronounced malaria, but there were many people who said that I had been poisoned. One day my uncle had come out to my bungalow, had bundled my emaciated body into a motor-car, and had packed me off home via Japan and America.

My Malayan venture had brought me neither credit nor cash. But now, twenty-five years afterwards, in the futile London of Fleet Street, it was to Malaya, the golden Chersonese of the early voyagers, the Insulinde of the poets, that my thoughts turned, and not to Russia or to Central Europe where I had spent what most people would call the exciting years of my life. "Lockhart in Quest of his Youth" seemed an attractive dream.

British Agent and, in a minor degree, my enthusiasm for Loti were instrumental in giving material shape to my dream. *British Agent*, which provided the financial substance of my voyage, was begun at the old monastery house of Millicent, Duchess of Sutherland, in Anjou. It was to her tiny villa in the Vendée that I went to celebrate the book's success and to spend my first earnings as an author.

It was a pleasant holiday. There was good food and good wine. A huge Mercédès was at my disposal, and within easy range there was the whole of the Clemenceau country to explore. I made numerous visits to "La Bicocque", the little sea-swept cottage to which the embittered cynic of Versailles withdrew when his own countrymen repudiated him.

Clemenceau had carried his bitterness into the grave. In the cottage, where everything, even to the hair-wash and the toothbrush, had been left exactly as it was in his life-time, there was a little writing-desk. It was a primitive collapsible affair which pulled out from a window overlooking the Atlantic. On the desk were the quill pens with which he

wrote his books and a sand-box in place of blotting-paper.
On the immediate right was a large bookcase and in the
shelf nearest to his hand an English book entitled *The Man
Who Didn't Win The War*. The sub-title was "An Exposure
of Lloyd Georgism"!

It was a curious manifestation of the Tiger's egotism,
for "L. G." and he, united by the bond of courage, had
worked well together. And if both men had lost the peace
they had been indisputably the two chief agents of the Allies'
victory.

But it was not only the Clemenceau country which interested me. Within motoring distance was Rochefort, the
home town of my boyhood hero, Loti. The little Frenchman
had been the first French author that I had ever met and, indeed, after Andrew Lang, the first author on whom I had
ever set eyes. The meeting, like so many meetings with the
heroes of one's student days, had been something of a shock.
But it had not diminished my admiration for Loti as a
writer. I had read all his works, and *Le Mariage de Loti* and
Les Désenchantées had been the propelling force that finally
turned my footsteps Eastward. To Rochefort, therefore, I
made a pilgrimage of gratitude.

How well I remember that visit: the permission shyly
sought from M. Samuel Viaud, the author's son; the grey
November morning; the motor-drive through the bocage of
La Vendée; the marshlands of La Rochelle, where as a
schoolboy and Oxford undergraduate Mr. Anthony Eden,
the young British Foreign Secretary, used to come to learn
French from a Protestant pastor; the long alleys of tamarisks,
and then just before Rochefort itself, the superb view of the
Atlantic with the tiny Ile d'Aix, where Napoleon spent his
last days on French soil before surrendering to the captain of
the *Bellerophon*.

During the first half of the eighteenth century, when
France still held her colonies in the New World, Rochefort
was a great port. To-day, the town has lost its ancient glory.

It has ceased even to be a naval base, and the neighbouring town of Brouage, still famous as the home of Champlain, the founder of Quebec, is now a ruin left high and dry by the receding sea.

But, if the remote past is dead, the immediate past is very much alive. The spirit of Loti haunts the town. There is a fine Loti street, a Lycée Loti, and several Loti charities. And at No. 141, in the street which now bears his name, is the Loti house, kept piously to-day by the son in the same exotic state as the father left it.

At the door I was received by a fine old servant in a black and yellow waistcoat. He was not "Mon Frère Yves", the sailor hero of Loti's most successful novel. But he was the next best thing—an old rating who had taken part with Loti in the Tonkin and Boxer campaigns. He bowed me into a room full of family portraits, waved an arm towards the Japanese room heavy with Buddhas and Samurai armour, piloted me through a gimcrack Louis XVI salon, and left me standing in a vast banqueting hall with a high roof, a stair-case, and an inside balcony. I surmised correctly that this was the medieval hall. At this point in came M. Viaud, a dapper, slim Frenchman, very neatly dressed, with small black moustache, deep-set, very earnest eyes, and a charming modesty.

Under his guidance I now made a complete tour of the house. Upstairs there was another period room with old oak doors and stained glass windows taken mainly from local ruins. I felt as if I were being conducted through an antique store. At every moment I expected to come face to face with a waxwork figure of Loti himself. M. Viaud, however, was upset because the house was undergoing repairs, and it was to an accompaniment of polite apology that I made my way over rubble and loose stones to the top floor.

Here was Loti's Turkish room fitted up as a mosque with the actual stones from the famous ruined mosque at Damascus. This was the best room in the house, and the presence of praying mats and Turkish coffins was a reminder not only of

Loti's love of the East, but also of his morbid interest in Death. Here, too, dressed as a Turk, he used to sit for hours in search of atmosphere. I ought to have been impressed, but in Rochefort so much exoticism seemed out of place. Instead, I marvelled at the filial devotion of M. Viaud, who lives with his wife and sons in this literary mausoleum.

Like most authors Loti was an egotist. His son is a devout Protestant whose name in Rochefort is a synonym for unselfishness and good works. There are three Loti grandchildren. Two are boys. They wish to go into the Navy. Fifty years ago, when Loti was at the height of his fame, a Paris professor asked his class to put down on paper their choice of profession. Forty out of fifty put down "sailor". To-day, the highbrows affect to ignore Loti, although it is less than twenty years since Anatole France said "de nous tous, il est le plus sûr de durer".

From the Turkish room we passed into a little attic with white-washed walls. At one end was a small iron bedstead with a crucifix above it; at the other a tiny washstand, a chest of drawers, and a wooden bench covered with a white cloth by way of toilet table. In the midst of this austere simplicity there hung on the wall a set of fencing foils and two masks: a useful reminder that this amazing little man, who in the salons of Paris wore high heels and rouged his cheeks, was a great gymnast who did his physical exercises daily until almost the last months of his life. Above the chest of drawers, too, was the "citation du jour", the French equivalent to "mentioned in despatches", commending the work in the war of the Commandant du Vaisseau, Julien Viaud. The "citation" was signed by Marshal Pétain. Julien Viaud was Loti's real name.

This was the proper room for a Viaud with several generations of sailors behind him. A Viaud grandfather of Loti, a naval gunner, had died in Tarifa hospital from wounds received at Trafalgar. A Viaud uncle had perished on the *Medusa*, the ship which was bearing the new French Governor to the Senegal in 1817, after we had returned that colony to France after the Napoleonic Wars. The wreck, marked by a combination of bravery and cowardice almost unparalleled in the history of the seas, is immortalised by Géricault's picture, "The Raft of the *Medusa*". A brother, a naval doctor and twelve years older than Loti, had died of fever in Saigon.

A man of this stock had no need of all this exotic junk to remind him of his voyages. Here in this tiny white bedroom was the real Loti. Here, too, was the neatness which comes naturally to a naval officer whose life has been spent in confined space.

In the room there was one extraneous object: a box containing a cast of Loti's tiny woman-like hand and a collection of his gloves. The box had belonged to Madame Barthou, the wife of the statesman who was killed by the assassin of King Alexander at Marseilles. After her death it had been sent back to the Loti house as an exhibit. It was a token of the affection and hero-worship which Loti could inspire in women.

I have a capacity for making pilgrimages. I know none which has made me so dissatisfied with myself as that visit to Loti's house in Rochefort. Its immediate effect was to translate my dream of going East again into reality. And when in 1935 temptation presented itself in concrete form, I fell resolutely. For twelve years Lady Rosslyn has been my sheet-anchor and my better conscience. Five feet two inches of Irish Catholic saint, she is a woman who in spite of constant disappointment still believes that every moment of time is an opportunity for a fresh start. One afternoon she told me that Lord Rosslyn and she were going to Malaya for the winter. I looked out at the grey November sky and found it comfortless. Then I banged my fist decisively on the arm of my chair. "By Saint Andrew," I said, "I'll go with you."

The next thing to do was to obtain the necessary leave of absence. That same evening I sat down and racked my brains for a sufficiently good reason to enable me to retain my job

B

and at the same time to be away from London long enough
in order to make the tour I had already contemplated. The
excuses seemed futile and unconvincing. A friendly consulta-
tion with the managing director of my newspaper brought
me good advice, and the next day I sat down to write the
plain truth to Lord Beaverbrook. I told him that after six
and a half years in London I was sick of the sight of its buildings, the smell of its fumes, and the sound of its traffic. I
stressed the desire for the Eastern sun. I asked for three
months' leave of absence. His reply to my letter was not only
favourable but friendly. It ended with the words: "I suppose
you are going in search of the little wooden shoes."

The remark flattered me as much as it surprised me. The
flattery came from the fact that after an interval of three
years Lord Beaverbrook should remember the episode of
the little wooden shoes. It refers to the passage in *British
Agent* when my uncle comes out to my bungalow in Malaya
to lift me from my sick-bed and to take me away. It is the
hour of my parting with Amai. As the motor-car turns the
corner of my compound, my last view of my Malayan
home is of Amai's little wooden shoes on the steps at the
entrance to my bungalow.

I was surprised, too, by Lord Beaverbrook's prescience. I
had not forgotten Amai. After the war I had made inquiries
through one of my highly-placed official friends in Malaya
and had been informed that she was dead. The information
had left a permanent if shadowy regret, tinged sometimes
with remorse. But not until I read Lord Beaverbrook's letter
did I realise how much my desire to re-visit the East was influenced by memories of Amai and by a Loti-esque sentiment to pay a last tribute to her grave.

The days passed rapidly and pleasantly in the planning of
my voyage. For with the comparatively short time at my
disposal I had to have a plan. My programme was to land at
Singapore, revisit my old haunts in the Malay States, go up
through the new states to Bangkok, cross from Bangkok to

Saigon, taking Angkor *en route*, proceed by steamer from Saigon to Batavia, visit the native states of Java, make a tour of the Outer Islands of the Malay Archipelago to seek for fresh Conrad material, and on the way back "do" Bali and as much of Sumatra as my time would permit.

It was an ambitious if slightly hackneyed programme. It might have to be cut down. But Bali was an integral part. True it is that all my friends, both British and Dutch, who had spent a life-time in the East Indies, showed little enthusiasm about the place, holding one tropical island to be very like another. But Hollywood or Mr. Roosevelt had "discovered" Bali, and social America was in the process of going Bali-mad. In the United States there was already a considerable literature dealing with the various seductions of this last Paradise on earth. The fever had communicated itself to London. Obviously, I should have to visit Bali.

I spent some delightful and expensive hours in ordering a new tropical outfit from my tailor. As this artist commented on the growing circumference of my figure, my thoughts went back to General Mackensen and to Berlin in 1931. The general was then eighty-two. He was in a new uniform when I met him. Someone complimented him on his figure. It was his boast that he had not had to have his waist-line altered since the day sixty years before when he ordered his first uniform as a subaltern. Twenty-five years ago I had possessed the huge tropical outfit which every extravagant young man acquires in the East. Where it was now nobody knew. But I knew and my tailor knew that, if it were found, it would be of no use to me to-day.

Before I was safely away from London, I had one last-minute agony of suspense. I had completed all my arrangements. I had equipped myself with a bagful of letters of recommendation, including an extraordinarily useful one from my old friend Sir William Oudendijk, the former Netherlands Minister to Russia, who had arranged my exchange for Litvinoff after I had been imprisoned by the Bolsheviks at a critical moment in my existence in 1918, and had subsequently been made a K.C.M.G. for his services in securing the release of arrested British officials. I had taken and paid for my steamer ticket, when a week before sailing I walked into the shipping agency in the Haymarket to see the list of passengers. The first name on the list, opposite a whole string of cabins, was "Lord Beaverbrook and party". My heart thumped twice and then seemed to stop. Lord Beaverbrook has many qualities. When the sun in his world is shining, he is a brilliant conversationalist, witty, entertaining and instructive. When the clouds gather, one feels his presence even when he is not in the room. Not even his greatest admirer would prescribe him as a rest-cure. I was seeking an escape from Fleet Street. Here was Fleet Street descending on me in the person of its Napoleon. It was too late for me to react against this disturbing coincidence, for the remedy was now beyond the powers of human agency. Fortunately, Lord Beaverbrook had also reserved accommodation for other parts of the world. In the end he went to South America.

Early in January I took the train at Victoria for Genoa, where I was to join the Netherlands steamship *Oldenbarnevelt*, specially selected because its Batavian stewards and "boys" would provide me with the opportunity of repairing the ravages which time had made in my knowledge of the Malay language. There was a lilt in my step and a fierce exultation in my heart. There was a contraband talisman in my bag: a packet of home-made Esthonian marzipans which I had to post from Paris to Mr. Somerset Maugham, then living in his beautiful villa at Cap Ferrat. This vicarious homage to the greatest living English writer on the East or, for that matter, on any subject, seemed a good omen. The fates would be propitious. I had shed my worries as easily as a snake sloughs its skin. For three months I should be as free as a man can be in this modern world of ours.

CHAPTER TWO

THE PERFECTION OF organisation has ironed all the creases out of modern travel. To-day, it is easier to go without a hitch from Southampton to Singapore than from London to Littlehampton or from New York to Newark. There is, too, more punctuality and less excitement. When I crossed through the Fascist-guarded barrier at Genoa and set foot on board the *Oldenbarnevelt* I knew that, unless I was on my guard, I should be drawn into the hum-drum routine of ship life in which one day is exactly like another.

It was Goethe who said that the English carry their tea-caddies with them round the world. To-day, the tea-caddie has been replaced by a gramophone, a cocktail shaker, and the latest best-seller from the Times Book Club. Otherwise, the aphorism stands. The English who can afford to travel run true to pattern. As far as their external behaviour is concerned, they have come through the same sausage-machine. This unimaginative uniformity is their strength and their weakness. One can tell without mental effort what they will say, what they will wear, what they will eat and drink, at any given hour of the day. With rare exceptions they are uninteresting as travel-companions. They have seen everything. They are not interested in history. On the big liners, at any rate, ninety per cent. of them are semi-religious maniacs in search of the twin English gods of Health and Sunshine. Their temple is the sports-deck. Their ceremonial robes are shorts and a sleeveless cricket shirt.

They are extraordinarily competent. Without fuss and without undue extravagance they secure the sunniest spot on the sun-deck when it is cold and the coolest spot on the shady deck when it is hot. They know exactly how much to tip and at the same time they obtain the best service no matter by what line they may be travelling. And they have the knack, acquired by birth and by education, of making all other races, including even Scots and Irish, feel uncomfortably in-

ferior in their presence. This inferiority complex is responsible for most of the rude comments which foreigners make
about the English.

Rudeness rightly has few defenders, but in the story of the
two English peers and the American naval officer, my sympathies have always been with the American. The two peers
met on board the old *Mauretania*. The one had seen everything in the Northern hemisphere; the other everything in
the Southern. As they leant against the cocktail bar, they went
through the long list of the places they had visited in a drawl
which was limp with boredom. As gloom settled over the
room, an American naval officer, who had done himself
proud in side-cars, interrupted them. "Say, have you boys
ever had delirium tremens?" There was no answer.

The question was repeated. This time one of the Englishmen replied rather coldly: "No, Sir, and I don't want
to."

"Then let me tell you", said the American, not a whit
abashed, "you've never been anywhere and you've never
seen anything."

On the *Oldenbarnevelt* the bulk of the passengers were English with a handful of Americans and Dutch thrown in by
way of ballast. There was, too, one German, and he was the
most interesting figure on board. A world-famous chemist,
he had invented the substitute for nitro-glycerine in 1917
when Germany ran short of that essential product for explosives. As he himself said, he was the man who had prolonged
the war for another year. He had received the Iron Cross for
his services. He was not so proud of them now. On board
ship he played bridge and smoked his cigars. He was courteous, kind and gentle—above all, gentle. He did not look as
if he could ever have robbed a bird's nest or put a pin
through a butterfly.

The interest and, indeed, the charm of a voyage depend
almost entirely on the liveliness of one's imagination, and
to mine I had made up my mind in advance to give free rein.

Here was the Mediterranean, the home of the gods and the immortals, with more history in one of its waves than the Atlantic has in the whole expanse of its 24,000,000 square miles. Here were scenes to be re-visited and first impressions of one's youth to be recaptured: queer, delightful impressions, sometimes obscure, sometimes altering their form, yet constantly recurring through the turmoil of the changing years. There was Bonifacio, the little Corsican town perched like an eagle's nest on the cliffs and guarding the Straits between Corsica and Sardinia. Most people remember the place as the garrison town of the young Napoleon Bonaparte. It was here that on January 21st, 1793, on the same day on which Louis XVI went to the guillotine, Napoleon himself was nearly murdered by mutineering sailors. He had taken part in the ill-fated Sardinian campaign. Badly prepared and with troops recruited mainly from the revolutionaries of Marseilles, it had been a failure. At Bonifacio there had been a revolt. The French sailors of Admiral Trugnet had quarrelled with the Corsican volunteers. The Commandant Bonaparte had tried to intervene. The sailors had replied with "Ça Ira", had hurled the epithet "aristo" at him, and had struck him. Napoleon had been saved in the nick of time by the arrival of the local sheriff with reinforcements.

But in my mind it is not Napoleon whom the place invokes but Alphonse Daudet, the first real French author whom I ever read and whose *Lettres de Mon Moulin*, in spite of its grim associations as a school-book, is still one of my bedside favourites. At the entrance to Bonifacio lie the barren reefs of Lavizzi. You remember now Daudet's story of "The Agony of the *Semillante*", the French ship which, carrying 600 troops to the Crimean War, was broken to pieces on these needle-shaped rocks with the loss of all on board. You remember, too, the distinctive thrill of the story. Three weeks before, a French corvette had run ashore in the same way and in the same place. On that occasion the troops on board had been saved but only after hours of terror and ex-

posure. They had been sent back to Toulon. They had been
re-embarked on the *Semillante*, and their dead bodies were
found by the same Bonifacio peasants who had rescued them
three weeks before.

This is one of the stories which by early association with
the place are far more clearly, far more grimly imprinted on
my memory than all the horrors of the Russian revolution of
which I was an eye-witness. I did not see Bonifacio on my
way East. But on the return journey a Dutch captain, who
knew by heart every great story of the sea in literature, sailed
his ship right up to the cliffs until one could distinguish the
faces of the inhabitants on shore. In the stillness of a perfect
spring day both Corsica and Sardinia with the islands of
Maddalena, the Italian Gibraltar of the Tyrrhenian Sea, and
Caprera, the last home of Garibaldi, guarding the Strait,
looked peaceful enough. But I have seen them when the sun
is covered, and dark clouds accentuate the jagged, angry
edges of the rocks. Then French Corsica and Italian Sardinia
look like two war-scarred bulldogs who would be at each
other's throat.

Here in this queen of all seas were a thousand memories to
be revived. They should have begun at Genoa, which had
been my first port of call on my voyage East, twenty-seven
years ago. I tried to attune my mind to the past. But the blue
sky played havoc with my dreams. Behind the town the hills
were sprinkled with snow. I was like a schoolboy going
home for the holidays. In that moment the sunshine meant
more to me than sentiment. Genoa was the birthplace of
Columbus. There was even a Columbus house. But I was not
interested in Columbus. He had sailed West.

Garibaldi, too, had sailed from here on his Sicilian expedition. In my mind I saw his "red shirts" and thought immediately of the Genoa Conference of 1922. If I had played my
cards better in Russia, I should have been present in an official
capacity at that Conference. Against my will the ridiculous
figure of Chicherin kept obtruding itself before my eyes.

Then I remembered. It was at Genoa that Chicherin had appeared before the world in his famous morning-coat.

I knew the history of that morning-coat. For months on end in 1918 I had seen Chicherin every day in Moscow. He had always worn the same hideous, yellow-brown, tweed suit which he had brought to Russia with him from England. He had worn that suit so long that even his Bolshevik colleagues had rebelled against it. When the time came for him to represent the new Russia abroad at an international Conference, they felt that it was time to act.

One night Radek, the arch-jester of Moscow, had crept quietly into Chicherin's bedroom, had stolen the old brown suit, and had left in its place a well-cut morning-coat with striped trousers, white shirt, and all the other appurtenances of male vanity. He had then rushed back to the Kremlin, assembled the Commissars, and telephoned to Chicherin to tell him that Lenin wanted him immediately. A quarter of an hour later Chicherin, the most dutiful of all Lenin's lieutenants, had appeared with a hang-dog expression on his face and the new morning-coat on his back. From that moment the coat became the centre-piece of his wardrobe.

My frivolous mood lasted throughout the whole of that first day. I scanned the coast with my binoculars in an attempt to recognise the spot where Byron and Trelawney had watched Shelley's funeral pyre. But my heart was not in this Baedeker business, and when in the evening we passed Elba I was still under the influence of my improper levity.

In vain I tried to approach this altar of forgotten greatness with submissive respect. In summer one can see the statue erected by the Italians to Napoleon. But now the island looked like a black hippopotamus lying in the sea. Round the coast a few scattered lights shone from the various lighthouses. A cluster of electricity marked the position of Ferrajo.

I thought of all the Napoleon worshippers I had met in my life; of Lord Northcliffe telling Tom Clarke, then his news editor and subsequently author of that diverting book, *My*

Northcliffe Diary, not to miss Napoleon's hat at Fontainebleau and saying naïvely that he had tried it on and found it fitted; of Rabel, the Cuban, who had been my companion in my student days at Douai and who had spent the bountiful allowance of his millionaire sugar-planter father on Napoleon books, Napoleon pictures, and Napoleon relics; of Sidney Reilly, the Odessa Jew who was Britain's master-spy in the war and who had ruined himself in buying Napoleana.

By hazard I had picked up the night before in Paris a copy of Masson's *La Journée de Napoléon*. I had been painfully impressed by the small number of the Emperor's servants who had remained loyal to him in the hour of his adversity. Even Rustoum, his Mameluke whom he loved like a favourite dog, deserted him in 1814. I fell to wondering how many of any great man's henchmen would stand by him if he fell on evil days. I had been amused by the story of Napoleon's surgeon who, when the Emperor suddenly showered a pension, a title, and a lump sum of money on him, was so excited by this unexpected access of fortune that he took a horse from the Imperial stables at Fontainebleau and galloped off to Paris in the middle of the night. The inhabitants of Sycophantopolis are not renowned for their loyalty.

Among the domestics who remained faithful to Napoleon was a valet whose main usefulness to Napoleon was the fact that his foot was the same size as the great man's. His task in life was to try on and buy shoes for the Emperor. Great men are alike in the externals of their make-up. Lord Beaverbrook's valet, Albert, is much the same size as his master and is commonly supposed to try on and buy Lord Beaverbrook's suits. Nearly every day, too, I see a painting of that great gambler with life, the Earl of Rosslyn. It portrays, indeed, the head of its titled subject. But the body is the body of a groom whose figure resembled the once sylph-like figure of the noble earl. Lord Rosslyn puts comfort before pride. He would not have sat more than once for Titian himself.

This habit of engaging substitutes, now so popular with

the picture stars of Hollywood, goes back to the dawn of civilisation. One of Lord Carnarvon's most valuable discoveries at Luxor was the life-size mannequin of Tutankhamen, which now lies beside the Tutankhamen mummies in the Cairo museum. The mannequin was used by the Egyptian tailors for trying on the costumes of a monarch who was, doubtless, as restless as other great men have been, are now, and will be always.

After my first night on board I put a brake on my frivolity and settled down to follow the programme which I had prepared for myself. With characteristic egotism I had decided to take no part in the communal life of the ship. I should not waste my time on sports or cards. Indeed, I should rise with the sun and go to bed before the jazz-band started. I should work all morning on my Malay language and my Malay history. In the afternoons I might swim. In the evenings the panorama of the tropical sunset would be my only cinema. Above all, I should eschew the pleasures of the table and of the bar. I had wasted many opportunities in the past. On this occasion I should extract the maximum amount of pleasure from the old receipt of high thinking and plain living.

As far as my life on board ship was concerned, I stuck with a fair measure of success to this priggish programme both on my outward and on my homeward journeys.

When, therefore, on the afternoon of my second day on board we approached Stromboli I was in a more serious and more receptive mood. The weather, it is true, had broken, but I had made friends with the captain. With that attractive indifference to detail which characterises the English, one of my compatriots had told him that I was a successful writer of spy stories. The effect was magical. I was given the run of the bridge. The captain himself was an encyclopaedia of sea lore. When every now and then he threw out a feeler about secret service, I would assume the proper look of embarrassment and turn away. Then I would counter heavily with questions about the exact position of Scylla and Charybdis or the route followed by the Roman triremes. It was an admirable arrangement, for it was one-sided and the advantages were solely mine.

Stromboli I remembered very clearly from my first voyage East. Then I had passed it at night, and the red glow from the crater had induced a respectful awe. Now an innocuous-looking white smoke issued steadily from the top. Our approach was towards the crater side. Beneath the crater itself was a steep slide worn away by the lava and running sheer into the sea. It would have made a fearsome toboggan run. We passed within a stone's throw of the island, and at the most westerly point we came suddenly on a picturesque village with a score or two of flat-roofed villas. They seemed to be nestling in the very jaws of the crater.

Closer inspection, however, reveals a thin grass on the rocky slopes, some olive trees and a few vineyards. The inhabitants live on their wine and olives and on the fish they catch. There is another village at the south-east corner. Both afford a remarkable object-lesson of the diminishing effect of familiarity on danger. Stromboli, the mythical home of the wind god Aeolus, is an active volcano. Every now and then the seismographical station in Rome issues warnings to the islanders. Only a few days before we passed there had been a report of a threatened eruption and a government ship had been sent to take off the inhabitants. Very few had gone. Like many people in this noisy world I have, or fancy I have, a passion to own a small island. Stromboli would not be my first choice.

A hundred yards or so to the east of Stromboli is a little island which in the distance looked remarkably like one of those Italian brigantines which frequent these waters. The island is called Strombolini or "Little Stromboli". Mussolini, I suppose, means "Little Musso", although I doubt if the Duce would like to be considered in terms of the diminutive. Away to the south-west there was physical evidence of his power in the group of the Lipari Islands, looking very grim and barren in the grey winter light. They have played a grim part in history. Here in the first Punic War the Carthaginian Fleet fled for refuge after its first encounter with the Roman raven, the famous grappling machine invented by the Romans, in order to bridge the gulf between their own inferiority and Carthaginian invincibility on the sea. In these waters, too, Michael de Ruyter, the great Dutch admiral and hammer of the English, received his mortal wound. Now the islands serve as the internment camp for the political opponents of Fascism. Here, too, is or was interned Guaglino, the former Italian artificial silk king, part of whose wonderful picture collection now adorns the walls of the Italian Embassy in London. Doubtless, the islands have a better climate than France's "Devil's Island". But they are forbidding enough, and it must be tantalising for the prisoners to see the liners pass almost every day carrying free people to freer countries.

Formerly the big liners used to pass between the islands. Now they are not allowed to follow this route, because these waters are reserved for the Italian navy. I imagine that the real reason is that the Duce does not want any foreign ships plying too near his political prisons. Certainly the world hears very little about them. I remember an exalted official of the German Embassy in London once complaining to me that the British Press always raised a storm of abuse over Hitler's concentration camps, but never referred to Mussolini's Lipari Islands. Herr Hitler, to a large extent the creation of the post-war policy of the Allies, has perhaps some reason to complain. But, apart from the fact that he has persecuted the Jews whereas Mussolini has not, he suffers from one great disadvantage. He is a German. And in its attitude towards both races the British public, which reacts more to instinct than to knowledge, draws a sharp line between Germans and Italians. When Mussolini says "We must darken the skies with our airplanes", we laugh. The English have not yet learnt to take Mussolini seriously.

When Germany begins to be truculent or even mildly assertive, we react immediately. We are afraid of Germany. That is perhaps why to-day Mussolini believes that the British are a decadent race whose Empire is ripe to fall into Fascist hands, and why the Germans regard us as the most cunning and far-seeing diplomatists in the world.

I have passed through the Straits of Messina four times in my life, the first being just before the great earthquake of 1908. They are one of the great sights of the world, associated in my mind with rather terrifying boyhood memories of Turner's "Ulysses Defying Polyphemus". But they have never shown themselves to me in their best colours, and on this occasion not even Mt. Etna was visible, still less a Cyclops' cave.

The time of our approach could not have been more favourable. There should have been a perfect sunset. But, as we left Stromboli, a thin drizzle began to fall, and, although it stopped before we entered the Straits, the distant view was obscured. Just as we were swinging round to negotiate Scylla and Charybdis, we passed the P. & O. steamer *Kaisar-i-Hind* or Cæsar of India, a title of our own King handed down through the centuries by the great Roman, who, although more renowned for his victories on land, doubtless sailed through these Straits on his way to Egypt and to Cleopatra.

Many famous men must have used this highway of the ancient world: Hadrian and his boy-love Antinoüs; Pompey, the scourge of the Mediterranean pirates, and Hannibal himself on his retreat to Africa after the failure of the greatest military exploit in history. There was one famous man who longed to use it but was frustrated. From the bridge the captain pointed out to me a small village on the Italian side with a background like a Patinir landscape. On the map it was called San Giovanni. "That", he said, "is where Murat was shot." After the failure of his expedition to Calabria in 1815 he had lain in concealment there, waiting for the English ship which was to carry him to safety.

It is one of the strangest coincidences of history that Napoleon's two greatest marshals, Ney and Murat, were both shot by their compatriots or former subjects, that in both instances the English had promised to save their former enemy, and that on both occasions they had come too late. Doubtless, if ever we go to war with France, a French Ministry of Propaganda will revive and re-edit these stories in order to show that these heroes of France were betrayed by an Albion too perfidious and too cunning to allow two such great soldiers and potential enemies to remain alive. The poison gas of governments is a clearer sign of the white man's decline than the chlorine of the soldiers.

As we passed Messina itself in the fading twilight, I could just distinguish the dirty-grey funnels and strange lopsided masts of a modern Italian warship hedged in by a flotilla of destroyers. Then, as we were opposite the huge one-hundred-and-fifty-feet-high statue of the Madonna at the end of the mole, the lights began to appear, slowly at first and then increasing in rapidity until presently the whole hillside was like a black cushion studded with luminous yellow pins. High up on the mountainside was a group of lights which came from a cluster of villas. They were so high that they seemed to belong to the sky and looked like stars. This combined effect of man's ingenuity and Nature at Messina is very similar to lighting-up time at Hong-Kong and at Nagasaki. It is attractive but slightly artificial. It reminds me of the love scene in the first act of *Madame Butterfly*.

CHAPTER THREE

LET NOT THE reader suppose that my whole time on board
was spent in the meditation of my past or in a rigid aloofness.
If my mornings were devoted to study, they had their moments of relaxation during which I aired my Malay on Djo-
Djo, my cabin steward. Most of the native stewards were
Javanese. They were grave, dignified men with small ankles
and tiny, graceful hands and beautiful kain kepala, a headdress wonderfully tied from a coloured square of silk or
cotton. They spoke a Malay which differed considerably
both in words and in pronunciation from the Malay spoken
in the Malay States. And they spoke it badly. Djo-Djo, however, was what is called in Malay an "anak batawi", a son of
Batavia. This meant that Malay was his native language and
not a foreign tongue. He divided all Europeans into two
categories: those who spoke Malay fluently and those who
spoke not a word. With my collection of Malay books, my
ability to read, and my halting speech, for in twenty-five
years one can become almost dumb even in a language
which one has once spoken well, I was both a puzzle and a
source of amusement to him, so that I soon broke down the
barriers of his natural reserve. I used to engage him in long
conversations about his life on board ship, in his kampong
at home, and in the ports of Holland. And in this manner
my tongue was loosed and my Malay came rapidly back to
me.

Everyone who wishes to study seriously the life and customs of the East Indies must be able to read Dutch. The
Dutch are the experts. I therefore wrestled with their language.
Although I made no attempt to speak it or even to master its
guttural and difficult pronunciation, I brought my studies so
far that by the end of my trip I was able to read a Dutch history with moderate ease. In the afternoons I swam in the
luxurious swimming bath and strove to penetrate the mysteries of a new Leica camera which a friend had given me

before my departure. In the evenings there was a quiet laugh to be extracted from a distant inspection of the human comedy.

It is true that, as far as life on board ship was concerned, the comedy itself had changed vastly since my first voyage in 1908. Then there was youth on board. We had carried a small detachment of German naval officers and ratings who were going out to relieve their colleagues in a German cruiser at Samoa. There had been quite a number of young girls, including the two daughters of a British shipping magnate in Shanghai. There had been the dashing and vivacious wife of a German banker in Kiao-Chow. Above all, there had been a diaphanous vision of French loveliness, married but temporarily unattached and going back unwillingly to rejoin a husband in the French civil service in Cochin-China. I had written a poem in the approved fashion of "ships that pass in the night" to one—or was it both?—of the two daughters. I had danced once with the vivacious German lady. I had surprised a blond young German naval officer kissing the diaphanous loveliness in the moonlight and had been thrilled. To my breathless innocence it all seemed very romantic. There was no talk of slumps or of yellow perils or of Japanese competition. We were six years away from August, 1914. And to a youth of twenty-one six years seemed the last milestone before eternity.

Now everything was changed. Our ship was not more than half full. There was no youth and no romance among our passengers. Only age and gout and nerves and hard-lined faces. People were travelling either for health or for business. Amusement had to be sought in other directions than romance.

I found it in the comic difficulties encountered by the English passengers in ordering food from the Javanese stewards, in the perspiring but praiseworthy efforts of the Dutch officers to keep their guests amused, and in the strange contrast between the clumsy antics of the Europeans

c

on the dance floor and the quiet reserve of the lissom Javanese
who stood by waiting, their limbs motionless, their eyes gaz-
ing vacantly into space. Did they think at all? Did they see
the same lack of dignity as I did in the gyrations of gym-
nastical old gentlemen trying to recapture their schoolboy spirits? Or did they take this nightly travesty for granted
as part of the *adat*, or custom, of the superior white race?
Their own *adat* taught them to respect rank and titles. Perhaps life on board ship, with its different classes and categories of food and cabins, had increased the feeling of respect
and had taught them to regard all first-class passengers as
demi-gods or at least as supermen.

Strictly speaking, there were in our ship only two passengers who could properly be viewed in that light. They
were not exactly demi-gods. But they were, at all events,
English peers. Nor were they of recent creation. Both
had behind them a background of knight-errantry and romance.

Lord Rendlesham was a direct descendant of the famous
Peter Thellusson, a Huguenot merchant who came to London in the middle of the eighteenth century and was naturalised. Like most naturalised British subjects he became fabulously rich and immortalised himself by making an eccentric
will which left his large fortune to accumulate for several
generations. The will was challenged, but was held valid by
the Lord Chancellor. The next year an Act of Parliament
was passed prohibiting such accumulations for the future.
Lord Rosslyn, known to half the world as "Harry", was a
direct descendant of the Scottish kings, and the owner of
Roslin Chapel, the finest architectural jewel in the realm of
Scotland. Sir Walter Scott has sung in verse the exploits of
his ancestors. Harry's own exploits have been confined
mainly to the racecourse and the card-room. He has broken
both himself and the bank at Monte Carlo. He takes his title
from Lord Loughborough, Lord Chancellor during the
reign of George III and first Earl of Rosslyn. It was Lord

Loughborough who as Lord Chancellor pronounced the Thellusson will valid.

There were, therefore, strong historical grounds why our two noble passengers should be good friends. To the historically sentimental reason must be added the bond of the same school tie. As boys the Earl and the Baron had been at Eton together. The course of schoolboy friendship, however, had not run smoothly. During a game of football the future Lord Rendlesham had emerged from a bully and, neglecting the ball, had hacked the future Lord Rosslyn on the shins. There had been retaliation of the usual schoolboy kind. They did not speak on board our ship, holding each his separate court in the smoking-room to the bewilderment and chagrin of a rich American banker, who wished to invite both peers simultaneously to his Texas ranch or his Wisconsin homestead.

There were other comedies of a similar nature which, however, need not be chronicled. I was easily amused. My chief joy was not merely freedom from work, but freedom from responsibilities. If I wanted to be alone, I could be so in the certain knowledge that no one would disturb me. When one has worked for seven years, almost without a break, in a newspaper office where everyone sits together in a babel of tongues and telephones, solitude becomes a craving that is stronger than wine or women or opium. The knowledge that for three months not only should I take no part in the making of a newspaper, but that I should not even read one was in itself the most delicious and most necessary of holidays.

This disregard of the newspaper habit made me a new acquaintance. Actually, there was a newspaper on board—a roneo-printed sheet produced by the wireless officer. It contained a column of English news devoted mainly to the doings of the M.C.C. cricket team in the West Indies and of the English women's cricket eleven in Australia. I rarely looked at it. But on my way down to the saloon one day I stopped before the notice-board and saw chalked up: "England 3 pts. Wales 3 pts." A powerfully-built Englishman stood by my side. He was clean-shaven and grey-haired. I judged him to be about sixty. "I give full marks to the Dutch", I said. "Fancy their giving us the result of the 'rugger' international."

"I did that", replied my neighbour briskly. "Have you seen the ship's newspaper? Full of ridiculous accounts of women's cricket and thunderstorms, and not even the result of the international. I complained to the wireless officer."

Actually he had done more. When the wireless officer was unable to pick up the result, my new acquaintance complained to a director of the steamship company who was travelling with us, and the director had telephoned to England for the result.

The director's action was typical of Dutch politeness. But I could not help wondering what an English captain would have said to an Italian or a Czechoslovak who, in similar circumstances, had demanded the result of the Italo-Czechoslovak " soccer" match at Rome for the so-called championship of the world. But obviously "civis Britannicus sum" has still the virtues of a world passport.

My new friend's name was Hewan. I discovered that, like myself, he had been at Fettes, that Scottish nursery of "rugger" Blues and scholars. The ruling passion of "rugger" has remained with him to this day.

His period at Fettes coincided with that of Sir John Simon, and once again I imbibed from the fountain-head the knowledge that no subsequent great man is a hero to his schoolfellows. Sir John, I learnt, had been more of a master's darling than a rugby football stalwart. He had scraped his way into the cricket eleven, but even the *Fettesian*, the school magazine, had lapsed from its customary kindness in its criticism of his performance as a wicket-keeper. In manhood the brilliant scholarship is forgotten or taken for granted. But

the sins against the Sport God are remembered against us by
our schoolboy contemporaries until death.

Forty years ago Hewan had gone out to Singapore to
Boustead's, the well-known shipping and export merchants.
He had become a partner and had retired after the war. Now
at the age of sixty he was going back to have a look at the
scene of his life's activities and to see his son, the Marlborough, Cambridge and international hockey player, who
had just started his career in the East. The father was a man
who during the course of his life had amassed a vast store of
knowledge about all kinds of curious people and places. He
had the rare power of imparting information without being
boring. I had many talks with him and learnt much about
Singapore life at the end of last century.

That night I went up to the bridge before dinner. The sea
was dead calm after a cloudless day, and a moon that was
almost full was shining. Far away on our right lay the long
island of Crete. I rushed downstairs to eat a rapid dinner, and
came up again on the top deck. From nine to eleven we
steamed parallel to the island. From the ship it looked alarm-
ingly precipitous. There were very few lights or other signs
of habitation, but the snow-capped mountains stood out in
astonishingly clear relief in the moonlight. After the warmth
of the day it was surprising to see snow so far south. Two
peaks, almost side by side, over-topped all the others.

Unconsciously my thoughts turned to St. Paul, whose
ship, bearing him to his trial in Rome, was struck here by a
typhonic wind with such force that the crew had to pass
ropes round her frame to keep her straining timbers together. I was alone, and there was something eerie about
these mountain wraiths. It brought back all that charm of
the unknown which in great cities is nearly always absent.

A little later we passed a small island which, standing out
clearly in the opalescent highway made by the moon, looked
marvellously like Napoleon's hat. Venizelos's skull cap
would have been more appropriate, for Crete had just sur-

vived another revolution. As the ship changed her course, moon and shadow combined to give to the mountain slopes the appearance of a vast cemetery. The scene reminded me of El Greco's "The Agony in the Garden". Here, too, were the same wraith-like figures, the same moonlight, the same rock, and the same colouring of mother-of-pearl. Like Venizelos, El Greco was a Cretan, although his name Domenico Theotocopoulos defeats most candidates in a general knowledge paper.

Vaguely I wondered how many Cretan revolutions Venizelos had inspired or provoked during the fifty years of his political career, and how many ignorant peasants had been induced to lay down their lives for the restless ambition of this turbulent Cretan. El Greco would be a living name when Venizelos's existence had been forgotten even by the historians.

CHAPTER FOUR

AT QUARTER TO six in the morning we berthed at Port Said. The town takes its name from Mohammed Said, the Viceroy of Egypt, who gave to Lesseps the concession for the Suez Canal.

I was already awake and, my cabin being on the port side, I had a perfect view of the dawn. At ten minutes to six the night was still encased in the darkest of dark-blue skies. Far away on the eastern horizon was a faint line of grey. At six the stars were still out. The grey light in the east was slightly clearer and was now streaked with the palest pink. By a quarter past six the stars had disappeared; the sky was the lightest of pale blue; the horizon was a riotous maze of colour ranging from dark gold to the rosiest pink with intervening layers of mauve and saffron. At six-thirty the horizon was still suffused with a pink which was growing rapidly fainter. The sun had not yet shown itself, but, with the light, scores of "feluccas" with their single swan-winged sail slid gracefully out to sea. High up in the sky, looking not much larger than one of the kites which surrounded our ship, was an air-plane, still more bird-like because the throb of her engine was drowned by the raucous shouting of the native dockers who were already loading our ship. It was the Eastern dawn such as I should now see it every day for the next ten weeks. Its beauty, almost painful in its effect, gave me exactly the same shiver of emotional expectation as it had given me twenty-seven years before.

Neither age nor custom has staled my capacity for sightseeing. By seven I was already on shore in the place which in my youth was labelled the wickedest in the world. My memory sharpened by the renewed association, I suddenly remembered the donkeys which met one on going ashore. They were always called after the latest favourites of royalties: "Mrs. Langtry", "Mrs. Cornwallis West", or "La Belle

Otero". The names were a startling reminder that even in those days gossip travelled far afield.

These donkeys were then the only means of conveyance, and before the hirer realised where he was going he found himself being carried off to some exhibition of vice. The brothels worked day and night to suit the coming and going of the passing steamers. There were, too, gambling dens where even if one made money at the tables one was certain to have it filched from one's pocket before one returned to the ship.

At that time Port Said used to be called the Gate to the East. To-day, it is more like the gate to the East End of London or to the East Side of New York. Gone are the donkeys and gone to a large extent is the vice. The town was cleaned up during the war for the benefit of the Australian troops, and, incidentally, for the safety of the native scoundrels who provided vice's victims to the vicious. It has been kept tolerably clean ever since.

I do not mean to suggest that Port Said or, for that matter, Egypt has become a monastery of virtue. The moralities still sit lightly on the shoulders of the Egyptians who have the worst faults of the East and the West, and Port Said still has native gentlemen who surreptitiously proffer various forms of illicit pleasure. They are well hobbled by the police.

Otherwise, the town seemed to have changed little since my first visit. Simon Artz, the Selfridge's of Port Said, has a new store and a wider and better selection of goods, including the beauty specialities of Elizabeth Arden. These latest symbols of modernity were displayed in a large glass case on which stood incongruously a cheap, embossed portrait of Mr. Ramsay MacDonald. New, too, were the electric signs dominating the skyline with drink advertisements. Strangely enough, the teetotal brands held their own with the beers and brandies. Under a cliché caption of "East is East and West is West" Van Houten's Cocoa disputed pride of place with a well-known French cognac. Mr. Bell of Perth and the proprietors of White Horse have arranged that whisky has not been forgotten. But the highest and largest sign in Port Said is supplied by Horlick's Malted Milk.

Down on more sordid levels the advertising is more primitive and more comic. The pitfalls of the English language have no terrors for the commercially-minded polyglots of Port Said. "Sport Shirts 3/9 each. Be a Sport and Buy a Few" might receive the approval even of Sir Charles Higham or Mr. Jesse Straus. But "Never Change Your Shirt If The Quality Is Good", which I saw displayed above a counter in Simon Artz's, is bad hygiene and bad advertising. Doubtless, Mr. Artz meant something different.

The universal prevalence of the English language in a town which was once predominantly French should reassure those pessimists who are mourning the decadence of the British and the decline of their world power. The "Mrs. Langtrys" and the "Mrs. Cornwallis Wests" may have gone, but more than ever Port Said clings to its quaint affection for English manners. In the main street there is a George Robey Store with a George Robey electric sign. On the front a modest shop exterior bears the name of "The Old Firm. Jock Ferguson." Needless to say, both George and Jock wear a fez above a hooked Semitic nose.

Port Said will always have a certain attraction for me. Apparently there are a few other eccentrics who share my affection for it. During my visit I made a pilgrimage of respect to a villa which stands at the north end of the town not far from the Lesseps statue. It belonged to a Scot who was one of the pioneers of British Malaya. His name was Grant Mackie. A son of the manse, he began his Eastern career sixty years ago in Ceylon. From there he went to seek a fortune in the Malay States and after many vicissitudes found it in tin. He was a great character and a firm believer in his own generation. I had seen him at home some years before. He was hurling anathema at the post-war Englishman. Victory had ener-

vated the English. They were no good at home. They were
worse in the East. "In my day", he grunted, "every young
man kept a horse and a woman. Now a motor-bicycle does
for both." In the end the old gentleman had retired to Port
Said as a kind of half-way home between the Scotland which
had bred the grit in him and the Malaya which had given
him wealth. And there he died three years ago.

When my car reached the front again, I paid the taxi-man
off and walked. At once I was surrounded by an army of
fruit-sellers, carpet-sewers, cigarette touts, "gilly-gilly" con-
jurers, and purveyors of pornographic literature, all eager to
press their wares on the visitor. The pornography merchants
have a limited knowledge of English, but their attack is persistent and is directed against both sexes. Indeed, the most
forbidding spinster is as likely to have dirty photographs
flaunted before her eyes as the most obvious old rake. Perhaps the pornographers are indiscriminately energetic. Perhaps they know their market.

On my first visit these irrepressible touts had one stock
phrase for a sex-scene photograph or a lascivious book. It
was "very nice; very French". To-day, everything from a
radio set to a necklace made of Birmingham bone and guar-
anteed as uncut ivory is proclaimed as "good for the stomach". Just what this means I could not discover. Probably it is
some catch-word which the touts have picked up from an
English patent medicine advertisement in a local Arab newspaper. But I do remember very clearly that experienced colonial administrator, the late Sir Ernest Birch, telling me
many years ago that the fault made by nearly every British
official when he first went East was to form his impressions
of the Oriental instead of concentrating on trying to discover what the Oriental was thinking of the English. On the
external evidence alone the Port Said natives cannot have a
very high opinion of the European. They are a rascally im-
portunate band. But they deserve some reward for their
energy. When they sleep I do not know. Ships arrive at every

hour of the day and night. The native is always there to meet them. His shops are always open.

My last impression of Port Said is of the front at 10 a.m. As I stroll back to the ship I am joined by "Tommy" and Harry Rosslyn. Harry is dressed in grey flannels and Deauville shoes. He has a yachting cap on his head. There is a cigarette with a long amber holder in his mouth. He carries a heavy malacca cane in his hand. There is a grave and solemn expression on his face, for the hour is earlier than his wont. He is the tallest, stateliest figure between Jerusalem and Cairo.

A monkey-faced follower of the Prophet interrupts his lordship's stride. He flashes a set of dirty photographs before Lord Rosslyn's eyes. "Buy smutty photographs, sah. Good for the stomach, sah!" The man's face is unpleasant. What is more dangerous to his safety, he causes Lord Rosslyn to stumble. The noble Earl recovers and flourishes his cane. Then in a voice which drowns the rattle of the derricks, the shrieking cacophany of the street vendors, and the siren of a passing steamer, he roars: "Get out at once! How dare you speak to me!" The effect is instantaneous. Our rat slinks away. The statuesque police suddenly come to life. The other pornographers hide their wares in their long sleeves.

I am amused and slightly envious. All the morning these fellows have pestered me, and I have been too self-conscious to deal adequately with them. Rather sadly I realise that if all Europeans were to combat this nuisance in the same way as Harry Rosslyn did, their prestige would stand higher than it does throughout the East.

To-day, Port Said is still picturesque enough to give a mild thrill even to the most unromantic traveller. But the new world of speed is rapidly destroying what is, in effect, a somewhat artificial charm. In a few years' time its fezes and its palm-trees will be as commonplace to air-bus travellers as are the electric signs of Piccadilly or Broadway to the city pedestrian.

It will be a new world in which man will move faster than the sunsets. It will be a different world with different standards of beauty, a world in which strange rocket and cylindrical figures will take the place of the Aphrodites of the classical period and of the Madonnas of the Renaissance. And in a hundred years' time Lesseps, whose statue to-day is the most imposing monument of Port Said, will be faintly remembered, like the half-forgotten Pharaoh of 1500 B.C., as the man who built a canal which is no longer used.

Above all, it will be a world of change. And the greatest change will be the effect of this constant shortening of time and distance on the countless millions of the East who for centuries have been the servants of the white man and who to-day are awaking from their long sleep.

My passage through the canal provoked a mental struggle between reality and imagination. In vain I sought to see the canal in its proper setting as one of man's greatest triumphs over nature. Vaguely I remembered the previous efforts of the ancients: the canals of Darius and Trajan, Venetian dreams of piercing the isthmus in the fifteenth century, the great project of Napoleon. With less strain I succeeded in visualising that inaugural scene on November 17, 1869, when after a Te Deum celebrated on the banks of the canal an international fleet, preceded by a cruiser carrying the Empress Eugenie on board, sailed solemnly through the sand-walled ditch.

There was no Washington ratio in those days, and British naval supremacy was accepted by all nations without demur. It was adequately reflected in the composition of the international fleet on that day. Britain had twelve vessels, Egypt and France six each, Austria seven, Germany five, Spain and Holland two each, and Russia, Denmark, and Sweden one apiece. There were no Italian ships. At the last moment the sudden and grave illness of King Victor Emmanuel had prevented the appearance of the Italian flotilla.

On my way home through the same canal I was to pass

Italian warships bearing raucously exuberant Fascists to the barren coasts of Eritrea. But now there were no shouts of "Evviva l'Italia" to disturb the peaceful monotony of the scene.

I tried to concentrate my mind on the war period of which an imposing memorial at Gebel-Miriam was a reminder. My brother had been one of the few British officers wounded in repelling the Turkish-German attack on the canal in February, 1915. But my imagination rebelled against activity. The day was pleasantly cool, and there was no excuse for my lethargy except the canal itself. Since I passed through in 1908, it has, I suppose been widened. But the general impression remains unchanged: a surfeit of sameness which is not relieved by efforts of the imagination to visualise Joseph in the Land of Goshen or Moses leading the Israelites across the Red Sea.

Incidentally, modern Biblical scholarship has slightly amended the site of the crossing. As the Red Sea varies from sixty to two hundred miles in breadth, the experts have sought to bring the miracle within the bounds of a more reasonable probability by fixing the actual point of the cleavage of the waters in the Great Bitter Lake which now forms part of the canal.

The Sinai peninsula affords another opportunity for the imagination to run riot, not merely because of Moses, but because here, five thousand years before the birth of Christ, man first discovered the use of metals. From the copper mines of Sinai came the chisels which were used to shape the Pyramids. And if the first-class tourist, looking down from the seclusion of the promenade deck on the toiling natives below, is inclined to feel complacently superior, it will be good for him to remember that he is passing through the source of all civilisation and that here Egyptians were ploughing with domestic cattle and raising wheat and barley, making linen clothing, producing pottery, working metals and inventing letters at a time when the European was a savage hunter. Six thousand years is a fragment of time in the life of the world, and, as Herodotus says, "many states that were once great have now become small; and those that are now great were small formerly." And, assuredly, for it is the rule of life, will be small again.

To most Englishmen the one salient feature of the canal is unknown. At the Port Said end stands the statue to Lesseps, who is admittedly the hero of the whole venture. At the other end, at Port Tewfik, is the statue, rarely seen by passengers, to Lieutenant Waghorn.

This brilliant young Englishman was the man who in 1837 opened the overland mail route to India. His chief ambition, however, was to secure the sea route to the East for Britain by linking the Mediterranean and the Red Seas by a canal. He spent the rest of his life preaching his project to a deaf and uninterested British public. He died in poverty in London in 1858, the same year in which the subscription lists for shares in Lesseps' company were opened to the public. The British public bought no shares in a canal to which Lord Palmerston more than once referred as "the foul and stagnant ditch."

Nor did English hands raise the statue to Waghorn. It was erected at the instigation of the generous-minded Lesseps. Waghorn was not the first Empire-builder to be ruined by the apathy of the British public. From now on the reader will find the names of British colonial administrators, beginning with Raffles and ending with Swettenham, whose greatest achievements were accomplished in face of the passive and sometimes even active opposition of the British Government at home.

CHAPTER FIVE

IF I FIND it hard to enthuse over the Suez Canal, I have a minor passion for the Red Sea. To most travellers it recalls a nightmare of stifled breathing and sandy suffocation. But its reputation as a kind of sea-hell is undeserved, and in a modern liner equipped with electric fans and refrigerators its worst heat has now few terrors. During nine months of the year the weather, on board ship at all events, is not unpleasantly hot. At times it can be unpleasantly cold. On the occasion of my present voyage the officers wore their heavy blue uniforms until we reached Perim.

My youthful memories of the Red Sea were vague and unpleasant. The vagueness meant that I took no interest in my surroundings. The unpleasantness was the enforced cessation, owing to the heat, of those various forms of violent physical exercise in which, like my fellow Britons, I then indulged and occasionally excelled. Now in the maturer reflection of middle-age I accepted both the inactivity and the sea itself with gratitude. There was, first, the ebullient feeling of relief, which since my prison days in the Kremlin I always experience in escaping from a bottle neck into the open. And on the present occasion the sense of escape was magnified by the knowledge that Europe, landlocked by the isthmus, was safely behind me, and that now I was at the beginning of my real journey. For, long before Diaz and Vasco da Gama rounded the Cape, the Red Sea was the starting point of the first sea-journey East, and as far back as the year of Cæsar's death the merchants of Alexandria were sending fleets of 120 ships by way of the Red Sea to India.

Then, too, there was the fascination of being for three days in sight of land, represented in the case of the Red Sea by numerous islands and by two lines of coast which throughout the centuries of history have been and still are to-day the scene of as much human wickedness as the imagination can devise. To-day, it is hard to believe that this Arabian coast

39

was one of the most fertile areas in the world. Yet at the dawn
of history this was one of the five lands in which civilisation
started and probably the first from which a boat was sent out
upon the sea.

During our transit I spent much time on the bridge with
the captain, who laughed at my enthusiasm over the various
groups of islands and corrected my romanticism with accurate details of their physical unattractiveness. Common sense
compels me to admit that for the city-sick European misan-
thrope they would be about the hottest home on the earth.
They are all alike: volcanic formations devoid of vegetation
and even of water. In the day-time they resemble reddish
cones more than anything else, but in the kaleidoscopic background of a Red Sea sunset they stand out like great black
sentinels. One we passed so close that I might have thrown a
stone on to its rocky shore. It had a lighthouse built on the
summit of the rock and exposed to the full glare of the sun.

The numerous lighthouses in the Red Sea are manned by
Greek Levantines of the same type as the gentlemen who run
the hotels and stores of Massawah and Djibuti. There are
generally four men to each lighthouse. On my voyage home
one of the lighthouses signalled our ship for a doctor. He
went off with his instruments in a boat and returned in half-an-
hour. The four Greeks had quarrelled over a game of cards.
It had finished with knives. One of the keepers had had his
face slashed open.

We were too far out to see Jeddah, the pilgrims' port for
Mecca, but the captain who in the past had taken many a pilgrim ship there from Java, gave me an apposite illustration of
the hard times which had overtaken the Dutch East Indies
since the world "slump" of 1929. Seven or eight years ago,
when economic conditions were good in Java, his line used
to carry as many as 25,000 Javanese pilgrims to Jeddah in a
single year. In 1934 the number had fallen to less than 2000.

Involuntarily, my mind went back to my early days during the rubber boom in Malaya when at Pantai I had carved

a ground out of the jungle and had taught my Malays football. They had learnt quickly. Within two years I had entered
them in the local state league. I remembered with irritation
how they fell away during the fast of Ramazan. Still greater
was my disgust when two of my best players had returned
their shorts and jerseys and in the middle of the season had
announced that they were leaving on the pilgrimage which
every Mohammedan hopes to accomplish once. Mecca was
their goal.

In those days when my mind was fixed on terrestrial goals
I found this itinerant interference with my ambitions both
galling and ridiculous. Why could they not postpone their
pilgrimage until their fleetness of foot had departed and the
hot blood in their veins had cooled against earthly temptations? Now their impatience seemed not only natural but
essential. The pilgrimage had to be made as soon as enough
money was saved or inherited, because, once accomplished,
it deprived death of all its terrors. There is no faith so strong
as the Mohammedan's. That is why throughout the centuries
he has always defied conversion by the Christian missionaries. It is almost the only European temptation which he has
resisted. It must be counted to his credit and to the merits of
Mohammedanism as a religion for Orientals.

I was full of compassionate understanding. Here was where
my full-back and my inside-left had landed twenty-five
years ago. I wondered if they were still alive. I wondered how
many of my old football team were now Hajis. Mecca would
not prevent them from petty pilfering, from sponging on
their relatives, from minor deceptions against the British raj,
from excesses of sensual pleasures, or from all the other
Malayan venialities, but it would establish complete confidence in their minds for the future, and leave their souls at
peace for the rest of their earthly existence.

As we drew nearer to Perim, the number of islands increased. The Harnish group, now made famous by the
French writer, Henri de Montfreid, is still the centre of the

D

Red Sea pearl-fishing industry. The islands, too, afford a refuge and a shelter for the slave-traders and gun-runners who ply their nefarious trade between Abyssinia and the Yemen coast. Having just re-read de Montfreid's *Secrets of the Red Sea*, I was prepared to transfer the label of the world's wickedest spot from Port Said to the shores of the southern end of the Red Sea. I had been interested in Montfreid for some time. I had met many of his enemies and several of his friends. More than once friends in Paris had arranged for me to meet him. We had even exchanged letters. But Fate has always intervened to prevent our coming together. His books are extraordinary and are an indispensable guide to the life of the Red Sea coasts. But they are no more extraordinary than the man himself, who as self-confessed gun-runner and pearl-smuggler has made himself the enemy of every government, including his own, with which he has come into contact. Yet this amazing man has won and kept the friendship of some, at least, of the officials who have been ordered to dog his footsteps.

Montfreid inherits his love of the sea from his father, Georges Daniel, the painter, whose name has been immortalised by his friendship with Gauguin. It was to Daniel de Montfreid that Gauguin wrote his letters from Tahiti. Like Gauguin, Daniel was a great sailor and owned a little schooner in which he used to sail from the South of France as far as Algiers.

Henri carried his adventures farther afield, and a long period of early manhood spent among the pearl-fishers, the gun-runners, and dope-smugglers of the Red Sea coasts, not only made him a picturesque figure but gave him an unrivalled knowledge of one of the least-known corners of the earth.

Like most adventurers of artistic temperament he was always up against officialdom. On one occasion he fell foul of the British authorities at Perim. There was no real charge against him, but a cross-examination might have been awkward. Montfreid, however, entertained his potential captors so wittily that as a reward for an amusing evening they let him go.

During the Italo-Abyssinian conflict de Montfreid threw in his lot with the Italians and became more or less an official propagandist for Signor Mussolini. For a man whose life had been spent in playing a lone hand against all governments, including his own, this change of front struck me as a ghastly anti-climax.

The captain interrupted my thoughts about Montfreid in order to point out to me Mocha with its white minarets glistening in the sun. In the distance it looked like the picture of the Celestial City in my old illustrated edition of *The Pilgrim's Progress*. To the Dutch and to the Viennese, Mocha is synonymous with coffee. Indeed, in the Vienna cafés the order for a black coffee is "ein Mocha, bitte".

Mocha is not the original home of the coffee tree, but it was long held to be by Europeans and perhaps the Arabs themselves. At all events there is a pretty Arab legend which the "gurus" tell to the children. In the waste land behind Mocha there once lived an erudite hermit. He was kept alive by a small herd of goats who brought him milk every day. The leader of the herd was an old billy-goat who had long passed his youth. One day the hermit was surprised to see the billy-goat springing in the air and performing the antics of the gayest and youngest of goats. For some days he studied the goat's movements instead of the pages of his Koran, and he noticed that, whenever the goat browsed on the leaves of a few low trees which had appeared from nowhere in the desert, the light-hearted antics began again. The hermit took the leaves, boiled them in a pot, drank what he had brewed, and found that, if he could not skip, at any rate he did not want to sleep. This, the Arabs say, was the origin of coffee. Certain it is that from Mocha, coffee was transplanted to Java and other Eastern countries, but, as a matter of fact, the tree was introduced to Mocha from Kaffa in Abyssinia.

Of Abyssinia itself I saw nothing, and even at the point
between Eritrea and French Somaliland where the Abyssinian frontier comes nearest to the sea even the captain could
not tell me whether the mountains we saw on the horizon
were in Ethiopia or not. In any case Abyssinia was then little
more than a name to me. Vaguely I remembered from my
schooldays that it had been responsible for the death of the
greatest man of the ancient world and that Pericles had died
of the Ethiopian plague. Adowa meant more to me as the
name of the steamer in which Conrad wrote a chapter of
Almayer's Folly than as the scene of an Italian colonial defeat.
Addis Ababa I should like to have seen once, if only in order
to remind myself that the most correct of diplomatists can
be human and that there is no strong man in the world who
has not some strain of weakness.

It was to Addis Ababa that my old friend and former chief,
Sir George Clerk, came as a young diplomatic secretary
nearly forty years ago. This undelectable post had been of his
own seeking. He had gone there in order to economise after
a disastrous race-meeting at Doncaster. Perhaps it was the
habit of self-denial and self-discipline then acquired which is
responsible for his elevation to the highest post in the British
diplomatic service.

At different times he had told me of his adventures there
in Menelik's time: strange tales of the comic and the savage
sides of Abyssinian life, of barbarous justice and of a man,
who had had both hands and both feet hacked off for theft
and who had put out his tongue to his official torturer,
screaming: "Cut it out. I can steal with that, too." Twice the
young British diplomatist had had to intervene to save the
life of a tribesman who had struck him, as he rode past on his
pony in a lonely district, with the long wooden stick which
all Abyssinians use to push away the scrub on their narrow
riding tracks. The first time Sir George had to save him from
the clutches of his Abyssinian escort who would have dealt
summarily with the offender there and then. Later, when the

man was brought before Menelik, who ordered him to be
flogged, Sir George had to intervene again to prevent the
man's back from being torn to ribbons by the hippopotamus lash used with expert precision by the official flogging
master.

Decidedly, Abyssinia was not my affair. Only that morning I had picked up the ship's news bulletin. It contained a
short paragraph of three lines announcing that M. Bernard, a
French Somaliland administrator, together with eighteen
native troopers and eighty-eight Somalis, had been mas-
sacred in French territory by marauding Abyssinian tribes-
men.

Perim we passed as the light was beginning to fade. But
it was not too dark for me to see the barren rockiness of the
place and to pity the handful of white men who man its guns
and its oil station. Back to my mind came an ugly story told
to me by a French officer in Russia during the war at four
a.m. in the morning in the garden of the Aquarium, a Moscow night-haunt owned and run by a negro called Thomas.
It was a story of Perim and perfidious Albion. Nearly a hundred years ago a small French fleet arrived before Aden on
its way to Perim in order to take possession of this deserted
island for France. The same evening the British Governor
invited the French officers to dinner. During the banquet the
Frenchmen were persuaded to state the purpose of their mission. When they arrived at Perim the next evening, they
found the British flag flying. During the banquet a British
sloop had been sent off in order to forestall the Frenchmen!

It is not a pretty story. But then one does not expect pretty
stories in the Straits of Bab-el-Mandeb. The Straits themselves are well-known to shipping companies and, best of
all, to the P. & O., for it was here that during a dance at which
most of the officers were present the S.S. *China* went on the
rocks. Since then the P. & O. officers have not been allowed
to take part in the passengers' dances.

CHAPTER SIX

THE DUTCH BOATS do not call at Aden, and on this occasion I saw only the lights of the town. There are queer people—exotic government servants and lean, hungry "sappers"—who profess a love for Aden and ask to be sent there as a favour. I do not share their passion. Nevertheless, three reasons combine to keep the place warm in my memory. Aden was the first place where I saw native boys diving for pennies. All my life I have felt an unwilling fascination for the turns of trapeze acrobats and other artists who risk their lives for the amusement of the public and for their own gain. High in this category of performer I place the native divers who recover small silver and copper coins almost from the teeth of the waiting sharks. I always imagined the sharks were waiting, although I doubt now if the loss of life was ever as great as the Mr. Know-all passenger who is on every ship always tells us. At least, when I arrived in Singapore, there was an old Kling gentleman who dived all morning with a burning cigar in his mouth and rarely missed a coin. He told me that he had been at the job for thirty years.

Secondly, since my childhood Aden has been associated in my mind with a tune which is known officially as "The Barren Rocks of Aden". It is the tune which the pipe band used to play at Inverleith when Scotland took the field against England in the "rugger" internationals. It was supposed to strike terror into the Sassenach's heart and to inspire the chosen of Scotland to reckless deeds of valour. In those days its grandeur overwhelmed me. Later, when I went to school at Fettes, I found that the tune had a new name and that on Pop nights the whole school sang to it a ribald chorus about a lady called "Mrs. Grunt". My respect for Scotland's football hymn diminished. But even to-day the tune wakes savage emotions in my heart, and I feel that if there were another war and I had to take part in it I could go over the top more bravely to the skirl of "Mrs.

Grunt" than to "Scots Wha Hae" or any other patriotic anthem.

And finally Aden to me meant Jean-Arthur Rimbaud. To-day the great French literary adventurer has become the favourite poet of European diplomacy. M. Paul Claudel, the most literary of modern French ambassadors, sees in Rimbaud the martyr who has redeemed himself by suffering, and has now elevated him almost to the footstool of a saintly throne. Already in his Oxford days that precocious young statesman, Mr. Anthony Eden, had read everything Rimbaud had ever written, and even to-day, when he flies to Geneva, there is generally a copy of Rimbaud's poems in his pocket.

There are other distinguished diplomatists who regard him as little better than a gifted crook and homosexualist. But there is not one who has not read "Le Bâteau Ivre" or who does not know that "Les Illuminations" was finished in a cheap London boarding-house where the poet shared a furnished room with Verlaine.

But in the early part of this century Rimbaud was far from being a popular figure. By the merest chance I had come across his work when I was little more than a boy. In 1906 my father sent me to Douai of all places in order that I might perfect my French before descending on Paris and the Sorbonne! I had boarded with a young French professor who taught French literature in the local college and whose classical orthodoxy was fortunately tempered by a taste for the exotic. He introduced me to Rimbaud's verse. I embraced it with the ardour of a youthful lover. The life-story thrilled me. When two years later I made my first voyage East I was already steeped in Rimbaud. I had imbibed a little of the Rimbaud melancholy and much of the Rimbaud rebellious attitude towards mankind.

The knowledge, too, that I was going to the Malay Archipelago and that Rimbaud's first Eastern adventure had begun there, when in order to see the world he had taken the Dutch *prime d'engagement* and had enlisted in the Dutch East Indian army, seemed to give me one of those vague personal contacts which like shadows follow the traveller for the rest of his life. The fact that he had deserted almost immediately after landing at Batavia merely enhanced his romantic value in my eyes.

Something of these feelings came back to me at this moment. Abyssinia had been the last of Rimbaud's adventures, and the adventure had begun in Aden.

Here nearly fifty years ago he had arrived after having walked the length of the Arabian coast in a vain search for work. Here in Aden had been the headquarters of the French coffee merchants who had given him employment.

Fortunately for the world, M. Bardey, the head of the firm, had understood his strange poet-clerk and had sent him to take charge of the agency in Harar.

But at Harar the poet, who had scouted every convention for the sake of his art, wrote no poetry. He had no time for dreams. He was too busy extracting ivory from the savage tribes, selling arms to Menelik, and saving money. He learnt a number of native dialects. He formed some sort of a harem. Doubtless, the intimacy helped his philological studies. But money—money to enable him to return to France and to marry—was his main object. And after eleven years he had achieved prosperity. Then Destiny had played him a cruel trick.

The story is too well known to be retold at length. One day the poet awoke with a swollen knee. He diagnosed rheumatism and tried to cure it by exercise. The knee defied treatment. The leg began to shrivel. The pain increased. Furious because he had not gathered in the fortune which lay almost ready to his grasp, he was forced to leave the country. He made an agonising calvary to Aden, and here in the town hospital the last act of the tragedy began.

The English surgeon could do nothing for him. He advised an immediate return to Marseilles, and Rimbaud sailed in the first available steamer. Thirteen days later the Marseilles doctors removed the afflicted leg. Although they did not tell him, the operation was of no avail. Gradually the cancer invaded his whole body. He was tended by his sister Isabella. In his last hours came the death-bed conversion which has so impressed M. Paul Claudel and other Rimbaud admirers, and the rebel poet, who for years had been a blasphemer, returned to the faith in which he was born. Was his recantation a genuine disavowal of his atheism or merely the easy way out of a dying man who longs to be left in peace? Death has put a seal for ever on the truth. The end came exactly six months after his last departure from Aden.

As I stood alone on the top deck, my imagination stimulated by the warm beauty of the night, I tried to unravel the complexities of this strange life: the contrariness of a Fate which left Rimbaud unknown and neglected in his lifetime and which to-day has given him perhaps a greater influence over modern poetry, both French and English, than any other poet; the contrast between de Montfreid, who began life as a commercial adventurer and is now finishing it as a writer, and Rimbaud, the poet-adventurer, who from the day on which he became a man of business never wrote another line of verse; and, lastly and most curious of all, the spell which a vagabond like Rimbaud can weave round a man so immaculate in thought, word and deed as Mr. Anthony Eden.

For Mr. Eden's expert knowledge of Rimbaud I found an explanation. The appeal of beauty unites all kinds and conditions of men. The influence of heredity is perhaps even stronger, and from his father, an eccentric squire and painter of distinction, Mr. Eden has inherited a highly developed artistic sense, which is revealed to-day not only in his taste for poetry, but in his expert knowledge of modern French painting. Rimbaud, too, was perhaps even more an adventurer in the realm of ideas than on the face of the earth. It is mostly women and poets who are prepared to sell reality for a dream, but there is no progressively-minded man who does not profess himself an adventurer in ideas. The fact that at Oxford Mr. Eden took the highest honours in Oriental languages is sufficient proof that in his case the adventure in ideas began early. It has not ceased and, as an admirer, I hope that it will never cease.

Since that night of passage off Aden I have made the pilgrimage to Charleville, the little industrial town in the Ardennes, where Rimbaud was born and where he is buried. To-day, many of the chimneys are smokeless, for depression has laid a heavy hand on the valley of the Meuse. There is a fine square with old-fashioned arcades and below the town a picturesque mill-tower overlooked by a hill called Mount Olympus. Beneath it flows the Meuse, in winter turbid and swollen, where the young poet, clad in the blue-slate trousers of the French working-man, used to play with boats and found his inspiration for his "Bâteau Ivre". There are trees in plenty: lime-trees in the town; poplars, willows and osiers by the river; silver birches on the hills. Crows and magpies abound in the fields. But the general impression is one of grey slates, grey houses, leaden skies and poverty. The inhabitants are Socialists. There are many unemployed.

Of Rimbaud himself many of the local traces have now disappeared. The college on the square of the Holy Sepulchre, where he went to school, has been pulled down. The square itself has been re-named La Place de l'Agriculture in honour of the cart-horse fair which is held there every year. But there is the cemetery and the house in which he was born, and his memory is not forgotten.

When I visited the cemetery, I was the only visitor. It lies on the top of a small hill and, although well tended, has a look of haphazard growth which is not unattractive. The tomb, which stands in a small family grave, is on the immediate left of the main path close to the entrance. The grave is encased by a low grille and contains two standing stones and a flat slab. A small box-tree in a tub stands before each stone. Rimbaud's is on the right. It is very simple and has a small floral design with two stars. The lettering, which has recently been re-gilded, runs as follows: "Jean-Arthur Rimbaud, 37 ans. 10 Novembre, 1891. Priez pour lui." Beside him lies his sister; beneath is the grave of the mother who never understood him. Just across the path is a large chestnut-tree with spreading branches which in summer cast the long shadows of the setting sun on the poet's last resting place.

From the cemetery I went to the Rue Thiers, a shopping thoroughfare in the centre of the town. In a room on the first floor of No. 12 Rimbaud was born. A stucco plaque on the outside wall commemorates the birth. The house is owned by a bookseller and printer. The bookshop has been there for over a hundred years. It is still stocked with a better collection of books than one could find in even a large provincial town in England. But hard times have forced a reduction of its frontage, and half the shop has now been let as a bar. It is the bar-keeper and his wife who now occupy the Rimbaud room.

During the first years of the war Charleville was the headquarters of the German Kaiser. Later, the Crown Prince established himself here. From an inspection of the records of the occupation I drew the conclusion that never before in history perhaps had so many important Germans been gathered together in one small town. Here came Hindenburg and Ludendorff and all the German Generalitaet to report progress to their Imperial master. Here were assembled all the numerous minor royalties and princes of the Reich.

Indeed, the people of Charleville, who within the memory of the oldest inhabitants have had their town twice destroyed by the Germans, can talk of little else except the occupation. Even for Englishmen the place evokes sad memories, for its station was one of the main arteries of the German railway system, and the soil of Charleville covers the bones of English soldiers, wounded prisoners who died in the station on their way into captivity in Germany.

I hired a car, owned by a war-veteran chauffeur, and drove out to the Château Belair, which was the Kaiser's residence. It stands by itself on the top of a hill. Its present owners were absent, and its heavily shuttered windows added a certain grimness to its general gloom. Leading away from it is a lonely country lane, bordered by an English hedge and still remembered as the Crown Prince's road.

As we drove back, my chauffeur pointed out to me a large house opposite the station. "That house", he said, "was the Kaiser's first residence—until a bomb drove him to the château."

"I suppose in summer you have many visitors who come to see the Kaiser's headquarters?" I asked.

"No," he replied. "We have very few tourists—more's the pity. Those, who do come, come to see 'that'." He waved his arm towards a little railed-in park with a bandstand. "That" was a small bronze bust of Rimbaud with the words "Bâteau Ivre" engraved on the pedestal. The bust is perhaps appropriately placed, for the square is the same as that stigmatised in Rimbaud's poem "À la Musique":

"Sur la place taillée en mesquines pelouses,
  Square où tout est correct, les arbres et les fleurs,
  Tous les bourgeois poussifs qu'étranglent les chaleurs
  Portent, les jeudis soirs, leurs bêtises jalouses."

The bust, however, is a fine achievement and shows the poet as a young and attractive collegian. It is a post-war work. The original was taken away by the Germans during the war and was melted down.

"Monsieur is interested in Rimbaud?" said my chauffeur. "The family was from Roche. It is my country. I knew the brother well when he was a waiter at Bataud's in Attigny. He, too, was very clever."

I paid him off and walked across to the rather dingy station, marvelling that any tourists should come to Charleville at all. In a world which has temporarily lost its sanity the fact that they should come to reverence Rimbaud's memory and not to speculate on the past glories of the Kaiser seemed to me a consoling thought for the future of mankind.

CHAPTER SEVEN

ONLY A SAILOR who sails a sailing ship can derive genuine enjoyment from a sea voyage in which no land is sighted. I confess without shame that to me the six days from Aden to Colombo in a modern steamship will always be a period of chafing restlessness. Work and even reading are impossible. By now the passengers have shaken down together. Everyone knows his neighbour. All restraint and shyness have vanished, and, unless one is prepared to be definitely rude, one is forced into a community life from which there is no escape. It is the gala period for deck games, children's sports, bridge tournaments, fancy-dress dances, and captain's dinners.

Two virtues I concede willingly to the Dutch. They are extraordinarily kind to their children, and on this occasion we carried almost as many children as grown-ups. Their ship's officers are not only unfailingly courteous but also exceptionally good linguists.

A captain's dinner on board a Dutch liner is an experience which is well worth undergoing once. There is a present for every guest. There is a dramatic moment when the lights go out and from the quadrangle above the dining saloon the procession of Javanese boys, spotless in white drill relieved by their gaily-coloured head-dresses, bring in the ice in ceremonial stateliness. Each ice-dish is lit up by a fairy-lamp, and the effect of these ghostly figures, barefooted, impassive, and mysterious, is unforgettable. After the ice come the speeches, and the Dutch captain makes his speech in as many languages as there are nationalities among his guests.

On this occasion Captain Potjer spoke in Dutch, English, French, and German. In each language—I take his Dutch for granted—his accent was almost impeccable. Doubtless, he had made more or less the same speech on numerous occasions. Nevertheless, the performance was impressive. It was infinitely better than that of the passengers who responded, although I must make an exception in the case of our English speakers. Both Lord Rosslyn on the voyage out and Lord Pembroke on the voyage home made excellent speeches. They spoke with good humour and with commendable audibility. They paid exactly the appropriate compliments to the Dutch and to the other nationalities represented among the passengers and they delighted their audience by a brevity which was lacking in the other speakers. The English aristocracy excels at this kind of oratory and in this respect has not outlived its sphere of usefulness. It is helped by its rank, for, if other aristocracies can boast of more quarterings, an English title has still a higher value, especially in republican and democratic countries, than that of any other nation.

Indeed, much as I like the citizens of the United States and admire their achievements, I have never been in a liner, which has carried an English peer on board, without noticing that the richest Americans invariably hustle to make his acquaintance. That they rarely fail in their endeavour is a tribute to the good "mixing" qualities of the average British peer.

I should be untruthful if I were to give the impression that these landless days were entirely without satisfactory compensations. During the long afternoons I found an endless delight in leaning over the side and watching the flying fish and the torpedo-shaped porpoises. Alas! they showed themselves less frequently than in the days of my youth. The experts maintain that the speed of the modern liner and the oil-fuel which is now burnt are responsible for the decline. My own opinion is that the speed of modern life is the real culprit and that, whereas in pre-war days time moved slowly, to-day one wants one's enjoyment quickly and frequently.

Then, at half-past five there was the daily "trek" through the second class to the stern of the ship to watch the sunset and to try to catch that elusive green ray which is supposed to show itself just as the sun ball of fire sinks below the horizon. I never saw it. I do not think that I have ever seen it. One evening, however, I was witness of a curious sight which even the captain did not remember seeing before. As the sun was nearing the rim of the horizon, it disappeared behind a bank of white cloud which looked strangely like an English fog. For some ten minutes or so the combination of sun and cloud turned itself into a series of caricatures, all in zigzag, first of a Chinese lantern, then of a large brown mushroom, and finally of a Chinaman with a red back, a black head, and a large cone-shaped straw-hat. The effect was so extraordinary that had we not known it was there, no one would have believed that what he saw was, in fact, the sun.

I resumed, too, without any difficulty my old Eastern habit of rising with the dawn. In the mornings, before my fellow-passengers were stirring, I found time to re-read my Conrad, more especially, the Malayan novels like *Almayer's Folly* and *An Outcast of the Islands*. Their appeal to me was just as strong as when I first read them in Malaya twenty-seven years before.

I was, however, heartily glad when on the fifth day we sighted Minikoi. The island, which lies half-way between the Laccadives and the Maldives, is like most other tropical islands. There are the same coconut trees and other palms waving gently to the sea breeze. There is the same line of golden sand washed by a thin line of white breakers. There are the same greenness and the same white lighthouse. But Minikoi has a special place in my heart. It is the first island one passes on the journey East which has the same rich, warm vegetation as the islands of the Malayan Archipelago. And for twenty-seven years it has remained clear-cut in my memory.

It is not the great scenes of life that are most easily photographed in the mind. In my varied career I have witnessed the living dramas of history. Of all the great figures of the Russian revolution with whom I was closely connected the photograph which stands out most sharply before my eyes is of Kerensky, but not of the Kerensky of Russian days. One November afternoon two years ago I was walking, towards dusk, with a friend in Kensington Square. As we were making our way up to Kensington High Street a gaunt figure came striding down the pavement. His head, covered by a soft black hat, was bent forward until his chin almost touched his chest. His coat collar was turned up. His hands clutched a paper-bag. As he brushed past us, I caught sight of his face. "Good God," I said to my companion, "that's Kerensky." Although I have known him intimately now for nearly twenty years, I did not stop him but turned to watch him until he disappeared in the gloom and the sharp click of his shoes on the pavement was lost in the frosty air. I was so overwhelmed by the contrast between the Kerensky of 1917, the all-powerful dictator of Russia to whom the Allied Governments would have offered any honour he desired, for keeping Russia in the war, and the ignored and forgotten Kerensky of to-day, that I shall remember every detail of that scene until I die.

I carry in my mind the same memory picture of Minikoi, and whenever I dream that dream, so popular to-day, of a tropical island, it is Minikoi that I see. It has now the additional attraction of the hulk of a wrecked German ship which lies off its eastern point, and which without undue strain on the imagination can be made to suggest buried gold and the other appurtenances of a treasure island.

The next day, a Thursday, we anchored in Colombo harbour. Captain Oliver, the Governor's aide, came on board to meet the Rosslyns, and at 2.30 I went ashore with Lady Rosslyn in the Governor's launch. The sky was cloudless, but there was a cool breeze from the sea, and I found my first contact with the tropical sun for twenty-five years both pleasant and invigorating.

As we walked from the pier to the shopping centre I had some inkling of the changes which I should find in Singapore. Colombo has altered vastly since my first visit. The shopping part of the town might be Brighton or, perhaps more accurately, any south-eastern European town. The

E

shops themselves were filled with shoddy and, as in most
English provincial towns, there was no good bookshop. On
the other hand, there were several stucco and very English-
looking cinemas. Down the main street, too, marched an
army of sandwichmen parading huge placards announcing
the forthcoming visit of C. de B. Mille's "Cleopatra".

There is only one adjective to describe the pictures or the
placards. They were flaming. I shall have more to say about
the effect of the flaming cinema on the East.

Meanwhile, after much bargaining, we allowed ourselves
to be inveigled into hiring a car for the afternoon by a Tamil
owner of antiquated open cars. His English was picturesque,
fluent, and tolerably good. Turning to Tommy Rosslyn, he
said: "Colombo very like London, lady." Tommy asked
him if he had ever been in London. "No," he answered, "but
I've seen it often at the pictures." Colombo is not like London, but, whereas twenty-five years ago there was no resemblance, there is to-day enough stucco and, I gladly admit,
enough cleanliness and other sanitary improvements which
British civilisation brings in its train, to suggest a comparison
even to British, let alone, native minds.

In our hired Ford we drove out to Mount Lavinia. Here,
too, the trail of Western civilisation had blazed itself right
to the doors of the huge new hotel, complete with jazz-band
and a railway station, which now dominates this once attractive and peaceful bay. Neither the vast array of cars nor the
pernicious hoarding, advertising Ceylon's "Lido," could quite
destroy the natural beauty of the place. The golden stretch
of sand with its background of palms was picturesque
enough. But not even the old Tamil gentleman fishing
patiently off the rocks nor a graceful catamaran, beaching
at break-neck speed its catch of yellow fish, could impart a
proper Oriental colour to the scene. Colombo and Mount
Lavinia have become westernised, and the process has
brought with it some of the worst features of American
tourism. Even in the shops Tommy, who wished to buy

some socks for her husband and who turned in disgust from some clocked monstrosities, was told by the polite Cingalese shopman that they were the latest American fashion.

One stroke of fortune came our way in Colombo. Our chauffeur was a Malay who came from Menangkabau in Sumatra, which is supposed to be the cradle of the Malay race. He spoke very much the same Malay as that spoken in Negri Sembilan, my old state in the Federated Malay States. I found him easier to talk to than the Javanese boys on board our ship and told him so. His face beamed with pleasure. "The orang Jawa and the orang Malayu don't get on together and never will", he said. There is some truth in this statement. It should be consoling to Imperialists, for in the Malay Archipelago there must now be nearly 90,000,000 people of various races who can be listed under the general heading of Malays, and of whom the vast majority has a common bond of unity in the Islam faith.

This chauffeur and cicerone was a smart young scoundrel. Four years ago he had come to Colombo as a chauffeur, not knowing a word of any language except Malay. He now spoke Tamil, Cingalese, English and French. I soon discovered how he had developed his linguistic abilities so quickly. He was evidently accustomed to showing the town to visitors. "Here", he said, pointing to some well-built houses with attractive 'stoeps', "is where the Dutch used to live. Now all Scots gentlemen." Farther on we passed more bungalows, luxurious enough but less tidy. "Here", he said, "is where the rich Klings live." In his melodious voice there was the same natural accent of contempt which is common to all Malays in referring to the races of India. As we continued our drive, the number of Christian churches and church schools increased very noticeably. Our Mat Saleh pointed them out with the sure knowledge of an expert: "Dutch Reformation Church, Scotsman's Church, American Methodist Church and School, English White Man's Church, Tamil Catholic Church, Cingalese Catholic

Church—Eglise française avec école." The few words of French impressed Tommy. "You speak French?" she asked. "Ah oui, lady. I learn four languages in four years. Colombo very good place to learn languages. Go one year French church school, learn French language. Go one year English church school, learn English; one year Catholic Tamil school, learn Tamil. Very good method."

When I was in Japan twenty-five years ago, the young Japanese were learning languages by the same method. To-day, like Japanese goods, the system seems to have spread all over Indonesia.

Our Malay hopeful, however, was still a good Mohammedan. As we passed the mosque, he pointed it out with obvious pride. "To-morrow", he said "is 'hari Jema'at' (Friday). There will be many people here."

After driving round for an hour or two we went to the Galle Face Hotel to pick up Harry Rosslyn. We found him in Macan Markar's jewellery store together with Lord and Lady Pembroke, who had been staying in Ceylon and were going on to Java in our ship. The motto of Macan Markar is "known for reliability". The epithet is no exaggerated boast. The firm has an international reputation, and for many years has done a regular business with the leading jewellers of London, New York and Paris. Some idea of its standing may be gained from the fact that when it opened its new premises in 1928 the inauguration ceremony was attended by the British Governor in his official capacity.

The firm possesses the finest sapphire in the world, a stone whose shimmering blue is rivalled only by that of the Indian Ocean on the calmest and sunniest of days. It was found in a rice-field and is valued at £50,000, but until the United States turns that elusive corner of prosperity it is never likely to fetch this price or to be sold at all. To-day the owners still talk with grateful awe of the last great sapphire purchased in Colombo. It was found in 1907, weighed 466 carats, and was bought by the late Mr. J. P. Morgan, Senior,

when he passed through in his yacht. The price paid was a
good one, but it was very much smaller than the price fixed
on the present stone, which bears the music-hall name of
"The Blue Belle of Asia". In spite, however, of the depression, or perhaps because of it, the East is still the East, and
the firm's methods of trading and bargaining are still
pleasant and entertaining.

When we entered the shop, we found a sleek and im-
maculately dressed manager heavily engaged in trying to
persuade Harry Rosslyn to buy various kinds of sapphire
and aquamarine settings at prices ranging from £300 to
£3000. The temptation to this born gambler must have been
irresistible, but Tommy arrived in time to prevent what
would have been an injudicious purchase, not from the
point of view of the value offered, but of the state of Harry's
finances. With clever diplomacy she switched him off to an
inspection of the jewels of the old Cingalese kings of Ceylon.
They must have been attractive old gentlemen, for their
personal adornment consisted of ear-rings with jewels set in
the most delicate filigree work, anklets, bracelets, a turban
tiara studded with sapphires, and a bejewelled breast-
plate.

Meanwhile Lady Pembroke had just concluded an excellent bargain. She had been staying at the Galle Face Hotel
for the past week, and on the day of her arrival had gone
into the store to complain about a slight defect in a stone
which she had bought in Colombo some eight years before.
The manager was apologetic. "I'll put everything right, my
lady. We want our customers to be satisfied. I'll make you
one big bargain." He had then produced a ring, a sapphire
bracelet, a sapphire and diamond necklace, and a magnificent
sapphire stone fit for the finest tiara in the world. He then
placed them, first, on a black velvet cloth and then on one of
a faint yellow. Then, piece by piece, in order of value and
beauty, he had lifted them lovingly to reveal their qualities
to every angle of the light. A faint sigh had escaped his lips.

Then, suddenly, he had turned to the window. "£—— for the lot, my lady, and cheap at the price."

The figure mentioned was substantial, but would not have been considered exorbitant in London or New York. Lady Pembroke had looked at the collection and had liked it. But she had kept her head and with great firmness had offered a sum rather less than half the manager's original price. The manager had smiled politely as if to convey his appreciation of Lady Pembroke's joke, but for the next six days he had never left her. By the second day he had reduced his price by twenty per cent. By the third day, with tears in his voice, he had announced his willingness to come down another ten per cent. On the fourth day with sobbing protests that he was giving his precious stones away he had knocked off yet another ten per cent. On the fifth day, with the mournful tones of an undertaker, he had resigned himself to a further reduction, pointing out that his sole object was to retain the goodwill of so august a customer and that he was losing money on the deal. Lady Pembroke had stuck resolutely to her original offer. Finally, that very morning, which was to be the day of her departure, the manager had made his last price. It was still a little higher than Lady Pembroke's bid, but about fifty-five per cent. below his own original demand. After consulting her husband, Lady Pembroke accepted.

The deal had just been concluded when we came into the store. Both customer and salesman were smiling with the respect and contentment born of a bargain which has given satisfaction to both sides, and from its yellow-white velvet throne the great sapphire sparkled and beamed on everyone. The whole deal was a remarkable refutation of the foolish Western adage that in the East time is no object. On the contrary, time—and lots of it—is all-important in every Oriental transaction whether of high diplomacy or of more common-place commerce.

From the Galle Face we went to tea at Government House, or rather at a temporary Government House, for the official residence was being restored. The approach was by green fields where young Cingalese students were playing cricket with the graceful ease common to all Indians. The house itself exhaled an English summer atmosphere of afternoon tea and lawn tennis. Actually, Miss Dorothy Round, the English champion, who also was going on with us to Singapore, was playing an exhibition match on a court close by.

Sir Reginald Stubbs, the Governor, was on board our ship attending the captain's "jamboree" for the Colombo locals. These functions, incidentally, are only one of the numerous Dutch methods of advertising their liners. Lady Stubbs, grey haired, tall, very English, very gentle, and full of poise, looked tired. She had been working night and day superintending the battle against the malaria epidemic which was then raging in the low-country districts of Ceylon.

There were two explanations, she told us, for the scourge which had suddenly descended on the island. The official one was that it was caused by the unprecedented drought which not only had ruined the crops but had dried up the streams leaving everywhere pools of stagnant water as fertile breeding-grounds for mosquitoes. The natives had, of course, a very different explanation. A few months before the outbreak of the epidemic King George had graciously given back to Ceylon the old Cingalese throne which had been kept for years at Windsor. I do not suppose that King George or any member of the Royal Family ever sat on it. But the Cingalese were firmly persuaded that the plague was a visitation sent by the throne-god, who was enraged because his throne was empty. Apparently, when it was filled he was warm and happy like a gourmet's stomach after a good meal. Now that it was empty, he was angry.

Be this as it may, the superstition had a serious effect on Cingalese patients who, believing that they had been struck down by a supernatural power, made little or no effort to recover.

It had been an exhilarating day. Looking back with the soot of a London fog boring its way through the curtains of my study window, I feel that Ceylon is a country which I should like to know better and where I could gladly spend a year. But when we sailed that night I had no regrets. Singapore was only five days' journey ahead, and the spell of Malaya was already upon me. My nerves tingled with impatience, and I made myself a nuisance to everybody trying to work out time-tables which had seemed simple in theory but which in practice could not be made to fit. Reluctantly I decided to omit the Indo-China part of my tour. Desire had outrun the time-limit at my disposal.

CHAPTER EIGHT

FIFTY-SIX HOURS LATER we arrived at Sabang, the port of Pulau Wei, the most Western island of the Malay Archipelago. I rose at six to see the ship steering its way in a rose-pink dawn into a picture-postcard bay studded with islets. The perfection of the approach was marred by a huge unsightly hoarding, placed on the most attractive headland and advertising the virtues of a well-known mineral water. I am, I hope, no crank, but were I an out-of-work millionaire in search of a hobby, I should certainly try to form a world society whose members would be pledged to boycott all goods which are advertised in places where they are an eyesore on the face of natural beauty.

The port of Sabang has little to recommend it. It is only ten years old and is used mainly as a coaling and oil station. Most of the port buildings consist of long, corrugated iron sheds. Close to the jetty, shoals of goldfish swim leisurely in the lukewarm water.

The Achinese, a race of warriors who for forty years defied all efforts of the Dutch to subdue them, form the indigenous population. Like most other members of the Malay race, they have no aptitude for, and no interest in, commerce. In the town itself the shops are owned by Chinese and Japanese. There are a small garrison and some comfortable-looking Dutch bungalows. Every house, Dutch, Chinese, Japanese, and even Achinese, has a gramophone which plays at full blast from early morning until late at night.

After watching for a few minutes a strenuous football match, played on the local padang in the full blaze of the noon-day sun between the crew and the passengers of our steamer, I took a car and made a tour of the island. The road, gratefully shaded by lofty trees, was a switchback in which steep gradients alternated with pleasant glades with butterflies of every size and colour fluttering over the green grass.

65

Away from the immediate neighbourhood of the town there was little sign of cultivation. A small fresh-water lake, quite unspoilt by the handiwork of man and reflecting in its unruffled waters the green shadows of the hills, added a picturesqueness to an island which, as far as scenery is concerned, should be as attractive to a modern Gauguin as Tahiti. But, for all their warrior qualities, the Achinese are not alluring physically, and this is, doubtless, the reason why the island has attracted none but Dutch painters.

Sabang has one institution which I inspected and which gives to the island a special importance in Dutch eyes. This was the lunatic asylum which is one of the largest in the Dutch East Indies. The patients, over a thousand in number, are given a considerable amount of freedom. The establishment is excellently run, although with its barrack-like bungalows and its barbed-wire entanglements it looks more like a German internment camp than an asylum. There are coconut plantations and a vegetable garden run entirely by the patients. The institution is close to the road and fully exposed to the public view.

I found it hard to distinguish between warders and patients, a difficulty which fills the foreign visitor with a feeling of insecurity. In my youth my father and mother were intimate friends of the head doctor of Broadmoor, the great British criminal asylum. As we lived close by, I was expected to take part in cricket matches against a combined team of warders, chaplains, and patients, and to dance at the annual ball with the more innocuous of the female patients. Asylums have furnished the theme of a series of humorous and successful novels written by an old pupil of my father. But on me their effect has always been shattering, and I find these personal contacts with people who are in reality exiles from life itself, more macabre than meeting those lingering on the brink of death.

Since my visit to Sabang I never think of an asylum without recalling the story, told to me by a former member of his cabinet, of a well-known Dutch minister, who throughout his life refused persistently to contribute to the upkeep of any institution for the mentally deficient. The minister was rich. He was a generous giver to other charities. Above all, he was a foremost exponent of that policy of social welfare which has made Holland the one country in the world today without slums. His idiosyncrasy was therefore a puzzle to his colleagues. At last one more daring than the others put the question to him:

"Excellency, why do you contribute so generously to other charities and yet refuse your aid to what is surely one of the most deserving causes of suffering humanity."

"Gentlemen," said the Minister gravely, "I am in favour of asylums, but were I to contribute to them personally my opponents might conclude that I believed that everyone outside them was sane."

In this institution I saw a case of a strange Malayan disease known in the vernacular as "latah". I suppose it is caused by some lack of muscular control like St. Vitus's dance. In the case of a "latah" victim this lack of control takes the form of an involuntary muscular reaction which forces the patient to imitate the movements of anyone who engages his attention. Someone raises his hand or makes a face. The patient does the same.

It is an affliction which lends itself to the propensities of practical jokers. I remember from my early days in Malaya an old Malay woman who used to sell sweet drinks and fruit at the Seremban railway station in Negri Sembilan. When a train came in, she used to walk along the platform with a tray. Sometimes, when we were going to Kuala Lumpur or Kajang to play hockey or football, we would amuse ourselves by pulling faces at her or laughing loudly. She was forced to respond. Then someone would pretend to be throwing things on the ground, and the poor old lady would begin to throw her fruit on to the platform. I am bound to say that the practical joker always paid her handsomely. But it was a cruel form of amusement, and to-day the thought of it fills me with shame.

Here in Sabang the patient was an elderly man, lean and scraggy. I could not make out whether he was patient or employee, for he was quite sane and worked a full day as a vegetable gardener on the asylum farm. I expect that he was kept there in order to spare him from the mockery of his fellow creatures, although Malays, as a rule, are kind to "latah" victims and reprove the thoughtless youths who attempt to make fun of them.

Sabang has a permanent place in my memory, because during this voyage it was the scene of my only adventure into which the element of danger may be said to have entered. Having heard much of the fish to be caught in the bay, I determined to try my luck. The Dutch, as usual, gave me every facility, and on landing at Sabang on my way home I took a car and drove out to a tiny fishing village where a small dug-out with two Achinese fishermen was waiting for me. They were little more than boys. The bay was full of sharks. One of fourteen feet had been caught the previous day, and I had seen its carcase rotting in the sun. I had, however, no tackle for such heavy fish. My quest was the "ikan tenggiri", a long, narrow fish with a blue-green skin. It can move faster than a salmon, and it is a great sight to see one travel fifty yards or more on the top of the water in pursuit of the small fish which are its prey.

Trolling two lines, baited with small fish, we paddled towards the far side of the bay. Once or twice the bait was hit hard, but I was either too slow or too fast, and I could never strike the hook home. When I struck too quickly, the fishermen would say: "You must wait, Tuan." If I waited, there was a gentle reprimand of "Too slow, Tuan."

Doubtless, the time of day was unpropitious and the sun too bright. It was also unpleasantly hot, and the frail dug-out, far too narrow for my bulky figure, imposed on me a stationary restraint which cramped my body. By eleven o'clock the sweat was streaming down my face, and I ached in every limb.

We were already nearly an hour's paddle away from our starting place and, irritated by the heat and by my lack of success, I gave the order to return. We turned and proceeded leisurely homewards. Bent forward in the centre of the dug-out with my eyes closed, I was mopping my face with my handkerchief, when suddenly the two Achinese began to splash so violently with their paddles that the water soaked my coat and the boat began to rock with a rapidity that made my balance precarious. "What are you doing?" I shouted sharply. "Sharks", said the two boys and continued their splashing. Two long shadowy figures came up beside the dug-out, swam slowly alongside for a few seconds, and then, disliking the splashing, turned and disappeared in the deep water. The fishermen pushed the dug-out forward with a few rapid strokes. Then, relapsing into their normal leisurely pace, they grinned. "Dangerous?" I asked. "Oh no, Tuan," they said. "They are stupid fish. But if one hit the boat by accident it would be unpleasant." They grinned again. But I was not amused. My discomfort was rendered more acute by fear. It continued until we reached the shallow water near the shore.

Fishermen, however, are alike all the world over. When we were within twenty yards or so of the fishing village, the locals came out to see us land. At once our boys began to announce the catch. We had hooked the biggest "ikan teng-giri" ever seen in the bay. The paddle was held up and the exact length of the fish denoted with a thumb-nail. The tenggiri has pulled us half-way across the bay. It had broken the tackle and gone off with half of a brand-new line.

This piece of fiction was received by the onlookers with interest and apparent credulity. There was no mention of the sharks which had disturbed my equanimity. Doubtless, they were an every-day incident in the life of a race which laughs at all dangers, except the supernatural, and especially at those with which from infancy it has been familiar.

The next morning we arrived at Belawan Deli, the magnificent modern port at the mouth of the Deli river. It is the outlet for the products of Eastern Sumatra, and through its wharves pass the vast quantities of tobacco, rubber, palm-oil and tea which in less than fifty years have turned a virgin jungle into one of the richest areas in the world.

Here we stayed twelve hours, and, as Belawan itself is a flat and dreary hell-hole, I took a car and made the trip to Medan, the seat of the East Sumatra Government. It lies about fifteen miles inland and but for the Sultan's palace is more like a Dutch provincial town than an Eastern city.

The Sultan's palace was a disappointment. I had seen photographs of it in various Dutch books and had been enchanted by the slender form of the minaret of the mosque and the apparently beautiful gardens. The reality, however, brought disillusionment. The palace and the mosque were horribly new, and the gardens with their artificial lake lacked even a suggestion of charm. The whole surroundings gave me the impression of a temporary jerry-built structure put up for a colonial exhibition.

The place, however, was a concrete proof of the wealth of the Deli district. Thirty years ago the Sultan of Deli was little different from a Malay peasant, and his income could not have exceeded £300 a year. To-day, the development of Deli as a rubber and tobacco-growing centre has multiplied his income a thousandfold, and now he owns a fleet of motor-cars and a stable of racehorses and has acquired a number of other European vices.

Over 200,000 coolies have been imported for the development of these two planting industries, and the district produces about one-fifth of the world's total output of rubber. British capital as well as Dutch has played an important part in the development of this fabulously wealthy territory.

Medan itself is the Mecca of the European planters and in the days of the rubber boom it was the scene of orgies of a kind which is more commonly associated with gold rushes in the West of America. The Dutch are good spenders and good drinkers, and a farewell to a planter going home for good or even on leave left a trail of broken glass and sore heads behind it. I saw one such farewell on my way home. In spite of the prevailing bad times half the Europeans in Medan turned up at Belawan Deli to deposit the departing guest on the steamer, and the din and cheering which greeted his departure could not have been exceeded even by the exuberance of a Yorkshire crowd welcoming home its football team after winning the coveted English Cup.

Medan, too, is the departure point for Brast'agi, the finest hill station in the Malay Archipelago. The drive up the mountain pass to the Batak country with its curious villages built with enormously high roofs, and to Lake Toba is an experience which stirs the enthusiasm of even the most jaded sight-seer, and the range of view from the top of the pass is unexcelled by any other vista in the world.

But this visit I deferred until my return journey. Although Sumatra is probably the Eastern country with the greatest future, the truth is that at this moment I was unable to concentrate my thoughts on these new surroundings. We were due in Singapore the next morning. That night I slept little, but paced the top deck alone, my mind swaying between the past and the present, in the excitement of anticipation. At one moment my enthusiasm was as eager as that of a youth embarking on his first lone voyage in life. I saw myself again in Pantai, meeting old friends and picking up from them the threads of Amai's story and of her subsequent fate. Then the doubts of middle age would obtrude themselves, preparing me for the possibility of disappointment. One thought, however, dominated all others. I was on the point of realising a dream which had never seemed more than a dream. On the morrow I should see again the blue hills of Malaya.

BOOK II

A STRANGER RETURNS

F

"EVEN SUCH is Time that takes in trust
Our youth, our joys, our all we have,
And pays us but with earth and dust."

CHAPTER ONE

THERE MUST ALWAYS be something exotic in the return of a man to a foreign country which he had known in his youth but which he has not re-visited for a quarter of a century. The geographical progression is in the inverse direction to that of the exile who is returning home after long service abroad. Yet the sentimental reaction is not dissimilar, and in both cases there is likely to be the same disillusionment over ties which have long since been broken and which exist only in the romantic background of the memory. For weeks I had invested this return to Malaya with a gaily-coloured cloak of romance. I had steeled my heart resolutely against the danger of dwelling too lovingly on the past. Change I was prepared for, and I realised that I should return as a stranger in a community to which I was not even a name. For a period of twenty-five years in the East covers most men's careers, and of the friends of my youth I knew that few were left. But enthusiasm is the mainspring of adventure, and I had set high hopes on a journey that was to recapture the glamour of the days that were gone.

If I was not disappointed, the reality of my arrival was very different from the dream.

True, the approach more than fulfilled my expectations. I awoke before six and from my porthole saw the shadowy line of the Malayan coast, slate grey in the early dawn. As the sun rose in a cloudless sky, the land, green-blue where sea and shore met, stood out in bold relief. And in the background were the mountains of Malaya as blue, as languorous, and as majestic as my fancy had ever pictured them. The scene was unchanged. I could detect no houses. Like an ant-heap seen from the distance, the land seemed motionless and uninhabited.

I dressed with feverish haste and went on deck. We were

75

somewhere off Malacca, but the town itself was invisible. The sea was as calm as a lake on a windless day. I tried to recapture the impression of my first voyage, but the effort defied my memory. Instead, I found my thoughts turning to the countless Europeans who had sailed down these straits: from the great heroes of Portugal, the early Dutch traders and sea-captains, unappreciated Imperialists like Raffles, and Catholic missionaries, turning their backs for ever on the Old World, to the cheerful youths who, like myself attracted by the new plantation rubber industry, had set out in the early years of this century in search of quick fortune and a pleasant life.

But no Portuguese dom of the sixteenth century, not Sequeira nor Albuquerque himself, had made so emotional an approach to this Golden Chersonese as Joseph Conrad in modern times. It was in 1883, three years before he became a naturalised British subject, that the *Palestine*, a barque of 425 tons on which he had shipped from London as second mate, had caught fire in the Indian Ocean and after four days had been abandoned. And it was from an open boat that the future author, then a young man of twenty-five, caught his first glimpse of Singapore and found safety in its friendly harbour. No wonder that the prose which was in the man had to find its outlet in an Eastern theme. Doubtless, too, the experience helped him to form his magnificent philosophy towards life. "Man is only a feeble light in the storm, but this light resists and this light is everything." It was a sailor's philosophy, but it could be adopted with benefit by every white man in the East.

My musings were soon interrupted. Passengers were now lining the side of the ship. Boys were hustling along the decks, collecting chairs and forgotten books. There was the laborious business of tipping to be done. There were the goodbyes to be said to people whom one had learnt to know more intimately in three weeks than if one had lived beside them in England for a life-time, and yet whom one realised instinctively one would never see again. These duties finished, I went on to the promenade deck to find Hewan, who as an old shipping man knew every inch of these waters and every story connected with them.

We were now approaching the numerous islands with which the entrance to Singapore is studded. The islands themselves were an indication of the new Singapore. Where formerly all had been greenness were now great patches of hard yellow soil disfigured by huge oil tanks. Bungalows, many of them occupied by officers, held the best points of vantage. Beside a small wharf, before we reached the entrance to the harbour, we came upon a destroyer. Naval ratings, clad in topees, shirts and shorts, were scrubbing the decks. It was a new and strange aspect of the British Navy. Three airplanes, shimmering like quicksilver in the bright sunlight, whirred above our heads.

But neither the noise nor the unseemly advertisement hoardings could spoil the beauty of a harbour which, just because it has so few of the stereotyped features of most harbours, never grows stale. As we steamed slowly alongside the Nederland wharf in the huge Tanjong Pagar dock, I was thrilled by the sight of the countless small craft which form the units of Singapore's world-famed mosquito fleet. Not since the war had I seen so much shipping in one port. There on the quay was Commodore Mark Wardlaw to meet the Pembrokes. There, too, to greet me was my old friend, Freddie Cunningham, who lived near my former home at Port Dickson and with whom I was to spend what I had rightly expected would be the happiest part of my visit.

I felt a lump rise in my throat. And then came the inevitable anti-climax. Wardlaw and Freddie were soon on board. But we were not allowed ashore. Its new importance as a great military, naval and air base has given to Singapore a perhaps necessary vigilance against spies and communists, and we were in the grip of the British bureaucratic machine.

In this case it was operated by a single passport or immigration officer, who did his job with a patient courtesy, but with a thoroughness and slowness which in any foreign port would have roused the British passengers to the usual explosion of invective against the inefficiency of foreigners.

With the Rosslyns and the Pembrokes we sat down at a table in the smoking saloon to await our turn. Freddie, always in his element as a host, produced cocktails, and while he gave the local gossip to the others, Reggie Pembroke told me a story of Wardlaw, a slim, rather silent man who impresses by the quiet efficiency with which he gets things done.

Reggie was in the "Blues" and fought all through the war. Through his grandmother he has Russian blood, and had his father cared to change his nationality Reggie would now be the head of the princely family of Vorontzoff. On account of his Russian connections he was sent on a temporary mission to Russia during the war and was received by the late Tsar. "You are wearing the wrong uniform," said the Ruler of all the Russias. Reggie, who is particular about these matters, was taken aback. "You should be wearing a Russian uniform," said the Tsar, releasing him of his embarrassment.

What Reggie might have worn but never has is a British naval officer's uniform, for he is a born sailor who is never happier than when he is on the bridge, examining charts, taking bearings and doing all those other little mysteries in which sailors delight. Some years ago he was on a world cruise and, as is his wont, spent most of his time on the bridge. There, every day, he noticed a man who, like a hawk intent on its prey, hovered for hours with compasses and pencil over his own charts. They became friends. The man was Wardlaw. He was then a commander in danger of the government axe which during those post-war years of British disarmament ended the career of so many brilliant naval officers. Reggie asked him what he was doing. "Taking a busman's holiday," was the quiet reply. "I'm checking our charts. May be useful some day." Reggie was impressed by this devotion to duty, and soon the story of the commander's keenness on his job reached the ears of a famous Admiral. Wardlaw was given command of a flotilla of destroyers at Hong-Kong. To-day, as Senior Naval Officer in Singapore, he shares a large part of the responsibility for the most ambitious overseas defence scheme which the British Empire has ever undertaken.

I looked at Wardlaw with a new respect. I looked, too, with some trepidation at the third Bacardy cocktail which, during the telling of this story, had appeared mysteriously beside my elbow. The passport queue still seemed as long as ever, and, as it was already past one o'clock, we decided to lunch on board. Our party was breaking up, but only temporarily. The Pembrokes, who liked the sea, were going on by steamer to Java and then to Bali. The Rosslyns were to stay a few days with Freddie Cunningham. Then their course was set leisurely for Bali. We all had planned to meet in Singapore in five weeks' time. Luncheon should have been, and to the others probably was, a gay and amusing meal. But I was restless and ill at ease. I wanted desperately to talk to Freddie, and during the two hours he had been on board I had not had a word with him alone. At last I got him into a corner by ourselves. He looked at me rather seriously and put his arm on my shoulder. "I've some news for you," he said. "She's alive and she knows you are coming." I understood at once that he meant Amai.

There was neither elation nor regret in my heart, but only a feeling of clammy nervousness. I was not helped by the reflection of my figure in the glass mirror of the saloon. With startling vividness I pictured to myself the ravages of twenty-five years of tropical sun on the former beauty of a young Malayan girl. I remembered Amai's aunt, an old hag with betel-stained lips. She must then have been between forty and fifty. Amai herself must now be over forty. There would be no Loti-esque farewell in a Malayan graveyard. Pantai was the living cemetery of a romance that was dead. Here was a complication, rich in its possibilities of ridicule, which had never entered my mind.

Fortunately, my reflections were cut short with welcome abruptness. All was now ready for us to leave the ship, and in a few minutes I was driving along Anson Road, alone with Freddie in his car. As we passed through the business quarter of the city, I noticed with surprise and admiration the many new splendid offices. But I was still more amazed by the silence of the streets. They seemed strangely deserted. We pulled up at the Singapore Club where Freddie wished to cash a cheque. With a bewildered sweep my eye took in a magnificent building, new of course since my time and stately and large enough to dominate Pall Mall if it were transferred to that centre of London clubland.

I turned to Freddie with a gasp: "Gosh, it's like Liverpool —except that Liverpool has more Chinese!"

"You're right," said Freddie. "The Chinese are in the back streets playing with dragons, squibs, crackers, and other explosives. You've struck the last day of Chinese New Year."

The sun beat down on us fiercely enough. But there was none of the old enervating humidity in the air. Here was another miracle. I had arrived in the middle of a drought almost unprecedented in the history of Singapore Island.

As we passed over Anderson Bridge, hundreds of junks and sampans, jammed close together in an apparently inextricable maze, lay idle and unattended. But from the river itself came a breath of the old Singapore—that stew of Oriental smells which is responsible for the last word in the trinity of the city's nickname of "Chinks, Drinks and Stinks". Now the old landmarks began to reveal themselves. There, looking down from Empress Place close to a group of Government buildings, was the statue of Raffles, the founder of the city and the most inspiring figure in the history of the British rule in the East. It looked a little be-

draggled, a little in need of a bath, for, although the name
of Raffles is never forgotten in any speech in Singapore, no
one would accuse the British, and, least of all, the sport-
loving British in the East, of an exaggerated reverence for
statues. `

Perhaps this apparent indifference to externals is a healthy
sign. The memory that is passed down from generation to
generation is of more value to a race than any attempted per-
petuation in stone or marble.

There, too, on the left was the Cathedral of St. Andrew,
very English and in its stately greyness conveying an atmosphere of more permanence than any other building in Singapore. Here on the right was the old "padang" with the
British Singapore Cricket Club at one end and the Eurasian
Recreation Club at the other, a striking symbol of the
British attitude towards the colour question and of the fact
that the field of sport is the one place where British and
Eurasians meet as equals.

Suddenly the car pulled up, and a tall Indian chasseur,
magnificent in black beard, turban and red sash, came forward to open the door. We had arrived at Raffles Hotel,
known from Port Said to Wei-hai-wei as "Raffles", and,
now that the old Europe Hotel is gone, more than ever the
centre of Singapore life for tourists and for planters down
from the Federated Malay States for a "jolly". My first
cinematic view of the city was over.

It was the old Raffles of my youth, but so altered, so re-
equipped and so enlarged as to be almost unrecognisable.
Gone were the Sarkies, the former Armenian proprietors.
Gone, too, was "Joe", the old Armenian manager, the cultivation of whose acquaintance was worth many amenities,
including an occasional tip for the races.

There were other changes. I remembered with poignant
vividness my first arrival at the hotel twenty-seven years before. Then my ignorance of a single word of Malay had left
me in a state of irritating helplessness. Now that I knew the

language it was of little use to me. Every Tamil clerk and even the youngest Chinese "boy" not only knew English, but used it with an insistence which defeated all my efforts to break it down. The population of Singapore is now 550,000. It includes a vast diversity of races, of whom over 400,000 are Chinese. There are fewer than 70,000 Malays and only 9000 Europeans. Yet to-day there are Singapore-born Chinese who speak English as their first language. Some day, perhaps not very far distant, English, and not bazaar Malay, will be the *lingua franca* of Singapore. In one sense it may well be the most significant triumph of a British rule which, in spite of certain criticisms, some fair and some unfair, is still administered with an instinctive sense of justice and fair-play, and with a happy balance of solicitude for the interests of the various races under its care and protection.

When we arrived, the huge verandah with its dancing floor and its score of small tables was deserted. It was the hour when all sensible people, who do not have to work, were resting. I was well pleased with the spacious lofty room which Freddie had engaged for me. With relief I in-spected the huge electric fan with blades as large as an air-plane's propellers. Here was a modern innovation which I could appreciate. But when I came to the bathroom my face fell. There, firmly set in the tiled floor, was a European bath of the latest model with hot and cold water complete. Al-though the Raffles managers still tell the story of the old lady who stuck in one, the old Siamese jar with its tin-pan for sluicing one's self was evidently a thing of the past. I felt a pang of regret, and after my experience of the Dutch East Indies, where the Siamese jar is still in use, the regret remains. In my opinion the sluice-bath is by far the most invigorating and refreshing form of bath in the tropics.

We sat down and began to talk, trying to bridge over the gaps in the past. Freddie and I were brought up as boys to-gether. He was the youngest of a family of four brilliant brothers. Jim, the eldest, passed first into Woolwich and was rejected on account of his eyesight. It was not too defective to prevent his joining up in 1914, and both he and his second brother, Charlie, were killed in France. George, the third brother, who was at Fettes with me, is the former Oxford and Scotland "rugger" captain and ex-scholar of Magdalen. He passed high into the Indian Civil Service, and was Lord Irwin's private secretary during the period of his Viceroyalty. To-day, at the age of forty-eight, he is Sir George Cunningham, Governor of the North-West Province of India.

Freddie, the youngest son, was supposed to have fewer brains than his brothers. He was therefore sent to Glen-almond. By this time we had become family connections, my uncle, a rubber pioneer in Malaya, having married his first cousin. When, in 1908, it was evident that plantation rubber was about to come into its own, I went out to join my uncle in Malaya. Freddie followed me six months later. We had both been stationed in Negri Sembilan, and Freddie had succeeded me as a "creeper" on the Third Mile estate at Port Dickson. Freddie has remained in Port Dickson ever since. The story of the so-called brainless son of the family has run true to type. A shrewd Scot, with the same capacity as Maurice Baring for balancing glasses on his head in his hours of relaxation, he has prospered exceedingly. Now, with his own rubber estate and interests in coal and jute, he is the freest and probably the most successful planter in Malaya.

We had so many interests in common that we should have talked until dark had not Freddie insisted on my un-packing and on my having a lie-off. We were to meet again at five-thirty and to dine later at the Sea View, a new hotel on the sea-front outside the city. I lay down on the bed, but rest was impossible, and presently I made my way to the reception office to find out where I could order some Malay "sarongs" and "bajus", which in my day were the regulation undress uniform and sleeping-suit of the up-country planter and official. There was an Indian shop in the hotel arcade, and there, at a trifling cost but still many times higher than I should have had to pay up-country in the old days, I ordered myself three modestly coloured "sarongs" and three white silk "bajus". With the customary despatch of the Eastern outfitter, they were ready for me the next morning.

When Freddie came to fetch me, I had bathed and changed and was ready for anything. First, we went to the Singapore Club to collect Harry Rosslyn. Taking the lift, we went up to the top floor and from the terrace had a superb view of the harbour. Between us and the pink and saffron-coloured horizon ocean liners, merchant ships, and the slender forms of Buginese sailing "prahus" lay motionless on the glass-surfaced water. Farther out at sea, closing in the whole scene, a line of British cruisers and destroyers, headed by H.M.S. *Kent*, stood out like black swans in the fading sunlight. I could have lingered long over this imposing and unforgett-able picture. But the others were impatient. Freddie had asked some friends to meet us. The Rosslyns had to dine with Wardlaw. Back we went to Raffles to indulge in the Singapore habit of "pahit" drinking. "Pahit", incidentally, is the Malay word for bitter. In Singapore English it means a whisky or a gin in a wine glass taken with bitters and a little water. It is a cleaner and less harmful drink than the American cocktail.

By this time the verandah terrace was beginning to fill up and, as we took our places, couples were already dancing on the floor to the latest American and English tunes played by a jazz-band composed, like most bands in the East, of Austrians and Russians. There were almost as many women as men, and some of the women at any rate drank "pahit" for "pahit" with their male companions and with appar-ently less effect on their composure.

It was one more proof of what I believe to be the most fundamental change in Malaya during the last twenty-five years: the huge increase in the number of white women and the passing of the directing force of social life into their hands. It is a change which impresses the old-timer very forcibly. Even admitting its inevitability, I cannot think that it is a change for the better. As I watched the scene, exemplary in its decorum, I put a brake on the natural tendency of the man who comes back to criticise adversely. For better or worse, this was the life of these people, and who shall say that they are not capable of ordering it more wisely and more in accordance with their own need than the tourist and the passing stranger. It is as much the natural tendency of the British exile to long for the lights of London and to seek the best imitation of them that local conditions can afford, as it is for the man chained to a London office stool to sigh for the green fields and placid streams of the English countryside.

I shall permit myself only one adverse observation. Throughout Malaya the hours from six-thirty to nine-thirty are the period, to-day rather extended but yet prescribed by years of tradition, for social relaxation. It is the time when these small British communities foregather in club, in hotel, or private bungalow after their daily tennis and golf and other games. It involves, perhaps, an exaggerated concentration on alcohol, which is not merely the fuel of conversation, but tends occasionally to become its sole topic. The concentration is certainly not greater than in my time and the alcohol is weaker. But it means a late dinner, and its chief drawback is that it entirely absorbs those hours of the day which are best suited for more profitable recreation. It is, in fact, mainly responsible for that absence of intellectual interests which is a defective feature of British colonial life in tropical countries.

I found that my capacity for "pahit" drinking was not what it used to be, and I was glad to get out into the cool night air and drive to the Sea View Hotel. Here, with the surf lapping the steps of the hotel, we dined in a spacious pillared hall. There was a dancing-floor in the middle, the inevitable jazz-band, and a cabaret show with a Russian singer and a blonde dancer in a transparent evening dress that suggested the lily of the field comparison with Solomon in all his glory. But it was the dinner itself which provoked my amazement. *Hors d'œuvre*, almost as numerous as the eighty varieties of Caramello, the famous Riviera restaurateur, were wheeled up to our table. I dined off an excellent *petite marmite, homard à l'américaine*, and roast pheasant complete with bread sauce and *pommes pailles*. Here I stopped, but had I wished I could have ended my meal with *pêche Melba* and angels on horseback. My mind went back to the stuffed eggs, the tinned mulligatawny soup, the "ikan merah", and the scraggy chicken which in the old days had formed the staple menu of every gala dinner. Here was a revolution. Indeed, cold storage, electricity, and the motorcar have entirely changed life in the tropics and have robbed it of nearly all its discomforts. To-day Singapore gets fresh meat from Australia, fresh butter from New Zealand, swede turnips from Sumatra, potatoes from Palestine, tomatoes from Java, rhubarb from New South Wales, oranges from China, and cabbages, lettuces and salads from the Malayan hill-station of Cameron Highlands. Soon, too, this Scottish-sounding resort will provide Malaya with fresh trout, for the ova which were put down in its mountain streams have given excellent results. Fishing, however, is not likely to be permitted before the end of 1937, and to my regret I was unable to add a Malayan specimen to the trout which I have caught in different parts of the world.

After dinner we went into the garden for coffee and brandy. The scene was enchanting if slightly artificial. The streams of light from the hotel gave an unnatural vividness to the grass and shed queer zigzags of a ghostly white on the sea before us. From the dining-room the strains of "Smoke In Your Eyes", pleasantly diminished by the distance, floated across to us through the night air.

Freddie's two friends, who completed our party, were a Dr. and Mrs. Hanna. Both are Americans and both are known throughout the length and breadth of British Malaya. Their popularity is merely one of countless proofs of my contention that, whatever political differences may exist between the two nations, British and Americans form a natural affinity whenever they meet abroad. They stand together in every scrap. In these circumstances, at any rate, they are the only two races in the world who can criticise each other's shortcomings without ill-feeling, and who can chaff each other without any barrier of national restraint.

"Doc" Hanna is a racing man in his spare time. As he had recently won a big race, most of our conversation was about the turf. I recalled the up-country racing of my early days: the raw Australian "walers", the auction sweeps, the amateur jockeys. There was, I think, only one well-known "bookie", an Australian called Tully, who went all over the country from meeting to meeting. Back through my mind floated a verse from a topical song written in Malay by one of the best linguists among our Government officers and sung at a smoking concert in my first year in Malaya:

> "Kelau suka mendapatan kreja—
> Untong besar sěkali,
> Dan patut menjadi bookmaka'
> Matcham Artie Tullee."

> "If you're seeking a job that is 'cushy'
> With profits as large as can be,
> Then you'd better start in as a 'bookie'
> Like the great Mister Artie Tullee."

Racing in those days had been a haphazard affair. Everybody had his little flutter, and the verse of the song was an accurate reflection of the empty pockets with which most of us, totally ignorant of form and of horseflesh, came back from our local meetings.

To-day, racing must be nearly the most profitable by-industry in Malaya. Singapore has a magnificent race-course equipped with the most modern of stands and a giant totalisator. The big meetings are attended by a vast crowd of all nationalities, and form the scene of a fashion parade not only of the European women, but also of the Chinese, whose modern Shanghai dresses with straight-cut frock slit on both sides from the ankles to the knees, has inspired many of the recent creations of the great costumiers of Paris, London and New York. There is, too, a whole army of thoroughbreds, professional jockeys, and trainers ; and Sultans like the Sultan of Perak and the Sultan of Johore spend large sums on buying horses. The most successful owners, however, are the rich Chinese who, apart from their innate love of a gamble, have become shrewd judges of form. Both the betting turnover and the stake money have increased a thousandfold. This progress of pleasure, which probably gives to the disgruntled champions of the past an excuse for their growls about the dangers of decadence and luxury, has been on the same scale in the smaller towns of Malaya.

I began to descant on my first impressions after my return, stressing particularly the immense improvement in the amenities and security of life, and adding a personal sigh of regret for the consequent loss of Oriental colour and atmosphere.

"I'm not so sure about the security," said Hanna thoughtfully. "And as far as local colour is concerned it depends on what you mean. Do you see that bathing 'pagar'?"

He pointed to a small enclosure of sea, fenced in with a palisade of heavy stakes, just below us.

"Well", he continued, "a young Australian girl, a tourist passing through, was picked off there by a shark in broad daylight only a few years ago."

I looked knowingly at Freddie. I had spent a long enough apprenticeship in the tropics to know that supplying tall stories to travellers, especially if they were writers, was a favourite leg-pull of the local experts. Their joy was renewed when they saw their best efforts perpetuated in print. The story of the Nigerian chief who on seeing the sea for the first time rushed forward to drink it in the belief that it was crème de menthe; the first-hand account of the traveller who, having been regaled with roast monkey, believed that he had taken part in a cannibal feast; these and many similar stories could be ascribed to the pleasant game of hoax, which is as old as man himself and which goes back to the days of the first traveller in history.

That night, before going to bed, I began to read some recent copies of the *Straits Times* which Freddie had left with me. Turning over the pages, I came across an account of a tiger which had swum across the straits of Johore and to the consternation of the native population taken up its abode on Singapore Island. I had spent three years of my life in a lonely district where tigers were far more numerous than they are now and had never seen one alive. Other men, who had spent their lives in the Malayan jungle, had had the same experience. Yet even to-day a tiger might walk into Government House, and no one except the Governor himself would be unduly astonished. At all events no one can say that such a visit is beyond the bounds of possibility.

My first comparison after landing now seemed foolish. Singapore is not like Liverpool. Except for the thin surface layer of Western civilisation imposed by the industry and energy of a few thousand Englishmen and maintained by the might of Britain's sea power, there is nothing European about it. Six hundred years ago a flourishing kingdom in Singapore was destroyed by foreign invaders from Java, and the island went back to jungle. In the light of the thousand new problems which confront the East to-day it is just conceivable that in another six hundred years it may go back to jungle again.

G

CHAPTER TWO

IN THIS CHAPTER I give a short summary of the geographical situation and of the most important statistics of British Malaya as a complement to the map which will be found on the end papers of this book. I assume without arrogance that some of my readers will be glad of this information, for even members of the British House of Commons are strangely ignorant of the geography of the British Empire for whose administration they are in the last resort responsible.

When, in 1935, the Dindings, a narrow strip of territory on the west coast of the peninsula, which formerly belonged to the Straits Settlements, was retroceded to Perak, one of the Federated Malay States, a member of the House of Commons put down a question to ask if the wishes of the Sultan of Irak had been consulted about this important matter. Although by the cognoscenti the "k" in Perak is not pronounced and the "e" has a Continental value, the member of Parliament had probably pronounced the word as it reads in its English transliteration and had confused it with Irak. It is perhaps unnecessary to add that Irak is some thousands of miles distant from the nearest point of British Malaya. Such geographical aberrations have been not uncommon in the history of British politics, and every Canadian knows that in the delineation of Canada's frontier with the United States the ignorance of British statesmen cost the Dominion more than one valuable strip of territory.

Let me state at once that Malaya is a peninsula lying between latitudes 1° and 7° north and a longitude of 100° to 105° east. It is situated in the south-eastern corner of Asia, roughly half-way between India and China, and comprises for purposes of administration the Colony of the Straits Settlements and the Protectorate of the Federated Malay States and of the Unfederated Malay States. The total area is a little larger than that of England, and the population is approximately four-and-a-half millions.

There are just under two million Malays, one million seven hundred thousand Chinese, and over six hundred thousand Indians. The Indians are principally Tamil coolies employed on the rubber estates. There are approximately twenty thousand Europeans and seventeen thousand Eurasians. The rest of the population, forming a fractional percentage of the whole, is made up of a motley collection of other Eastern races, including an important but relatively tiny Japanese colony. The diversity of races, especially the almost equal division between Chinese and Malays, is a great asset to the British administration, for it enables it to hold a fair balance between the widely divergent interests of the two main groups.

The Straits Settlements are composed of the four settlements of Singapore, a small island now joined to the State of Johore by a causeway; Penang, another island which includes in its administrative area Province Wellesley on the mainland; Malacca, historically the most interesting city of the Malay Archipelago; and Labuan, another small island off the north-east coast of Borneo. The Straits Settlements, administered as a Crown Colony, have a population of over a million. The Federated Malay States comprise the four States of Perak, Selangor, Negri Sembilan, and Pahang. They have had British advisers for the last sixty years, were federated in 1895, and were administered, in practice if not in theory, from the federal capital of Kuala Lumpur in Selangor. Since 1933 a new decentralisation scheme has conferred a greater measure of control over local affairs to the individual State Governments. The states form a British Protectorate and are ruled nominally by Sultans. The actual control, however, is in the hands of a very competent British civil service. The population of the F.M.S., as it is always called locally, is one million seven hundred thousand.

The Unfederated States are composed of the States of Johore, Kedah, Kelantan, Trenganu and Perlis in the Malay

Peninsula and of Brunei in Borneo. They have accepted British advisers to assist them in administrative matters and are bound by treaty relationship to the British Government. But their Sultans have more freedom of action than those of the Federated Malay States. The population is just over one million six hundred thousand.

For the purposes of a ready calculation the Chinese may be said to outnumber the Malays by more than two to one in the Straits Settlements, to have a slight numerical superiority in the Federated Malay States, and to be themselves outnumbered by the Malays by more than three to one in the Unfederated States. The Chinese predominate wherever industry and commerce exist. The Malays, ex-warriors who under British rule have become poor gentlemen of leisure, live mainly on their land.

From a practical point of view British influence in Malaya is a nineteenth century growth. Singapore itself, a creation of Sir Stamford Raffles, was founded in 1819. Since then the sphere of British influence has been slowly extended. It has been established with very little fighting, the great period of development in the Malay States during the last quarter of last century being distinguished by a marked ability on the part of the early British administrators in playing off one Sultan against another. The Governor of the Straits Settlements is also the High Commissioner for the Malay States. His dual capacity involves an inevitable, if only partial, centralisation of Government in Singapore. The Straits Settlements, the Federated Malay States and the Unfederated Malay States are known as Malaya.

In the early days of European colonial expansion the Malay Archipelago was the centre of the lucrative spice trade, and provoked what Lenin would have called the inevitable capitalist conflict between the Portuguese, the pioneer discoverers of the East Indies, and the Dutch; and later, between the Dutch and the English, who came last of all.

Malaya still exports spices of various kinds, but the twin gods of her wealth are Tin and Rubber. In 1933 she exported two-thirds of the world's rubber and nearly sixty per cent. of the world's tin. Die-hard Imperialists and supporters of economic autarchy should note that the United States took fifty-five per cent. of the rubber and fifty-eight per cent. of the tin. The United States is Malaya's best customer, her normal purchases representing from thirty-five to forty per cent. of Malaya's total exports. Britain is the next best customer, but whereas the United States sells to Malaya only a tiny fraction of what she buys, Britain buys less from Malaya than she sells to her. To-day a complicated system of import duties and quotas have further reduced American and other foreign imports into Malaya.

There is a definite clash of commercial interests between the Straits Settlements and the Malay States. The Straits Settlements live largely by the vast trade of the two great *entrepôt* ports of Singapore and Penang. Free trade has been the breath of their existence, and although Japanese competition has made many converts to protection, there are still free-traders to-day among the great mercantile houses, some of them over a hundred years old, of Singapore and Penang. The Malay States are producing countries. They are in favour of protection.

Taken together, the Straits Settlements and the Malay States are, for their size, the richest of all Britain's overseas possessions. In 1934 the overseas trade reached the huge total of £126,000,000. The figures for the same year for Ceylon, the senior Crown Colony, were only £25,000,000. Malaya, however, has suffered severely from the world economic depression, and it is only thanks to the international restriction schemes now in force for both rubber and tin that the country has been nursed back to a partial and perhaps only temporary prosperity.

Let it be added that in spite of quotas and duties the competition of Japan and China is making itself more strongly felt every day in almost every class of goods which formerly the British manufacturer used to supply, and the reader has a general idea of the racial and economic lay-out of a part of the world of which, sooner rather than later, he is likely to hear more.

Tucked away in the eastern estuary of the Strait of Johore and guarded by islands and Changi Point are the vast military, naval and air defences which, erected at enormous expense, have made the island of Singapore the greatest citadel of the world. At Changi, guarding the entrance to the Strait, are the shore batteries mounted with guns whose range is said to be over twenty miles. A somnolent Malay village in my time, Changi to-day is a garrison town complete with artillery, engineer, and infantry barracks. A few miles farther down the Strait is the new naval base. A bridge over a narrow arm of the sea connects it with the air base. Farther inland at the apex of a triangle of which the line from the air base to Changi forms the base is the Admiralty wireless station. A network of admirable roads connects all these vital arteries of the new defence scheme.

It is true that in my day also Singapore was a garrison town. There were small units of "sappers" and garrison artillery. A British infantry battalion and an Indian regiment enabled the Governor to add the title of Commander-in-Chief to his subsidiary title of High Commissioner. But there was no imprint of militarism on the life of the local British resident. The officers infused an added zest of rivalry into the local games and gave valuable support to the Singapore "rugger" and cricket teams in their matches against Hong Kong and the F.M.S. To the officers themselves their three years in Singapore was an exotic and not unpleasant interlude in the ordinary duties of soldiering. They were welcomed by the local British for the colour and distinction which they lent to the social life of the colony. It was rarely, if ever, that military matters obtruded themselves into the garrulous conversation of "pahit" time.

The war, the mutiny of 1915, and, above all, the disturbing menace of the awakening East, have shaken the foundations of this pleasant security. To-day, defence questions and spy mania obsess the minds both of the armed forces and of the local British, and the base is on everybody's lips. It is true that the millions of pounds which have been and still are being spent on the new defences have brought a welcome prosperity to the commercial community, both Chinese and British, and especially to contractors, builders and architects. Indeed, the housing problem is causing acute anxiety to the much harassed Government officials, who have already had to provide nearly ten per cent. of the area of an island only twenty-five miles long by sixteen wide for the accommodation of the armed forces.

While I was in Singapore I saw barracks being erected in feverish haste for the second British battalion which has already been added to the local strength. A third battalion is to join it as soon as the necessary accommodation can be provided. But apart from the pecuniary advantages which the defence scheme has brought to the local community, there is a new seriousness behind the cheerfulness and apparent levity of Singapore life. Twenty-five years ago a few planters and officials played at volunteer soldiering. Playing is perhaps an unkind epithet in reference to men who showed a public spirit in advance of their times. But their example attracted few recruits from among the vast majority of selfish and easy-going residents who, like myself, saw little use and no amusement in devoting part of their spare time to drills and shooting practice in the heat of a tropical sun. To-day, every young Englishman, be he planter, miner, or merchant, is urged to join the local volunteer forces which now include tanks and also local flying units attached to the Royal Air Force.

I doubt, however, if the passing tourist has more than the vaguest impression of the vast transformation which has taken place or if, apart from the occasional air-planes which

fly over his head, he realises the immense activities which are
being carried out within a few miles of his hotel. For the
defences, perhaps for political as well as for strategic reasons,
are hidden in a secluded part of the island which no one can
enter without a permit.

It is an imposing sight to come suddenly on the naval base
after a drive through palm groves and shady trees inter-
spersed with market gardens and peaceful kampongs. It is as
if one were suddenly to find a Portsmouth, equipped with
naval yard, wharves, huge oil and ammunition depots, and a
seven-hundred-yards-long quay, in the middle of a Highland deer forest.

The glory of the base is the great floating dry-dock which,
built by Swan, Hunter of Wallsend-on-Tyne, was towed on
its long journey from England to Malaya by Dutch tugs,
and which is large enough to accommodate the largest
battleship or, for that matter, the *Queen Mary* herself. As the
dock was being towed into her final resting-place, more
ballast was required. It was supplied by Japanese. For only a
few miles up the west coast of Johore is Batu Pahat, the centre
of the richest iron deposits in the Malayan Archipelago.

The Japanese exploit this iron field, having obtained a
concession from the Sultan of Johore. And now, every
second day, a Japanese steamer goes out from Batu Pahat
carrying away from under our very noses the ore which
Japan lacks in her own country, and which she doubtless
uses for some form of naval or military armament.

In 1935 Japan took 1,500,000 tons of iron from this Johore
concession. She has recently obtained a second concession in
Trenganu, one of the Unfederated Malay States, and this is
expected to yield 1,000,000 tons a year.

Nor is iron the only war material which Japan receives
from Malaya. There is another product of that rich and fertile country which is rapidly being bought up by the vigilant
Japanese. This is ilmenite, of which tens of thousands of tons
are to be found in the slag-heaps of Malaya's tin-mines.

Hitherto the product has been neglected, and in 1934 the total export to all countries was only fifty tons. Now the Japanese are buying it in thousands of tons. The reason is that ilmenite is used for the manufacture of titanium tetra-chloride, a liquid which fumes on contact with water. It provides the quickest and most efficacious smoke-screen for battleships.

To a neutral observer the fact that a country which adjoins the Singapore Base should be supplying the Japanese Fleet not only with the sinews of defence, but also with the means of invisibility, might present some of the elements of a comedy. But as I watched the swarm of Chinese coolies working on a huge graving dock then nearing completion, I could not help wondering how difficult it must be for a European to control the identity and even the nationality of these Oriental labourers, and how easily a determined fanatic might do irreparable damage to these costly constructions. I was re-assured by the sight of the contracting British engineer-in-charge. He must have weighed twenty stone—a grandiose figure of a man for a grandiose job.

How far is the defence scheme likely to justify the huge cost to the taxpayer of Great Britain and to the citizen of Malaya, for Malaya contributes more per head of population to Imperial defence than any other unit of the British Empire? A layman's criticisms of the strategic reasons which have dictated this conversion of Singapore into a modernised and impregnable Gibraltar are of little value. It is a soldier's job to discover sound strategic reasons for defending almost any place under the sun, and as a vital link in the chain of our sea and air communications with the Far East and with Australia the importance of a strong Singapore is self-evident. There is Australia, determined to keep herself white and already obsessed by the fear of a coloured invasion. There is India, for just as Changi guards the entrance to the naval base, so too Singapore is the sentinel of the Indian Ocean

The psychological reasons in justification of the scheme are more within the layman's province. They are strong. The white man's rule in the East is based on native recognition of his physical and mental superiority. Mainly as a result of the war the prestige of the white man all over the East has declined in startling fashion. Of all the changes which have taken place during the last twenty-five years this is the most important and the most far-reaching in its consequences. Through the imposing seriousness with which Britain has set her military house in order and the rapidity with which the defence scheme has been carried out, British prestige in Malaya has recovered much of its former glamour.

But even if every favourable argument is accepted at its face value, the fact remains that the scheme itself is primarily defensive and not offensive. Given that Britain can maintain two powerful fleets at the same time, a fleet, based on Singapore, could afford reasonable protection to the outlying islands of the Malay Archipelago. These are mostly Dutch possessions, and for that reason the scheme is welcomed by most Dutchmen in the East, although I met some Dutch business men who regarded it as an unnecessary and provocative challenge to Japan. It would be able to maintain communications with the eastern coast of Australia. But its operative radius would be limited. It would be powerless to protect British trade and shipping beyond an extreme limit of Hongkong, or to do anything to prevent Japan from taking whatever action in China she may decide to take.

It is as a defensive measure that the scheme justifies itself. Britain has reached the territorial limits of her Imperial expansion. Her possessions are coveted by ambitious nations in the East no less than by nations in other parts of the globe. In the face of the potential menace of Japanese conquest and of the already existing menace of Japanese trade competition Britain may one day have to make a stand in the East. If the British Empire is to survive, it is unthinkable that this stand should be made at any point west of Singapore. In the opinion of the experts the island has already been made impregnable to every form of attack from outside.

It would, however, be foolish to close one's eyes to the fact that the defence scheme has placed a new and heavy responsibility on the shoulders of the local British administration. There is the problem of the presence of large numbers of British troops in what is, in effect, a Chinese city and of the influence of their behaviour on the present loyalty of the Oriental population. I should not like to contemplate the sending to Singapore of Australian troops with a colour prejudice stronger than our own. Yet this is a potential eventuality, for Australia has a vital interest in the maintenance of the Singapore defences.

There is the more curious problem of the effect of a climate, which if not deleterious to health is nevertheless enervating, on the fighting efficiency of white forces, whether of the army or of the navy or of the air force. These are not necessarily insurmountable difficulties, but they are definitely problems which will have to be carefully watched.

I found it hard to resist a certain atmosphere of artificiality about the whole scheme.

This impression was strengthened by a glimpse of a squad of air force units awaiting the landing of a machine. The men were dressed in topees, khaki-coloured shirts and khaki shorts. With their knees browned by the sun, they looked fit enough. Without a doubt this dress is the most efficient that human ingenuity can devise for soldiering in tropical countries, but to me it seemed unnatural and slightly undignified. Here again was another startling change. Twenty-five years ago every Chinaman in Singapore wore a pigtail, the Tamil had a loin-cloth, the Malay Government "peon" his sarong and a khaki coat, and the European was covered in spotless white from chin to toes. To-day, the Orientals from the rich Chinese to the most junior Malay office boy are dressed in European clothes, while the European's undress uniform, seen almost invariably on the golf course and occasionally even in Raffles, is the shortest of shorts, a sleeveless shirt, and white stockings or socks.

It is true that in the evening the Singapore European is more "dressy" than he used to be, and that in the daytime he has not yet adopted a loin-cloth. But at first sight this inversion of the old order of things is startling, and it is permissible to doubt if the motto of comfort before prestige is altogether a sound policy for the white man in an Oriental city.

CHAPTER THREE

UNLIKE THE DUTCH, who have made a religion of tourist propaganda, the British in Malaya do little to attract the passing stranger. But to old friends, or to anyone bringing letters of recommendation from old friends, their hospitality is almost overwhelming. In spite of the fact that many of my contemporaries of twenty-five years before were dead or had left the country, I was in this happy position, and, had I accepted all the invitations that I received, I should have had to abandon all thought of visiting the Dutch East Indies and to cancel my passage home.

In Singapore I was especially fortunate. The Governor and his family were away on a tour of inspection in the F.M.S., but in the shadow of Government House I found two old friends in high official positions. One was Sir Andrew Caldecott, who had come out to Malaya a year before me, and who as Assistant District Officer in Jelebu had been almost my nearest white neighbour when I was at Pantai. The other was Gordon Ham, a former Cambridge hockey Blue, who had been Assistant District Officer during my first year at Port Dickson and who, as a serious and sober-minded young man, had been the confidant of my first literary ambitions.

I took the earliest possible opportunity of seeking out both. Gordon, who was now in the Secretariat of the Straits Settlement Government, was just leaving Singapore. Andrew, however, was at home, and he came at once to Raffles to carry me off in his car to luncheon. Although we had not met for twenty-five years, I had no difficulty in recognising him. In the old days we had played fierce home-and-home matches of football, transporting our teams of Malays by bullock-cart and by bicycle; in my case up the steep mountain pass to Jelebu, and in his case down the precipitous Bukit Tangga, where in those days we always wondered if the brakes of our bicycles would hold and what would happen if they did not. With one white man on each side, they had been

Homeric battles in which quarter was neither asked nor
given. We played opposite each other at centre half, charg-
ing like bulls and exhorting our barefooted Malays with
stentorian roars of "lekas-lah" and "jangan takut" ("Quick
there! Don't funk!").

There were not more than half-a-dozen motor-cars in
Negri Sembilan in those days, and, the journey being long,
we had stayed the night at each other's bungalows. Andrew
was a delightful host. He was already a good Malay scholar
with literary tastes and a genuine interest in the poetry and
folklore of the language. He had a piano and played it well.
More wonderful still, his bungalow was decorated with attractive water-colours of his own painting. Although he was
the prince of "good mixers" and a host in himself at a party,
he was a very exceptional figure in a community which in
those days, and even now, is chiefly remarkable for its
healthy low-browism. And, although he is probably unconscious of the fact, he, too, had a preliminary influence on the
shaping of my literary destiny.

Outwardly our re-union was unemotional. After years of
separation even the closest friends meet more or less as
strangers. He looked tired and overworked. Indeed, I was
lucky to catch him in Singapore, for he was leaving in two
days' time for a short and well-earned local leave at a Java
hill-station. During the last four years he had had nine different jobs, including those of Resident or Acting Resident
in several states, Acting Chief Secretary of the F.M.S. Government, and Acting Governor in Singapore. His present
official post was that of Colonial Secretary of the Straits
Settlements, the official on whose shoulders falls the detailed
work of administration. In his case it had been complicated
by the additional burden of piloting a new Governor through
those difficult initial months of a new term of office.

Luncheon, served in the cool dining-room of the Colonial
Secretary's official residence, which occupies one of the best
hill sites in Singapore, was a pleasant meal. Only Lady

Caldecott was present, and she let us talk our fill. It was great fun to discuss old times, and informative to me to hear Andrew's views on the changes which had taken place since my time. I gathered that routine office work had increased beyond all standards of comparison, and that if a Colonial Secretary were to do all he was expected to do he would have to forgo not only all relaxation but even sleep.

After luncheon I went down with him to his office. He had kindly offered to arrange certain facilities for me, including a visit to the Singapore Jail. A great stack of papers, neatly arranged in piles, lay on his desk awaiting his attention. Native clerks came noiselessly in and out, bringing more papers or seeking instructions. The telephone rang incessantly. Someone at the Air Base wanted to know if a visa were required for Siam. An artillery major sought information about accommodation for a married officer who was arriving next week. I realised that wet-nursing the various units of the defence forces until they found their tropical legs had not exactly decreased the labours of the civil service. Andrew dealt with the questions and fixed up my arrangements with an unruffled composure and efficiency which were impressive. It was in this atmosphere that he proposed to settle down to a quiet afternoon's work of clearing up all outstanding matters before his departure. It certainly was a he-man's job.

Both at home and during my visit I heard many complaints from old-timers about the decline in the quality of the British colonial civil servant. He was now recruited from a new and inferior type. He was spineless and, content to get through his work without reproof, took little interest in the country. Above all, he lacked the presence, the dignity, and the other he-man qualities of his predecessors of the old days. In short, the criticisms were much the same as those one hears every day from old gentlemen in the London clubs about the delinquencies of the present-day youth of England.

There may well be some truth in these assertions. It is the

weakness of all government services that they do not get rid of their inefficient officers. Because of their widespread spheres of activity this is especially true of the diplomatic and colonial services, and, doubtless, there are inefficients to-day in Malaya as there were inefficients yesterday. Certainly I saw one or two men in responsible posts who, more particularly in the matter of dignity, fell far short of the standard set by the high officers of the service in my time, not to mention great colonial servants like Sir Frank Swettenham, Sir Hugh Clifford and Sir Ernest Birch, all of whom began their careers as youngsters in Malaya.

It is also true that, like the Indian Civil Service, the Colonial Service does not make the same appeal to the best type of young man in Britain as it used to do. The rewards are less attractive. The sense of security has been weakened. At the same time the glamour of adventure has diminished and the chances of advancement have been normalised by the absurd bureaucratic system of promotion by seniority. The pioneer days are ended, and to many, including myself, the loss in attractiveness of life in Malaya is immeasurable.

But in fairness to the present-day colonial servant I must point out that his work is infinitely harder and more complicated than that of the colonial servant of a generation ago. He deals as a matter of daily routine with countless problems of modern civilisation, any one of which would have puzzled his more virile but mentally less well-equipped predecessors.

He is, too, enormously handicapped by official restrictions on his liberty of action. This was not the case in the early days of Malaya's development. In Singapore Harbour there is an island called Pulau Brani. On it stands the huge tin smelting plant of the Straits Trading Company, a British-owned concern started in 1883 by a Scot and a German! To-day it and its rival, the Eastern Smelting Company, smelt all the tin ore mined in Malaya and sold in the open market as well as ore from Siam and other producing countries. But in 1903 an astute American company nearly succeeded in cornering this huge business for the United States. At that time the Americans were doing a rather unprofitable shipping business with the Philippines, which they had acquired after the Spanish-American War. Their ships came from the States with passengers and freight and had to return empty to their home port.

It was then that the American group conceived the idea of buying the Malayan tin ore, carrying it back in empty ships to San Francisco and smelting it there. Their object was to obtain control of Malayan tin by paying high prices for the ore. When the control was assured and competitive buying and smelting killed, they could then buy the ore at their own price and put a high duty on all block tin imported into the United States.

They went to work quickly and had spent £30,000 on the erection of a smelting works in the United States before the British tin industry in Malaya realised what was happening.

The consternation among the British was great. The plantation rubber industry was then in its babyhood, and the capture of the whole tin production of Malaya by the United States would have been a crippling blow to the country's fortunes. In its distress the British commercial community appealed to the Governor, Sir Frank Swettenham.

That brilliant colonial administrator took immediate action. He met and squashed the attack by imposing an *ad valorem* duty of 35 per cent. on all tin ore exported from the F.M.S. with a rebate of the duty on all ore smelted in the Straits Settlements and sold in the open market.

Sir Frank informed the Colonial Office of his action, but did not consult it beforehand. He was promptly hauled over the coals. But, fortunately, Joseph Chamberlain was then Colonial Secretary, and when he received Sir Frank's letter of explanation he gave his full approval to the duty. It remains in force to this day.

H

Pulau Brani means the Island of the Brave. The epithet is a happy one. The British company which has its chief smelting plant on the island owes its prosperity to a Governor who was resolute enough to take his own line of action.

There are many people who say to-day that just as Joseph Chamberlain was the last great Colonial Secretary, so Sir Frank Swettenham was the last great Colonial Governor. But I think that this splendid pro-Consul would be the first to admit that in his day the machinery of Whitehall moved with a slowness which was not without certain compensations to the local Governor. To-day, the speeding-up of communications by air and by wireless has enabled Whitehall to spread its tentacles over the local administration in almost every corner of our Colonial Empire. Ministers, too, descend out of the sky by air-plane, spend a feverish week in touring the country, and return home with a little dangerous learning, and even if he be blessed with the rare qualities of a Swettenham the local Governor is, like most British Ambassadors, little more than a human post-box for receiving the instructions of the Home Government.

The system has serious defects. It puts a premium on the promotion of yes-men and destroys initiative. The defects are magnified in the case of the British Colonial Office, which, for some strange reason known only to the sacred circle of Cabinet Ministers, has been a neglected department. When in the Cabinet reconstruction after the general election in November, 1935, Mr. J. H. Thomas was transferred from the Dominions Office to the Colonial Office, he spoke of "going into retirement". The remark was made jocularly in an after-dinner speech, but it reflects accurately enough the present standing of the Colonial Office in the eyes of ambitious Ministers. The fact remains that since the war there has not been a British Secretary of State for the Colonies of any outstanding ability.

The canker in the body politic of all empires is want of spirit and lack of direction of intention. The decline of the

Roman Empire began when the civil servants of Rome started to suppress every symptom of energy, initiative and enterprise shown by the local administrators. The modern bureaucratic methods of Whitehall and the inability of the Home Government to select the right man and to leave well alone may have the same disastrous effects on the future of the British Colonial Empire. To-day, the local British residents in Malaya look for many qualities in a new British Governor, but the supreme test by which they measure his abilities is: how far will he stand up to the Colonial Office?

In the circumstances it is perhaps unfair to draw a comparison between the pre-war and post-war Governors of Singapore. But most residents, I think, would agree that Singapore has not been altogether fortunate in her post-war Governors. Some of the appointments were in the nature of the square peg in the round hole. One, which should have been the most successful, was frustrated by the intervention of a cruel fate. Sir Hugh Clifford, who was appointed in 1927, was, with his brilliant administrative record and his unrivalled knowledge of Malaya, the obvious man for the post. Soon after his arrival he began to show signs of the breakdown in health which ever since has kept him a secluded invalid.

The restrictive disabilities from which a modern Governor suffers extend also in a minor degree to all the members of the colonial service. But, as far as Malaya is concerned, and in spite of all my romantic interest in the past, I noticed no decline in the mental equipment of the average British civil servant. His achievement stands there for the eyes of every passing tourist to see in a land, which, if no longer flowing with such a prosperous "spate" of tin and rubber, has reached a standard of civilisation, comfort, racial tolerance and happiness which has not its like in any other colony in the world.

Much of this development has taken place since the war. To-day the civil service is much nearer to problems which twenty-five years ago were only vaguely dreamt of—problems connected with the huge strides made by the Oriental in education, with the maintenance or removal of the colour ban, and with the menace of conquest from outside and even of native nationalist ambitions from within. Although the tendency is to stifle individuality by routine, the general standard of ability in both the administrative and the professional services is of a very high order.

The one menace to the continued efficiency of the service comes not from the civil servants in the East, but from the young men at home who, in recent years at any rate, have shown an ominous reluctance to go abroad, preferring any profession that will keep them in England to a life which, however attractive it may sound, means more or less permanent exile.

Here again I believe that sex psychology is partly to blame. With the emancipation of girls young men to-day form attachments with young women of their own class at a far earlier age in life than they used to do. It is, I think, these premature attachments which keep young men at home and which make them cling to the towns and centres of Western civilisation, when they do come East, in preference to the up-country life. In my time every healthy young man preferred the "ulu" to the town, not merely because he found the life more attractive in itself, but also because it offered greater chances for promotion.

It is also my opinion that the civil servant in Malaya works harder to-day than he did in my time. And this, I think, is true of the planter, the miner and the merchant. The passing tourist may find little attraction in the life of the British community. He may detect even signs of a certain lack of virility in the ease and luxury of a mode of living which to him may seem to invite comparison with that of the Romans in the later period of the Empire. But his conclusions are almost certain to be wrong, for the truth is that the British resident in Malaya is suspicious of the unknown stranger in his midst and resents immature criticisms formed after a motor-drive from Penang to Singapore between steamers. He wants to live his life his own way, and on the whole he makes a good job of it.

He is not a highbrow. There is in Malaya no prize for colonial literature as there is in the French colonies, and, although both Sir Frank Swettenham and Sir Hugh Clifford have a number of books to their credit, no British resident in Malaya has yet produced a work of outstanding merit. How vividly I still remember the romantic enthusiasm which I brought to my first reading of Sir Hugh Clifford's *In Court and Kampong* and *The Further Side of Silence*. Alas! their glamour has now gone beyond hope of recapture, and the accurate portrayal of local colour is no compensation for the stilted artificiality of the language in which Sir Hugh makes his Malays talk. To-day I should divide the first prize for literary merit between Sir Frank Swettenham's *The Real Malay* and Sir George Maxwell's *In Malay Forests*. But the fact remains that the best literary interpretations of the Malayan East are the works of a French planter called Fauconnier and of Joseph Conrad, a Pole, whose knowledge of the Archipelago was limited mainly to the ports which he visited as a ship's mate and captain.

I have not forgotten Mr. Somerset Maugham. That greatest living English man-of-letters has also written several books with a Malayan background. But he cannot be called a local resident, and through most of his stories runs the theme of the deteriorating effect of a moist tropical climate on the life of the white man and white woman in the East. No British resident can deny either the accuracy or the brilliance with which Mr. Maugham has described certain exceptional aspects of European life in the East. But no one will agree that these aspects are in any way a true reflection of British life in Malaya as a whole.

The British resident reads Mr. Maugham because there is no other writer who commands his interest in the same manner or who jogs his complacency so usefully. But he has never quite forgiven him. Other British writers who have passed through his country he has frankly disliked. He has, in fact, all the Englishman's mistrust of brilliancy, and like most Englishmen at home he sets a higher store on physical fitness than on intellectualism. And, in spite of certain changes in his attitude towards life, his physical fitness is even more in evidence than it was in my day.

There is certainly nothing effeminate about the vigour with which the inter-state "rugger" matches for the Malaya Cup are fought out every year, and there is surely no race in the world except the British who would make rugby football their favourite game in a country only a degree or two removed from the Equator. Nor is there any lack of virility about the young men who spend their spare time in man-œuvring tanks and learning to fly in the heat of a tropical sun.

It is true that many changes have taken place in the life of the British community since 1910. In my day everybody knew everybody, and there were few men who had not received a public school education. The large increase in the numbers of the white population has altered this happy state of affairs, and the advent of motor-cars has destroyed that privacy and solitude which to my mind was the great charm of the old life of Malaya. To-day, there is a new bridle of social discipline which forces a man to do as his neighbours do, and, except in the outlying unfederated states, the day is nearly past when a white man can live his own life as he wants to without paying the consequences for his flouting of British social conventions.

There is, too, among the British a division of classes which was unknown in my time, and which has been sharpened by the large increase in the number of white women. It is a replica of the same social life that exists in Britain, but in the East it is a disturbing and undesirable feature. Indeed, the presence of a white woman in the tropical East sets a problem for which a satisfactory solution has yet to be found.

The disadvantages are obvious; an enervating climate, a multiplicity of servants to attend to her wants, and nothing to do all day except to seek amusement. As far as the amusements are concerned, she plays golf and tennis with the men, but in other cases she sets the course of pleasure. Dancing, a rare form of amusement in my time, is now a weekly or daily part of the social life of the British community, and even up-country it is a commonplace event for a young planter to motor fifty miles to the nearest town to provide a partner for the wife of some official or business man who prefers his bridge and his "stengah" to the gyrations of a one-step.

There are some women whose lives are little else than one long round of pleasure-seeking from their morning bridge to the moonlight drive at night with their young admirer of the moment. There are, I admit, many others whose activities are both healthy and useful, and who add definite aesthetic and intellectual values to the life of the white community. In particular, I should like to pay a tribute to the beautiful gardens with which they have surrounded most European houses and bungalows, for there are few British women in Malaya who have not the national love of gardening and who have not translated it into practical results which gladden both the eye and the soul. But in spite of the accessibility of hill stations and the improvement in health conditions, I doubt if the white woman will ever be suited to long residence in a tropical country like Malaya, and I cannot resist the contention that her presence in such large numbers is responsible, at least to some extent, for the decline in the white man's prestige.

I should not like to give the impression that I am comparing the present unfavourably with the past. Such is neither my intention nor my belief. Indeed, I should estimate that to-day the percentage of expatriated officials, miners and planters living on drink, tobacco and their nerves and blaming their subsequent ill-health on the climate, is lower than it was twenty-five years ago. The general atmosphere is still refreshingly invigorating if sometimes unnecessarily noisy, and there is still a good deal of the public school and Empire spirit about it. Since my time the old school tie has added many new stripes and some queer spots to it. There are few Etonians, but there are still a host of those Haileybury, Cheltenham and Marlborough boys who, as Kipling maintains in *Stalky & Co.*, are the most successful bearers of the white man's burden in the East.

The public school system has certain drawbacks, and a time may come when the advance of the Oriental towards political maturity will demand new methods and a new type of English product. Nor can I deny that the white man's rule in the East has at times been cruel and harsh, with gain as its chief motive. But I know of no other country which has devised a better system. The proof of the whole matter is to be found in the sometimes grudging but generally flattering admiration of statesmen of other nations. This admiration is neatly summarised in the following story which is taken from the unpublished correspondence of M. Jules Cambon, the great French ambassador, and which through the kindness of one of his relatives I am able to reveal.

In 1908, during one of the difficult moments of the Moroccan crisis, Cambon, then French Ambassador in Berlin, was asked by his Government to make representations to Prince Bülow, the German Chancellor, regarding the aggressiveness of Germany's attitude. Bülow, a great courtier and a greater cynic, diverted the dispute into a safe channel.

"My dear ambassador," he said, "why all this fuss about Morocco? Let us be frank. You know very well that if we both were condemned to spend the rest of our lives in a colony, you wouldn't live in a German one and I certainly shouldn't live in a French one. We'd both choose an English one."

CHAPTER FOUR

A VISITOR WITH friends among the local British residents could spend a very pleasant month in Singapore. At the end of it he might be exhausted, but he would not be bored, for the amenities of life are amazingly varied. Sport is the mainspring of the social life of the city, for with an illogicality that is typically British the same Singapore Englishman who will hardly deign even to undress without the aid of a Chinese servant will spend his afternoons in beating or kicking some kind of ball with a vigour which seems to defy both the climate and common sense.

To-day the hall-mark of British civilisation in the East is a bag of golf clubs, and in Singapore the modern caddy is a slip of brown or yellow humanity, sometimes male, sometimes female, but as keenly appreciative and occasionally as contemptuous as a St. Andrews caddy of the white man's standard of play. The island has half-a-dozen golf-clubs, and in Bukit Timah a course which, both in the quality of its turf and in its test of golf, has no superior in the East. There are also facilities, extensively used every day, for tennis, cricket, polo, "rugger", "soccer", yachting, rowing, and private flying, and since my time there has been a boom in bathing. Indeed, on a Sunday the scene at the Singapore Swimming Club pool, fenced off from the sea and said to be the largest in the world, is an unforgettable sight. The costumes of the women lose nothing by comparison with those of Paris Plage and Deauville, and iced-beer softens the rigours of sun-bathing. At night, apart from dancing, the social round has few attractions, and the visitor is likely to find time hang heavily on his hands. Amateur theatricals are amateur theatricals all the world over: a trial and an infliction unless one is taking part in them or has a personal interest in one of the performers. There is, too, more discomfort than pleasure in the official dinner parties at which on gala occasions at any rate a boiled shirt and a tail-coat are obligatory.

In this connection my admiration goes out to the present King of the Belgians, who during his trip to the East some years ago was invited to dinner at Government House. Suffering considerably from the heat of Singapore and learning rather late in the afternoon that he was expected to put on what is, in effect, the hottest rig in the world, he refused point-blank. The local Belgian Consul had to explain the situation as best he could to the Government House staff, and almost up to the last minute an unfortunate secretary had to keep his mouth glued to the telephone in order to warn the other guests that on this occasion they might appear, by the Prince's grace, in a soft shirt and a white dinner jacket.

Singapore, however, is a Chinese city, and I had not travelled seven thousand miles in order to see my compatriots preparing themselves for an Eastern Waterloo or Trafalgar on the playing fields of Singapore. I arranged my programme so as to have as much time as possible to myself; for sight-seeing, like shopping, is best done alone. Moreover, a long experience of foreign countries has taught me that there is more lore and more atmosphere in shop-signs and in the streets than in a thousand guide-books.

Finding a sympathetic Malay chauffeur, I engaged him more or less permanently and used his car in my spare hours both by day and by night. I would rise early in the morning and go out to watch the native population preparing for its day's work: Chinese and Japanese shopkeepers waiting passively for custom behind the counters of their windowless shops, fat Bombay "Chetties" with Japanned boxes full of notes ready for the day's moneylending, lean and hungry Arab capitalists plying the same trade, French and Portuguese priests in black alpaca robes, and, later, a whole army of Eurasians, Chinese and Malays, dressed in white drill coat and trousers, the former regulation kit of the European, and hurrying on "push-bikes" to their daily task at the Government offices, the schools, the hospitals, and the other middle-class institutions of Singapore. Mosquito buses, Chinese-owned and with their destinations marked in half-a-dozen languages, commercial vans, also Chinese-owned and illustrated with a tiger's head or some other equally vivid advertisement sign, ply through the streets with a reckless energy. And all this human and mechanical traffic is controlled and shepherded by a combined force of tall, bearded Sikhs and Pathans, and tubby, square-shouldered Malays with the quiet efficiency and white armlets which are the hall-marks of the police of London.

The scene is fascinating in its animation, but it has changed considerably since my time. The shops in North Bridge Road have still the same attraction of cheapness and of Oriental bargaining for the European visitor. The quality of the goods, in fact, has improved. Silk shirts of excellent texture can be bought for a quarter of the price which they would fetch in London or New York, and, provided that you can leave a European model, Chinese and Japanese tailors can turn you out a Palm Beach suit, excellently cut and sewn at a trifling cost, in twenty-four hours. Chinese silk pyjamas with trousers wide enough for an elephant are another good investment and, incidentally, have replaced the old Malay sarong and baju as the favourite sleeping costume of the local European. And in the Japanese shops, by some strange perversion of economic law, you can buy such European goods as, for instance, a Leica camera at a lower price than in their country of origin. The Japanese are few in number and have increased very little since my time, the actual figures being 1400 in 1911 and 3215 in 1931. But they are very active commercially. Their goods fill the Chinese shops as well as their own. They sell anything from a cheap fountain pen to the finest flower-seeds in the world, and their fishing fleets have pushed the noses of their barks into every bay of the Malay Archipelago.

But with the Westernisation of the East much of the local colour and much of the old glamour have departed. Gone is the pig-tail and with it the picturesque robes of the old Chinese towkays. Gone, too, is the former seclusion of the better-class Chinese women, and to-day Chinese girls, some bespectacled, some passingly beautiful, but all serious, all with bobbed and permanently waved hair in place of the former glossy straightness, and all dressed in semi-European fashion, walk vigorously through the streets on their way to their studies or to their games.

Indeed, with the general adoption of European dress by the Oriental middle-classes it is extraordinarily difficult even for a European resident of long standing to recognise at once the nationality of a Malay, a Chinese, or a Japanese. For Singapore has now a large middle-class. It is the product of a city which is exceptionally rich in educational institutions and which possesses its own university, its technical colleges, and its medical school. These institutions have turned out scores of young Chinese, Malays, Indians, and Eurasians, all trained on the traditional British educational lines of work and games. The young men and women have the same passionate urge for education which characterises the peasant youth of new countries like Jugoslavia and Czechoslovakia and the new proletarian intelligentsia of Soviet Russia, and already they present a problem which is certain to become even more serious in the future. To-day the supply of candidates for jobs is far in excess of the demand, and when the various government services and the business houses can no longer absorb them, these educated Orientals may find an outlet for their discontent in political agitation. They will be far more dangerous than the present uneducated communist agitators who try to spread the gospel of Moscow among the coolie class.

No former resident, returning to Singapore after an absence of many years, can fail to be struck with the numbers of cinemas which now obtrude themselves in every thoroughfare of the city. They are of all kinds and for all classes. But they have one common characteristic: the glaring blatancy of their advertising. Above the entrance there is a huge hoarding which, apart from its text matter printed in English, Chinese, Malay and Tamil, generally carries some flaming picture of Hollywood's latest "flicker" favourite either dressed in the flimsiest of underclothes or clutched in a fierce embrace with the wrong man.

There is a board of film censors in Singapore. It is severe on films in which revolutionary scenes are depicted. It banned the film of my book *British Agent*. Let me hasten to add that I have no grievance about its action. But it does tolerate sex-appeal, both in the film itself and in advertisements cruder than the actual picture, in a form which I cannot help thinking is detrimental to the white man's prestige in a country where, however incredible it may seem to Europeans and Americans, the Oriental's respect for the white man's woman decreases in inverse proportion to the amount of her body which she exposes. When he sees the alluring semi-nudity of a film houri duplicated in the strangely scant attire of fashionable tourists passing through Singapore, he can scarcely be blamed if he concludes that the white man is not the man he was.

In Malaya bananas grow like weeds. Now that the arboricultural experts have discovered that the fig-leaves with which Adam and Eve clothed themselves in the Garden of Eden were in reality full-sized banana leaves I feel that the censors might appropriately enforce the banana standard on the Singapore cinemas.

But perhaps the greatest change in Malayan life is the emergence of the modern Chinese capitalist and industrialist. Singapore has always been famed for its rich towkays. But the towkay of to-day is a very different being from the courteous, pig-tailed gentleman of two generations back. Externally, at least, he is Westernised from the soles of his brown shoes to his tie and collar, and in the evening he can wear his boiled shirt and dress-coat with the best European. More often than not he wears horn-rimmed glasses. If he is the son of a rich father, he is almost certain to be a university graduate and perhaps a bencher of one of London's Inns of Court. If he is self-made—and among the Singapore towkays there are still amazing examples of men who began life as an ordinary coolie and became dollar millionaires—he soon acquires the outward attributes of his better-educated compatriots. But in both cases he is a fully-equipped industrialist with the money-sense of a Jew, the gambling instincts of a South African Rand magnate, the modern methods of a Bat'a or a Ford, and the tireless, persevering energy of an old-time Glasgow Scot. He runs banks and newspapers. He has the stock exchange quotations of the world's bourses at his finger-tips. He is an authority on commodity prices. He owns rubber estates and tin mines. His factories turn out boots, cheap clothing, food stuffs, including canned pineapples, building materials, medicines, soaps, toys and articles made from rubber, and by the latest methods of modern salesmanship he contrives to export his goods to nearly every country in the world.

Outside of his business hours he plays a considerable part in the social life of Singapore, owns houses, takes his wife to the races, and plays golf. He is air-minded, and on the first flight of Imperial Airways from Penang to Hong-Kong the only passenger was a Singapore Chinese called Ong Ee Lim. He is, too, a patriotic citizen and a keen Rotarian, is grateful to the British raj which protects him, and gives valuable service both to the Government Legislative Council and to the various municipal boards of which he may be a member. Above all, he is a generous giver to local institutions, and like American millionaires is fond of endowing hospitals, colleges and other educational institutions.

He is expatriated, and in some cases is afraid to return to China in her present state. But, although he feels himself at home in the Straits Settlements and is proud of what he has done for Singapore, it would be a mistake to imagine that he has forgotten his homeland. One day some Straits-born

Chinese may rise with the same ambition as the Austrian-born Hitler to raise his fatherland from the depths of defeat and revolution. Already some of his profits go to help his struggling country, and there is more than one university, including Amoy, in China that has been founded with Chinese money from Singapore. His services to Malaya have not been forgotten by the British Government, and one of King George's last acts before his death was to confer the first knighthood ever given to a Singapore Chinese on the person of Sir Song Ong Siang, a dignified lawyer, who has devoted the best years of his life to municipal work and to volunteer soldiering in Singapore.

The modern Singapore towkay lives on a scale commensurate with his wealth. His house is a compromise between the traditions of Chinese architecture and the exigencies of modern European comfort. On occasions he likes to entertain his British friends, and the entertainment is both lavish and European, with a dancing floor specially laid down for the evening and tables on a terrace planted with orchids. Indeed, the only strikingly Oriental thing about his house is the Chinese lettering which one still sees on the gates of some houses. More often than not it conveys, to the Chinese at all events, the information that the house belongs to Koo Foh Soon, and that the owner is rich, honest and virtuous.

Incidentally, these Chinese signs are a pitfall for Europeans. When that former pioneer rubber planter, Colonel "Teddie" Bryce, who won the rare distinction of a D.S.O. with two bars during the Great War, was in Johore, the Chinese painted a sign in Chinese on the outside wall of his servants' quarters. It stood there for months before "Teddie" bothered to ask what it meant. When he did, he was told that the literal translation was: "The owner of this house is an Englishman called Bryce. He has a good heart, but a very bad temper." To-day Hylam servants have other means of informing each other of the merits or demerits of their white employers.

British diplomacy, too, has a story rich in its value as an illustration of the dangers of acquiring beautiful objects decorated with Chinese symbols of whose meaning the purchaser is ignorant. Although it has, doubtless, been embroidered in the telling, this story is true, and has its setting in Peking in the days of the Chinese Empire. At that time the brightest star in the diplomatic firmament of the Chinese capital was the wife of a British Secretary. She was a daughter of an ancient and aristocratic family, and a beautiful and high-spirited woman whose independence of action was sometimes a little trying to a Minister who had risen to his exalted position from the ranks of the Consular Service. Above all she was artistic, with a passionate interest in the treasures of Chinese art. It was her artistic sense that led her astray. One day she returned to her house in raptures over a new purchase. It took the form of a beautifully lacquered rickisha. It had a Chinese "puller" with the torso of a Greek athlete. But its chief glory was two lanterns, borne by two picturesquely-dressed bearers and decorated on the one side with an idyllic moonlit scene featuring a pagoda, a bridge, a river and a garden, and on the other side with exquisitely painted Chinese symbols. This brilliant turn-out was not bought as a museum-piece. It was intended to add lustre to the glories of British diplomacy, and in order to give greater effect to the lanterns and the lantern-bearers it was used mostly at night. And the arrival of its owner reclining gracefully on a background of red lacquer and preceded by her lantern-bearers was, indeed, an impressive sight well calculated to drive the iron of envy into the heart of every other diplomat's wife in Peking.

The last person to see it was the British Minister, a sound Chinese scholar, who encountered it one evening as he was entering the compound of the French Legation. The next morning he sent for his Oriental Secretary, then Mr. Barton and now Sir Sydney Barton, who was British Minister to Abyssinia during the recent Italo-Abyssinian War. "Barton," said the Minister, "have you seen Lady X's rickisha?" The Oriental Secretary nodded. The Minister hesitated, debating the difficulties of an intervention which should properly have been undertaken by himself. "Well," he continued, "I think you'd better go and see her and explain things."

Soon the Oriental Secretary was facing his colleague's wife fortified behind a tea-table.

"I'm sorry," he said, "but His Excellency thinks that you ought to give up using your rickisha."

The secretary's wife sat up. She foresaw a social battle, and was at her most formidable best in such encounters.

"I do not see what my rickisha has to do with the Minister. Surely I can use any kind of vehicle I like?"

"Yes, I agree," said the Oriental Secretary with diplomatic suavity, "but it's not a question of a rickisha or a carriage, but of the kind of rickisha. Yours is not at all suitable for the wife of a diplomatist."

"That again is my business and not the Minister's. As long as I behave myself, I do not see what right he has to dictate to me in a personal matter like this."

"But there's the lettering on those lanterns. Do you know what it means?"

"No, and I don't care. But you can tell me if you wish."

"Well," said the Oriental Secretary, "the lettering on the one lantern means 'I belong to the First Class Order of Prostitutes', and on the other 'My Price is Five Yen'."

Thirty years ago similar lanterns could probably have been bought in Singapore, for in those days legalised or semi-legalised prostitution flourished throughout Malaya. Indeed, eighty years ago vice was so rampant that, rather than allow ship's crews on shore, foreign Consuls in Singapore and in other East Indian ports used to arrange for boatloads of inspected prostitutes to be sent on board for the duration of the sailors' stay in port. Even in my time Singapore deserved a certain reputation for vice. The vice itself was never at any time so lurid or so glamorous as it is still painted by certain

I

travellers and by the scenario writers of Hollywood. The
reputation may die slowly, but now it is certainly not deserved. Here, too, change has worked a minor miracle.

Singapore was the first city in which I had ever seen at
first-hand the sale and purchase of vice, and the temptation
to revisit what had then seemed the street of adventure was
irresistible. Accordingly, just after sunset on the evening of
my third day I ordered my chauffeur to drive me to Malay
Street and Malabar Street, where formerly the white wrecks
of European womanhood and young Japanese girls, silent,
immobile and passionless, traded their bodies for the silver
dollars of Malaya. As I drove down the beach front, the
lights began to appear on the ships in the harbour like so
many little lives which would vanish in the morning, for
Death is still an early caller in these tropical parts. There was
the faintest of cooling airs from the sea. By the time I
reached Malay Street it was already dark.

I had chosen this hour intentionally for my attempted recapture of the spirit of a past which had eluded me ever
since my arrival. Recognition returned with a momentary
thrill, as I made my way into the district inhabited by the
poorest Chinese. Somewhere in these narrow streets were
houses where secret societies still held their meetings and
where another set of laws and moral codes held sway. Somewhere in this teeming ant-heap of yellow humanity were the
political agitators and the gang-robbers whose raids and
hold-ups from time to time stirred a complacent European
community to demand an increased vigilance from a police
force which is both efficient and remarkably well-informed.
But the illusion was only temporary. Malay Street itself
brought me face to face with the new Singapore. Gone was
Madame Blanche with her collection of Hungarians, Poles
and Russian Jewesses—the frail army of white women recruited by the professional pimps from the poorest population of Central and Eastern Europe, and drifting farther East
as their charms declined, *via* Bucarest, Athens and Cairo,

until they reached the *ultima Thule* of their profession in Singapore.

There had been no English girls among them. On political grounds the British administration has always maintained a ban on the British prostitute. But here in the past, ship's officers of every nationality, and globe-trotters, travellers, miners and planters from up-country wasted their money on an orgy to which drink and noise and occasional brawling supplied a discordant orchestra. Sometimes, a Malay princeling or Chinese towkay would make his way discreetly to this sordid temple in order to satisfy an exotic and perhaps politically perverted desire for the embraces of the forbidden white women.

Gone, too, were the long rows of Japanese brothels with their lower windows shuttered with bamboo poles behind which sat the waiting odalisques, discreetly visible, magnificent in elaborate head-dress and brightly coloured kimonos, heavily painted and powdered, essentially doll-like and yet not without a certain charm which in romantic youths like myself inspired a feeling more of pity than of desire. In those days the trade in Japanese women all over the Malay Archipelago was on the same kind of hire-purchase system as the trade in gramophones or motor-cars is to-day. Japanese contractors travelled the poorer country districts of Japan, picked out families where money was scarce and young daughters too numerous, and made an offer to the father. If the father accepted, he signed a contract and received a lump-sum down from the slave dealer. The purchase price, supplemented by a further sum for outfit and travel fees, was marked down as an advance against the girl. When she had worked it off, she was free to regain her liberty. Till then she was to all intents a slave, and, more often than not, unless some European planter bought her out in order to minister to his loneliness, her thraldom lasted for the rest of her earthly existence.

In those days this traffic in human souls had roused in me

feelings of resentment both against the Japanese and against the existing social order. I had seen the system working in various parts of Malaya. I had known several of these Okomasans and Omitsans. With other youths as irresponsible as myself I had taken part in jollifications after football matches—jollifications which generally ended with a visit "down the street" and much drinking of Japanese beer and the singing of ribald songs like "Potiphar's wife" and "She was poor, but she was honest". The Japanese dolls had laughed and clapped their hands, while the fat mistress of the house raked in our dollars, gauging her charges by the state of our hilarity and occasionally beseeching the more sober of us to make less noise. I had picked up a few words of Japanese and a verse or two of Japanese poetry, and had learnt to twang a three-chord accompaniment on the sami-sen. But in my moods of reflection I had been disgusted by this cruel and senseless wastage of human life, and in the first short stories which I ever wrote one of these young Japanese slaves always figured as the sympathetic and self-sacrificing heroine. The stories have never been and never will be seen in print, but they were based on facts. There was one up-country gold mine which then employed several thousand Chinese coolies. Two Japanese brothels served the needs of these primitive proletarians, whose sole education consisted in a knowledge that money was hard to come by and in a determination to extract the fullest value from what they spent. The mine-manager had told me that the girls had to be changed on an average of once in every three months.

To-day all this tolerated sordidness has vanished. The Japanese Government has stopped the sale of Japanese girls abroad. League of Nations vigilance has done the rest, and throughout Malaya the licensed brothel has been stamped out, the white prostitute has been repatriated, and the semi-professional amateurs who under various guises strive to ply an independent trade are quickly moved on to other countries and to other ports where League of Nations resolutions are not observed with the same nicety.

That drive through Malay Street will remain in my memory for longer than the previous visits of my youth. Then one had been drunk and in the company of others. And together we had taken possession of the place. Or else one had driven down the street furtively, with the hood of the rickisha up, afraid lest any pair of eyes behind the shuttered windows were witnesses to the white man's secret shame and not daring to emerge until one had ascertained if Rose or Madeline or Wanda were free.

Then there had been discreet and obsequious touts at the doors to show the way and to carry messages. Now I felt no sense of self-consciousness because the feeling of shame was absent. The street was the same street. The houses, too, looked old, and must have been the same houses that I had known a quarter-of-a-century before. But they had been reconstructed. The ground floor was now a row of open booths, where small shopkeepers plied their trade. The Europeans and the Japanese had vanished. Like an army of ants the Chinese had taken possession of the district, removing all vestiges of its former occupants. In one booth a whole family of husband, wife, sons and daughters, were ironing the day's washing. In another an old man, consumptive-looking and almost hairless, was working an antiquated model of a sewing machine. Around him, squatting Buddha-wise on the floor, were half a dozen assistants patiently sewing buttons on to khaki suits.

It was a peaceful and infinitely remote scene. Although at my request we moved at rather less than walking pace, no one stared at the white intruder. There was no reason to stare. These shops had nothing to sell to a European. Their owners had no possible interest in me. I was merely one of these mad-dogs of tourists who poked about in the humdrum quarters of hard-working Chinese, and who thought they were finding the glamour of romance.

"Which was Madame Blanche's house?" I asked my chauffeur. His eyes looked vacantly at the row of sordid buildings. He jumped out of the car and went over to the tailor. The old man looked up from his machine and listened gravely for a moment. Then, shaking his head, he resumed his sewing.

At a loss to understand why I should spend good money on driving slowly up and down Malay Street and Malabar Street, the chauffeur took the initiative. "The Tuan wants a woman?" he said. "There are none here. I know a house in Bencoolen Street."

I shook my head. "I am looking for the past," I said, and I made a reference to "zaman dahulu" (the times that are gone) which figures frequently in Malay pantuns. I think he understood, for he replied: "Singapore very big city now. New houses every day, and the past is soon buried."

Before going back to Raffles I told him to drive me out by the Botanical Gardens and towards Bukit Timah. The cloying smell of the narrow Chinese streets was still in my nostrils, and fresh air had become a more urgent desire than passion in retrospect. As we turned down Orchard Road, we passed at intervals the shadowy figure of a Malay woman, her head covered by a sarong, her eyes and teeth flashing a greeting through the semi-light of the street lamps. "Perempuan jahat, Tuan," said the chauffeur contemptuously, "ta' guna—busoh sěkali." ("Bad woman, Tuan. No good—rotten with disease.") Their presence was a proof that in an erring world perfection is unattainable.

As we drove through the cool night air leaving the light of the city far behind us, my thoughts were busy with this new aspect of a puritanised Singapore. How far did it represent progress? From conversations both at home and now in Singapore I knew that local doctors, forced by their profession to adopt a realist attitude towards morals, often expressed grave doubts regarding the wisdom of abolishing controlled vice. I am aware that their apprehensions are shared by many naval and military officers, who are responsible for the hygenic welfare of several thousands of young British soldiers and sailors and airmen.

It is a fact, little known but undeniable, that one of the chief technical objections against removing the British troops in Egypt from Cairo and Alexandria to the Suez Canal zone is the difficulty of maintaining discipline and contentment among large bodies of young men established in exotic surroundings and shut off from all intercourse with the other sex. In a semi-puritanised Singapore the problem is one of hygiene.

These facts, proved by centuries of experience, must be stated, for they are frequently ignored by well-meaning reformers. Nevertheless, even among old-timers there can be few who will seriously deny that in every respect except sanitation, for the old "stinks" remain, the new Singapore is a cleaner, healthier city than the Singapore of quarter-of-a-century ago.

The next day I lunched in the Singapore Club. Still under the impression of what I had seen on the previous evening, I was eager to check my own observations by the first-hand knowledge of local European residents. Experience has taught me that the best method which a traveller can employ in order to obtain local criticism is the use of indiscriminate praise.

Before I went to Chicago a few years ago, I had been warned by an American friend that the Chicagoans were sensitive about gunmen and, more particularly, about the sensational stories of gangster rule which from time to time filled the front pages of the British popular press. In the company of a local crime expert I had made a tour of the worst quarters of the city. I had visited the garage, now a flower-shop, in which Mr. Capone's henchmen had mown down the gang of Mr. O'Bannion. I had inspected Capone's headquarters in the Lexington Hotel. I had seen Mr. William Collins, brother of the famous Irishman, Michael Collins, and then superintendent of the Des Moines Police Station, interrogating some of Chicago's lowest down-and-outs. I had noticed nothing half so sordid as I could have witnessed by myself, at any hour of the day, in Glasgow or Birmingham. I had returned to my headquarters at the Drake Hotel convinced that Chicago was the most orderly city in the United States. As I stood in the hall saying goodbye to my guide, I said to him: "Well, I don't believe you've ever had a gunman in Chicago. All these stories must be just a newspaper racket."

His face fell in pained surprise. "Why, Mr. Lockhart, right here where you're standing now a bunch of gangsters held up the whole hall, shot down the head porter and a couple of cashiers, and walked off with all the cash in the hotel till,—in broad daylight, too, and only a year ago almost to a day."

In the Singapore Club I used the same method. I told my hosts of my Singapore rambles. I told them how my illusions had been shattered. I described the dancing at Raffles and my descent into Malay Street. Where was all this Singapore vice so exotically portrayed in the books of post-war globe-trotters? Raffles had appeared to me to be more decorous and more middle-class than any Bournemouth hotel on a Sunday. As for vice I defied even an American journalist to land himself in trouble, let alone discover an exotic charmer, without the aid of a policeman or a tout.

Once again my shaft found the mark. One of my friends, a man of erudition and high standing in the city's affairs, hit back immediately. "Ah," he said, "life in Malaya is not so innocent as it looks on the surface." And then came a story of an exalted Government official whose wife had been having an affair with a European business man. The speeding-up of life in the tropics is a double-edged weapon in these Eastern triangles. If the motor-car has facilitated illicit meetings, the telephone has strengthened the defences of the cuckold. In this story the husband official became suspicious.

He enlisted the aid of his servants. They were to let him know by telephone whenever the lover came to the house. One day the husband went to an official luncheon, and in Malaya official luncheons are long and soporific affairs. It seemed an admirable opportunity for the lover to profit by the husband's absence, and he took it. A discreet telephone call brought the husband back from his luncheon. He hurried into the house, and the next thing seen was the business man retreating towards the road in his shirt and using his trousers as a shield against the niblick onslaught of the enraged official.

Like other parts of this imperfect world Malaya has its adultery, both dignified and undignified.

CHAPTER FIVE

MY VISIT TO Singapore jail will be one of the landmarks in my memories of my Eastern tour. As I had to meet the prison governor at the jail door at seven a.m., I rose early. My way led me by Sepoy Lines, where there is one of the queerest golf-courses in the world. It was made as a course for Government officials, and, although it should have been built over long ago, it is, of course, sacrosanct.

In spite of the early hour several enthusiasts were already practising iron shots with that grim seriousness which the Englishman reserves exclusively for his games. The course has only nine holes, but each hole has its distinctive landmark. These landmarks include two mortuaries, a maternity hospital, an infectious diseases hospital, a lunatic asylum, a powder magazine, the prison itself, and a Chinese graveyard. In the case of the graveyard there is a serious breach of the rules which does not commend itself to those true golfers who stand or fall by the rigour of the game. In order to soothe Chinese susceptibilities niblick shots are not or used not to be permitted between the gravestones.

Alongside the sixth tee there used to be a scaffold. It was on the golf course of Sepoy Lines that the battle against public executions was finally won. This is the story. Away back in the dim "nineties" Sir Charles Mitchell, the Governor of Singapore, was playing golf one morning with his aide. As he was playing off the sixth tee, there was a frightful noise of hammering. The governor missed his drive. His eyes blazed. "What the blank hell is that outrageous noise?" The aide explained that the scaffold was being strengthened for a public execution the next morning. The governor continued his round in silence, but his mind was busy with weighty affairs. That afternoon he took a momentous decision, and from then onwards public executions were stopped throughout the Colony. There has been only one since. That was in 1915 when the ringleaders of the Singapore mutiny were shot outside the prison wall before thousands of native spectators.

The British public has always been told that the Singapore mutiny was organised by local Germans. The story was one of the propaganda lies of the war. Actually, the mutiny, which was confined to an Indian regiment stationed on the island, was organised entirely by agitators from India. The soldiers, who were about to be transferred to Hong-Kong, were told a mass of falsehoods, one of which was that they were to be taken out to sea and dropped overboard. For a few hours the situation was desperately serious, and several European civilians as well as the white officers of the regiment, who were shot down in cold blood, lost their lives. Retribution came swiftly and severely. The executions were carried out in three batches. The first batch was shot by naval ratings, and the second by regular soldiers. The third batch was reserved for the local volunteers, most of whom had never fired a shot at anything except a target. They lost their nerve. There were many misses, and the unfortunate victims had to be finished off by the prison warders.

As I made my way to the jail gate, I had time to reflect on the incongruous attitude of the English towards our Scottish game of golf. I thought of the golf course near Cairo where there is a green at the very base of Cheop's Pyramid. I shuddered to think what will happen when golf becomes really popular in Jerusalem.

When I reached the jail I found Captain Bloxham, the governor, waiting for me. Attended only by a warder and an interpreter, we set off on our tour of inspection. My previous prison experiences had been few. I had been shown over the French convict prison at Fontevrault, where some of the Plantagenet kings and queens of England lie buried. I had inspected the prison on the Ile de Ré off Rochefort where Dreyfus was nearly mobbed by the crowd in 1896, and where unfortunate criminals spend their last night on French soil before being shipped to Devil's Island. During a fishing holiday on Dartmoor I had once attended mass at the grim Princetown prison, and had even had a cut in my head stitched by the prison doctor. And, of course, I had spent a week in the dreaded Loubianka in Moscow and three weeks in the Kremlin as the political prisoner of the Bolshevik Government. But this was my first visit to a prison in a British colony.

Externally the jail is not unlike any European prison in that it is a barrack-like building impressively ugly and large. But it is not big enough for its purpose, and a new jail is now being constructed. A few years ago, when the prisoners numbered 2000, there was serious overcrowding. On the day on which I made my visit the total was just over 1000. The reduction was the result of the world slump in rubber and tin and in the repatriation of thousands of Chinese coolies. In 1927 there were eighty-nine murders in Singapore; in 1935 only thirteen. For this improvement credit must be given to the police for increased efficiency. To-day there is an effective co-operation between the French, Dutch and British colonial administrations in controlling the movements of Chinese criminals and communists. Most of the prisoners in Singapore jail are Chinese.

I was taken first to a corridor of cells segregated from the rest of the prison. The control of crime in Malaya depends largely on informers. Occasionally these Chinese informers get into trouble themselves. When they are sent to prison, they are kept in a separate ward. If they were sent into the main prison, they would be murdered by the other Chinese prisoners.

As I passed through the various rooms and rows of cells I was struck by the spotless cleanliness. Most of the cells were empty. In the day-time the prisoners work together in large rooms. The work is strictly utilitarian. There are rooms for weaving, shoe-making and book-binding, and a great laundry establishment where all the washing of the prison is carried out by prisoners.

The interior of any prison is a sad sight, and here, too, were many corners where the impression was one of melancholy unrelieved. The sick ward with its rows of open beds occupied by men suffering mainly from open sores made me shudder. In the book-binding room I found a white man working together with better-class Chinese. He never raised his eyes from his work the whole time we were in the room. Fortunately, there are few European prisoners. Most of them are men who have misappropriated funds or who have tried to obtain money under false pretences. I met, too, a strange European, a vagrant from Shanghai, who claimed to be a Pole, but who had no passport. His only crime was vagrancy and a total inability to give a satisfactory account of his antecedents. He, too, was lumped together with the other prisoners.

This lack of differentiation seemed to me entirely wrong, and was the only blot on an administration which, so far as I could see, was as humane as any colonial prison system can be. Certainly the governor himself was a first-class man, who went among the prisoners with as little fuss as possible and gave to every man the right to complain to him personally. Several prisoners took advantage of this excellent rule while I was there. I admired, too, the governor's courage. The heavy gloom which had settled on me changed to a sinking feeling of fear when, attended only by our unarmed and rather corpulent warder, we entered an iron-barred room not unlike a lions' cage in a zoo. Here were kept the most dangerous criminals in the prison: professional gang-robbers, who in cruelty and in the efficacy of their methods had nothing to learn from the gangsters of New York and Chicago. There were about eighteen of them. They were working on looms. Their expression was sulky. They looked as villainous a collection of cut-throats as I had ever seen.

I was already sweating with the damp heat of an overcast tropical morning, for the drought had broken. But now inside this cage, with the door locked behind us, the beads of sweat began to drop from my brow, leaving a slate-coloured damp mark on my white coat. My mind went back to the gang-robber stories of my youth in Malaya. Vividly I saw in my imagination the famous Pahang murder, when an English planter taking back money from the town in order to pay his coolies had been tripped up by a wire stretched across the road. Foolishly he had forgotten his revolver. Even more foolishly he had persuaded the local English doctor to accompany him. The two Englishmen had been set on by a band of Chinese gang-robbers. The planter had escaped. The doctor, a powerfully-built man, had fought heroically and had knocked out half-a-dozen men with his bare fists before he was finally knifed to death. He had disfigured one man so badly that the gang-robbers killed their colleague and buried him lest his bruises should lead to their detection. At the time of my first arrival in Malaya the story had made a deep impression on my mind. It used to come back to me sometimes when, after an occasional late night in the club in Seremban, I was cycling back to my lonely home in Pantai on a push-bike through the ten miles of jungle. And now in this gang-robbers' cage in the Singapore jail it came back to me again with an unpleasant sensation of reality.

When we came out, I asked the Governor if these men ever gave any trouble inside the prison. "Oh, yes," he replied, "ten days ago these fellows in there tore out a bar from one of their weaving looms and murdered a fellow-prisoner.

" Why? We never really knew. Probably he had betrayed one of his pals. They have their secret societies even in the jail. We try to keep them together as far as possible: gang-robbers in one section, communists and political prisoners in another. Occasionally we have minor mutinies. Gang-robbers still exist; they use all the modern American methods, motor-cars and revolvers, and a few of their own as well."

We went over to another room which was full of Chinese

communists. In type they differed considerably from the gang-robbers, being less villainous-looking and of poorer physique. Most of them had been convicted of spreading seditious literature. During my stay in Malaya I was shown several examples of these communist pamphlets. They were mostly to the address of Chinese coolies on rubber estates and tin miners. The script was in Chinese, but the language was the language of Moscow. "Sons of the soil. Now is the time for us to unite. The coolies working on estates are suffering because the price of rubber has fallen. Wages have been reduced. Although we have to live, the government demands a licence for carrying on business. Kings fight with each other and try to squeeze money out of us. There is a surplus of rubber on all estates, and disputes about restriction are going on between the British Government and other governments. This is the white man's doing. Continue to make more and more agitation." Occasionally these pamphlets and proclamations are printed in several languages. One printed on coloured paper ran as follows: "Oppressed toiling masses of all races unite and rise with one accord. Assist revolution in the colonies. Oppose the increase of customs duties, licence fees, land revenues, and especially exploitation by the enforcement of rubber restriction by British imperialists."

While the governor talked in quiet, matter-of-fact tones to these yellow disciples of Moscow, I made a careful scrutiny of their faces. I was struck by their impassive composure. Some of the men looked intelligent. They made no complaints. Only a certain dignified surliness revealed a hate which seemed deep-rooted. My memory went back to my own experiences in the Moscow Cheka where I had been imprisoned with gang-robbers and capitalist political prisoners. There the communists had been the jailers. The prison methods had been very different. In Moscow there had been a very short shrift for the robbers. For the political prisoners there had been the nightly torture of ruthless cross-examination and other third-degree methods. Over their heads was suspended the constant shadow of death. The Bolshevik jailers carried guns and even hand-grenades. Here in Singapore there was little interference and considerable tolerance. The warders, all Englishmen brought out specially from Britain, looked sleek and good-natured. There were no arrows or other marks on the prisoners' clothes. In humaneness and, above all, in cleanliness the bourgeois-run prison of Singapore seemed like a well-run school compared with the insanitary horrors of the Loubianka. And yet I suppose to the political prisoner whose sentence is indefinite and whose fate even after release is uncertain the different methods of prison administration seem very much alike.

My reflections were disturbed by the governor, who drew my attention to a talkative and rather frail-looking prisoner. His whole face smiled. There was a light in his eyes which seemed to invite the fullest confidence and to stimulate even a cynic's belief in the ultimate goodness of human nature. I thought him the kindest-looking man I had ever seen. "This", said the governor quietly, "is our best prisoner and our most dangerous communist. He planned and very nearly pulled off the assassination of a Chinese minister on his way through Singapore some years ago. I call him 'Little Sunshine'." 'Little Sunshine', who probably understood every word, beamed more benevolently than ever.

From the communists we went to inspect the cells where prisoners unfit for work and suspects awaiting trial were confined. There were two Japanese in neighbouring cells who had been arrested in connection with a recent spy case which had caused a sensation in Singapore. It was a story of an attempt to smuggle out documents, presumably relating to the Singapore base, in an antique table. The spies had a duplicate table with secret drawers and by substituting it for one which they had bought in a Singapore antique shop they had very nearly succeeded in getting the dealer to ship it to Japan in the ordinary course of business. A prominent

Japanese business man, who had been concerned in the case, had committed suicide. The two prisoners, who were now before me, were suspected accomplices.

Strangely enough, of all the prisoners whom I saw in the jail they were the most voluble and the most truculent. They complained about the food and about the lack of exercise. They threatened, they cajoled, they whined. Bloxham listened to them with reasonable patience. He never lost his temper or tried to bully the men. He said a few words to the warder. Then he continued his rounds. Personally I should have been very short with these men. Their exhibition was one which I should never have expected from Japanese. Perhaps they were trying to impress on us the might, majesty and dominion of the Empire of the Rising Sun. As far as the might and dominion are concerned, the sun is indeed rising, for to-day in the East it is Japan's writ, and not that of Britain, the United States, and the League of Nations, which runs, and there are very few Japanese who are not conscious of this fact.

I also talked with our warder, who told me something about his life in Singapore. The full strength of the British warders in the Singapore jail is about fifty. They form part of a regular service recruited in Britain and carrying at the end of it a pension. They are picked more for character than for physique. Their life is not without danger, but has few excitements. Most of the men are philosophers performing their duties with clock-like regularity and dreaming of the day when they can retire and go home. British warders in Malaya seem to have incongruous names. At one time the three chief warders in Kuala Lumpur, the capital of the F.M.S., were Currie, Rice and Fish.

Crossing from one block of buildings to another, we passed a narrow oblong strip of grass surrounded by high windowless walls. The grass was of the same vivid green that one sees on the west coast of Ireland. There was an atmosphere of cloistered seclusion about the place. I half-

K

expected to see an altar, so peaceful and so silent was the setting. And yet there was something uncanny and sinister about these high grey walls which shut out everything except the stretch of sky overhead. The plot is not an architect's whim. It has its uses. Sometimes its walls resound with the dull, heavy sound of the lash and with the screams of prisoners. Sometimes, too, they echo to the strokes of the carpenter's hammer, and in the early morning a small band, composed of the governor, the prison doctor, and a warder or two stand silently while the hangman does his grim work. Since Sir Charles Mitchell's game of golf this plot has been used for floggings and hangings.

When we had finished our inspection, the rain came down in torrents. I refused the governor's invitation to breakfast and drove back to Raffles. My clothes were wet with rain and sweat. My appetite was gone. Ever since the Russian revolution opened my eyes to the cruelty of life, I have had an unalterable sympathy not only with the toiling masses, whose lives are at the mercy of an out-of-gear economic system, but also with the misfits and outcasts of society who are its victims. The whole conception of prison seemed senseless and soulless, and the conservatism of man, always opposed to change because it was change, strangely unimaginative. My mind went back to Thucydides, whom I had re-read so carefully during my own imprisonment in Russia: "In settled times the traditions of government should be observed; but when circumstances are changing and men not compelled to meet them, much originality is required."

Since 1918 there has not been much originality in political thought; only cruelty more cruel because it has been caused by stupidity more than by wickedness.

CHAPTER SIX

DURING MY FIVE days in Singapore I could have had all the hospitality that a man can desire. There were two reasons why I avoided it. For the past five years I seemed to have been meeting new people every day and every night. A holiday was not merely a rest from work. It was an escape from people. But a stronger reason was my almost passionate desire to keep this return to Malaya to myself and to let my impressions form themselves without the interference of extraneous agencies.

For three days I succeeded in going my way. Then an Englishman from the *Straits Times* came to interview me. He was an intelligent young man. He had a brother on the staff of the London newspaper for which I wrote. He produced a column of matter in which he referred flatteringly to the Malayan chapters of *British Agent*. He touched on Amai, and apparently had taken pains to obtain the latest information about her, for in his paragraphs he predicted that, having seen Malaya for the first time through the eyes of romantic youth, I should now experience a profound disillusionment. And to give point to this truism he added that "the girl Amai was now a betel-stained hag".

I have no grudge against the young man. He treated me well and fairly. But the publicity which he gave to my presence in Singapore made a hole in my privacy. During the next twenty-four hours I received messages and visits from an amazing variety of people. There was an invitation to dinner from a girl whom I had known at home in my youth, and who was now married to an Englishman in Singapore. There was a visit from Major A. Neate, who had been military *attaché* to Bulgaria when I was in Jugoslavia, and who was now doing a "gunner's" job in Singapore. There were gentlemen from the local Chinese newspaper, who wished to know my views on everything from Stalin's personal appearance to Mr. Noel Coward's favourite hair-wash. Serious business presented itself in the person of the Far Eastern representative of Messrs. Warner Brothers, the film magnates. He had been having trouble with the censors in all the Eastern countries, including China, over the film of *British Agent*. Couldn't I take the governor or the censor or Chiang Kai-shek by the scruff of the neck and tell him where he got off? There were telegrams from old friends in the F.M.S. asking why the hell I was wasting my time in a lousy hole like Singapore and why hadn't I let them know I was coming out East.

Unable to satisfy either my friends or my business acquaintances I decided to pack my bags and go. Actually I had no regrets, for, if Singapore is still colourful, it lacks all the hall-marks of historical antiquity. It is an international Liverpool with a Chinese Manchester and Birmingham tacked on to it. Its finest buildings are modern; it has no ancient monuments and, apart from the Raffles statue, very few monuments to the past.

There is no monument to Sir Frank Swettenham in Singapore. I went up to Government House, a pretentious rather than imposing building with colonnades and pillars which give to it the appearance of a Jockey Club, and tried to picture that great man in the days of his Governorship. He had gone home several years before I first went East in 1908. My uncle had known him in the nineties, and I remembered an old drawing of a man with a long silky moustache, heavy eyebrows, and attractive penetrating eyes. This, no doubt, was the Swettenham, lean, tireless, and with all the attraction of the cultured man of action, whose *Unaddressed Letters* had captivated both Bloomsbury and Mayfair.

The Swettenham I knew was a dignified old gentleman with a sallow complexion which spoke of a life-time spent in the East, although he had been home for thirty years. But the brain and the memory were as active as ever; and the handwriting was as clear and as neat as a German schoolboy's. I had had tea with him soon after his eighty-sixth birthday in his flat in Great Stanhope Street in London. Surrounded by glass cases of Eastern curios, he had talked of my return visit and of the changes that had taken place in colonial administration. At eighty-six he was still far more alert mentally than many colonial servants of half his age. Swettenham would have been a remarkable man in any epoch and in any country. Although perhaps never heard of by the masses at home, he is still remembered in Malaya. It will be a sorry day for the British colonial empire when his name and his example are allowed to lapse into oblivion.

The administrative creators of Singapore and the Malay States were mainly Englishmen. In the building up of the commercial prosperity of British Malaya the Scots have played a part out of all proportion to their numbers. Nor have their activities been confined to such supposedly Scottish activities as banking and insurance. In the great tin and rubber industries of the country they have been pioneers, thus disproving the theory that the Scot is canny and pawky in business. The truth is exactly the reverse. There is no man more willing to stake his capital on a hazardous, but not necessarily reckless, speculation than the Scot. From the time of Law he has been the great adventurer of finance, and it has been his readiness to risk that has been mainly responsible for the development and the peopling of the British Dominions.

I do not think that there are in Singapore to-day as many Scots in proportion to Englishmen as there were in my time. Perhaps Malaya no longer offers a big enough or a quick enough reward. With the decline of British shipping there are certainly fewer Scottish engineers. As a Scot I regret the gradual disappearance of the man who has done more to spread the fame of Scotland over the seven seas of the world than anyone since Burns. And I still get a thrill out of the old story which the local captains used to tell when I first came out to Malaya. The steamer is going through a typhoon, and in natural anxiety some American lady passengers turn to the captain with an appealing cry: "What can we do to be saved?" And the captain answers gravely: "Say your prayers to God, ladies. And if God fails you, trust the Scottish engineer."

I should have liked nothing better than to have made the trip from Singapore to the F.M.S. by boat. But there was no convenient steamer at the moment. Freddie, who had the Rosslyns staying with him, was urging me to join them at Port Dickson, and it was by train that I decided to make my departure on the following evening.

My last night in Singapore I kept to myself. It was to be devoted to a return to the past. I should engage a rickisha puller, preferably one who could speak no known language, and the rest of the evening would be left to the whims of his mechanical jog-trot. Like a leaf before the wind I should go wherever he chose to pull me.

I put my plan into effect after an excellent dinner. There had been a thunderstorm during the afternoon. But the skies had cleared, and under the starlit heavens there was a delicious coolness in the air. My rickisha puller was a scraggy, toothless old man. Like the harper in the *Lay of the Last Minstrel* he was admirably suited to perform the rites at the last rickisha ride that I shall ever take. For even if I ever return to the East, the rickisha will soon be a vehicle of the past.

I had some difficulty in clambering into my seat. Perhaps I had lost the knack. I had certainly added several stone to my weight since the days when a husky sweating giant used to pull me the long ten miles out to my estate at Pantai at ten cents a mile. Then I could sleep the whole way. But this was an uncomfortable ride. My puller spoke no Malay and no English. From his lips came a stream of unintelligible labials. I waved an arm towards the night. With a grin he seized the shafts, and off we jogged. Twenty-five years ago we should have pulled up at a brothel, for your rickisha puller, even if he is inarticulate, knows instinctively the tastes of the tourist,

and in those days Malay Street was the obvious destination
of a European setting out alone at night.

Fashions, however, have changed, and after a gentle trot
my puller stopped before a gateway with a huge electric
sign in English and flashing the words, "The New World".
I got out and rather shyly followed the throng which was
streaming through the open gates. Inside was a huge fair
with theatres, opera, cinema, dancing-hall, side-shows,
booths, refreshment stalls, and even a stadium. The crowd
was of all classes and of all races. Naval ratings towered over
squat Malays. If Chinese predominated, there was a fair
sprinkling of Europeans and Eurasians. Tamils, Japanese,
Arabs and Bengalis completed the racial conglomeration.

The noise was deafening. Next door to an open Chinese
theatre with the usual accompaniment of gongs, a Malay
operatic company was performing *Mashdur*. From the side-
shows came an endless broadside of chatter and laughter. In
the booths in the centre, Japanese and Chinese were selling
toys which would have delighted the heart of any European
child: voracious-looking dragons, clock-work crocodiles
and snakes, miniature baby-carriages, wooden soldiers, and
the quaintest of domestic animals.

Avoiding the cinema where alluring posters of Miss Mae
West revealed the fact that *I'm No Angel* had been passed by
the Singapore Board of Censors, I went into the dancing-
hall. There was an excellent orchestra, hired, I think, from
some liner. It was playing *Aufwiedersehen* when I came in, and
a crowd of dancers, mostly young Chinese, the men in white
European clothes with black patent-leather dancing shoes,
the girls in their semi-European dresses slit at the side, filled
the dancing-floor. Many of the dancers had their own partners. But when the dance was over I noticed a number of
girls who left their partner as soon as the music stopped and
went to join other girls in a kind of pen. They were the
professional Chinese dancers who can be hired for a few
cents a dance.

There were other Europeans dancing, and after asking an attendant how the thing was done I plucked up my courage and, as soon as the music started for the next dance, went over and engaged a partner. More intent on information than on pleasure I ambled slowly round the floor. I had no reason except my own clumsiness to feel self-conscious. My Chinese partner danced with the ethereal lightness of a Viennese. Her name was Tiger Lily, and she told me some of the secrets of her profession.

These Chinese girls are engaged by the management. They are very carefully selected, and breaches of discipline are severely punished. They are paid about eight cents a dance. Each dance is registered on a card, and at the end of the week the cards are vigilantly scrutinised. Girls who are in great request, and who can show a high average of dances, may be promoted. Others, whose engagements are below the fixed average, have their wages reduced. In the dancing-hall, at any rate, there is no social intercourse between guest and professional dancer. At the end of each dance the professional goes back to her barricaded seclusion. The decorum, indeed, was unimpeachable, and could not have been criticised even by a Wee Free minister in a North of Scotland parish. To me this model seemliness was even more extraordinary than the almost complete waiving of the colour bar in a British colony.

After dancing a slow waltz with another Chinese professional partner, I left the hall, and presently I found myself before a turnstile in the side of a high wooden wall. It looked like the entrance to a football ground. A notice intimated that the champion team of the Shanghai Tung Ah Girls School was playing a side of Singapore men at basket-ball. I paid fifty cents for a stand seat and went inside.

The arena, surrounded by stands, was lit by powerful electric arc lights. The place was packed to capacity with Chinese. In the middle the two teams were practising. The Chinese girls dressed in white shirts and the shortest of black shorts, and with sturdy, muscular thighs showing almost up to their buttocks, were the finest physical specimens that I have seen outside of Nazi Germany. Perched on a stand, a cinema operator was filming the scene with monotonous persistency. In the arena itself was an army of reporters and camera men. Presently out came a young Chinese in cricket shirt and white trousers. With his closely cut hair and his horn-rimmed spectacles he looked like a medical student. He was the referee and, as such, fully conscious of his importance. He examined the ball carefully while the girls and men did some physical jerks to loosen their muscles. The camera men fired a last battery as they left the arena. The umpire looked at his watch and blew his whistle, and to shrieks of encouragement from the stand the game started.

I have seen less fuss and less ceremony at an English Cup Final or at the biggest American baseball game. The skill of the players thrilled me. Their speed was only less marvellous than their accuracy. The Shanghai girls won easily. They would have beaten any team in Europe. Although they thrashed the local favourites, they were cheered tumultuously by the Chinese spectators.

To me, who in the days of my Malayan career had hardly ever seen a Chinese woman outside of the coolie or the easy virtue class, here was a change indeed.

When I came out, I found my puller anxiously scanning the faces of the Europeans at the main exit. In the old days in Negri Sembilan he would not have cared if he had been bilked. He would have known where to find his man. Here in Singapore with its ten thousand whites such confidence would have been misplaced.

The basket-ball match had exhilarated me. I felt no desire for sleep, but was at a loss where to go. Apart from Raffles Singapore is as dead at midnight as a Highland village in Scotland on a Sunday. Suddenly an old memory revived an old desire. "Satai", I said. "I want eat 'Satai'." I dipped a tooth-pick into an imaginary dish and raised an imaginary piece of meat to my mouth. The puller grinned and set off at a steady trot until we came to a narrow street close to the sea. Here, occupying various pitches like the men who sell hot Frankfurter sausages in the vegetable market in Prague, were the Malay "Satai" cooks.

I got out and went over to an empty stall kept by a plump Malay gentleman, who obviously enjoyed his own cooking. He had a couple of boxes set on end. On one of them he had a small charcoal fire. On the other were the various dishes containing respectively a curry, too hot for the uninitiated, a milder curry, and a delicious kind of onion sauce.

"Satai, Tuan?" he asked and, when I nodded, he began the ritual. With a small straw-plaited fan he began to stir the charcoal to a bright flame. While it burnt he chopped up onion and cucumber on a plate. When the fire was at the proper glow, he produced from his box pieces of chicken meat fixed on little sticks in much the same way as the Russians prepare "shashlyk". Then, dipping the sticks of meat into a can of fat, he grilled them for several minutes on his fire. He bowed. The "Satai" were ready. I took a stick and dipped it into the dish with the milder curry and ate with gusto, gradually working up to the strongest curry and keeping my mouth cool with the cucumber and the onion.

I do not profess to know the origin of "Satai". In Singapore it is always said to be a Chinese dish, but in Java it is to be found in every village, and certainly the Javanese prepare it hotter than anyone else. "Satai" are insidious, and there are Europeans who at cocktail parties or after a dance can eat incredible numbers of them. The stall-keeper pays little attention to how many you eat. All he watches are the sticks. At the end of the meal he collects them and charges, I think, two cents a stick. For a dollar you can gorge yourself on what, to my mind, is by far the most appetising of Eastern dishes.

On my way home to Raffles I saw a sight even more startling than the basket-ball match that I had seen at the

"New World". As my puller turned into Beach Road, I passed a string of Chinese running down the streets in Indian file. Until I noticed their shorts and their stockingless legs, I thought that they were pursuing some thief. The hotel clerk told me that they were Singapore Chinese training for the Malayan All-Chinese Olympiad to be held in 1937.

I was impressed and slightly bewildered. Only that morning I had read a letter in the *Straits Times* protesting against the fact that the State of Johore was proposing to spend 100,000 dollars on a golf course instead of on agriculture. It seemed a reasonable criticism. Yet perhaps, after all, the British were wise in their own way. It was, I think, the late C. E. Montague who said that boredom was the first sign of decadence in a nation. The British in the East were certainly not yet bored by sport. Their Empire might survive for many a long day because of the games which they had taught to the races under their protection.

While it lasted, it was a consoling thought. Then came the reflection that Greece had taught the world not only most of its games, but nearly everything else that it knew. And Greece had no empire to-day. Nor was there anything in the character of the modern Greek to remind one of his great forbears.

I spent my last day in Singapore in driving out to Johore Bahru, the capital of the State of Johore. The drive takes about forty minutes, and the road runs pleasantly through rubber and cocoanut plantations, occasional strips of jungle, and acres and acres of pineapples.

In my time Singapore *was* an island. To-day, the narrow strait which separates it from Johore is bridged by a broad and impressive causeway. The town itself is picturesque enough, and is a favourite with tourists. It has a fine mosque and a palace which houses the famous Ellenborough Plate, once destined for a British viceroy of India and now the property of a Malay Sultan. Like many Eastern buildings, both mosque and palace look better in photographs. To the naked eye they seem like inferior imitations of the Brighton Pavilion.

Apart from tigers, which abound but are rarely seen, the most interesting thing about Johore is the Sultan Ibrahim. I had met him twenty-seven years before. He was then about thirty-five, and was a bit of a tiger himself with a long string of escapades, mainly connected with racing and women, to his discredit. He has the blood of Danish sea-captains in his veins, and in those days was a fine figure of a man, full of the joy of living and with a special penchant for the lights of London and Paris. His great friend at that time was Colonel "Teddie" Bryce, whom I have already mentioned and who was then living in Johore. One of the trials of Teddie's life as a hard-working, early-rising planter was being woken up in the middle of the night to drink champagne with the Sultan.

To-day the Sultan has more or less settled down. He still likes the good things of life, and has a fund of racy stories which he tells well and likes telling. On this occasion he had only recently returned from a world tour and was full of his reception by the Prince of Wales, now King Edward VIII, in London, and by President Roosevelt in Washington.

There is a good story of his visit to the White House during the crisis of the American depression. The President was perhaps rather hazy about the whereabouts of Johore. At least he gave that impression to the Sultan, who at once replied:

"Mr. President, I'm ruler of only a very small state, but my treasury's full and I can balance my budget."

Sultan Ibrahim is by far the most Europeanised of the Malayan sultans. To his natural shrewdness he has added a considerable store of knowledge acquired during his travels. As he still enjoys more independence than the other Sultans, his goodwill is of some importance to the British authorities. He has given many proofs of his loyalty, the latest being his Jubilee gift of £500,000 towards the cost of Singapore's defences. His wife is the daughter of a Scottish doctor. The Sultana, who travelled home to England on the same ship as I did, is a quiet, dignified woman with a wonderful collection of jewellery. Very fair with a creamy complexion, she spent most of her time on board playing bridge. She has considerable influence over the Sultan, and has used it wisely. It is well that she has poise, for her life cannot be easy.

That same night I left Singapore for Port Dickson. I took my departure from Singapore's new and florid station. I travelled in a modern sleeper, better equipped and more comfortable than is to be found in any other Eastern country except Siam. To me Singapore had never been more than an exotic island. I was an F.M.S. man, now returning after twenty-five years of absence to the land of my youth. I felt the same emotional reaction as I always feel on the all-too-rare occasions when I can leave London for the Highlands. Only when the water begins to flow north does home begin.

BOOK III

ROMANCE IN RETROSPECT

"THOUGH WE attain not, yet we shall have shared
Together for a space the bread and wine;
Have stood together on the peak of dreams
And seen afar the mystic city shine."

CHAPTER ONE

I ARRIVED AT Seremban, the capital of Negri Sembilan, just before dawn. Kassim, Freddie's Malay chauffeur, was there to meet me, and in a few minutes I was being carried smoothly along a perfect road towards Port Dickson. As we drove through Seremban I could just see in the feeble light of the pre-dawn that the town had grown greatly. Soon we were out of its precincts and racing past acres and acres of rubber, most of it planted since my time. I owe much in my life to the generosity of my relations. They, in turn, owe the ability to be generous to rubber. But no one can say that a rubber plantation is a thing of beauty. Coatless in an open car, I was as cold as a charity child on a winter's day. The old landmarks had vanished. There was little or no jungle by the roadside.

My first feeling was one of disenchantment. Then, with the rising sun, my heart warmed. As we approached Port Dickson I was aglow with excitement. There before me was the sea, pearl-coloured and calm till it lost itself in the horizon. There, too, was the little township itself with the island of Pulau Arang, still uninhabited, still unspoilt, lying off the point of the harbour.

Here there was almost no change. I told the chauffeur to stop and stood up in the car. There before me was the padang in which I had played my first game of football in Malaya. There, beside it, was the post-office where my Chinese puller had deposited me, dressed in football kit, after my first ricki-sha drive. I could see the whole scene before my eyes: the young man, little more than a schoolboy, rather shy and helpless in his ignorance of the language, that was myself, the lusty Chinese puller gesticulating by the side of the road. I had given him a dollar—about three times his legitimate fare—and he had asked for more. As I stood, stupid in my dumbness, little Hussein, a Malay half-back, had come up and smiled. He had said some phrase in which I caught the word "football".

I had nodded, held up my dollar, and pointed to the coolie. Hussein, diminutive beside the muscular Chinaman, had taken swift action. Before I could realise what had happened, I had received fifty cents change, and the Chinaman had slunk off with the bare foot of the Malay planted firmly in the middle of his short pants to help him on his way.

Hussein had become my firm friend. And where were all my old friends now? I could recognise the old buildings, but among all the passers-by there was not a face that I knew. I was at home and yet I was a stranger, a junior Rip Van Winkle returning to a new world.

As we set out along the coast road towards Freddie's bungalow at the seventh mile, there were more deceptions in store for me. The sea-front was studded with bungalows and sanatoria. There were private yachts anchored in the bay. High on the cliff and marring the whole landscape was a huge kind of Moorish palace, the home of a son of Loke Yew, the famous Chinese millionaire who had begun life as a coolie. In my time Loke Yew himself had been content with a modest bungalow on the sea-shore which he used to lend to British planters for the week-end. This was not Port Dickson. It was Brighton.

At the third mile I passed the spot where my old bungalow had stood. There was nothing to mark the place in my mind. In place of the wooden barrack with its "atap"-leaf roof was a splendid new building, more like a Riviera villa than a bungalow. The steps, the hedge that had shut off the house from the road, the casuarina tree that had stood in the untidy compound, where Abdullah, our Mohammedanised Tamil gardener, used to pick the ticks from the dogs, had been cleared away. In their place was a garden with grass plots and an avenue for motor-cars leading up to the front door. I passed a golf course, the barracks of the new Malay regiment, and other signs of civilisation.

Sad at heart, I thought of Kingsley's verdict on *Westward Ho!*" which was named after his novel. "How goes on the

Northam Burrows scheme for spoiling that beautiful place with hotels and villas?" Like Kingsley I wanted a new planet without railways and motor-buses and pretentious projections. And then the car turned sharply to the right, and I entered into Paradise. We passed through a hundred yards or so of "blukar" or scrub, and there on a cliff before me and overlooking the sea on the finest site in all the East was Freddie's bungalow. On each side a strip of jungle with enormously high trees shut off the civilisation outside. All around us was Freddie's garden, heavily-scented and riotous with colour. Every tree seemed to be in bloom. There were temple flowers, flame of the forest, tulip tree flowers, crotons, Indian laburnum, Honolulu creeper, oleanders and three different kinds of bougainvillea. A long stair of steps neatly carved in the red laterite soil led down to a strip of beach with a Malay fisherman's prahu nosing the golden sand. Between house and sea was a grove of coconut palms. Far away on the right was the point of Port Dickson harbour and the lighthouse of Pulau Arang. Otherwise there was not a house to be seen. Beneath us was the broad panorama of the sea, placid, opalescent, and in spite of the sharks which haunt its depths, bewitchingly inviting.

Too much travel blurs the memory, but with every man and woman in this world there are certain scenes which remain as long as life itself. During the last seven years I have known little genuine happiness. But for that first view from Freddie's bungalow I shall always be grateful. It meant something much more than the recapture of a past that had seemed gone for ever and the instinctive realisation that my trip had been worth while. At the moment I thought of none of these things. I was content to know that for the first time in my post-war life I had felt an emotion which satisfied me completely.

I had little time to linger over it. Tommy Rosslyn and Freddie were already having their morning tea on the verandah. Even Harry, who in London rarely rises before midday, was shouting greetings from his room. There was Freddie's house to inspect, and my arrival had coincided with the most important day in its history: the introduction of a running water system. Built high off the ground on brick supports, its whole front facing the sea, was a long verandah which served as the living-room. Behind were the dining-room and three large bedrooms. A red-tiled roof tempered the heat of the sun. To give more air the rooms were separated, not by walls, but only by partitions, so that by raising one's voice one could talk from one room to the other. Below each bedroom and leading from it by steps was a bath-room or rather a bathing-place complete with Siamese jar and tin can for sluicing one's self. Connected to the main building by a covered passage were the kitchens and servants' quarters. The bungalow had belonged to a friend of Freddie's who had made a fortune in Malayan coal and had died during the worst year of the slump. Furnished by an expert, it would make an idyllic home.

Before I was allowed to have any breakfast, I had to be introduced to the domestic staff: the head Chinese boy and his buxom, trousered wife, a diminutive and intelligent Chinese "ketchil" (assistant boy), the staid and dignified Chinese cook, the Malay chauffeur and the chauffeur's Malay wife, the Javanese gardener, for gardeners in Malay are nearly always Javanese, and—Buntak. Strictly speaking, Buntak should have come first, but he remained standing in the background, his teeth showing in a broad grin and his arms motionless by his side. Buntak had been the first Malay to whom I had ever spoken. He had been the Malay head-man on my old estate at the third mile. He had taught me my first steps in Malay and everything that I knew about rubber-planting, and much more wordly wisdom besides. When the estate was refloated as a public company, he had gone to Freddie. He had remained with him ever since. In twenty-five years he had changed scarcely at all, and there was a lump in my throat as I shook his hand.

I have an immense affection for Malays. I bristle with resentment when Europeans refer to them as black men. More than any other oriental race, they have qualities akin to our own, and there are few Englishmen or Scots who have lived alone among them and who do not like them. They are proud, courageous and independent. Their sense of humour is keen. By nature they are courteous and cheerful. They have a profound respect for their own "adat" or law of custom, and as companions on a shooting trip they are unflinching in danger. As befits a race that lived formerly by piracy and war, they like most of the white man's games, especially football, and play them well. Ninety-nine per cent. of the English in Malaya prefer Chinese to Malays as house servants, and in every respect except one the Chinese are infinitely more efficient. But if you are living alone and you fall ill, your Chinese servants leave you. A Malay will stand by you in good times and in bad, and after my first year in Malaya I had a Malay boy. When I was at death's door fidelity was cheap at the price of a buttonless shirt or an unpunctual meal.

Not even his most perfervid admirer, however, would claim that the strong suit of the Malay is concentration on work for work's sake. He is a philosopher who lives by agriculture and fishing, and in a country where the British administration has safeguarded his land he labours as little as he can. Occasionally, if something interests him, he will work both intelligently and industriously. But the effort is generally spasmodic, and neither education nor adversity has developed in him any commercial ambitions. Buntak, however, was an exception. In his own rather jerky manner, for he is a man of few words, he told me the story of his life during the last twenty-five years. He had learnt Chinese and Tamil. He could swear in half-a-dozen languages. Times had been difficult, especially on account of rubber restriction, but thanks to Allah he had not done so badly. He was now getting a hundred dollars a month and had a motor-bicycle. His family were well. No, it wasn't the same wife as I had known. I remembered her vividly—a wanton young lady with sloe-coloured eyes which wandered. He had been married half-a-dozen times since then. I must see his new house—and his new wife.

A great and wise man is Buntak to-day. He now runs Freddie's estate and, during Freddie's frequent visits to Europe, is in sole charge of all his rubber interests. He is worth half-a-dozen European assistants, for even during the worst period of the slump Freddie has managed to make his rubber pay.

After breakfast we all went down to the sea for a swim. It must have been the first time that Harry Rosslyn had bathed in the open sea for many years. I was already some way out when he strode majestically into the water, his gigantic figure, impressive but slightly top-heavy, brushing the waves aside with an easy grace. After a few steps he stumbled forward, and I shrieked with laughter as his arms beat the waves in a flail-like movement. I thought he was fooling, but Freddie looked serious. In a few swift strokes he was at Harry's side and had helped him to his feet. The noble earl had been unable to regain his feet and had been in danger of being drowned before our eyes in three feet of water.

This *contretemps* successfully liquidated, I sat down on the beach, where Ah Ling, the nine-year-old daughter of Freddie's Chinese "boy", was playing with a young Malay companion on the sand. I watched them lazily. They were lying opposite each other at a distance of about fifteen paces. Each held a stick pointed at the other. Before each of them was a small channel dug in the sand. My curiosity aroused, I sat up and took notice. They were playing soldiers. The sticks were rifles, the little channels trenches. I spoke to Ah Ling. Yes, she was playing soldiers. She was Chiang Kai-shek, and her young Malay opponent was a Japanese general. She was defending China against the Japanese Imperialists. In the persons of these young children of different oriental races the military spirit had penetrated even into this sheltered haven of peace. Human nature in the East did not seem very different from human nature in Europe.

When we had dressed, Freddie took us for a drive in his car. The car was not too big, and in order to make room for his bulk Harry Rosslyn had to sit in the front seat next the driver. On my way down from Seremban I had formed the conclusion that Kassim, Freddie's chauffeur, was the most staid and silent Malay I had ever met. I was right. He was. But suddenly I saw him bend over his wheel, his whole body shaking with laughter. Freddie pulled him up sharply. In stammering tones he confessed that the sight of the big Tuan (Harry) trying to lift his legs over the windscreen had been too much for him. It had never struck us in that way before, but on second thoughts we agreed that the spectacle justified the internal explosion. Harry will live for ever in that chauffeur's memory. The humour of those long, unwieldy legs never staled, and on every subsequent occasion when Harry entered the car the chauffeur had to perform contortions of self-control in order to restrain his laughter. I think he gave Harry as much amusement as Harry gave him.

We drove slowly in to the town, Freddie pointing out the new landmarks and I plying him incessantly with questions about the past. Freddie told me the names of the new bungalows and of their new owners. That—he waved an arm towards a building on the left—was the Port Dickson Club. Here was the Railway Sanatorium, there Clovelly, and there Magnolia Bay. But I saw only the ghosts of my youth. Where was old "Hairy-Belly"? Where the good-natured Robert Engler? "Hairy-Belly" had been an Australian surveyor, Robert Engler, a mystery German of good family, who had been an officer in a crack cavalry regiment and had become a remittance man. In my time he lived on a coconut estate with a stout, middle-aged Tamil lady for a paramour. He never did a stroke of work, but drank beer by the gallon. I had often met him driving back from Port

Dickson in a rickisha, his hand holding a bottle of beer and his Tamil lady clasping him round his plump stomach in order to prevent him from falling out. "Hairy-Belly" and Robert were dead.

We passed the old Tamil burial-ground, and suddenly, as in a film scene, I saw Harry Cumming, drunk but a born elegant, conducting a Tamil funeral, sprinkling lotus-flowers on the grave, and wailing in unison with scores of Tamil coolies. His Tamils worshipped him. I believe they thought he was a God. Harry, the brother of a great rubber magnate, had been another failure. Yet he had died at Gallipoli.

As we approached the fourth mile, I saw a bungalow on a site which I recognised. "Where's Jimmie now?" I asked. "Jimmie" was James McClymont, a Scot with the broadest of Girvan accents, who had begun his career as a clerk on the little railway which runs from Port Dickson to Seremban. He was a character who would have appealed to Kipling. In my early days in Malaya he appealed to the handful of young Englishmen in Port Dickson for quite different reasons. From small beginnings he had amassed a large fortune in rubber and in other speculations, but he still kept on his small agency in a store just beside the harbour. Here, when we were thirsty before "tiffin", we would find him in white trousers and singlet counting cases of whisky and thumbing bills of lading. The first greeting was generally gruff. "What are you young rascals idling aboot for when ye should be wor-r-king? Yon's no the way to get rich." Then out would come a bottle of champagne.

Like most successful Scots "Jimmie" was a strict presbyterian who exercised a rigid discipline over his family. In 1909 he went home for his first holiday for years, enjoining all of us and, more particularly, my then manager, "Monkey" Holland, to look after his son Quentin. During Jimmie's absence Quentin celebrated his twenty-first birthday. It was a royal celebration and the host's health was drunk with Highland honours. After dinner we had a jumping competition over rows of long chairs placed side by side on the verandah. Quentin smashed himself up rather badly, and the rest of the evening and the early morning were spent seated for the excellent reason that everyone was past walking. Apart from the birthday "bust" Quentin made full use of his freedom, and when "Jimmie" returned he married the boy off as quickly as possible. "Jimmie", one of the definite successes of Malaya, retired long ago. He died at Girvan last year. His daughter Bella is now the wife of Andrew Agnew, one of the British oil kings, and another Scot who from humble beginnings in Malaya has risen to the highest heights in commerce.

I shall not weary the reader further with the necrologies of my former Malayan friends. In my youth they seemed to me to be important, and I saw them as men of resource and determination and possessed in rich measure of that spirit of adventure which has peopled the four corners of the world with Celts and Anglo-Saxons. I realise now that they were probably rather ordinary people who owed such prominence as they achieved to the circumstance of the time and place in which they lived. They were pioneers with all the advantages and discomforts of their peculiar position. The advantages were those of opportunity. There was all the wealth of a new land to be had almost for the asking. There was, too, all the glamour of a prestige which in those days stood high and made even the youngest white assistant feel like a governor. The discomforts were real. The motor-car, which has changed the heat and burden of travel in the tropics to a deliciously cooling relaxation; cold storage; electric fans; all these luxuries were unknown thirty years ago.

To-day, the average young Englishman who comes out to Malaya tries to keep as near as possible to the comforts of the towns. He has lost much of the former spirit of adventure. The men of my day may not have worked hard. But they did go out into the uncomfortable districts and never hesitated to break new ground. It may have been largely a matter of necessity, but on the whole they preferred life in the "ulu" (up country) to life in the towns like Kuala Lumpur and Ipoh. And personally I have no doubts about which life I should choose even to-day. The only important fact to remember about Malaya is that, whereas Singapore and Penang are ports built and peopled largely by Chinese and which have played their part in world commerce for over a hundred years, the Malay States were uncivilised less than sixty years ago. Piracy and internecine warfare between the neighbouring states flourished almost unchecked. Out of this jungle chaos and with almost no bloodshed the British rule has created a model adminstration with admirable roads, hospitals, law-courts, schools, and all the appurtenances of modern civilisation. Under this rule various Eastern races which a few decades ago were engaged in slitting each other's gizzards now live happily and contentedly. Even their ambitions are carefully nurtured, for the administration has already made a considerable advance towards that dual partnership of Briton and native, which is the foundation stone of modern British colonial policy. All this has been accomplished within the last fifty years, and for this achievement much credit must go to the pioneers of my time and before it, although many of them would certainly turn in their graves if they could see to-day just how quick has been the emancipation of both Malays and Chinese during the last ten years.

I saw startling proofs of this acceleration while Freddie drove us through the main street of Port Dickson. I have said that the town proper had changed little since my time. In one sense it has gone back. In my time the coast road beyond the fifth mile was mostly uninhabited jungle. But in the town itself we had an English district officer and his wife, an English assistant D.O., an English police sergeant, an English customs officer, an Australian surveyor, and a Scottish engineer in charge of the Public Works Department. To-day, the coast road may be lined with the week-end bungalows of European planters and business men, but of all this white officialdom in Port Dickson itself, which was the very kernel of the British administration and the guarantee of justice and incorruption, only one Englishman is left, and he is a junior customs officer, who without an adequate staff is expected to control and check the smuggling which goes on across the Negri Sembilan and Malacca frontier.

For Negri Sembilan is in the Federated Malay States and Malacca in the Straits Settlements, and, strange as it may seem, each state has a different tariff.

The Port Dickson District officer is now a Malay. Much as I like the Malays, I was not impressed. There is one cardinal principle which should govern British colonial policy. And that is that the right of self-government should be given to those states which are capable of exercising it properly and should be firmly refused to those which are not. Malaya is still far from ripe for self-government, and in their effort to prepare the Malay for his eventual assumption of this right I only hope that the British authorities are not trying to make him run before he can walk.

There was not much to see at Port Dickson, and we soon drove home. On our way back we stopped at a bend on the road. "Do you remember this?" asked Freddie. "This" was where we used to shoot "punai", a small green pigeon which is hard to hit and which at flighting time gives very good sport. And from "punai" we got on to tigers.

I am aware that tigers, especially Malayan tigers, are a subject which should be approached with diplomatic caution and reserve. The Malayan jungle racket is getting played out. American authors, cinema directors, and "catch 'em alive" zoo proprietors have very nearly exhausted its possibilities. It is certainly astonishing what the reading public— especially the American public—will swallow in the form of travel tales. The finest travel book written since the war in any language could not find a publisher in the United States until it had become an established success in England. It was

refused by scores of publishers. I have seen their letters. The
same note ran through all of them. The story was not exciting enough. Had the author not had some personal adventures? Personal adventure was what the American public
liked—personal adventures like those of X or Y. Mr. "X"
and Mr. "Y" were generally professional globe-trotters
whose adventures were self-manufactured. Sometimes, too,
they are borrowed. There is one American author who writes
on tropical life and who has lifted his personal adventures
straight out of the books of more famous writers. He has not
even bothered to paraphrase his borrowings. Yet his books
have done well and at least one of them has been filmed. One
day, however, the public will be better informed and will
rebel. For, although tigers abound throughout the Malay
Peninsula, the Malayan jungle is too thick for the staging—
and the filming—of spectacular adventures.

Seeing a Malayan tiger is a matter of luck. One may spend
a life-time in the country and never see one. One might arrive at Penang for the first time, drive down by car to Kuala
Lumpur, and run over a cub on the way. Does not the best
and most truthful of all Malayan tiger stories relate how a
young English girl straight out from home saw a tiger washing its face by the roadside and said nothing about it to her
parents because she had been told that tigers were as common in Malaya as rabbits in England. Nevertheless, the odds
are heavily against such meetings. I have seen fresh tiger
spoor within a hundred yards or so of my bungalow at Pantai. I have been out tiger-shooting with the chief police
officer of Negri Sembilan, that is, with all the chances in my
favour, and I have never seen a live tiger outside of captivity.
I remember meeting a procession one morning close to my
bungalow. It was headed by a group of road "coolies" carrying on poles the dead body of an old tiger, a "man-eater"
for whose corpse the Government had offered a reward of a
hundred dollars. Behind the tiger walked a skinny little Indian superintendent carrying a gun. A chattering crowd of

Chinese, Tamils, and Malay boys and girls brought up the rear. The Indian had been in charge of a gang a mile or two up the road. The tiger had walked across early in the morning, and the Indian had killed it with a home-made cartridge, full of slugs and nails, fired from the single-barrel of a villainously cheap Belgian shotgun. The gun had knocked over both the tiger and the man, and now he was a hero with riches in his grasp, for in addition to the Government reward he would sell the skin to a European—who later would tell his friends and his children how he had stalked the monster through the depth of the jungle—the flesh to the Chinese as a table delicacy, and the claws and whiskers and other extremities to Malays as charms for courage or as ingredients for making love-philtres.

This preamble will have prepared the reader for the tall but true story which now follows. As we drew near to Freddie's home, he said to us: "You've heard the story of the seventh mile tiger, of course?" We hadn't. The whole coast looked far too civilised for tigers. I suggested to Freddie that it was no good trying to pull our legs. He laughed. "Oh, yes! there are still tigers even here. The government has a forest reserve behind Sendayan. The tigers come over on to the rubber estates occasionally. A year or two ago there was one which made quite a good bag of coolies on your old estate. When the number of victims reached eighteen there was something like a revolution in the 'lines'. The coolies were afraid to go out to work. Although we sat up all night on numerous occasions and set scores of traps, we never even as much as got a sight of the man-eater. When the nineteenth coolie was found badly mauled and dead one morning, the estate manager came to see me.

"We decided that drastic action must be taken. We sent in for the Indian dresser at the Port Dickson hospital and told him to bring out all the strychnine he had. We then took him to the place where the corpse was lying and made him fill it up with strychnine. We then withdrew, hoping that the tiger would come back to the scene of his kill. He came back all right. We found him the next morning quite close to the sea. His mouth was full of bamboo shoots and grass. In his death agony he had trampled everything down for a radius of about twenty yards.

"The story had a sequel. Although the coolies on the estate were delighted that their enemy had been destroyed, the strychnine incident became known and received a wide publicity. It was taken up by the Indian Immigration people and by prominent Orientals of all races. There were questions in the Federal Council. It was suggested that we would never have dared to take such liberties with a European's corpse. For a bit we had quite a bad time, but I took the line that the safeguarding of the living was more important than the sanctity of the dead and that the addition of a little strychnine to his body would not interfere with the coolie's chance of salvation. After all, old boy, you wouldn't mind your dead body being used to save your fellow-countrymen."

It was a nice point. I could have quoted a case where Europeans in Europe had used human bait to destroy, not a tiger, but other human beings. In 1925 I was in the Balkans when the communists tried to blow up King Boris and the Bulgarian Cabinet during the funeral service for General Georgieff in the Cathedral of the Sveta Nedelia in Sofia. In order to provide themselves with an opportunity of trapping the King and his Ministers under one roof, they had murdered General Georgieff, a harmless old gentleman. The bomb which they exploded killed nearly two hundred people. But the King was not among the victims. He was away attending the funeral of his favourite gamekeeper. As that great sexagenarian sportsman, Mr. "Gerry" Weigall, would say, it was another illustration of the advantages of taking up sport.

As for the use of my body for such humanitarian purposes as the destruction of a local scourge, I was not prepared to argue the question. For the moment I was not interested in tigers. They would not worry me. The only sound of wild animals that I was likely to hear during my present tour was the chattering of monkeys in Freddie's two strips of jungle.

That evening, as we sat on the terrace watching the rose-yellow reflections cast on the sea by the last embers of the dying sun, Freddie was full of plans for my future delectation. To-morrow we should spend the whole day at Malacca. The day after there was the first inspection of the new Malay Regiment by the Governor. It would be a *"Hari bĕsar"* (*big day or holiday*) in the history of Port Dickson. There would be a luncheon. We should have to go.

Then he had arranged a fishing expedition for me, an all-night affair with the best Malay fisherman in the district to look after me. After that we could. . . . But for the moment I was not interested. Lying back in a long chair with some kind of scented fumigating oil burning at my feet to keep off the mosquitoes, I had my eyes glued on the sea. Many a time I had seen it lashed into foam by a "Sumatra", the western gale whose approach was generally preceded by a terrible stillness and which came with a fierce sudden rush, lifting the atap roofs off the top of the Malay houses and even off the old-fashioned European bungalows. But now the Straits were as still and as mysterious as a shadow.

How often had I watched the same skyline and the same stretch of water! In those far-off years sea and sky had been cinema and theatre and news-reel to me. I could see new worlds in them every evening, could read anything I wanted into them. They were the only visible things that had not changed in this country during the last twenty-five years. They had been the same sea and the same sky when the first Portuguese came. They would be the same sea and sky when the Dutch and the British had disappeared in the limbo of lives which have accomplished their alloted span. In their relation to the forgotten past, the present, and the unborn future, they alone gave an impression of eternity in a land where life was still amazingly evanescent and was as uncertain as the flame of a candle flickering in the wind.

I did not want to talk but was content to be alone with my own thoughts. I knew that my stay in this Lotus-land would be all too short. I wanted to make its best moments last as long as possible. Suddenly I realised exactly why I hate big cities. It was because there one never sees the sun rise or set.

CHAPTER TWO

OUR VISIT TO Malacca was a complete success. We set out early in the morning and from then until our return long after dark I enjoyed every minute of what was undoubtedly a strenuous day. Twenty-five years ago I had made my first entrance into Malacca from the sea. To-day, we went by car, making the seventy-five mile journey by a coast road which ran through rubber estates, Malay kampongs, and rice fields, with alternating strips of jungle to remind us of what the country had once looked like, and occasional glimpses of the sea. Soon after we had started Freddie pulled up at the side of the road. He wanted to show us a bungalow built by an English artist. We went down a path towards the beach, and there, invisible from the road and with a little bay all to itself, was a bungalow modelled on a Siamese house with a well-kept grass terrace overlooking the sea. The artist was in England, but the Malay caretaker was at home and he showed us over the house. It was very simply furnished. The walls were hung with attractive oriental studies by the owner. Had I been a rich man I should have bought the place as it stood. It was peaceful and secluded. It would have made an ideal home for an author.

While I was admiring the angular concave roofs, I noticed that the Malay caretaker was watching me with concentrated interest. His eyes never left me as I went from room to room, but it was not until we were about to leave that he made any attempt to satisfy his curiosity.

"Tuan Lockhart?" he said, tentatively. "The Tuan doesn't remember me. I'm Haji Sabudin. I used to play in your football team at Pantai."

I didn't recognise him, but I didn't tell him so. For a few minutes we talked about our old Malay friends in Pantai, who were dead and who were still living. We parted after a firm promise from me that I should revisit Pantai and should allow him to make the arrangements for my reception. He was obviously pleased. As for me I went away with my head in the air and my feet walking on the clouds. Haji Sabunin had recognised me after twenty-five years without any prompting from Freddie or anyone else. There is no limit to the various manifestations of human vanity. One of the most curious is the vanity of being remembered. It is also one of the most satisfying.

The rest of our drive was uneventful. As we drew nearer to Malacca, the number of Malay kampongs increased. There were more rice-fields and, although in many places the rice was ripe for harvest, there were a few backward patches of that vivid green which is the reposeful adjunct to every Malayan landscape. We passed many water-buffaloes wallowing up to their neck in muddy pools by the side of the road. They look both stupid and placid and, indeed, can be led literally by the nose by a Malay child of ten years old. But they are the most violent nationalists in Malaya, for they dislike the smell of a white man. The dislike is returned, but ever since I was chased by these animals twenty-six years ago I have an instinctive respect for them. We stopped, too, at the Linggi River which in my youth I had visited with Roger Swettenham, a nephew of the famous Sir Frank, in the Government launch. In those days the river was alive with crocodiles. Freddie told me their numbers had scarcely decreased. It was a strange emotion to feel that close around one were crocodiles, tigers, wild pig, deer, not to mention snakes, iguanas, lizards, and other smaller animals and insects, both dangerous and harmless, for the surrounding country gave no indication of their presence, and we saw no signs of animal life. On the other hand, all the ugliness which Western civilisation always brings in its train was there in full measure: motor-buses, motor-bicycles, road-drills and other noxious and noisome tools of modern engineering.

The monotony of the landscape was just beginning to pall when we caught a glimpse of the sea. We began to pass rows of large houses with walled-off grounds and gates with

Chinese signs. They belonged to the rich Chinese merchant. of Malacca. Presently we were in the town almost before I was conscious of it.

This was a great moment, for, although the British now pay little attention to Malacca, the town has more atmosphere than any other place in the East Indies.

> "Still further onward thou wilt come to know
> Malacca for emporium famed and strong,
> Where every Province on the mighty sea
> Can send its merchandise of rarity. . . .
> 'Twas Chersonesus called, and the rich ore
> Of gold, which by the land produced had been,
> Added the title 'golden' to its name;
> Some have imagined Ophir was the same."

So sang Camoens in the Lusiads, and his judgment is supported by the testimony of all the early European travellers. The first Englishman to sail through the Straits of Malacca was Drake in the *Golden Hind*. But the real heroes of the place were the Portuguese who captured it in 1511, established it as the greatest emporium for trade between East and West, made it the first Christian centre in the East, and held the place for over a hundred and thirty years or longer than we British have held Singapore.

The Portuguese captains and merchants failed with the course of time. But the missionaries remain. The angelus has been rung and mass has been said here daily for over four hundred years, and in the sleepy old-world atmosphere of the town it is easy to re-create in the imagination the glories of the Lusitanian colonial empire.

After the Portuguese had come the Dutch, and after the Dutch that great Englishman, Stamford Raffles. It was from Malacca that Raffles organised the conquest of Java for the British in 1810. It was to Malacca that Lord Minto, the Governor-General of India, came with British troopships to take command of the expedition, and it was from Malacca that the expedition sailed. I do not suppose that any Englishman has ever captured or ever will capture the affection of the Malays in the same degree as Raffles succeeded in doing. In the Hikayat Abdullah, the autobiography of Raffles's Malay secretary, and one of the most entertaining books in the Malay language, the author pays a Malay's tribute to a man whose greatness is only now being fully recognised by his countrymen. To-day, Raffles is claimed by die-hard Imperialists as one of their own. Actually, like most great proconsuls, he was ahead of his times. Like Swettenham, he was a champion of the Malays and a great advocate of a liberal policy towards all native races. He was severely censured by the directors of the East India Company, who then administered India and other British possessions in the Indian Ocean, for abolishing slavery and for thus reducing their profits.

When the Portuguese took Malacca first, it was said to have a population of 100,000. The figure sounds fantastic, although long before the arrival of the Portuguese the place had become a great *entrepôt* centre and a stronghold of Islam, from which the followers of the Prophet went out to preach his gospel in every part of Insulinde. To-day, the population has sunk to a modest 39,000. The harbour, once so highly prized by the British Government for its geographical and strategic position, is useless, and even small steamers cannot approach within a mile of its walls. Most of the inhabitants are Chinese, and, as in all the large cities of Malaya, they dominate the industry and commerce of the place. They have even taken possession of Herren Street, where the charming early eighteenth century Dutch houses remain intact. Looking down from the hill you see the long rows of tiled Dutch roofs extending down the narrow street. You go down into the street, and the interiors are Chinese with Chinese lacquer cabinets, Chinese idols, Chinese joss-sticks, Chinese children, and Chinese smells.

I could write a whole book on Malacca, for its attractions are endless. But I must follow the sequence of my pro-

gramme, for Freddie, who is a great organiser, had made a
programme for us. We were to lunch with George Wiseman, the head of the Dunlop Rubber Company in Malaya.
After luncheon we should have a swim in his outdoor swimming-pool and a siesta. Then in the cool of the later afternoon we should climb the hill and from the site of the old
fort and the ruins of the old church watch the sunset over
the harbour.

It was a good programme. We went first to Wiseman's
office where we found him surrounded by charts showing
the rubber production of each of the numerous estates under
his charge, the cost per lb., the average yield per tree, and a
mass of other statistics. In a neighbouring room was a whole
army of accountants, both European and Chinese. The Dunlop Rubber Company has 85,000 acres of planted rubber in
Malaya. I thought of my own early days of rubber planting
in Negri Sembilan, when accounts were of the simplest description and the only kind of office work consisted in entering up the check-roll at the end of the day. As I listened to
Freddie and Wiseman discoursing eloquently on such technical problems as bud-grafting, I felt somehow that times must
have changed since my dilettante days.

The Chairman of the Dunlop Rubber Company is Sir
Eric Geddes, Britain's Minister of Transport, Secretary of
State for Air, and First Lord of the Admiralty during the
Great War. Of all my conversations with Mr. Lloyd George
none has impressed me more than his story of how he discovered Geddes. "L. G." had then taken over the organisation of munitions. In his search for men he used to walk
round the department. He would ask for a piece of information. Nearly always the unfortunate official would attempt
to supply it himself and would search wildly among the
mass of papers on his desk, until Mr. Lloyd George's patience
was exhausted. Then one day he went into a room where a
heavily-built man with the shoulders of a "rugger" forward
sat at a large desk. The desk was bare. There was not a single

file, not a despatch, on it. Its sole accoutrements were a piece of blotting paper, a telephone, and a set of three bells. The man was in charge of bicycles. Mr. Lloyd George asked for the latest production figures for Birmingham and for Coventry. Could he have the statistics for motor bicycles and ordinary bicycles? A large forefinger pushed two bells. As if to the rubbing of Aladdin's lamp two black-coated genii appeared simultaneously. "Mr. Jones," boomed a deep-bass voice, "bring me immediately the motor-bicycle production figures for Birmingham and Coventry up to last night. Mr. Smith, let me have the same figures for push-bikes." The genii retired. Within sixty seconds they were back with the information. Mr. Lloyd George was impressed.

This was the beginning of the meteoric official career of Sir Eric Geddes. He could delegate work. Ever since Mr. Lloyd George told me that story I have pictured Sir Eric sitting in a huge office in London and pushing bells in different parts of the world in order to find out if people are working. Occasionally he comes East, and because he is a big man both physically and metaphorically, the Dunlop Rubber Company have the biggest bungalow in Malaya. The spacious comfort of its high-ceilinged rooms, the beauty of its gardens, the mown elegance of its private golf-course, and, above all, the Roman opulence of its marble swimming-pool, modelled on the swimming-pool in Sir Eric's house in Wimbledon, raise it to a peak of luxury to which neither Carcosa, the Chief Secretary's residence in Kuala Lumpur, nor Government House in Singapore has ever been able to ascend. And because Sir Eric is a heavy man who cannot stand the heat the bungalow has electric fans in every room, including even the *cabinets de toilette*.

Wiseman, who is also a big and heavy man, receives the full benefit of these Augustan luxuries, and he deserves them. For, after a luncheon in keeping with the glory of his palace, he went back to his office in order to ascertain whether in the last twenty-four hours Dunlops had made a profit of 1.935d.

per lb. of rubber or whether they were a fraction of a farthing on the wrong side. This devotion to business in the heat of the day was not the least surprising change in the white man's life in the tropics. In my day we led a more wisely regulated existence. But then there were no overseas telephones and no bell-pushers in London.

With the free run of the place to ourselves, we had our siesta in luxurious beds; we strolled through the richly scented garden; we reclined lazily in the shallow end of the Roman swimming-pool. And then towards four o'clock we set out to explore what remains of the old part of Malacca.

We made our way down Herren Street and Jonkers Street. We examined the gate of the old Portuguese fort. We saw the silver collection at the old Dutch Church. We inspected the old cemetery with its dates going back four hundred years and we admired the luxurious Chinese houses, for Malacca, strangely enough, is also the cradle of the Straits-born Chinese who are known locally as "Babas" and were originally Hokkiens. They are very intelligent, have probably a good deal of mixed blood in their veins, and frequently speak no Chinese. Their languages are English and bazaar Malay.

We should have called on the Resident-Councillor. We should have seen many more sights, but I grew tired of poking about smelly streets, and after an exquisite view of the river meandering through the town and giving to it a kind of Venetian effect we made our way up the grassy slopes of the hill to the old ruined Church of St. Paul. Here was the view over the whole town and the harbour. Here we could rest undisturbed until it was time to go home. Here, too, was the historical heart of Malacca.

The white-washed walls of the church are solid and well-preserved. There is a clump of trees beside it and a tall flagmast where on the King's birthday the Union Jack flies to proclaim the might, majesty and dominion of the British Empire. But otherwise the British have done nothing to dim the glory of its past. The grass is well tended. Within the roofless walls is a stone which marks the former grave of St. Francis Xavier, that ascetic Basque who helped Loyola to form the Jesuit order.

There was a time when Montmartre meant to me champagne, French ladies of easy virtue, and the most foolish kind of night life. I never go to Paris now without visiting it. But I go by day, and the object of my pilgrimage is the Notre Dame of Montmartre, where on Assumption Day, 1534, Loyola revealed to his six companions his dream of the militant order of Jesuits. And of the seven men, St. Francis, who on that day renewed his vow of poverty, chastity, and pilgrimage, was to be the most militant and the most ascetic. Europeans who know the East well hold very conflicting views about the work of Christian missionaries, but I have yet to meet one who does not at least respect the asceticism, the industry and the self-denial of the Jesuits, who, when they come East, turn their back for ever on Europe. The example of this self-denial was set by Francis Xavier, who to-day figures in every missal as St. Francis Xavier, Apostle of the Indies. And every year, on December 3rd, the anniversary of his death, every good Catholic throughout the world says the following prayer:

"O God, who, by the preaching and miracles of blessed Francis, wast pleased to join to Thy Church the nations of the Indies, mercifully grant, that, as we venerate his glorious merits, we may also follow the example of his virtues."

St. Francis Xavier was a Basque, but he belonged to the great era of the Portuguese domination. What great men these early Portuguese adventurers were and how shamefully they have been treated by the Anglo-Saxon historians. Every schoolboy knows the name of Drake's *Golden Hind*, but he is never told that the first Englishman to travel East was carried on a Portuguese sailing ship. The United States has blazoned the name of Columbus over the world in much the same way as it has made a national god out of Lindbergh. But what Englishman can tell you the name of Albuquerque's ship? What American knows anything about Vasco da Gama, as great a man as Columbus, yet now in danger of being forgotten, just as the exploit of Brown and Alcock has been suppressed, even in the British Dominions, for the greater glory of the American flying hero? It is not the fault of Columbus and Lindbergh, who deserve their fame, that the others have passed into semi-oblivion. It is merely that history is written by the victors and the loud speakers. Ask an Englishman what he thinks of the Portuguese, and he will at once shrug his shoulders in amused contempt and refer to some aprocryphal incident of the great war. Tell him that Portugal was building an empire when we were still engaged in civil war at home, that alike in courage and in culture her captains and conquistadors were the foremost men of the sixteenth century, and that in the world to-day there are still 60,000,000 people who speak Portuguese, and he will smile at you sadly. These things are not in the English history books. Yet they are true enough. We have a great place in the colonial history of the world, but we came after the Dutch and after the French. The Portuguese showed the way to all three of us.

And of these early Portuguese the greatest viceroy had been Alfonso Albuquerque, the conqueror of Malacca and the builder of the Church of Our Lady where I now stood. As my eye took in the broad expanse of view with the town of Malacca lying below me like an ill-shaped mushroom with its legs in the sea, I pictured to myself that first arrival of the Portuguese. The city, now known to the English as "Sleepy Hollow", had then been very much alive. Men of almost every Eastern race, Hindus from every part of India, Arabs, Chinese, Gujuratis, and Javanese as well as Malays, composed its population. And then had come the first Portuguese, fanatical Christian warriors trained by years of fighting against the Moors in Africa and impelled hither as much by the zeal of the Crusader as by the cupidity of the merchant. This first squadron of five ships had come to trade and not to conquer.

It was at first favourably received by the Malay sultan, and a party of Portuguese had landed under the valiant Ruy de Aranjo.

But the instinctive jealousy of the Malacca merchants prompted the sultan to rid himself of these dangerous newcomers by an act of treachery. He would invite the Portuguese officers to a great banquet. In the middle of the banquet they would be murdered, and with their death the Portuguese ships would fall an easy prey to the Malays.

The plan promised well, and then fate in the form of eternal romance intervened on behalf of the Portuguese. A Javanese lady, who had already succumbed to the charms of one of the new white men, swam out to his ship to warn her lover. Thanks to this warning the Portuguese had been able to escape, although they were forced to leave Ruy de Aranjo and his twenty companions in the sultan's hands.

At that moment the great Albuquerque himself, then at the height of his fame, had come in his famous ship, *Flor de la Mar*, and with a squadron of seventeen other vessels, to rescue his compatriots and, above all, his friend Ruy de Aranjo. There had been negotiations with the sultan for the release of the prisoners, and Aranjo had written that gallant letter telling his viceroy to make no concessions in order to save the prisoners and that for himself he held it to be a good fortune that Our Lord had placed him in a state where he could die for his Holy Faith.

Albuquerque had waited until July 25, the day of his Patron Saint, St. James the Greater, before launching his attack. There had been fierce fighting. Like Hannibal, the Malays had used elephants in their charges. A second assault had been necessary in order to conquer the city. But in the end the Portuguese had prevailed. The prisoners had been liberated, and Albuquerque had shown his gratitude to God by erecting a Church to our Lady of the Annunciation and his trust in powder by building a fort such as the impressionable Orientals had never seen before. He had done more than this. At

one blow he had destroyed the Mohammedan commercial
route to Europe and had secured for his own country a monopoly of the lucrative spice trade of the East Indies.

Malacca has seen the Portuguese evicted by the Dutch and
the Dutch, in turn, by the British. Her square has been the
scene of grim executions and unbelievable tortures, for these
early white rulers believed that severity was the best guarantee for their own safety. The last occasion on which her harbour was animated by the bustle of naval preparations was
when the Minto-Raffles expedition which conquered Java,
sailed from it in 1810, and the watching natives were offered
an unrehearsed firework display when one of the British
ships took fire and her powder magazine blew up.

But long before this Malacca had ceased to be of any great
importance. Her trade began to decline when the Dutch began to develop Java, and it was finally destroyed by the rise
of Penang. Her glory belongs to the Portuguese period, and
it is to those early Portuguese that the mind returns again and
again when one visits Malacca.

Present at that first assault under Albuquerque was a very
young Portuguese called Fernâo de Magalhâes, better known
to the world to-day as Ferdinand Magellan. Camoens, the
poet of Portugal's great period, must have landed there more
than once. And to-day the traces of the Portuguese occupation remain not only in the stone walls of the church, but in
the living language of the people of Malaya.

Even to-day there are probably more Portuguese words in
the Malay language than the words of any other European
language, and the English or Dutch woman in Singapore or
Batavia who learns enough Malay to run her house, unwittingly uses as many Portuguese words as Malay, when she
requires more forks, is ordering butter, or is telling her boy
to open the shutters, to dust the wardrobe, or to give a ball
to the dog.

Albuquerque had several well-known successors in Malaya: Don Leonis Pereira, who defended Malacca against the

King of Acheh; Duarte de Silva, who distinguished himself greatly at the original siege; Fernão Pinto, and various de Castros and de Sousas. To-day, their names have come down to the present generation of Eurasians, for, although the Portuguese had a strict religious bar in relation to marriage, it was not extended to colour. Most of the early converts to Christianity were women. They were given to, or taken by, the Portuguese as wives, and to-day the Eurasian descendants of these Pereiras, de Castros, de Sousas, and even Xaviers, provide the British Government in Malaya with its best second-division clerks and very frequently with its best cricketers. My former assistant at Pantai was a Eurasian called de Silva, who could trace his descent back to Albuquerque's captain.

As I lay in the cool grass watching the little Malay prahus turning leisurely for home in the approaching sunset, I began to meditate on the transience of all empires. I found myself wondering if our Eastern Empire would last as long as the Portuguese Empire and if it would leave as many traces. These sixteenth-century Portuguese had been not only superb soldiers but men of vision and enterprise and self-denial. They had been drawn from a hardy peasant population which never exceeded 3,000,000. Their Empire had failed partly because the continual wars enforced a severe strain on the man-power of a small nation (the fleets for the Indian Ocean absorbed from 3000-4000 men a year), but mainly because the wealth which the Portuguese ships brought home from the East led all classes of the Portuguese population but especially the peasants, to abandon their simple virtues.

I saw again that glorious spring day when some years ago I paid my first visit to Lisbon. I had spent many hours in the richly decorated Gothic church at Belem where Henry the Navigator, whose mother, incidentally, was the sister of our own John of Gaunt, lies buried. I had seen the tower from which Vasco da Gama had set out. As a foreigner on whom

Malaya has cast a spell which will never be broken I had paid
my tribute to the tall white pillar on which stands the statue
of Albuquerque surrounded by flowering Judas trees.

True, in his life-time the Portuguese had not treated him
well. The king had censured him as the British "John Company" had censured Wellington in India and Raffles in Malaya. He had superseded Albuquerque, and the news of his
recall reached the great captain a few days before his death
and made him exclaim: "In bad repute with men because of
the King and in bad repute with the King because of men it
were well that I were gone."

But in death the king and the Portuguese had relented,
and to-day the conqueror of Malacca looks down on his
present-day compatriots from one of the most imposing
statues in the world. I should like to think that it might
serve to revive the adventurous spirit of the Portuguese and
to give a new stimulus to their colonial enterprises. But I
doubt its efficacy. As a colonial power Portugal has long
since passed into decline. One day the British Colonial
Empire may reach the same stage.

To the average British subject who sees the Empire as a
conception as permanent as the world itself, my reflection
may seem like a lack of faith equivalent to high treason. But
there is no permanence to any empire. Nor is there much
satisfaction to be gleaned from those comforting theories of
our modern historians about the advantages of climate and
the superiority of the northern races. The theories may seem
true enough if applied to the last two hundred years which in
relation to time are like a day in the history of the world.
Otherwise, they do not bear examination. Some of the greatest empires and civilisations have been built up by peoples
like the Hindus, the Egyptians, the Greeks, and the Romans
themselves, who lived in climates which to-day we profess
to regard as deleterious to races aspiring to world leadership.
No, a comparison between the Portuguese Colonial Empire
and the British Colonial Empire is strictly fair. Here in

Malaya, where the warning finger of history is already visible, it is even appropriate.

I continued my reflections during the long drive home in the pearl-grey light of the tropical moon. The fantastic shadows of trees across the road stimulated my imagination; the gentle murmur of the waves lapping on the shore lulled me to a generous complacency. The faults of the British in Malaya were easy enough to see. They consisted chiefly in a standard of luxury which was much higher than that of any other European race in the East or, for that matter, in Europe itself. The luxury was material and not intellectual. In all parts of the world the Englishman made a fetish of opening the pores of the body; he did less about opening the pores of the brain. Nowhere had he carried this fetish to such extravagant lengths as in the tropics. In his reading even the American felt an all-compelling urge towards self-education—even in a half-baked form. The Englishman was superior to all such urges. He flood-lit the old church in Malacca, but he did not read its history.

Yet he had great assets, and the two greatest perhaps were his inability to see himself as others see him and his convenient lack of imagination. The first came from the devil. Pride, none the less overweening because it was hidden by a mask of meekness and self-depreciation, was the Englishman's original sin. It exposed him to the charge, levelled against him for centuries by other races, of hypocrisy. At the same time it permitted him to believe that his scheme of things, above all, his sense of justice and his standard of conduct in public affairs, was the best in the world. Other nations professed the same faith, but in the case of the Englishman the belief was fundamental and had deeper roots of justification. His lack of imagination was a gift from God. It enabled him not only to keep calm in a crisis but to rise superior to it because, in spite of an increasingly hysterical popular press, he never saw it coming and refused to treat it as a crisis when it was upon him. I concluded that as a colonial empire we had reached an early middle-age rather too comfortable and complacent for our security, but still virile and far distant from senility.

When we reached Freddie's bungalow, we went down to the beach for a moonlight bathe. There is something eerily exhilarating about bathing by night in the tropics. Freddie's little bay is protected by a coral reef, but it has no pagar or staked enclosure, and there is always the danger, remote but never wholly improbable, of a shark or a stray crocodile or one of those numerous sea-snakes whose poison is more deadly than that of almost any land-snake. The water is still pleasantly warm. An instinctive caution puts a natural check on any exhibition of swimming prowess. Slightly apprehensive, but yielding to a temptation too exotic to be resisted, one lies in the shallow water a few yards out from the beach until every muscle is relaxed and the bloodstream is cooled to a delicious temperature.

It is a form of stolen pleasure akin in its emotional thrill to poaching. Only here one is trespassing not against man-made laws but against the law of primeval Nature.

CHAPTER THREE

IT MAY HAVE been the moonlight bathe or an infection contracted in Singapore. Be this as it may, I rose the next morning with a shivering feeling in all my bones. Like the sky above me my head was heavy and my usual cheery outlook slightly overcast. In my attempt to recapture all the emotions of my youth in Malaya was I to experience again the febrile sensations of a malaria which twenty-five years before had nearly kept me in the country for ever and which had altered the whole destiny of my life? I thought it more than likely, but I kept my feelings to myself.

We had a day before us which I was determined not to miss. That morning the Governor was to inspect for the first time the new Malay Regiment. This regiment is the latest accretion to the military strength of the British Empire and its present headquarters are at Port Dickson. In the past the only native regiments in Malaya have been regiments brought from India and Burma. One regiment has always been stationed in Singapore, and more recently another regiment has been quartered in Taiping in the Federated Malay States. Since the mutiny of the Indian Light Infantry in Singapore, in 1915, the British authorities in Malaya have altered their views about imported Indian regiments, and in 1934 a beginning was made with the formation of a Malayan regiment with a view to its replacing the Burmese regiment in Taiping.

Punctually at ten-thirty we made our way to the camp, which was only a mile or two away. There we met the Governor, Sir Shenton Thomas, and his wife and daughter, Mr. Hughes, the British Resident, and a small gathering of Europeans. After we had been introduced we were given seats on the edge of the parade ground and we sat down to watch the display.

Before us were a hundred and fifty recruits dressed in singlet and white shorts and the two hundred and fifty trained men, divided into three companies and looking very smart in their pale-green uniforms, with dark-green cap, pale-green web belt, shorts, puttees with Islam green tops, and well-polished black boots. From the laterite soil of the parade ground came a thin cloud of red dust. The air was charged with thunder. The heat was sweltering, and, as my head was splitting, I was prepared to be bored.

When the display started, I was pleasantly surprised. I am no soldier, but during my life abroad I have seen the cere-monial parades of most of the crack regiments of Europe. These Malay boys were marvellously efficient. They had the "swagger" of guardsmen. Drilled by a Scottish Sergeant-Major, a short, red-faced Cameron Highlander with a hoarse whisper of a voice which sounded just as if he had completed a three-months' lecture in the United States, they performed a series of complicated evolutions not only with machine-like precision, but also with exultant pride. At the end they formed up with fixed bayonets about forty yards away and directly opposite to us. An officer blew his whistle, and sud-denly the men charged with a chorus of blood-curdling yells.

I was quite sober, but as I saw this line of brown faces with open mouths, dilated nostrils, and fiercely gleaming eyes de-scending on us I was not quite sure what was going to hap-pen. I felt a sudden uneasiness which was increased when Harry Rosslyn gripped my arm. Then the whistle blew again, and the men pulled up a yard or two away from us. It was a magnificent and even terrifying spectacle.

After the parade we made an inspection of the temporary barracks. They were spotlessly clean and except for the plain unmattressed plank beds looked like the open dormitories of an English public school. The regiment is run on English lines, and every form of English sport, including hockey, "soccer", and cricket is encouraged. Tommy Rosslyn was so impressed that she presented the regiment with a challenge cup. It is to be competed for annually for inter-company cross-country running.

N

I inspected, too, the undress, or rather the walking-out, uniform of the regiment. It consists of white coat and trousers, a short green sarong worn short in the fashion of Malayan royalty, a green pocket handkerchief, an Islam green velvet songkok—a cap rather like a glengarry without ribbons and pompom—and a "swagger" stick. It is a kit to melt hearts, and the Malays are very proud of it. They have to buy it with their own money. They are paid fifteen Malay dollars a month or rather less than two pounds.

At first the Sultan of Perak was upset by the idea of the royal sarong being worn by ordinary soldiers and made an official protest. On being told that our King allows the Royal Scots to wear the royal tartan, he waived his objection. The regimental tie, I should add, is of three colours: green for Islam, yellow, the royal colour of Malay sultans, and a thin strip of red to mark the British connection.

About thirty per cent. of the Malays in the regiment speak English. Some of them speak it remarkably well. I met one or two of the Malay non-commissioned officers, including a son of the Sultan of Perak. He had been at Oxford and had married an English girl. Now he was a sergeant in the regiment and slept on a plank bed like the others. When he joined, his mother sent extra bedding. The Commandant of the regiment was spared the necessity of forbidding this breach of regulations. The young man refused the extra comforts.

In the regiment they tell a good story of this young Rajah. Shortly before my arrival a big British commercial man had come down to Port Dickson to see the regiment. He had heard of the Rajah and asked the commanding officer if he could speak to the young man. The officer agreed, and the following conversation took place:

Big English Visitor: "White man fire big gun—boom." He blew out his cheeks and emitted a blast of sound meant to imitate a cannon. "And every one run away—see?"

Young Malay Rajah: "Tuan."

B.E.V.: "White man eat too much rice, belly swell—see?"
This time he blew out his stomach to illustrate his English.

Y.M.R.: "Tuan."

B.E.V.: "White man soldier plenty button, plenty spit,
plenty polish—see?" Again he went through the appropriate
gestures.

Y.M.R., still standing at attention and without a smile on
his face: "Tuan."

His flow of baby English exhausted, the visitor walked
away.

"Fine-looking Malay," he said to the commanding officer.
"Intelligent too. He seemed to understand everything I said."

"Yes," said the officer, "I think he did. He was four years
at Balliol."

The young Rajah is a good example of the new Malay
princeling, for the old type of Malay sultan is rapidly vanish-
ing. The new generation is now trained at Kuala Kangsar,
the Malay Eton. On the whole the product of this college,
run on English public school lines, is excellent. But in the future it will create great difficulties, for with education and
travel will come inevitably national aspirations. Mixed marriages, too, are already causing awkward and undesirable
complications. Not long before my visit the Sultan of Kedah's
son had married a white girl. His father, or rather his father's
official advisers, tried to prevent the marriage by bringing in
an Order in Council that no member of the Sultan's family
should marry anyone who had not embraced the Mohammedan faith. The young man circumvented both his father
and the decree by taking his bride to an imam and having
her converted overnight to Islam.

The present Sultan of Perak is the first Malay sultan who
has graduated from Kuala Kangsar. I remembered him from
twenty-five years before when he was a young man in Government service in Kuala Lumpur and a keen polo player.
To-day, he diverts himself with racing, owns over a hundred
racehorses, and occasionally causes a little official uneasiness

by his extravagance. Probably his racing is an outlet from the
restrictions which British protection imposes on his powers
as a ruler. For, although the Malays have not yet acquired the
intellectual dialectics of nationalism, there is more than one
sultan, especially in the newer states, who remember the
good old days of the past and who chafe under British interference with their right of spending.

During my visit an unprecedented example of British interference had aroused considerable comment in British as
well as in Malay circles. Three years ago the British Government decided on a scheme of decentralisation for the Federated Malay States. Instead of central government from Kuala
Lumpur, the former Federal capital, greater powers were to
be given to the Sultans and the British Residents of the respective States.

It was a British Resident who first took advantage of his
powers under the new scheme. The Sultan of Selangor, a
fine type of the old Malay, was over seventy. His eldest son
and heir had long been regarded as an impossible successor,
and when Mr. Adams, the British Resident, proposed to
pass him over there were no complaints.

Mr. Adams, however, carried matters much farther. In
choosing a successor he forced on the Sultan, not his second
son, but his third. This action, supported by the Governor
and the Colonial Office, set tongues wagging all over Malaya. British officials, who disliked decentralisation, used it as a
stick to beat the scheme. Men like Sir Frank Swettenham,
who had played an important part in the negotiation of the
agreement whereby the Sultan of Selangor had first accepted
a British adviser, regarded the matter from a loftier point of
view. It was a breach of a definite pledge given to the sultans
that in giving our protection we should not interfere with
the religion and customs of the Malays.

Into the respective merits of centralisation and decentralisation it would be impertinence on my part to enter. It is an
administrative question which can be solved only by the ex-

perts. I shall permit myself only one observation. Several decades of centralisation created a new bureaucracy in Kuala Lumpur and destroyed the old type of independent Resident. Now that local powers have been restored, the men capable of exercising this responsibility are no longer there.

Time may justify Mr. Adams's action, but it has left three men with a sense of wrong in the Sultan's palace in Klang: the Sultan himself, his eldest son and his second son. And this is the first time that such a thing has happened in the history of Malaya by direct British interference. Even more extraordinary to an old-timer was the Resident's reason for his choice; the third son, he said, deserved the preference because he was widely travelled and had been in Europe.

I had some conversation with the Governor. Sir Shenton Thomas is a rather short, thick-set, clean-shaven man who, especially when he spoke, reminded me a little of the late Lord Birkenhead. He is fifty-seven and is a member of the Singapore Non-Benders Cricket Club. The members are presumed to have reached an age when they can no longer bend, but Sir Shenton looked active enough to get his hands down to the hardest drive. He has a keen, alert mind, talks very much to the point, and has a thoroughly business-like manner. He was quick to notice the weak spots in the parade. During his inspection he had noted that many of the new recruits had sores on their legs and other traces of skin affections on their bodies. The men who had been six months or more with the regiment had none and were as clean and as fit as trained athletes.

The creation of the Malay regiment is the work of Major G. M. Bruce, a Scots-Canadian, whose grandfather went out to Canada to join the Canadian Mounted Police and took part in the famous Klondyke gold rush known as "The Trail of '98". Major Bruce, a powerfully built officer who was wounded in France, belongs to that splendid type of man whom the Empire fortunately still produces, and in Malaya he has done a remarkable job. He is assisted in his task by

British officers who are sent out from England after a short course in Malay at the London School of Oriental Languages.

The idea of a Malay regiment for Malaya was first suggested nearly thirty years ago. It was officially put forward by my old friend, Stewart McClelland, one of the best brains in the Malayan civil service. The proposal was pigeon-holed. Had such a regiment been in existence in 1915, there might have been no Singapore mutiny.

But perhaps I had better avoid the subject of mutinies. In its short career the Malay regiment has already had a minor mutiny of its own. It was the result of too much zeal. On King George's Jubilee Day, 1935, there were sports at Port Dickson. The tit-bit of the programme was the tug-of-war between a picked team of the Malay regiment and a composite team recruited from the local "Bengalis". The Malays had made the mistake of under-estimating their opponents. They had been unduly boastful. On the day of days they had been ignominiously pulled over by the "Bengalis".

To an unbiased observer the result could have been no surprise. The "Bengalis", composed mainly of stalwart Sikhs and Pathans, must have averaged a stone or two heavier per man. But because of the preliminary boasting of the Malays, one of the "Bengalis" had cocked the Pathan equivalent of a snook at the defeated enemy. The warlike ardour of the Malays had been fired by this insult, and that evening part of the regiment had broken loose and had chased and beaten up the "Bengali" victors all over Port Dickson. Fortunately, there were no serious consequences. As soon as the commanding officer appeared, the Malays came to heel at once like well-trained retrievers.

That night Freddie gave a "pahit" party to some of the British officers of the regiment. They were pink-cheeked young men, who were still keen on their job and who had not been long enough in the tropics to have acquired that indifference to time and to work which is the essence of Eastern

philosophy. It ought to have been, and for the others doubtless was, a stimulating evening. But, try as I might, I could
not conquer the fever which already had me in its grip. The
next morning I awoke with a high temperature. My head
felt as heavy as lead. My eyes were sore. My throat was almost closed.

Freddie insisted on sending for a doctor and offered me a
choice between a British lady doctor with a private practice
and the Tamil doctor who was the head of the local Government hospital. "Give me the man," I said firmly, if ungal-
lantly. He came and at once diagnosed acute tonsilitis. I must
be very careful. It would be a week before I could move.
Reluctantly I decided to give up that part of my trip which
was to take me to the other states of the F.M.S. Abandoning
all resistance, I turned my face to the wall.

Two days later the Rosslyns left by steamer for Singapore.
Clad in my sarong and baju, I struggled out of bed to see
them off. I had been eager to meet the captain of their
steamer. I had heard much of him from several of my friends
in Malaya. He had begun life as a charity boy and had sailed
all the Eastern seas. Like most sea captains he was a great
reader with original views on literature and a special admiration for Mr. Somerset Maugham, who had once been his passenger. I had wanted to hear his views on Mr. Maugham.
Now to my regret I had to forgo this meeting.

I had my bed put out on the verandah in order that I might
see the steamer leave the harbour. With the reflected rays of
the afternoon sun the sea shone like corrugated zinc. The
wait seemed interminable, and in an orgy of self-pity I began
to review the various phases of my unrealised ambitions.
This stillness of land and water, deathlike yet eternal, which
composes the evasive atmosphere of the Port Dickson scene,
had been, and always would be, an influence in my life. In my
youth I had never grown weary of watching it. At many
moments in my life it had come back to me. To it I ascribed
my irresponsibility, my lack of self-control, my intense desire,

even when material success is within my grasp, to escape from the turmoil of city life and my unwillingness to follow the ordained paths. Circumstances had tried to make a man of action of me. Many of my acquaintances had credited me with an ability to carry things through in the face of great difficulties. The ability had never existed or, at best, had been a pretence exaggerated into a reality by the situations in which I had been placed. I had known from the beginning that I was a moral coward. Like Dan Leno wishing to play Hamlet, I had always pictured myself as a man of reflection. During the twelve years of my official career in Russia and in Central Europe there was only one thing on which I could legitimately pride myself, and that was a certain freedom from bias in my judgment of men and affairs.

It was here in Port Dickson that I had first learnt to observe and that I had made my first youthful attempts to write.

And now, with the shadow of autumn on the threshold of my life, here I was back again before the self-same scene and the self-same sea.

The distant blast of a siren interrupted my depression. At last the steamer was leaving, and in order to get a better view I raised myself on my pillows. The devil in me reasserted himself as I remembered the last time that I had seen anyone off by steamer from Port Dickson. My first Tuan Besar, *anglice*, senior manager, had been going home on leave after seven unbroken years in Malaya. Before his departure he had given a farewell party which had lasted for four days. It had been a carousal tempered by sea-bathing. Freddie, then just straight out from school and innocent as a lamb, had been shocked. The cliffs had echoed with the roar of ribald choruses. The piano had been oiled with beer. No "wild party" in the United States during Prohibition could have shown a more imposing array of empty bottles.

The house party had been composed entirely of Scots. All had been at Scottish public schools, most of them at Merchiston. I, as the only Fettesian, had been unmercifully ragged. Perhaps it was this ragging which upset my mental balance. But in an effort to get my own back I went into Port Dickson on the last day and by dint of bribery and diplomatic persuasion I ordered all the Japanese ladies of joy to turn up on the quay the next morning to give a ceremonial farewell to our host, and to ensure their presence I made them a generous gift of money.

The steamer left at six a.m. and we had some difficulty in getting our host ready for the three-mile journey by "rickisha" to the harbour. Eventually we arrived quarter-of-an-hour before sailing-time, and after a hilarious farewell he went on board. There was no sign of the Japanese ladies, but on the deck I noticed a high British official with his sister. He was known to us all as a rigid churchman and as the straightest-laced Englishman in the East. Our host, beaming but not yet restored to normal, was leaning against the rails. He would have greeted his executioner with the same urbanity.

My heart sank. Regretting my foolishness, I prayed that the Japanese would not come or, at least, would arrive too late. I had miscalculated the precision of that self-disciplined race. Just as the steamer was about to sail and as everyone was standing at the ship's side in a last exchange of farewells, a glittering procession of ladies, dressed in their brightest kimonos and with their little wooden clogs clacking on the stones, made their way along the quay. Our host caught sight of them at once and kissed his hand to them. The ladies twirled their parasols, bowed low, and kissed back. It was a touching and graceful scene. But I saw a thundercloud come over the dignified serenity of the high official's face. As he went below at once, I felt instinctively that I was in for trouble. I was. The story travelled round very quickly, and I was severely reprimanded by my uncle.

Now as I lay on Freddie's verandah, the whole scene came back to me with a vividness which the intervening years had been unable to dim. Instead of repentance I felt a glow of self-satisfaction. And when the steamer passed opposite the bungalow, I went to my bedroom and, taking a sheet, waved it to the Rosslyns. I should miss them, but as we were to meet again in Singapore a month later there was no sense of permanent loss in my farewell. When Freddie came back, he found a cheerful patient.

That afternoon, in fact, was the turning point in my illness. When the little Tamil doctor came the next morning, he was able to report progress. In three days I might go about again. Before he left, he delivered himself of one classic Babu gem. He recommended a course of light diet for some days to come. "What about alcohol?" asked Freddie with a grin. "Alcohol", said the little man, looking very serious and professional, "totally better not." He was a most efficient doctor.

CHAPTER FOUR

ALTHOUGH AT THE time I regretted the interference with my plans, I am inclined to-day to regard my tonsilitis as a god-send. Travel is like fishing. Its joys are not to be measured by the amount of water which one covers, but by the ability to linger at and to return to favourite spots. Hitherto I had been rushing round like a tornado, taking in very little in my desperate effort to see everything. Here, in Freddie's bunga-low, the enforced rest enabled me to sift the imperishable things from what was worthless and to sort and store them in my memory.

Now that the Rosslyns were gone I could talk freely about the visit to Amai. It worried me a good deal. Was it wise, was it kind, to scrape again the surface of a passion which had been dead for so long? Pantai, however, I must see. Singapore and Port Dickson were on the sea: one a city, the other a township, but both modern, both with nothing Malay about them. Pantai was a Malay village buried at the foot of the mountains. More than anything I wanted to see the old Malay life. With Freddie I planned a great tour which we should make as soon as I was better. We should motor round the interior of Negri Sembilan, which in English means "The Nine States"; we should cross the Gunong Angsi mountain range and spend a night at Kuala Pilah, a great Malay centre in the hills, where in spite of the heat by day one wanted a blanket to sleep under; and we should finish up by driving round the back of the range *via* Jelebu, and make the approach to Pantai by the Bukit Tangga Pass. And Pantai to me meant not merely my old home. It was Amai's home. It was also the home—and the thought was rather disturbing—of the aged father and mother of the Dato' Klana, whose ward Amai was, and who had so bitterly resented her flight to my house. The Dato' Klana was the Chief of Sungei Ujong, the most im-portant of the Nine States. It was his grandfather who in

1874 had first invited the British to assist him in maintaining his rule and in putting down the prevailing anarchy.

The three days of my convalescence passed pleasantly enough. By day I lay on the verandah looking out at the Indian Ocean and seeing on that vague horizon line where sky and sea seem to blend, the mirage of my half-forgotten romance. In the evenings I talked to Freddie or to Buntak.

There were moments of trial and disappointment. One of the trials was when one morning Freddie produced a durian with our early tea. I was not feeling very strong, and the smell was so nauseating that I was nearly sick. I am prepared to believe that the durian is the best of all tropical fruits. Europeans like Freddie who can get it to their mouths without fainting are unanimous in praise of its virtues. It is exalted in the prose and poetry of oriental literature as is no other tropical fruit. Chinese will sell their immortal soul and tigers will risk their life for it. And as an aphrodisiac its reputation holds sway from Colombo to Shanghai. Is there not the story of the old Scottish lady in Batavia in the 'sixties, when Presbyterianism was Presbyterianism, who seeing a newly-arrived fellow-countryman about to taste his first durian, exclaimed: "Maister Thamsan! Ye mauna eat that. It'll no agree wi' ye. And forbye, it's a maist unchaste fruit."

In spite of all these virtues it will never be my fruit, nor indeed that of anyone else who dislikes a smell which combines the worst odours of a rotten cheese and a sewage farm.

My chief disappointment was the visit of Haji Said, the fisherman, whom Freddie had engaged to take me out by night. I felt all the bitterness of regret when he held up his catch of glittering ikan tenggiri before my eyes, and said in his soft Malayan accent: "barang-kali besok, Tuan? Perhaps to-morrow, Tuan?" Twenty-seven years before, yesterday, to-day, and to-morrow and all the days after, had seemed exactly the same to me. Now time was all-important, and I knew that for me there would probably never be another fishing to-morrow at Port Dickson in this life.

I acquired a certain stoicism from the philosophical Buntak. He was a cheerful materialist with the cynical contempt of the successful man for human frailty. He told me that the Malays were much more careful about money than they used to be. Now that they had become mechanically-minded, they had begun to save up for motor-cars and motorbicycles. Japanese cars and cycles could be bought very cheaply. He himself had a super-British motor-cycle with all the latest gadgets.

Apparently the Malays have other more exciting, if less harmless, amusements. Between Port Dickson and Malacca, Buntak told me, there is still a good deal of smuggling. Sugar, piece-goods and matches are much cheaper in the Straits Settlements than they are in the F.M.S. The smugglers, he said, make a good profit, but not to be compared with what it was ten years ago, when the British had rubber restriction in Malaya and the Dutch in the East Indies refused to come into the scheme. He waved an arm towards the lighthouse at Cape Rachado, the nearest point to Sumatra. "That was the place," he said. On dark nights the Negri Sembilan Malays used to slip out from the shore in small boats loaded with rubber. A mile or two out a large Sumatra prahu would be waiting for them. There would be a deal in cash at the ship's side, and silently, as only a Malay knows how, the smugglers would steal back to the mangrove-girt shore. "That was a business," said Buntak, in matter-of-fact tones in which I thought I detected a faint accent of regret.

In my youth in Scotland I always had a natural sympathy with poachers, and to me smuggling by night on that still, phosphorescent sea, especially in the company of Malays in whom the old pirate instinct was obviously not dead, would have been far more thrilling than the capture of a salmon in the forbidden waters of some Highland river.

On the day before we were to leave on our grand tour, Freddie took me over various neighbouring rubber estates, including his own private estate. The contrast with my planting days was startling. In those early days of the rubber plantation industry we had had to carve our estates out of primeval jungle. We had foot-slogged daily in the sun. Then clearings were literally clearings. There was comparatively little fully-grown rubber, and therefore very little shade. Estate roads and very often estate bungalows were primitive. Now half Negri Sembilan was one solid block of rubber estates. Matured trees provided a welcome shade. Well-built roads gave suitable access by motor-car even to outlying parts of the estates. The very word planter was a misnomer. Planting had ceased. The planter of to-day was a manager equipped with far more technical knowledge than the pioneers. His hours of work were longer. He superintended far larger areas. But his comforts had increased a thousand-fold.

But if I saw bungalows lit by electricity, there were also signs of the slump which overtook rubber in 1929. Here and there I came across a European bungalow, derelict and deserted, and its timbers already gutted by white ants. In 1910 the price of rubber touched thirteen shillings per pound. To-day it is in the neighbourhood of sevenpence. Since the war it has been as low as one penny three-farthings. When an article which costs a few pence to produce can sell at thirteen shillings, there is little need of economy, and the planters of 1910 who thought the millennium had come never stinted expenditure. The fall in the price has meant a reduction of all costs, including the European planter's salary. The derelict bungalows which I saw had belonged to European assistants whose services had been dispensed with during the slump. They will never be reoccupied.

The sight of them was depressing. For there is nothing beautiful about a rubber estate—only a monotony of regularity which corrodes one's outlook on life, and in ill-health reduces even the most robust Philistine to a dangerous melancholy. If I were the High Commissioner of the Malay States, I should make a public protest against the building of planters' bungalows in the middle of huge blocks of rubber. Bungalows should be built on sites where a man can see beyond a forest of leaves and the mutilated trunks of rubber trees. In Europe men do not live in their offices or in their factories, and in Malaya there is neither reason nor commonsense in subjecting the European planter to this restricting and demoralising influence. And to-day when the motor-car —and every planter has a car or a motor-cycle—can take a man to his work in a few minutes, such callous indifference on the part of the large rubber companies to the housing of their employees is not merely an anachronism, but a hallmark of inefficiency.

If there is nothing attractive about a rubber estate, there is romance and comedy and tragedy in the story of rubber, of which commodity Malaya is the largest producer in the world. The romance, the comedy, and some of the tragedy can most graphically be told in the life-history of my grandmother and my uncle.

My Macgregor grandmother, who owned a distillery in Scotland, had a large family. Her third and favourite son was a good-looking young man, who excelled in running and rugby football. In his youth he had shown the same disinclination towards work which is common to most athletes. In the 'nineties my grandmother sent him out to Malaya, where she bought a coffee plantation for him. In those days most of the planters were proprietary planters. Nearly all had been to English or Scottish public schools. Their life ran on pleasant lines. There was cheap racing in which every man could be an owner for each meeting. There were no white women to interfere with the prevailing code of pleasure.

At this time there was a man called Ridley who was the director of the Botanical Gardens in Singapore. His great pride was a small collection of rubber trees. The trees had a curious history. Hitherto, the commercial rubber of the world had come from the *hevea brasiliensis* in Brazil. In 1876 the first seeds of this tree were smuggled out of Brazil by Henry Wickham and brought to Kew Gardens, where they were planted. In the same year twenty-two seedlings were sent from Kew to Singapore. Some were planted there and some in other parts of Malaya. The seedlings flourished exceedingly, grew into healthy trees, and in their turn produced seed. Ridley was the first man to conceive the possibilities of plantation rubber as a prosperous industry, and he used to visit the coffee-planters and urge them to plant his seeds. Some planters took them as curiosities. Some seeds were planted on Linsum, which was afterwards part of my uncle's property, and the oldest rubber trees in Malaya, I believe, are now those early Linsum trees, for the trees in the Singapore Botanical Gardens have disappeared before the encroaching demands of municipal building. Few planters, however, took Ridley seriously, and among the planting community he was generally referred to as "Mad Ridley".

The planters changed their minds when the slump in coffee, assisted by the ravages of the bee-hawk moth, ruined them. In their economic distress those who could afford the expense converted their coffee plantations into rubber estates. My uncle was among their number. But the consternation in the family circle at home was great. Four sons and four daughters of my grandmother's large family were still alive. Seven of them were up in arms against my uncle in Malaya. Rubber trees took seven years to come into bearing. During those seven years the estate would eat money. Whisky was then doing badly. My grandmother would be ruined. The family lawyer added his voice to the chorus of complaint. But my grandmother was a determined woman, and she loved her son. She continued to send money to Malaya.

In 1902 my uncle came home and tried to float his estates as a public company. He met with nothing but rebuffs. Serious financiers were suspicious of a proposition which on the figures seemed fool-proof, and which promised profits of hundreds per cent. He returned to Malaya and came home again in 1904. His personal situation was now desperate. There was an overdraft of several thousand pounds. The family opposition was more violent than ever. The estates would have to be floated as a company or abandoned. And then Arthur Lampard, a director of Harrison and Crossfield, came to the rescue. There were protracted hagglings and dealings. Lampard drove a hard bargain, but in the end a company known as Anglo-Malay Limited was floated in the autumn of 1905. My uncle's two estates of Tarentang and Linsum formed the bulk of the new property.

At that moment fate smiled on the destiny of the family fortunes. Under the pressure of the rest of her family, my grandmother would probably have sold the whole of the family interest for ready cash. The sum would have been comparatively small. But again, although unwittingly, Lampard was a deliverer. Rubber, he said, was an unknown adventure. The vendors must share the risk. A large part of the purchase price must be taken in shares. The Macgregors had little choice in the matter. They took the shares.

In the summer of 1910 the 2/- Anglo-Malay share had reached 40/-. My grandmother's £25,000 shares were then worth £500,000. My uncle, who had returned to Malaya, had made at least as much in buying shares and in promoting new companies. These were days of triumph and rehabilitation. From being a suspected black sheep my uncle became the hero of the family. In Edinburgh my grandmother was nicknamed the Rubber Queen. There was money for everyone, even for me who had gone out to join my uncle in 1908, and who was then grievously ill with malaria in Pantai. And when I was sent home in 1910, as I then thought to die, I was given £300 by my uncle and a like amount from home to make my passage easy.

In the autumn of 1910 there was a sharp slump in the price of rubber, and my stockbroker uncle Tom raised a voice of warning. But he had never seen a rubber tree. Alister, my

o

Malayan uncle, was still buying shares, and as his star was in the ascendant my grandmother backed him and also went on buying.

Her faith was of the kind which moves mountains. When I came home, she told me the whole story. I can see her now, her eyes searching me as always for the truth, her hands folded calmly on her lap, her mien austere, commanding, and slightly terrifying. "They criticised him," she said. "They told me I was a fool." The eyes flashed. Then came the all-conquering argument. "But what I say is this. Where would we all be now without Alister?" The only answer would have been: "Where might we all have been with Alister?" But my innate sense of diplomacy warned me that such a reply might be lacking in tact. I acquiesced. The facts were on my grandmother's side.

Alister himself came home in that same autumn. He had been hit by the slump, but he was still a rich man. Mr. J. G. Hay, the rubber expert, and now the head of Guthrie & Co., the great Singapore and London firm of merchants, was then a junior employee in the London office. He has often told me how my uncle arrived in the office, and wanted to arrange a loan of £30,000 so that he need not sell any rubber shares. Naturally Guthrie's asked for security, and my uncle said casually:

"I've got about £200,000 pounds worth of shares at the bank. You can send someone over to check them and arrange for the necessary security."

Hay was given this task. When he had finished it, he said to my uncle with all the astonishment of Scottish accuracy at such un-Scottish indifference to exact figures: "It's not £200,000 worth of shares you have, but £275,000." Optimism was the keynote in my uncle's financial scale.

He was, in fact, an easy-going man, charming in manner and generous to a fault. He came home for good at the age of thirty-six, believing in his star and in—rubber. He took a place in Scotland with fishing and shooting and, although he attended the board meetings of the various companies of which he was a director, he never really worked again.

His optimism was his undoing. He never sold a rubber share and, as the price of the commodity fell, his fortune dwindled. The place in Scotland had to be given up. Shortly after the war there was an improvement in his affairs, and he could have realised his rubber assets with a profit, smaller than that of 1910, but still comfortably substantial. He held on to his shares. Once again in the minor boom of 1924 he refused to sell. And that was the end.

There was something attractive about his courage. He never wilted under his losses. But finally his optimism reduced him to comparative poverty. In 1933 he was seriously ill, and during the next two years underwent a series of operations, borne with the same unfaltering courage which had characterised his whole outlook on life. I received the news of his death on my way home from Malaya, and with his passing one of the dominant influences in my life disappeared for ever. It was the inspiration of his success which in 1908 first set me on my way to Malaya. It was his generosity in sending me home when I was near to death which prevented me from leaving my bones to rot in that land of languor and of exile. To the end of his life he never refused an appeal for help from me or, indeed, from any of his other friends and relations. In spite of all my shortcomings I never heard an unkind word from him, and his death has left me with a sense of personal loss which remains poignant to this day.

I tell his story at some length because it is the story of the vast majority of the proprietary planters of those early days. Opportunity knocked at their door only to deceive their judgment. Rubber had brought them gold undreamt of, and their fidelity to it was pathetically disastrous. The same obstinate refusal to sell characterised nearly all, and only a few were wise enough to accept gratefully, and to cash in on, a gift which the god of financial chance brings perhaps only once in a hundred years.

Since then the whole plantation rubber industry in the East Indies has altered its character. When my uncle started on his crazy career of success in 1905, Malaya produced only 200 tons of plantation rubber as compared with the world output of 60,000 tons of wild rubber mainly from Brazil. To-day Malaya has a planted area of over 3,000,000 acres, and even under the restriction scheme now in force the annual export of plantation rubber is, approximately, 400,000 tons. The old proprietary planters have disappeared, and Freddie Cunningham, a shrewd and far-seeing Scot who has spent a quarter of a century in the East, is almost the only survivor. Public companies with headquarters in London now control the European-owned estates. They are finding it increasingly hard to compete with native-owned rubber, for so far from the native being exploited by the white man in the rubber industry, to-day the native holdings run into hundreds of thousands of acres, and in the opinion of some experts may one day dominate the world market. Throughout the East Indies over-production has made a return to the dream days of 1910 for ever impossible, and the white planter of to-day is a salaried official entirely at the mercy of his home directors. He will be fortunate if at the age of fifty he can save enough to retire with a few hundred pounds a year.

There is one interesting and little-known sidelight on the great rubber boom of 1910.

About that time a well-dressed American appeared in the office of one of the leading mercantile and shipping firms in Singapore. His credentials were excellent, and he had the backing of the Vanderbilts and the Goelets. In an atmosphere of war-time secrecy he unfolded his story.

The people for whom he was working had, he stated, acquired a new method for extracting the rubber from "Jelutong". This "Jelutong", which grows in large quantities throughout the islands of the Malay Archipelago, contains a large percentage of moisture and a very small percentage of rubber.

The American duly chartered a steamer to visit the Dutch Islands and also Sarawak, where he obtained a concession for the collection of "Jelutong" from that territory. His next step was to construct a factory at the mouth of the river which runs down from Kuching, the capital of Sarawak. The site selected was appropriately named "Gobilt".

After this factory had been completed at very considerable cost and had commenced to operate, a still larger factory was erected on the Kariman Islands, which lie about thirty miles to the west of Singapore and whose green slopes the traveller sees on his approach from Colombo. The factory was also duly completed, and at even greater cost than that at Gobilt. But it was never put into operation. Before the great dream could be realised, the bottom fell out of the rubber market. While it is conceivable that the company might have made a profit if the price of rubber had remained at 10/- per lb., it certainly could not do so when the price came tumbling down. It threw in its hand, and the factories were abandoned with, of course, a heavy loss to the proprietors.

Thus ended the second attempt of powerful American financial interests to capture one of Malaya's two greatest assets, rubber and tin. In the case of tin, American enterprise was frustrated by the masterful and independent action of Sir Frank Swettenham, the British Governor. In the case of rubber, Puck threw his cap on to the British side of the scales of chance.

CHAPTER FIVE

IT WAS LATE on a Monday morning that I took my farewell of Port Dickson. Although the sun was high in the sky, the air was dry and not unbearably hot. Like Singapore the F.M.S. had experienced an unprecedented drought. Here it had not broken, and the sea, like a horse-shoe mirror of mother-of-pearl in a frame of jade, was almost motionless.

After a two-course breakfast-luncheon I took one last look from the verandah. Then I went down the steps to the drive, where Freddie's heterogeneous staff of Chinese, Malays and Javanese was drawn up to say goodbye to me. Buntak came forward with presents of Malay handiwork, a straw-plaited cushion, two fans, and a tumbok lada, the smallest of Malay knives, very sharp and evil-looking, and made to strike home to the heart. A knife for lovers with dynamite in their blood. I seemed to be facing a squad of impenetrable brown relieved by a thin line of ivory set in a fixed smile. The biggest and widest grin was on Buntak's face. To him I should always remain the comedian among white men, the mysterious mad Tuan. Already I could see him repeating to his friends that night the very words of Conrad's Arab trader: "I know these white men. In many lands I have seen them; always the slaves of their desires, always ready to give up their strength and their reason into the hands of some woman." But I could not tell whether he or any of the others felt any emotion and, fearful of betraying my own feelings, I chatted nervously with them in a spirit of banter. As a boy in Scotland I had always felt a vivid emotion of home-sickness on leaving the Highlands after the summer holidays. I used to pray that the last day would be wet and misty so that my farewell to the hills should be less painful. But to-day I was glad that the sun shone and that the sky and sea and landscape were at their best. Twenty-five years before, sick in mind and body, I had made the same farewell. Then I was convinced that I should never see Malaya again.

To-day I had no such certainty. In any case, emotions, like life itself, cannot be repeated in the same person. In this second farewell there was no sadness.

On our way to Seremban we stopped at the Port Dickson hospital to say goodbye to my Indian doctor. Of course, we had to inspect his kingdom, and with justifiable pride he showed us a modern hospital, spotlessly clean and run entirely by Indians. The wards, spacious and well-equipped, contained mostly fever patients, for in spite of the immense and successful warfare against mosquitoes, malaria followed by pneumonia is still the chief disease of Malaya.

The new Malay regiment has a special ward in this hospital. It was surprisingly full. Most of the patients were new recruits suffering from sores. As we drove away from the town Freddie was saluted by Sikh policemen, Bengali watchmen, Malay officials, Chinese shopkeepers, Tamil coolies, the Eurasian post-master and a broken-down white planter. I had an impression of a sea of smiling faces. The whole scene was a cameo of British Imperialism in its best aspect.

Seremban itself was a disappointment. I recognised many of the old landmarks, but the little capital had swelled to four times its former size. Many Europeans, coming home to retire after a life-time spent in Malaya, feel that England is a graveyard. This cemetery is made up of the tombstones of their boyhood friends, who during the years of separation have drifted apart from them and with whom they now have nothing in common. Something of the same emotion I felt on returning to a town where formerly I had known every inhabitant, white, yellow, brown and black, and where to-day I was a total stranger. There was not a shopsign that I recognised. The character of the shopkeepers and, indeed, of all the oriental population had changed.

I went with Freddie to call on one of his rich Chinese friends. I recalled previous visits to Chinese towkays with my uncle a quarter of a century ago. The visit had always been arranged beforehand. The towkay had always received us in his house. I remembered the atmosphere of mystery and stillness. Somewhere behind the front room of teak furniture and lacquer cabinets were women-folk. But we never saw them. I could see again the towkay himself, his resplendent Chinese robes, his glossy pigtail, the long nail on his little finger, his series of profound bows. The bows had been frequent even during the conversation. We had sipped tea, fragrant yet almost colourless, from cups so fragile and so light that one had to be careful not to spill the tea by raising them too quickly. There had been ceremony elaborate enough to reduce me to a feeling of respect and inferiority.

Freddie's friend received us in his office or, to be exact, we just walked into his office. The towkay, his hair cut and neatly parted in European fashion, was sitting in European shirt and trousers. His coat was hanging on the wall. His shirt sleeves were rolled up. He was smoking a cheroot. His chair was tilted back, and his feet were firmly planted on the top edge of his desk in the manner of the late Arthur Balfour in the House of Commons. As we came in, he jumped up.

"Hello, Freddie", he said.

He shook hands, called for drinks, offered us smokes, and then sat down again with his feet on the desk. I remembered my astonishment when in my early days in Malaya I had stumbled on a Chinese bangsal or glorified shed in the jungle. It was inhabited by three Chinese, who had made a clearing and were growing vegetables on it. I had been out after deer and wanted to know the time. "Pukul brapa?" I said to them in Malay. One of them grinned. Then in a lazy drawl he replied: "Well, boss, I calculate by the sun it's a quarter after twelve!" The man had been a washerman in San Francisco and had wandered *via* Shanghai, Hongkong and Singapore into the Malay States.

In those days few, if any, Chinese in Negri Sembilan spoke English. But Freddie's friend spoke it as if it were his native language. He discussed rubber prices and the state of the American market with the knowledge of an expert. He was affable and racingly amusing. But he spoke as equal to equal. He was no rare exception. He was merely a superior example of the changes which time, the war, and the British system of education, have wrought in the character and outlook of the Chinese population of Malaya.

Seremban depressed me, and I wanted to leave it as quickly as possible. One visit, however, I had to make. On the outskirts of the town lived "Monkey" Holland, another old friend of my planting days. "Monkey", a brother-in-law of the late Lord Forteviot, had come out to Malaya from Ceylon in the early part of the century to join my uncle. When I arrived some years later, my uncle sent me to him to learn my job. He was another planter who should have made a fortune out of rubber. But he was too easy-going, too kind, and, above all, too generous and hospitable. His bungalow was always an open house to every lame dog, and when the bad times came he was hit harder than most planters. Like Freddie he was still a proprietary planter, but in a very small way. He now lived on a tiny estate in a bungalow perched on a hill overlooking a small lake and approached by a villainous road.

He was having his afternoon siesta when we arrived. But we woke him up, and I found him little changed. His hair had turned a little grey, but neither his optimism nor his cheerful outlook on life had altered. Like the Braddons he was one of the youthful old men who have made their home in exile, and who will never be happy outside of Malaya.

After an hour or two with "Monkey" spent in an exchange of reminiscences we set out on our journey to Kuala Pilah, where we were to spend the night. We took the road by Sĕkamat, the old mining village which twenty-six years before had inspired me with an eerie feeling of terror. In those days, when I lived on my lonely estate at Pantai, the shortest way to the Seremban club and to civilised pleasure was by Sĕkamat. At that time the village was the home of the worst scoundrels in the Chinese community of Negri

Sembilan, and various people, including my assistant, had been "stuck up" by gang-robbers. My only means of conveyance was a "push" bicycle or a native pony "gharry". I preferred the bicycle. Setting out from Pantai in a spirit of sober caution I always took the long way round. But sometimes coming home late at night with my courage fortified by late hours at the club, I would risk the shorter road. In any circumstances riding along a lonely jungle road by night is an uncanny experience. The senses quicken. Sight and hearing become more tense. Imagination sees a hundred ghosts beyond the orbit of the lamp's pale ray. The possibility of a wire across the road and a sudden attack by gang-robbers adds the fascination of fear to these ordinary terrors of the night.

Nine times out of ten the village would be in total darkness and as lifeless as a basking crocodile. But on the tenth occasion I would see light streaming through the chinks in the houses, and from afar I would hear the sound of voices raised in quarrel over some gambling game. Then I would pedal as if for life itself until the blood seemed to leave my thighs. Only when I was a mile or two past the village would I slow down and wipe the clammy sweat from my brow. Since then I have known fear on many occasions, but never in such an acutely prolonged form as in those days of my youth when life was a thing to be prized because it was all before one.

The Sĕkamat of those days is now a thing of the past and, as I drove through the place with Freddie in the afternoon sunlight, I scarcely recognised it. All that remains is a few deserted houses and a roadside shop with soft drinks and cigarettes for passers-by. The tin which gave the place its unattractive population has long since been exhausted. Unlike the coal-miners of Scotland and Wales, who in many districts have remained behind, workless and immobilised, long after the mines have been dismantled, the Chinese tin-miners had left and, in a land still new enough to afford opportunities to the adventurous in spirit, had gone to seek their fortune elsewhere.

Here was change indeed, but as we approached nearer to the mountains there was a complete transformation. The monotonous rubber estates gave way to acres and acres of padi fields with the rice almost ripe for harvest. Neat Malay houses took the place of Chinese shops. The air became cooler and sweeter. In a flash the barrier of the years was rolled away. This was the Malaya which I had known in my youth—a Malaya outwardly still unspoilt and surprisingly little changed.

As we passed the cross-roads at Ampangan, I felt a momentary pang of regret. Here on the right was the palace of the Dato' Klana, the Malay chief who had been Amai's guardian. There on the left was the road to my old estate at Pantai, where we had first met.

Involuntarily I touched Freddie's arm and pointed to the left, but the chauffeur kept on his course. Our visit to Pantai was to come later, and as we ascended the pass over the jungle-clad mountain range I had some compensation for the delay in one of those rare moments of beauty which leaves an imperishable memory in the mind and in the heart. On each side of us was primeval forest with thick, impenetrable undergrowth and trees superbly tall and femininely graceful. From our high vantage point we looked down on a vast extent of plain, its ugliness mellowed to a purple sea by the rays of the setting sun. The colour came from a heavy bank of cloud, and I had a curious feeling that the drought which had lasted for nearly two months, and which was almost unprecedented in this land of constant rainfall, would break when I came to visit Pantai.

We reached Kuala Pilah at seven in the evening, and at once I felt at home. Pilah is the seat of a District Officer and is still the most unspoilt part of Negri Sembilan. Since my time the little town has grown. There are more Chinese shops in the main street and a new Malay college where all the instruction is in English. But the district population is pre-dominantly Malay.

It is an ideal place for learning Malay, and here some of the best Malayan scholars in our civil service have acquired their knowledge of the language. Most of them have learnt it from their native mistresses, for the Malay women here are the fairest in the state. We had passed several of them on our way into the town, their head and the lower half of their face veiled by a sarong, their eyes, like ripe sloes, raised for a moment towards the passing car and then turned demurely to the ground.

Half the charm of travelling is in starting. Three-quarters of the charm of a Malay woman is in the difficulty of approach. As a Mohammedan she is guarded with considerable strictness. She may not be seen talking to a stranger in the road. Seclusion has whetted her appetite for temptation. She enjoys the secrecy of an illicit romance.

As I passed the secluded houses, my mind went back to the old Malay "pantun" or quatrain, scores of which—many of them of considerable antiquity—are known to every Malay. There is one which runs as follows:

> "Jalan-jalan sa-panjang jalan,
>   Singgah menyinggah di-pagar orang;
>   Pura-pura menchari ayam,
>   Ekur mata di-anak orang."

> *Wander, wander down the glen,
>   Stopping at the neighbour's fences;
>   On pretence to find a hen,
>   But his eyes are on the wenches.

Wandering towards Malay houses in search of romantic adventure has been, since the birth of time, the favourite

*The English version of this "pantun" is taken from Mr. A. W. Hamilton's attractive little book *Malay Sonnets*. It is published in Singapore.

recreation of young Malay bucks. The young European has indulged in it, too, although usually he has to employ a more furtive method of approach. If he is in a purely Malay district, he will engage the services of some aged feminine intermediary, preferably the court midwife. There will be long delays, some consultations of the omens, an interchange of messages and the bestowal of various presents. Only after this elaborate ceremonial will he meet the object of his desire, for immodesty is wholly foreign to Malays of both sexes. Doubtless, in these days of speed, the procedure of courtship has been expedited and commercialised.

Our headquarters at Pilah were the rest-house, which in this country takes the place of the hotel in the smaller towns. These rest-houses are under Government control, and are generally managed by a Chinese "head-boy". The Pilah one was a much more comfortable affair than in my time, with excellent service and better cooking than one can find in the average provincial hotel in England. There were two other Europeans staying in the rest-house: one, a young Scot, who had been a planter and had lost his job during the slump, and who was now employed under the Government restriction scheme as a controller of native holdings, and the other, an Englishman, and the biggest and heaviest man in Malaya. He must have weighed over twenty stone.

After dinner we sat down on the verandah and talked until far into the night. During his Malayan career our Carnera, who had a grievance and could express it fluently, had been most things: planter, engineer, commercial manager, and had spent the larger part of his time up country. He was now in middle age, and was critical of the present generation of Englishmen in the East and pessimistic about the future.

The main theme of his conversation was the decline of the white man's prestige. He attacked the civil service and the commercial community with equal vigour. Malaya, he said, was going to become Chinese one day, and the day was not very far distant. The Englishmen now in Malaya were of an inferior type to that of their predecessors. When they were offered a job, their first question was: how far away was it from the nearest cinema, the nearest dance-hall? As for the commercial fraternity, they had lost even their bounce. Their attitude now was: pray God the British raj will last until I have made my fortune.

The Chinese ignored the white man and were frequently rude to him. Certainly they no longer needed him. There were now no rich white men in Malaya.

My new acquaintance was, of course, a champion of the past. All his heroes belonged to the past. Pride of place he gave to great administrators like Sir Frank Swettenham and Sir Hugh Clifford, but the man after his own heart was Berkeley of Grik, a remarkable Irishman who at the age of seventy still hunts and never misses a Derby.

For years Berkeley was District Officer at Grik, a lonely, unspoilt outpost, where he was accepted by the Malays as infallible judge, counsellor, and father-confessor. Few men have ever handled Malays so successfully or been so loved by them, and for that reason he was never transferred. His privileged position gave him a feeling of security, and against Whitehall and, indeed, all his superiors he maintained a sturdy independence which to-day, alas! has few imitators.

In course of time civilisation invaded even this jungle fastness. A motor road was made to Grik, and a telegraph line immediately followed.

It was remarkable, however, how much more often huge trees fell across that road, thereby blocking it and destroying the telegraph wires, than across any other road in the country, and how sagaciously the wandering elephants seemed to sense the wishes of the District Officer.

Berkeley was the last D.O. who lived the life of a feudal chief. He abominates the motor-car to this day.

Another of my big friend's heroes was Grant Mackie, a Scottish son of the manse, who began his Malayan career as a road contractor and after many years of residence in the country struck tin and became a very rich man. In 1883 he was building the Pahang road when the volcano of Krakatoa erupted, obliterating its own island home and throwing up several new islands from the ocean bed. The sound of this terrible eruption, which destroyed 40,000 lives, was heard by Grant Mackie's Malays at a distance of some eight hundred miles. It sounded like a continuous cannonade, and the Malays, believing that the Chinese had risen and were attacking Kuala Lumpur, wanted to dash off immediately to the rescue of the British.

Grant Mackie, a great character in whom the spirit of adventure was strong, was known to all Englishmen in Malaya as "Father". Occasionally, in the Ipoh Club, youngsters, fresh out from home, would trespass too far on his good nature. "Father," they would say, "have a drink?" Then the eyes would flash. "Grant Mackie to you, sir," he would reply. "I'm not the father of every bastar-rd in this club." As I have already said, Grant Mackie retired to Port Said, where he died three years ago at the ripe age of eighty. He represented a type of pioneer, which, common enough thirty years ago, has now almost disappeared.

I listened to my bulky friend's tirade in silent attention. In my own mind I had already deducted fifty per cent. for exaggeration, and a wink from Freddie early on in the conversation made me take off another ten per cent. for the middle-aged grievances of a disappointed man.

Laudatores temporis acti have never at any time been lacking in the outposts of the British Empire, and to-day in Malaya their voice is strong. I should not like to give the impression that this Kuala Pilah Jeremiah was insincere or that what he said was wholly untrue. I think that much of the old pioneer spirit has disappeared, partly, but not entirely, because the opportunities which presented themselves to the old pioneers are no longer available. I am inclined to agree that, mainly because of increased control from London, civil servants in

Malaya to-day lack the self-reliance and readiness to take responsibility of their predecessors of a quarter of a century ago. I have no doubt that the influx of low-salaried Europeans and the great increase of one-man European businesses have had a deteriorating effect on the white man's prestige. I bear in mind that at all times and in all ages the old generation has wrung its hands over the failings of the new, and that the race has survived. Nor do I forget that, in the eyes of the European commercial community, all governors and high officials are good when times are good and that in bad times even the best official in the world is exposed to criticism.

What seems to me the weakest point in the British Imperial armour is the fact that since the war the middle classes, who are the bulwark of the British colonial system, have accustomed themselves to a standard of luxury and ease which in the face of modern competition will be increasingly difficult to maintain. The standard of pleasure in Malaya is much higher than in the neighbouring French and Dutch colonies.

Probably the young generation has an adequate reply to these criticisms. Almost certainly it will continue to ignore them as the young generation has always done, and, for its own self-respect, rightly done. The only thing that can be said with positive accuracy is that one day, when the decline which comes inevitably to all races sets in, the Jeremiahs will be right.

CHAPTER SIX

AT DAWN THE next morning Freddie left by car in order to inspect a native rubber estate across the Pahang boundary. Had I wanted to reach the same place from Negri Sembilan twenty-seven years ago, I should have had to take the steamer from Port Dickson to Singapore, change steamers there for an east coast ship to take me to Kuantan and then make my way across country. The journey might have taken the best part of a fortnight or even longer. Now it can be done in a few hours. Freddie was to make his inspection and be back again in Kuala Pilah in the afternoon.

I was not left entirely to my own devices. Freddie had arranged a programme for me. Its most substantial item was an inspection of the new English school. Slightly nervous, I hired a car and in a few minutes was put down before the entrance to a magnificent building. Alongside was a splendid playing-field with the greenest of grass and shut in by a neatly trimmed hedge. There was a flower garden, exotic in its contents but kept with a passionate tidiness that was unmistakeably English. The English headmaster was on leave, and the acting headmaster was an English lady called Miss Knapp. She was the only European on the staff. Her assistants were of various nationalities: Indians, Malays, Eurasians. All were men.

The school itself is of the co-educational type and is for boys and girls from the age of nine up to the junior Cambridge certificate standard. The school was built for Malays, who form about sixty per cent. of the pupils. Most of them pay nothing. But there are also Chinese and Indian pupils. These pay fees. The Chinese, I was told, make the best pupils. Miss Knapp ran the whole establishment unaided, organised the work and the games, imposed her British discipline, and settled with the proper admixture of tact and firmness the grievances and jealousies of her native staff.

She took me round each form-room. Our entrance was

marked by a ritual which was repeated with embarrassing monotony. I was introduced to the form-master. The class stood up and said a parrot's chorus of: "Good morning, Miss!" Miss Knapp smiled. "And now our visitor." The class, gathering confidence, redoubled its effort: "Good morning, sir!" I faced a barrage of ivory smiles from the boys and coy glances from the girls. Then in my presence and under the keen scrutiny of Miss Knapp, the unfortunate Indian or Malay teacher had to conduct his class in English, for all the teaching here is in English and the use of any native language is strictly forbidden.

The equipment of the school was excellent and, indeed, far better and more modern than that of many expensive private schools within a radius of twenty miles of London. I was less impressed by the teaching, which was rather mechanical and laid too much stress on mere memorisation. Rightly or wrongly, I formed the impression that the teachers themselves had memorised much of their work without understanding it.

I spent some time in listening to a history class, a geography class, and an entertaining lesson in mental arithmetic. The pupils, especially the Chinese, were very quick and accurate in their mental arithmetic, because it was something they could understand. Their written mathematical work was very neat—in some cases strikingly so—and far in advance of that of English boys and girls of the same age. But in the history lesson the master began in this wise: "In 436 A.D. the Romans left Britain. Why?" Up shot several hands. The master pointed to one boy who began: "Because a number of barbarous tribes called Franks, Vandals, and ——" The boy stopped. Memory had broken down. This time the teacher pointed to a girl who began again at the beginning: "Because a number of barbarous tribes called Franks, Vandals, and Goths were threatening the heart of the Roman Empire." The whole performance seemed to me strangely unreal and useless. What I wondered could a Goth or a Vandal represent to the imagination of a Malay schoolboy of twelve. Even more unreal was the geography lesson. "What", asked the teacher, "is the area of South America?" Then, having been given the correct answer, he asked again: "it is twice as big as what other continent?"

I come of a family of schoolmasters and have therefore a profound sympathy with the teaching community. But why, I asked myself, were these native children taught so much about Europe and almost nothing about their own country. At the time of my visit there was no English schoolbook of elementary Malay history in existence, although I understand that since then one has been published. The fault was not Miss Knapp's. The English curriculum in Malaya is based on the junior Cambridge certificate. Its inevitable effect will be to turn out thousands of clerks for whom there will not be sufficient jobs and who, sooner or later, will form a discontented white-coat native proletariat. The educational authorities in Malaya should know their own job best, but with all the good will in the world I cannot understand why this English education is not better adapted to local requirements and combined more fully with vocational training.

As the time passed, I grew tired of maintaining a serious demeanour, and I began to study the lighter side of Malayan child psychology. I was struck by the happiness of all the children—indeed, Malays bring their offspring up better than most Europeans—and, not least, by the beauty of some of the young Malay girls, already at twelve as developed as a European girl of seventeen. Most of them are of good family. They come to the school to learn English and do not bother very much about examinations or Cambridge certificates. Among them were two daughters of the Yam Tuan, the reigning sultan of Negri Sembilan. I remembered the late Yam Tuan very well. He belonged to the finest type of Malay, who spoke no English, but whose dignity impressed every European who met him. With his magnificent moustachios, famous throughout the East, he could never have been mistaken for a white man. Nor did he make any attempt to ape the white man's customs, let alone his fashions, but remained a true Malay to the end.

One little schoolgirl descendant, however, was surprisingly fair even for a sultan's daughter who does not work in the fields and who never goes out unveiled in the sun. She is transcendently beautiful and will break many hearts before she is twenty. But she is not wholly Malay. Her father, the present Yam Tuan, married a lady with white blood in her veins. Many of the pupils come to the school from long distances. Most of them have bicycles. The Yam Tuan's daughters make the journey daily by motor-bus from their father's Istana at Sri Menanti.

By noon I was in a muck of sweat, for, although Pilah lies high, the heat by day is fierce. With my respect for the admirable Miss Knapp greatly increased, I took my leave and made my way back to the rest-house to lunch and sleep until Freddie's return. In the evening after dinner we were joined by one of the Indian schoolmasters, and once again we sat down on the verandah in the cool night air and discussed Malaya's problems with more restraint than before, but nevertheless, with considerable freedom. This, too, was a change since my time and a change for the better. One of the problems discussed was the right of members of races, born in Malaya but not Malays, to enter the administrative branch of the Malay Civil Service. The Malay States, it must not be forgotten, are a protectorate run by the British in the name of the Malay sultans, and at present this right is reserved exclusively for Malays. It is a problem of which more will be heard in the future, for to-day there is quite an army of Chinese and Indians who have been born in Malaya and who learn English as their first language. Their legal nationality is at present undefined. If they are British-Malayans, they are without British-Malayan rights.

The next day, after an early luncheon, we set out for Jelebu, another Malayan district about twenty-four miles away and the last stage on our way to my old home in Pantai. We travelled by a road which ran round the north side of the mountain range. It was new since my day. Then this whole area was virgin jungle. Even now it is a lonely road with few habitations, but except for a strip of forest reserve most of the jungle has gone. Rubber estates, mostly Chinese-owned, have taken its place, and we passed one or two Chinese owners driving in ramshackle old cars.

I marvelled at the strides which Chinese penetration had made since my time. I conceived a new admiration and a new fear for this yellow race which can bring the most unlikely soil to cultivation and can endure the most gruelling discomfort for the prospect of material profit. Indeed, the Chinese and the motor-car have destroyed for ever that sense of loneliness and distance which formerly was the chief characteristic of life in Malaya.

As we approached Kuala Klawang, the district capital of Jelebu, the scenery changed to a background of rice-fields, coconut trees, and kampongs, which, before rubber, was the original, and is still the most attractive, feature of the Malayan landscape. All too soon we came into Kuala Klawang, an enchanting little mountain nest perched on a plateau and formerly the most delectable government post in Negri Sembilan. To me it was an even greater and more agreeable surprise than Kuala Pilah.

If progress in Pilah had been slower than elsewhere, Kuala Klawang had gone back. In my time there had always been six or seven Europeans in the place, including a British district officer. There had been even a European club where I had spent many a cheerful evening. Then it had been an important centre for tin, and Chinese coolies had added picturesqueness and sometimes rowdiness to the kaleidoscopic scene. My cousin, who owned a mine, had lived here for many years in an attractive bungalow with an immense banyan tree in the garden.

Now there was a Malay District Officer. The Europeans

had gone. There was only one left, "Abang" Braddon, who was living on an annuity in the former bungalow of the district engineer. My cousin was long since dead. His bungalow was deserted. Only the banyan tree, older than races and empires, its countless branches drooping to the ground like an enveloping shroud, remained to remind me of the past.

In the heat of the early afternoon sun the main street was almost deserted. The Chinese population had dwindled—a sure sign of vanished prosperity. The influenza epidemic soon after the war had made fearful ravages among the attractive Malay population of the district. The football padang, where Andrew Caldecott and I had once waged Homeric battles between his Jelebu Malays and my Pantai Malays, was now a neglected field with grass over a foot high. Even football had gone back. Certainly for me there would be no more wonderful evenings in Andrew's bungalow after the game, no more piano playing, no inspection of his water-colours, no more pleasant intercourse about newly discovered Malayan folk-tales with the most gifted Englishman in the Malaya of my time. Although I made a mental note to tell Andrew about the state of the football field, the impression of desolation conformed with my mood of the moment. The great tidal wave of progress had not merely passed Jelebu by. In its course it had thrown the little town far up on the beach of the past.

We went over to the local rest-house to leave Freddie's car and to have a wash. The Chinese boy was startled to see us. We went over the little building. There were cobwebs everywhere and myriads of flies. In the bedrooms the mattresses, rolled up like bales, looked stiff from want of use. We ordered drinks and sat down in rickety long chairs, their canes bent and twisted by the damp. Mine collapsed at once. Then, driven away by the flies, we strolled across the grass to "Abang" Braddon's bungalow.

As it was only half-past three, we disturbed the old gentleman's afternoon siesta. He appeared, however, in a minute, dressed in a Malay sarong and baju. A brother of "Adek" Braddon, the most brilliant doctor in Malaya and the pioneer whose work led to the discovery of the cure for beri-beri, the "Abang" had been the oldest British resident in Negri Sembilan when I arrived there twenty-seven years ago. He was now seventy-eight and did not look a day older than when I first knew him. His lean and spare figure was as erect as ever. His hair was grey, but all his faculties were unimpaired. The combined age of the two brothers is now one hundred and fifty. The combined total of their years of residence in Malaya is now close on a hundred and is, I think, a record for the tropics.*

The "Adek" is married and lives on the outskirts of Seremban. The "Abang" is legally a bachelor, although, doubtless, there have been coloured romances in his life. His visits home—or rather to Europe, for Jelebu is now his home— have been few and far between. Yet he has retained all the characteristics of a ruling Englishman. His bungalow, very comfortably furnished, was spotlessly clean and decorated with more taste than the average European bungalow. His servants moved with the quiet efficiency which only a Tuan who is respected can exact. From his open windows my eyes suddenly became fixed on a golf green with a neat flag. It seemed incongruously out of place. It belonged to a five-hole golf course built by the "Abang". The lonely old gentleman of Jelebu who had turned his back on Britain still played golf.

As we had tea in the hall downstairs with a glorious flame-of-the-forest tree casting a pleasant shade over the doorway, the "Abang" told us the tale of the decline of Jelebu in the terms of his own personal history. Jelebu was born from the Jelebu tin boom. The "Abang" had been a tin miner employing five hundred Chinese coolies. The mail used to arrive by bullock cart from Seremban. In those days, and, indeed, in my

*While this book was going to press, Dr. "Adek" Braddon died in Seremban.

day, the journey took twelve hours. Wages used to be brought by the same means of transport with two Sikh watchmen, armed with rifles, to guard the silver dollars. Only once had the cart been held up and the great cash box stolen. The thieves had never been discovered, for all proof of identification was missing. The Sikh watchmen, true to the universal characteristic of their profession, had slept peacefully throughout the hold-up.

Now Jelebu was dead. The tin was finished. The coolies had gone elsewhere. The journey to Seremban took only forty minutes by car and an hour by motor-bus. Yet few visitors came to the place. There was, indeed, no reason why they should come.

The "Abang" made no complaint. Probably he preferred things as they were. His criticisms were directed not to the past, but to the present. In the march of progress the Malays were losing ground to the Chinese. He thought that this was dangerous and undesirable. He was a champion of the Malays with whom the white man, and especially the Englishman, had more in common than with the Chinese.

I share his views. My sympathies, quite apart from racial prejudices, have always been with the people who live on the land and by the land. "He that maketh haste to be rich shall not be innocent", says the proverb, and I have always assumed that it refers to the town-dweller.

Not that the Malay works very hard on the land or is wholly innocent. If he lacks the commercial instinct of the Chinese, he is not without a certain amoral ingenuity. Not long ago the placid life of Jelebu was disturbed by a series of thefts of registered letters containing remittances of money from native town-dwellers to their relatives in the district. Suspicion fell naturally on the Malay postman, but there were no proofs. The system in force in Malaya for the delivery of registered letters is a simple one. The postman delivers the registered letter, and the recipient signs his name in the postman's receipt book. If he is illiterate, he makes an

inky thumbmark in place of a signature. In this case the postman had all the receipts for the missing letters. They were
properly provided with thumbmarks. The marks did not
correspond with the thumbprints of the addressees. Nor did
they in any way resemble the thumbprint or any other fin-
gerprint of the postman. For some time the police were
baffled. At last an enterprising detective, having noticed that
all the prints seemed to indicate a very large thumb, came to
the conclusion that the marks must have been toeprints. The
postman was made to produce his big toe. It was duly inked,
and as a result a much-chastened Malay is now meditating on
the truth of King Solomon's proverb at the expense of the
Malayan Government.

I could have listened to the "Abang" for a whole night,
but it was now after four, and we had timed our arrival at
Pantai for five o'clock. He came out to the door to see us off,
and my last view of him was as he stood beneath the flaming
petals of the tree, his face inscrutable, his arm stretched out in
a gesture of farewell, a motionless and scarcely living monument to the Malayan past. Realising that I should never see
him again, I felt a sudden uneasiness and insecurity. It had
been an emotional day. Within twenty-four hours I had met
the fattest Englishman and the oldest Englishman in Malaya.

As we set out on the fifteen mile drive to Pantai, we passed
a car driven by a Javanese. Freddie hailed him, and he stopped.
It was Hassan, the former head-man, who during my cousin's
absences in England had looked after his Jelebu interests with
unfailing fidelity. When my cousin died, he left Hassan fifty
acres of grown rubber, and to the careful Hassan these acres
have meant a towkay's wealth with all the comforts, including the inevitable motor-car, which a good Mohammedan
can desire.

The road from Jelebu to Pantai is one long descent down
the mountain slopes. In my youth I used to make the journey
from Pantai by bullock-cart sleeping on a mattress with my
bicycle strapped to the side. The return journey I made, of

course, by bicycle, free-wheeling most of the way. Here, too, there was no change and almost no traffic. Primeval jungle looked down on us from both sides. The road turned and twisted in tortuous, hairpin bends. Below us on the right was a steep precipice, dangerously deceptive because its terrors were hidden by a rich vegetation. Freddie pointed out to me the place where years before in the early days of motor-cars the "Adek" Braddon's car had skidded over the side and had been miraculously held up by a sturdy bush. The sun was still shining, but heavy clouds, harbingers of the coming storm, were banking up on the horizon. We should have a true Malayan sunset, but I realised that my forebodings about the end of the drought would come true.

At one corner of the road we passed an enormous tall trunk of a tree, erect as a steel girder, with its bark an ashen grey. Every branch had disappeared. Its jagged summit was black for twenty feet downwards—a grim reminder of the lightning which always is at its worst in these mountains. It looked for all the world like a gigantic match with which some pre-history Cyclops had lit his pipe, and which he had then planted nonchalantly in the ground.

From Bukit Tangga, at the top of the last hill which leads down into the Pantai valley, we had a superb view over the wide expanse of the Negri Sembilan plain. The old Government hill station where I sometimes used to spend a night in a homesick desire to sleep again under a blanket had been demolished. The advent of the motor-car has destroyed its usefulness, and to-day there is no trace even of its site, so quickly does the jungle re-assert itself in this warm and humid climate. But the view is the finest in the state, and to my impressionable mind it has always suggested a comparison with the view from the Cairngorms over my native Strath-spey.

Suddenly I caught a glimpse of a dark silver thread below me. It was the Jeralang River which had flowed past my old bungalow at Pantai. I became silent and nervous. My feelings were strangely mixed. Freddie was not a romanticist, and I longed to be alone. On the other hand, I was afraid lest without him my meeting with Amai should end in a fiasco.

Everything was going to be so different from what I had visualised when I set out from England. Then I had believed that Amai was dead. During the weeks on board ship I had attuned my mind to a harmonious sentimentality. Now she was not only alive but married—and married to the local muezzin, who from the mosque summons the faithful to prayer. While I had lain in my sick-bed at Freddie's bungalow, there had been mysterious comings and goings between Port Dickson and Pantai. Messengers had come from Pantai to know when I was to be expected. Freddie had prepared me for the worst. He had told me that the Malays had changed, that their memories were short, and that their attitude towards the white man had altered. Amai herself would be unrecognisable. She was now over forty, and a Malay woman of forty was an old hag with her mouth twisted out of shape by years of betel-chewing.

I knew that what he said must be true. I remembered Buntak's grin. I had an overwhelming dread that the whole visit would provide a rich comedy to everyone except myself and that Freddie's help would be not only welcome but necessary.

My second thoughts were best. Freddie understood my mood instinctively. He made no attempt to talk. He was the perfect companion. As we descended the hill all too rapidly, the old landmarks came back one by one. There was the rubber estate, most of which I had planted up myself from virgin jungle. The trees were larger, but otherwise Pantai did not seem to have altered. I was glad that there had been so little change. I did not wish to meet Amai in an atmosphere of cinema theatres and dancing halls.

But this consolation brought no relief to my emotional tremors. When we turned the last bend and came into the straight which led to my former bungalow, I was overcome by the same paralysing nervousness which always afflicts me when I speak in public and which not even the rigours of a lecture tour in the United States have been able to eradicate.

Whatever motive may have inspired my voyage to the East while I was in England, I realised now with that pellucid clearness which comes at one time or another even to the most indecisive of men that the focus point of my sentimental attachment to Malaya was Amai. The reflection that I was to see her again in the living flesh and to repeat the farewell which had been interrupted twenty-five years before by the sudden arrival of my uncle served merely to strengthen the conviction that she was the impulse which had directed the steps of my destiny.

CHAPTER SEVEN

FREDDIE WAS NOW driving very slowly. Hitherto he had been the guide and cicerone. But Pantai he knew only vaguely. Here I was as much at home as if I had never left the place. Our entrance into the village was marred by one disappointment. We pulled up at what should have been a gap in a high hedge. The gap had been the entrance of the short drive to my old bungalow. The hedge had screened my garden from the gaze of curious passers-by. Now both hedge and garden had disappeared and only the coconut trees, taller and more stately than in my time, remained. Where my old bungalow had stood was now a long row of Tamil coolie lines.

With Freddie I walked across the grass, while Tamil coolies, grinning and chattering, came slowly forward to stare at the white strangers. Here in this same compound I had first seen Amai. I had been the first white man to live in Pantai, and it had taken me some time to establish friendly relations with the local Malays. In the end the Dato' Klana's father and mother, who, although holding no official position from the British, still exercised a feudal authority over the whole district, had invited me to a "rong-geng", a kind of Malay dance in which two or more professional dancers provide the entertainment. In return I had invited them and, indeed, all the local Malay population to another "rong-geng". I had converted my compound into a Venetian garden with little lamps made of coconut shells. I had sat between the Dato' and his wife, a wizened old lady who feared neither man nor Allah and who had only to frown to be obeyed. And there in her suite of attendants I had caught my first glimpse of Amai.

As in a dream I walked across the primitive river bridge which had separated my bungalow from the rubber estate. The trees on the first clearing were wintering, and in their leafless branches I saw the symbol of my own dead past. Geographical reunion revived a thousand memories, and everywhere I saw the ghosts of my youth. Across this bridge had gone daily backwards and forwards my anti-fomes and anti-white-ant brigade composed of "Big Hussein" and "Little Hussein". They, too, were on my conscience. They had been great footballers. When I had started football in Pantai, I had brought them from Port Dickson to assist me in developing the local talent and had given them at my company's expense a very soft job which consisted in fumigating the rubber trees with a strange contraption worked by a hand pump.

I do not think that they ever earned the shareholders' money.

Across this bridge I had watched only too often Tamil coolies carrying the cheap white-wood coffin of some dead man, woman or child. For the death rate of my labour force had been high and the victims of malaria and dysentery numerous.

Across this bridge, too, I had helped Amai on that night when I had met her a mile or two down the river and had brought her to my bungalow. For some days we had stood a kind of siege. The old Dato's wife had both cajoled and stormed. Every kind of pressure had been brought to bear on me to give her up. But the difficulties had merely strengthened my obstinacy and my passion, and there she had remained for over a year until that day when, my health undermined by malaria or by poison, I had been bundled into a blanket and taken away in a car by my uncle and my cousin. The bridge, doubtless, had been renewed. But it was the same river, and yet how changed since my time. Then it had been a turgid stream, swollen by the continuous rains and muddy "tailings" from the tin mines. Now the drought and the absence of "tailings" had reduced it to a shallow silver trickle.

As I stood looking down on the water, Freddie touched my arm. We had still much to do, and the time at our disposal was short. Disconsolate and ill at ease, I went back to the car, but as we drove slowly along the road to the village

my spirits revived. Here there was no change. Pantai, like
Jelebu, had not shared in the general progress. Just beyond
the cross-roads we pulled up at Woh's house, and here a
great surprise awaited us. Woh, a local Malay who had
seen life in Singapore and Kuala Lumpur, had been something more than the stalwart of my Pantai football team.
From the beginning, and especially in my time of trouble, he
had been my friend and counsellor in all matters pertaining
to Malay laws and customs. And now there he was with what
was left of my old football team to welcome us. Many had
gone to their last rest. Big Hussein and Little Hussein were
dead. But there were six survivors to greet me. Here was my
old goalkeeper, now a Haji with a round, beaming face.
Here, too, was Haji Sabudin, who had made the thirty-four-
miles journey from Port Dickson in order to be present.
Here was Woh himself, once the best-looking Malay in
the district and now a bearded, grey-haired grandfather and
the oldest-looking of them all, but still unmistakably Woh.
In the background was a burly figure, now bald but as sheep-
ish as ever, his eyes cast on the ground as if expecting a scold-
ing. It was Drau, Drau the Habshi, with the black skin of
an Ethiopian, Drau once a fearless full-back and an even
more fearless pursuer of women, Drau, whom, twenty-six
years before, the beauty of a professional dancer had roused
to such a paroxysm of sensual frenzy that, foaming at the
mouth and roaring like a bull, he had broken the circle of
spectators and had tried to carry her off in the presence of
his Dato'. That had been a great scandal, although, assuredly,
it must have heightened his attractions in the eyes of the
village maidens.

Drau I recognised at once. He was delighted. "The Tuan
really recognised me?" he asked. "Or did someone tell him?"
I swore it was true. Indeed, it was. There was no one who
could have told me beforehand.

We were bowed into Woh's house—a new house since
my time, excellently built and with a verandah. If there was

little sign of change in Pantai, the Malays looked more prosperous. For the first time in my life I was taken into the women's quarters at the back, and there, bending down, I shook hands with Woh's wife, his sister, his son's wife, and his granddaughters. Then we came back to the verandah where Freddie and I were given chairs and served with tea, while the men stood round, dignified and silent.

Rather nervously I began the conversation, for the Malays are great formalists, and a false opening might easily have spoilt everything. Football seemed the safest subject. "How was the village team prospering?" At once the immobile faces became animated. Woh was the chief spokesman. Pantai to-day had no proper team. They were no longer in the league.

Freddie asked why, and again Woh took up the parable. When Tuan Lockhart was here, we had a captain to teach, to organise, and to spur us on. Now there was no one. In any case the young men were different. They now kept their money for clothes and bicycles and the cinema. Only the school-children played.

Like those greybeards in London who inordinately praise the past, Woh spoke scornfully. His words would have been more impressive had I not noticed, pinned to the wall behind him, a photograph of Jean Harlow and a Bat'a calendar: the two symbols of the new Malaya, for the American "movie" industry and the Czechoslovak shoe have conquered the whole peninsula. Involuntarily I looked down at Woh's feet. He was dressed in the traditional Malay costume, but, where formerly he had gone barefooted he now wore a pair of patent-leather pumps.

In my day the football field had been the centre of the village life. A "pawang", or magic doctor, had whispered the necessary incantations over it in order that the spirits which inhabited it might be propitious and not trip up our players in stride for goal. Now, as I saw from the annual government report, Directors of Education, and not "pawangs", opened football fields! I was mildly shocked.

"I'm sorry you have no proper football team", I said. "What about our turning out again and taking on the new generation just for the sake of example?"

I looked at Drau, who took my suggestion literally.

"Tuan", he said simply and very seriously, "my football days are done. I have put too many children into the world. My knees are too weak."

From football we passed to more personal topics: who was dead and who was still alive and whether times were good or bad. Times, they said, with all the conviction of pessimistic middle age, were not what they used to be.

By this time half the boys and girls of the village had assembled in the road outside Woh's house and were staring at us incontinently. White men who stopped to talk to Malays in Pantai were rare. My old rubber estate was now managed by an Indian. Only one white man had lived there since my time, and he had become a Mohammedan in order to marry a Malay girl. As I recalled how nearly I had embraced Islam because of Amai, I wondered vaguely if there was some romantic contagion in the atmosphere of this still unspoilt Malay village.

All this while there had been no mention of Amai. I had expected to meet her at Woh's bungalow and was relieved because his sense of the fitness of things had prevented what would certainly have been a calamity. Before I could muster my courage to put a direct question, he drew me into the back room on the pretence of showing me some Malay carving.

There had been a mistake and even a little trouble. He had expected me the day before, and now the whole village including Amai's "muezzin" husband knew of my arrival. There had been a scene between Amai and her husband. Amai had boasted that her Tuan was coming back to see her, and the muezzin's dignity had been offended. Amai, who as

Q

a young girl had defied the wrath of her highly-placed relations, had never lacked courage. She had made a spirited reply and, strong in her rights of possession, for in Negri Sembilan matriarchy is in force and the woman is the property-owner, had even threatened divorce.

Woh, seeing my embarrassment, assured me with a laugh that the situation was not serious but merely a little awkward. Now Amai could not come to his house. But she was waiting for me at the edge of the road and the rice-field at the ninth milestone.

I was now all impatient to be gone, and the ceremonial farewell to my Malay friends seemed interminable. At last we got into the car, and then Kassim drove us slowly past the little village. We went as far as the next kampong and must have missed her. I felt nervous and irritated. Freddie, however, was determined to show his ability as an organiser. He ordered Kassim to turn in his tracks and to drive back. Two hundred yards past the trysting-place, he stopped the car and let me walk back alone. This time she was there.

She was standing by the roadside at the same spot where in the days of my youthful infatuation I used to ride my bicycle up and down the road merely to see her pass, and almost exactly opposite the place where she had made her way by night through the fields to the strip of jungle in which I lay in hiding to meet her and to bring her to my house. The place had changed hardly at all. There was the same superb expanse of rice-fields, the rice golden-brown in the sunset and ripe for harvest, and the same mysterious background of blue mountains. A solitary palm, standing like a lone sentinel, added a wistful beauty to the scene.

Contrary to my expectations I had no difficulty in recognising her. She had changed but not so much as Freddie had led me to believe. As she came forward to meet me, she drew back her head sarong, and I saw that the beautiful oval face of her youth had become broader and more rugged. The skin, too, was darker and slightly weather-beaten. But her eyes, large and lustrous, still looked straight at me. Her figure was erect. There was a fine dignity in her carriage. She was old, but she had worn remarkably well for a Malay woman.

She spoke first. "Apa khabar, Tuan?" and, as she smiled, her teeth showed like ivory. "I thought you were dead", she added simply.

"Years ago", I replied, "I was told officially that you were dead."

"Who told you?" she asked.

"Tuan —— " I answered, mentioning the name of an old official friend.

Her eyes flashed. "He lied," she said vehemently. "He was always too stuck-up."

The fires died down. "The Tuan is married?" she asked.

"Yes."

"The Tuan has a child?"

"Yes."

"A son?"

"Yes."

"What does he do?"

I told her.

Question and counter-question followed each other in quick succession. Yes, she was married too. After my departure she had had to leave Pantai for some years. Then, like all Malay women who go with white men and survive, she had come back to the kampong and had married the "muezzin". She had been a good match. She owned her own land and house.

If she felt any emotion, she never revealed it.

"Have the old Dato' and his wife forgiven me?" I asked, suddenly remembering my fear of the old harridan who had stormed my house and demanded the surrender of Amai. The Dato' was dead. But the old lady was alive. She was nearly a hundred. She had not forgotten. Doubtless, the Tuan had seen her as he passed her house.

I had—an old, bent witch, like Gagool in *King Solomon's Mines*. I had no wish to meet her face to face again.

And the Dato' Klana, their son and Amai's guardian, with whom I used to play football? Was he alive?

Yes, he was alive. He was always kind. He was well, but he was like the Tuan. He had grown fat.

This candid comment was a rude shock to my self-respect. Since I had seen Woh, I had been priding myself how much younger I looked than my Malay friends. Now I was not so sure. Undoubtedly, I was fat. They were as lean and as straight as ramrods. In Malay eyes fatness was obviously a surer sign of age than grey hairs. Pathologically I think it is a correct conclusion.

"They say you have become rich and famous."

Amai was speaking again, and under my breath I cursed Freddie. He must have been talking.

I smiled sheepishly, and asked if times were bad. Could I help in any way?

No, times were not too good, but one could always live, and to-day desires were fewer. Her dignity and her composure were impressive.

Far away I heard the sound of voices. I looked up and saw half the village still maintaining a respectful distance, but nevertheless moving slowly forward, impelled by an irresistible curiosity. Once again the position threatened to become ridiculous. Then Freddie came back with the car. He looked at me inquiringly.

Amai understood at once. "Tuan mau jalan? The Tuan wants to go?" she asked.

I took the easy way out.

"Yes," I said, "I have to go. I leave for Singapore to-night. To-morrow I go to Java, to the islands—a long voyage. After that I am returning to my own country. Before I leave for Europe, I shall try to come back to Pantai."

The brown eyes looked into mine. There was an awkward pause.

"The Tuan has grown old," said Freddie with a nervous laugh.

"I am old, too," said Amai proudly, as though insisting that we belonged to the same generation and to the same period.

For the only time in our lives we shook hands.

"Go in peace," she said.

"Remain in peace," I answered.

I stepped into the car, and at Freddie's order Kassim drove away at top speed. I looked back only once. She was still standing there by the rice, her arm stretched out like a signpost. Huge angry clouds had turned the sunset to a fiery orange. Before we reached Seremban the soft tropical rain had fallen. The long drought had come to an end.

When we arrived in the town, I was still dazed. In a dream I said goodbye to Freddie, who was going back to Port Dickson. He had been marvellously kind and full of understanding. Even now he offered to stay and dine with me. My train for Singapore did not leave until eleven-thirty, and it was only half-past seven. But I refused, and would not even let him take me to the club.

In a dream I asked him to drop me at the rest-house. Then, after depositing my luggage, I went into the oblong dining-room and sat down by myself. Only two tables were occupied: one by an elderly man and woman, who were obviously tourists, and the other by a morose and slightly tipsy commercial traveller. Mechanically a Chinese "boy" handed me the menu—a long list with the same imitation French fare that one finds in the average provincial hotel in England. Mechanically I went through the performance of eating. Electric lights blazed above me, but the atmosphere was heavy with gloom. Nobody spoke, and in the silence the depressing tinkle of forks on the cheap china sounded doubly harsh. Presently someone in the serving room turned on the wireless. How incongruous and irritating at this moment was the Oriental's passion for the white man's music.

Away back in the 'eighties, in Conrad's time, it had been a musical box. Quarter of a century before Amai had driven me nearly mad by her incessant playing of my old phonograph with its hollow cylindrical records. Now radio was conquering even the jungle.

Here in this morgue of a rest-house it was playing a gramophone record—American, of course. Some famous crooner was singing "You Made Me What I Am", and as the sickly notes emerged the Chinese "boy", leaning lazily against a table by the side door, beat time with his foot. I was back in modern Malaya. Soon, I reflected, the Chinese would be beating the time and calling the tune all over Malaya.

My dinner unfinished, I left the room and went on to the verandah to look at the night. The rain had stopped. The moon was shining on the lake below me. There were still three hours until my train left. An irresistible temptation overcame me. I would go back to Pantai and have a last look at my old home by night. I hired a car and was there in half-an-hour. Telling the chauffeur to wait, I got out and walked slowly forward on foot. The road was deserted. The golden vanities of the sunset had given way to the solemn simplicity of the night, and in the moonlight the mountains looked like ghostly wraiths, distantly majestic and unapproachable. A slight mist rose from the rice-fields, and the damp, scented air combined with the eeriness of the tropical night made me shiver.

What a barrier of remoteness the interval of time had placed between me and my old friends. I had seen all that was best and worst in the modern world. They had never gone beyond this jungle village, and civilisation had not yet quite encroached on them. And yet between us was the bond of superstition common to all races who live among the mountains. There was many a ruin in the Highlands of Scotland where I would not spend a night alone for all the gold in Africa. Here in Pantai everyone still believed in charms, in evil spirits, and in were-tigers, strange animals who took the form of a human being by day in order to find their prey more easily by night. Even Woh, for all his boasted knowledge of the outer world, would regard a man from Korinchi with caution and suspicion, for it was Korinchi men who had special faculty of assuming the form of a were-tiger.

I stood very still. It is not wise to walk abroad unwarily in a Malay kampong by night. The village was almost in total darkness. Here and there the faint light of an oil lamp shone like a will-of-the-wisp through the chinks of wooden walls. One of these lights came from Amai's house. She was still up. She was there with her "muezzin" husband—wrangling or perhaps making love in a material Malay reconciliation. I did not know and should never know. Back to my mind came one of the Malay "pantuns" which she had taught me:

"Apa guna pasang pelita,
Jika tidak dengan sumboh-nya?
Apa guna bermain mata,
Kelau tidak dengan sunggoh-nya?"

"Why attempt to light a lantern,
If the wick should be not in it?
Why attempt to smile and wanton,
If you do not really mean it?"

My melancholy was complete. It was heavily tinged with regrets for Amai, for my Malay friends, for their dying civilisation, and for my own departed youth. Never again should I be so carefree, so exuberant, as I had been in this peaceful village. I tried to laugh at myself, to find something ridiculous in this spectacle of Lockhart in quest of his youth. There was no success to my effort. One sentiment dominated my thought. It was an immense tenderness towards the beautiful Malay girl of twenty-five years ago, who had stood by me in health and in sickness and who had braved the anger of her own people.

BOOK IV

JAVANESE INTERLUDE

"PERFORCE HIDE other vasty lands from thee
Until what time no land remains unfound;
But leave thou not those islands of the sea,
Where Nature rises to Fame's highest round."

CHAPTER ONE

IN ORDER TO save as much time as possible I had made up my mind from the beginning to fly whenever I could. Singapore to Batavia was an obvious stretch, for the journey by air takes less than six hours, whereas the journey by steamer wastes the best part of two days. The morning after my departure from Pantai and Seremban, therefore, found me on the Singapore air-field. I had booked my passage by the Dutch K.L.M. in preference to the British Imperial Airways. If it is unpatriotic to travel by a foreign line, then I am in good company, including that of Lady Chetwode, the wife of the former British commander-in-chief in India. The truth is that at the time to which I refer the Dutch K.L.M. service was faster and more punctual than that of Imperial Airways.

These criticisms have been made by other British travellers and residents in the East, and they are resented by the British company. Similar criticisms are made of the British steamship services to the East, and are resented by the companies running them. The fact remains that many British subjects prefer to travel by Dutch and German boats because they believe that they receive a better and faster service, that is, in plain language, better value of their money. I appreciate the difficulties of the British steamship and airway companies, but resentment of criticism will not help to improve the efficiency of their services. Stressing difficulties seems to have become a characteristic of the post-war Englishman. I know several brilliant young men in the British Civil Service who are past masters in drafting objections to every new proposal or new policy. The greatness of Britain was built up on her former capacity to overcome difficulties. I am, therefore, in favour of criticism where it is justified. I should like to hear it voiced fiercely and loudly by the whole British people, for a universal clamour would prove that the nation's will-power to advance had not atrophied.

But even the Dutch are not infallible; their airplane from Amsterdam was half-an-hour late. It had been held up by the storm of the previous night. During this slight delay I had time to take a look at the various units of the Royal Air Force, who were busily engaged in testing and tuning up their airplanes. They looked healthy and efficient. Of the three branches of our fighting services in Singapore the airmen suffer least from the rigours of the tropical climate. The sailors are cooped up in ships with limited space, and in the tropics limitation of space is the next stage to hell. While I was in Singapore there were some complaints by the ratings, mainly, I think, about the quality of the food. The soldiers have to carry heavy kit and to perform their exercises under a fierce sun. The flying men can soar above these terrestrial and oceanic disadvantages.

Presently my airplane, at first scarcely distinguishable from the local kites, appeared on the horizon, and in a few minutes had landed gracefully at the marked spot where I stood waiting with the Dutch officials. It landed two passengers, and I took my place. I had only three fellow-travellers: an Anglo-Canadian doctor, who was going to join a private yacht at Soerabaja, an amiable and enormously powerful German, interested in gold-mining, and a Dutch banker, who was returning to his post in Batavia. I travel by air merely for convenience. The sensation of flying gives me no thrills. It does not make me even sick. Unless we are flying very low, it gives me no aesthetic enjoyment. After a short and distorted view of Singapore island, I therefore lay back in my chair and began to study my Dutch language books, at which I had been working ever since I left England. I was not disturbed until we were approaching the coast of Sumatra. Then I was conscious of a voice addressing me in English.

"You're Bruce Lockhart, aren't you?" The voice came from Creighton, the Anglo-Canadian doctor. Presumably he had read my name from the label on my despatch case.

I said, "Yes," and he continued with a note of admiration in his voice: "You've done a lot of flying, I see."

"Not very much," I replied, with that smug modesty with which the average man reveals his vanity.

"Oh, yes! you have. Only a man who has flown for years could have read through that terrific storm. Why, you never even looked up when that jagged fork of lightning almost struck the wings of the plane."

I looked up now, and saw an inky black area of cloud gushing rain on the sea about four miles away on our right. Then I realised that, exhausted by my emotional experiences of the last few days, I had slept soundly through one of the worst storms that our much-travelled Dutch pilot had ever experienced. But I did not give myself away. For the first time in my life I had crossed the Equator by air and had been sublimely unconscious of the occasion. But with these men of different nationalities I have kept until now and, if they do not read this book, perhaps for ever a wholly undeserved reputation for courage and indifference to danger.

As we approached Palembang, where we stopped for twenty minutes, we came down lower, and I had a clear view of the surrounding country. Low-lying, swampy, and thickly covered with virgin jungle, it looked unattractive and singularly uninviting in the event of a forced landing. The assistant pilot pointed out to me a river where the local village council had forbidden the inhabitants to bathe on pain of imprisonment. This measure had been taken in order to reduce the number of gratuitous victims of the local crocodiles. With my passion for verification I checked this story later with the Dutch officials, and was given chapter and verse for the village order.

Incidentally, London and New York may soon be enjoying crocodiles' eggs, crocodile steak, and curried crocodile tail. Recent experiments in Singapore have proved that crocodiles' eggs taste like plovers', and that the flesh is rather superior to venison.

Palembang itself is a picturesque Malay Venice situated on the banks of the river Moesi. Many of the Malay houses are built on poles standing in the river, and there is quite a lively Chinese shopping centre in a water-street of rafts. But the place is hot and depressingly humid, and no one except a Dutchman intent on profit-making would want to live there.

Much more attractive was the approach to Batavia, called after the Batavii who fought against the Romans, and from whom the Dutch are descended. The airplane skirted the coast of Sumatra until it comes to the neck of the Sunda Straits. To the right is a mass of green islands. They look fertile and seductive; but they are uninhabited. They have a sinister name in history. Among them is Krakatau, ill-famed for the greatest eruption the world has ever known. Forty thousand human beings lost their lives in the eruption of 1883 and in the tidal wave which accompanied it. Krakatau is still active, still emits smoke and throws up great spouts of water. The giant who rained ashes over the greater part of Asia is building himself a new crater and gathering his forces for another attack on humanity.

Crossing from Sumatra to Java, one follows the Javanese coast for a little, looking down on tiny coral islands scattered like pin-heads in the sapphire-blue sea. Then, in order to reach the airport, one has to fly over the whole city. On my previous visit twenty-five years before, I had landed only at the docks and I had seen nothing. Now, as I looked down on the rows of red-tiled houses, the numerous garden-plots and open spaces, and neatly-cut canals, I felt as though I were in Holland. The impression was confirmed by closer inspection. Singapore looks like and is an international city. Batavia is provincial, and Dutch provincial at that.

The airfield was seven miles from the centre of the city. Soon the largest part of an air-journey will be the motor-car trips to and from the airports. But the efficiency of the Dutch officials impressed me. In contrast to my arrival in

Singapore, I was in and out of the customs and passport control within two minutes and was being whirled along at seventy miles an hour by a Batavian Malay chauffeur, whose break-neck indifference to the safety of himself and his passengers made the recklessness of our British Malays seem the acme of caution. Our destination was the famous Hôtel des Indes, which was to be my headquarters.

That night I dined with Miedl, my new German acquaintance from the airplane, and the Dutch banker. It was a long and late sitting. It began with gin "pahits" on the verandah overlooking the Molenvliet (Mill Stream), the main street which runs on both sides of the canal and links the new town with the old. It is the Dutch view that the English in the East are lazy because they drink too much whisky. But the English dilute their whisky and gin "pahits" with water. The Dutch drink their Bols gin neat, and they do not stint it. I must admit, however, that they stand their drink remarkably well, and that their capacity for gin does not affect their industry. After "pahit" drinking we dined downstairs, and again I marvelled at the Dutch capacity for eating. Then we went upstairs to watch a cabaret show.

The place was crowded, not by the hotel's clients, but by local residents. The cabaret show, provided by a troupe of Russians and Hungarian artistes, was excellent. But what interested me most was the crowd of onlookers. They were seated at tables in family groups. They were obviously well-to-do, for the prices in the Hôtel des Indes are far from low.

What impressed me most was the number of half-castes of both sexes. They included prominent business men and high officials. Here was the Dutch attitude, so different from our own, towards colour, manifest before my eyes. It has its advantages and disadvantages. Throughout the Dutch East Indies the number of half-castes is very large, but no statistics are available. Only one rough division can be made. The well-to-do Dutchman who has had a child by a native woman has, as a rule, cared for it, and sent it to school in Holland.

That child becomes Dutch, and is a supporter of the Dutch régime in the East Indies. The Dutch private soldier who has a child by a native woman cannot afford to do anything for it. It goes back to the kampong and, if subsequently conscious of its white blood, becomes a malcontent. It is from the large army of poor half-castes that most of the internal trouble in the East Indies has come.

The half-castes at our cabaret show belonged to the society which goes to the governor-general's receptions. On the whole the women with a dash of colour were more attractive and certainly slimmer than the hundred per cent. Dutch blondes. But all, both men and women, deported themselves with a stolid dignity that sent my thoughts back to the Dutch Calvinists. They drank innumerable cups of coffee and sipped their liqueurs. They clapped the various turns with the appropriate decorum. If they were amused, they expressed their gratification with a carefully controlled smile. When they danced, the men held their partners at the appropriately decorous distance. I saw no heads bent close together, no pressure of hand or arm. It was dancing without ecstasy and without temperament. When the most important party rose to leave, the others, including myself, followed.

I had the impression of a society brought up to observe a fixed book of rules as, doubtless, it had been brought up to observe the Bible. Subsequently I learnt that the Dutch, and especially the Dutch women, had hidden reserves of temperament which an onlooker that night would never have suspected. After my impressions of Singapore I felt a new respect for the Dutch, who, whatever their shortcomings in their private life, still preserve that external dignity which in an Eastern country is essential to the white man's supremacy.

The next morning I rose betimes, full of good resolutions and intent on mortifying the flesh by a rigorous and intellectual exploration of the city. My first visit was to the Governor-General, to whom I had a flattering letter of recommendation. As it was a Saturday, he had gone for the week-end to Buitenzorg, the permanent residence of the Dutch governors-general since 1745. The name is a Dutch translation of the French Sans-Souci. The little town, distant about thirty miles from Batavia, is world-famous on account of its botanical gardens. I saw the Governor-General's private secretary, who informed me that His Excellency would be back on Monday morning. I had letters to other prominent Dutch residents in Batavia, but, delighted to have two whole days to myself, I left their delivery till the next week.

Following my usual practice, I refused the services of a guide, and hired a car with a Malay-speaking chauffeur for the week. Fortune favoured me. My chauffeur, although born in Batavia, was of Sumatra parentage. He spoke much the same Malay as our Negri Sembilan Malays speak. He was a bright and intelligent young man with well-developed critical faculties. I sat beside him and carried on a lively conversation as he drove me slowly round the town.

Our way led by the Molenvliet. The canal was built over two hundred years ago, and was originally intended as a water route to bring the produce from the sugar mills outside Batavia down to the sea. To-day it is one of the liveliest centres of native life. In the canal itself men poling rafts dispute the right of way with countless bathers. The rafts are bringing building materials, and the building materials are the rafts themselves. For when the native wishes to build a house, he buys the bamboo, makes it into a raft and takes it to the site. Then he pulls the raft to pieces and begins to build his house with this timber.

The bathers are mostly boys and girls. Standing in the edge of the water are scores of women, clad only in a sarong skirt tied neatly over their breasts. Most of them are engaged in washing clothes, for the canal is the laundry of Batavia. Others are performing their own ablutions and brushing their teeth with the same water as that in which they wash their clothes. Others again are sitting on the banks dangling

R

their legs over the stone parapet and drying themselves in the sun. Green trees, white houses and red-tiled roofs, and yellow water, white-crested by the rays of the sun, blend together with the brown bodies of the boys and the variegated colours of the women's clothes to form as vivid and as picturesque a kaleidoscope as can be seen anywhere in the world.

The first feature of Batavia which impresses the English visitor from Singapore is the predominance of the various Malay races and the comparatively small number of Chinese. More than 400,000 of Singapore Island's half-million population are Chinese; Batavia's population of just under 400,000 is composed roughly of 300,000 Malays, 60,000 Chinese and 40,000 Europeans. In this respect the advantage is with Batavia.

My first objective was Tanjong Priok, for in this manner I should traverse the straggling length of the three cities into which Batavia is divided. Weltevreden, where the Hôtel des Indes stands, is the European residential town, and was built for reasons of health during the Napoleonic wars. The lower town is the old Batavia, and is the business centre both for Europeans and for the Chinese. Tanjong Priok is Batavia's dockland, and is nearly seven miles distant from the Hôtel des Indes. As we drove through the old town, Ahmat, my chauffeur, pointed out to me the leading banks and offices, including the building of the Netherlands Trading Society, a company which has supplied the House of Orange with the bulk of its private fortune, and in which the present Queen of Holland is a large shareholder. The buildings, spacious and well-equipped, were worthy of the capital of an island which, year in year out, has yielded untold wealth to the Dutch.

During my visit the signs of prosperity were to be seen only in tiles and plaster. The high exchange value of the Dutch guilder and the slump in agricultural prices, especially in sugar, had spread an economic blight over the land, and

Dutch, half-castes, and natives alike had had to draw in their belts. Only the Chinese and the Japanese merchants, underselling the manufactured goods of Europe, seemed prosperous.

Just how far the Japanese manufacturers have supplanted the British and the Dutch since 1929 can be seen from the following figures. In 1926 Britain supplied 29 per cent. of the textiles for the East Indies. Japan and Holland came second with 26 per cent. each. In 1934 Japan's share of the trade had risen to 76 per cent., Britain's and Holland's had fallen to 7 per cent. Nevertheless, several Dutch high officials, while resenting and fearing the encroachment of the Japanese, told me that the cheap Japanese textiles had been a godsend during the slump period. Otherwise, the discontent of the impoverished natives might have created serious trouble.

Ahmat, my chauffeur, spoke freely about the poverty of the native population. I told him that he must be glad to be a chauffeur, for cars in Batavia, and, indeed, throughout the Dutch East Indies, are not cheap to hire, and I was paying him a handsome price. But he shook his head. "I do fairly well," he said, "but ten people have to live on what I earn. They come from a country village and there is nothing for them there." Later, he took me to his own tiny house in a Malay kampong off the Jacatra Road, and introduced me to his father and mother and a band of other relations of all ages whom he was supporting.

Farther on we came to the Fish Market, picturesquely situated beside the river, where junks, many of them Japanese, and stately prahus, some bare-masted and others with their sails set, lay riding at anchor. The various kinds of tropical fish, laid out in baskets or thrown in a heap on the stones, the fishermen of different nationalities, and the native housewives buying and bargaining, add to the attractiveness of the scene, and I came back again and again to this colourful spot, which is at its best at sunset or in the early dawn.

Tanjong Priok itself was a disappointment. The docks are modern and magnificently equipped, but at the moment I was not interested in modern development, but was seeking historical landmarks. Captain Cook, one of my boyhood heroes, had landed here on his way home from his first voyage in the *Endeavour* in 1770. He had previously reported to the Admiralty that he had not lost one man of scurvy during the whole voyage. Batavia, true to its insalubrious reputation of those days, soon spoiled this record. Cook stayed eleven weeks in Batavia. When he left, seven of his crew had died, and forty were ill with malaria or dysentery.

Here, too, came Bligh of the *Bounty* in the small schooner which he had bought in Timor after his miraculous journey from Tofoa with the eighteen loyalists whom the mutineers had cast adrift in the ship's boat. Nor was Bligh more fortunate than Cook. He had not lost a man during the 3618 miles voyage from Tofoa. Three of his crew, the master's mate, the cook, and a quarter-master seaman, died in Batavia. It was in Batavia that he put up his schooner, which he had christened H.M.S. *Resource*, for auction. In Timor he had paid 1000 rix dollars for it. In Batavia it was knocked down for 295 rix dollars, and on top of this the Dutch tried to make him pay sale duty. The stern Englishman refused.

Ahmat, of course, had never heard of Cook or Bligh, nor could I discover any details about their stay in Batavia even from the Dutch officials and professors who, in striking contrast to the British in Malaya, have a profound knowledge of the history of the East Indies. Ahmat, however, was fully conversant with his own type of Malay history. As we approached the archway, known as the Penang Gate although no one could tell me why, he pointed out to me an old cannon sunk in a grass plot at the side of the road. The natives believe that this cannon has the power of making a barren woman fertile, and almost daily Batavian women come here to whisper a wish and to leave a floral tribute with the canon god. According to another superstition the cannon will one day be joined by its mate, and when this happens the Dutch rule in Java will end.

Ahmat, who explained these matters to me, told me of two other political superstitions, both modern and probably inspired by the Javanese nationalists.

"What will happen, Tuan," he said, "when Queen Wilhelmina and Princess Juliana die?" he asked me.

I confessed my ignorance.

"Why, Tuan, the Dutch will go. And what will happen, Tuan, when the whole world is encircled by wireless?"

I gave him the Malay equivalent for "I'll buy it."

This time he spoke with even greater assurance: "For sure, Tuan, the Dutch will be driven out."

This was my first insight into Javanese nationalism. Later I heard many similar stories throughout the Dutch East Indies, but at the time Ahmat's nonsense made a considerable impression on me. One could travel, I reflected, the length and breadth of British Malaya without hearing even a whisper of discontent from a Malay against the British rule. Yet here was a Batavian chauffeur talking the same kind of suggestive revolutionary superstition as the Russian peasantry talked in 1910.

Before we returned to the hotel for luncheon, Ahmat showed me two gruesome illustrations of the ancient and modern history of Batavia. Coming back by the Jacatra Road into the old town, he stopped close to the Portuguese church, although why it is so called I do not know, for it is an old Dutch church. He pointed to the wall, and I saw there a human skull, whitewashed and held in its place by a spearpoint. Beneath it was a tablet with a Dutch inscription, which in English runs as follows: "In execrated memory of the traitor, Pieter Elberfeld. Building on this spot is forbidden now and for evermore." The unfortunate Elberfeld, whose memory is thus perpetuated, was an influential half-caste who in 1722 formed a plot to massacre all the Dutch in Batavia and to set up a native government with himself at its head. True to all European historical legends in the East, be they Portuguese or Dutch or British or American, the plot is said to have been revealed by a beautiful native woman to her Dutch lover. Pieter Elberfeld's skull was the illustration from the ancient history of Batavia.

The example from the modern came a few minutes later, when Ahmat pulled up beside a long one-storied building with an extended roof which formed a covered verandah. Stretching out behind it a long queue of people stood waiting patiently. They were of all races: Chinese, Japanese, all the various Malay races of the Archipelago, and even broken-down Europeans. The Malays predominated. The queue included men and women of all ages, and even young boys and girls. There were old men, toothless and lean and scraggy as a starving horse. There were young wives with babies at their breasts. Everyone carried something: pots and pans, clothes, carved ornaments, pieces of embroidery, jewellery, and other gewgaws of the average native home, including even heavy articles of furniture. I saw one young girl staggering under the weight of a sewing machine. A native policeman stood by to keep the queue in line. But there was no disorder, no bustling, and very little chatter.

My first thought was that they were unemployed and out-of-works waiting their turn at some Dutch equivalent of our Labour Exchange. Ahmat soon corrected this impression: "Rumah gadai, Tuan (The pawnshop, Tuan)," he said, rather sullenly and with a kind of exasperated contempt: "It's crowded like this every day." He spoke no more than the truth. Perhaps because of its exotic background, the human tragedy of poverty made a more shattering impression on me than it does at home, and I went back to study it again and again. Whenever the office was open, the long queue was always there.

The pawnshops in Java are owned and operated by the Government. There are three hundred and seventy-five of them, and the annual sum lent or rather advanced, for in

many cases the pledged goods are never redeemed, is about
£20,000,000. The system is better, and probably fairer to the
native, than the *laissez faire* system of the British in Malaya,
where the "Chetties" or Indian moneylenders are allowed
to flourish. It was not, I reflected, a very good advertisement
for the capitalist system which, temporarily at least, had
broken down here even more calamitously than it has in
Europe and America. Even when I made every allowance
for the innate improvidence of the Malay, there was no mis-
taking the poverty of these long queues. They were testimony, more convincing than any accountant's figures, to the
extent to which the slump had shaken the economic foundations of the island.

Nearly seventy years ago Wallace, the great Scottish
naturalist and forerunner of Darwin, had described Java as
"the richest, the best cultivated, and the best governed tropical island in the world." It might still be all these things, but
for the moment, or perhaps for ever, something had gone
wrong. Economic development or exploitation—the choice
of words depends on the economic view-point—had brought
with it the inevitable result, an extraordinary increase in
population, and to-day Java with its 40,000,000 supports a
larger population than any other area of the same size in the
world. The Dutch had done their economic job with all the
organising talent and industrious genius of their race. They
had come from Holland in their thousands to take back the
wealth of the East to their own country. To-day there were
four times as many Dutch per every thousand head of population in the Dutch East Indies as there were British in British
India, and very nearly as many Dutch in actual numbers in
Java alone as British in India. But of these 275,000 Dutch,
how many were pure whites? No one knew. To-day in Holland itself one inhabitant in every hundred is said to have
Malay blood in his veins. And here in Java the proportion
was vastly higher.

When, too, did a half-caste become a Dutchman? The

Dutch themselves had a vulgar definition: when he wore shoes and made his water standing up. But there were many half-castes who had never worn shoes. I had seen some of them in the queues before the pawnshop. I thought again of that white-washed half-caste skull fixed to the wall beside the Portuguese church. Among the half-castes of to-day, perhaps even among the more successful, there might be other Pieter Elberfelds, more dangerous and more cunning because they were better educated. There were half-castes in the Volksraat, the limited parliament of the Dutch East Indies. They sat with the native Javanese in the nationalist bloc.

After my siesta I set out in the opposite direction to explore Weltevreden and the new suburbs extending to Meester Cornelis. Here are the government buildings, the offices of the great shipping companies, the museums, the spacious Koningsplein with its racecourse in the middle, the Waterlooplein with its football grounds, shady public gardens and pleasure grounds, row after row of red-tiled houses, very neat, very Dutch, rather uniform in style, and each with its well-trimmed flower garden, and scores of statues to the great Dutch governors-general and captains who had created the glory of the Dutch Colonial Empire.

The Dutch preceded the British in the East. They had been the distributors for Europe of the Eastern goods brought home by the Portuguese. About eighty years after the Portuguese conquest of Malacca they came to the conclusion that the wealth which hitherto they had only distributed might be captured on the spot.

The Dutch sent out the first expedition in 1595. It was a failure, but with the same perseverance which has enabled them to fight the sea at home, they stuck to their self-appointed task. In contrast to the British domination of Malaya, the story of their conquest of the East Indies is written in blood. They drove out the Portuguese, they fought and bested the British, they suppressed, sometimes with great cruelty, the resistance of the natives—a resistance which has manifested itself in numerous wars and rebellions lasting from the days of the first Dutch settlement right up to the beginning of the present century.

It is a fascinating story of triumph in the face of almost insurmountable difficulties. Had the men who won this triumph been Englishmen or Americans, their names to-day would be household words throughout the world. But when Holland lost her sea supremacy in the eighteenth century she became a small nation, and England and America, much to their disadvantage, for there is a lesson in the decline of former empires, do not read the history of small nations.

The Dutch have not forgotten their colonial heroes, and Batavia, exactly two hundred years older than Singapore and therefore far richer in historical associations, has many shrines to their memory. On the Waterlooplein there is a fine bronze statue to Jan Pieterson Coen, the founder of Batavia and the greatest of all Dutch governors-general. The town came into being as a result of a concerted attempt by the British and the Bantamese to drive the Dutch out of Eastern Java. They besieged the Dutch in Fort Jacatra and had nearly forced it to surrender, when Coen arrived with his fleet and raised the siege. On the site of the fort he founded the new capital of Batavia in 1619.

Coen, in particular, and indeed most of these early Dutchmen, had all the austerity, the courage and the rigidity of the early Calvinists. The Bible was their text-book, and in it they found a pretext and a justification for their frequent cruelties. In the tropics they wore the same sombre clothes that are portrayed in the portraits of Rembrandt and Hals. In their sugar-loaf hats, their black capes relieved only by their white ruffles and the sword-hilt at their side, and their square-toed shoes they must have presented a far more imposing and more dignified picture to the native than the white ducks of the modern Dutchman.

Farther out we came to the Entrée Gondangdia, and there I saw the finest European monument in the East. This is the memorial to General van Heutz, the Dutch Clive, who died at Montreux in 1924. The monument, grandiose in design yet graceful in its lines, is very modern, and its huge frieze of carved figures is reminiscent of the late Charles Jagger's artillery memorial opposite Hyde Park Gate.

Heutz himself, whom I met in Montreux after the war, was of the stuff of which modern dictators are made: a rugged plain-living soldier without frills and without illusions. He never asked his men to do anything that he was not prepared to do himself. There was very little that he was not prepared to do. "Goddam", according to local legend, was the longest speech he ever made. His favourite minute on reports from his subordinates raising difficulties to some new scheme of road-building or town-planning which he had put forward was "Start to-morrow". As the man who finally quelled the long revolt of the Achinese in Western Sumatra, he has become a legendary figure. Were he alive and in his prime to-day he would be without doubt the Fascist dictator of Holland. Dr. Colijn, the present Prime Minister and strong man of Holland, whose work on colonial administration is known to everyone as the "Colijn Bible", served his apprenticeship as van Heutz's adjutant in the East Indies.

At Gondangdia Ahmat suggested turning back. But I ordered him to push on to Meester Cornelis. He shrugged his shoulders as though to indicate that there was nothing worth seeing there. He was right. It was like any Dutch suburb. Its attraction had to be suggested by my own imagination. It was here that in 1811 the British expeditionary force had fought the decisive battle for the conquest of Java, then temporarily under the French-controlled Batavian Republic and administered by Marshall Daendels, a Dutchman who had taken service under Napoleon and had been made Governor-General by him.

The man who officially approved the British expedition was Lord Minto, the Governor-General of India. The soldier who led it to victory was General Auchmuty. But the man who advocated and inspired its despatch was Raffles, whose reward after the victory was the Lieutenant-Governorship of Java.

The modern Dutchman admires Raffles, but has no affection for him. Perhaps, if I were a Dutchman, I should feel the same. For Raffles saw the value of Java, and was heart-broken when, after the Congress of Vienna, Britain returned it to Holland. I smiled cynically when I turned to Meester Cornelis in my Dutch guide-book. The place was dismissed in one sentence—"nothing of interest here to the tourist".

Incidentally, supporters of the League of Nations and other believers in the progress of civilisation may be reminded that the Treaty of Vienna was in every respect a fairer and less vindictive treaty than the Treaty of Versailles. If we gave back Java to the Dutch because friendship with the Low Countries had become a first principle of British foreign policy, the return of Senegal and Corsica to France was a magnanimity which, in 1919, would have brought Mr. Lloyd George's Government to instant defeat.

It is perhaps unfair to the Dutch to say so, but the fact remains that the two greatest benefactors of Java were an Englishman and a Dutchman who preferred to serve Napoleon. During the six years of his lieutenant-governorship Raffles laid the foundation of much that is best in the administration of Java to-day. Daendels was the great road-builder of the island and the founder of modern Batavia. It was he who removed the European settlement from the malaria-infested lower town to the present Weltevreden.

On my way back from Meester Cornelis the clouds which assemble nearly every afternoon during the rainy season broke, and in the open car I was drenched to the skin. I went home, took a hot bath, and dined early and alone. Returning to my rooms after dinner, I ran into Miedl. He had spent a harassing day doing business with the hard-headed Dutch. He liked the English, but he spoke no word of our language. Because of my knowledge of German he clung to me. With German thoroughness he had planned a motor-trip for the next day—a three hundred kilometre circular journey over the Puntiak, including Buitenzorg, Bandoeng, Lembang, the famous crater of Tangkoeban Prahoe and the other mountain peaks of the Preanger district. He was starting at six in the morning. Would I go with him? I accepted without a moment's hesitation.

Elated by the prospect of a journey so much after my own heart, I sat down in my verandah sitting-room to smoke a pipe before turning in. The rain had long since ceased, and for a while I surrendered myself to the beauty of the star-lit night. Presently a terrestrial object arrested my attention. My rooms were in a corner of a courtyard behind the main building of the hotel. In the suite immediately at right angles to my own I suddenly caught sight of a white woman. Two white arms, leaning on the verandah ledge, supported a face whose pallor was exaggerated by the electric light above her. Her mouth was half-open. Her eyes, large and of a watery blue colour, stared vacantly into the night. She could not have been more than twenty-five. If not exactly beautiful, she was decidedly pretty. For five minutes I watched her. She never changed her position. Never have I seen boredom so epitomised in any human face. I went into my bedroom, undressed, and came out again to the verandah. She was still there, still as motionless as a statue. By now I was seriously puzzled. Was she mad? Had some sudden grief—the death of a child or a lover—afflicted her? My curiosity was soon satisfied. Presently I heard the sound of erratic footsteps stumbling along the concrete pavement which ran round the courtyard. A big heavy man, unmistakably drunk, was lurching and swaying towards me. He bumped against my verandah wall, steadied himself, and then entered the suite next door. The girl slowly raised her elbows from the ledge, turned her back, and went inside. I heard a thick voice say "Sorry, darling," and then silence.

I discovered afterwards that they were Australians on their honeymoon. The "pahit" drinking on the front verandah of the hotel had been too much for the husband. It was a cameo of European life in the East which would have provided the brilliant Mr. Somerset Maugham with the material for a short story.

CHAPTER TWO

MIEDL WAS PUNCTUAL the next morning, and a few minutes after six we set out in a high-powered open car. We had two Malay chauffeurs who, until they were restrained, drove furiously. The road surface, as nearly everywhere in Java, was excellent, but Miedl's seventeen stone, bobbing up and down on the back springs, made me both nervous and compassionate. By dint of frequent persuasion and, finally, of threats I succeeded in inducing the driver to slow down to a modest sixty miles an hour.

It was not as if we had the road to ourselves. Our way to Buitenzorg lay through flat country with rice-fields on every side and frequent native kampongs. In the early morning coolness it was fresh and green and pretty enough. But my sense of enjoyment was marred by our chauffeur's nerve-racking dodging between the hordes of natives on the road. Nowhere in the world have I seen what was, in effect, a country road so densely thronged. On the whole thirty odd miles stretch to Buitenzorg, I do not think that we ever went more than forty yards without passing someone.

There were men alone laden like beasts of burden and carrying huge weights on their "pikulan", a pliant bamboo pole carried across the shoulder. Similarly laden men were followed by their families, and a Javanese family is generally a cricket team. Boys and girls over ten carried little "pikulans". The wife brought up the rear with one child at her breast and leading the next youngest by the hand. Although it was Sunday, everyone was working. Cyclists, also carrying produce of some sort to the market, were numerous.

Every now and then, to add to the terrors of the road, a small red motor-bus, driven as furiously as our own car, would charge down on us and miss our mudguards by a last-minute miracle. The buses were Chinese owned. Curiously enough, their names were blazoned on them in English, and the name was always feminine: "Miss Canton" or "Miss Tiang Ho".

One contrast with British Malaya struck me forcibly. Our Malays are lazy, happy-go-lucky, cheerful aristocrats. Leisure is the keynote of their philosophy. They are loquacious. They have a love of words. They believe that a proper command of language is essential to good luck in fishing and hunting, which since the Europeans suppressed fighting and piracy are the only proper pursuits of a self-respecting Malay. Sustained work never appealed to them. Coolie work they despise. In British Malaya every Chinaman hopes to become a capitalist. But he starts as a coolie, and to-day, together with the imported Indian Tamil, he still provides the coolie labour. Here in Java the position is reversed. The Chinaman is the merchant, the shopkeeper, and the big and little capitalist. There are no Chinese rickisha-pullers in Java, no Chinese coolie class. The Javanese, the Sundanese, the Maduranese, and the other native races of the Island are the "coolies". Those whom we passed on our way to Buitenzorg were taciturn and uncomplaining. There was the same dumb sadness in their eyes that one sees in an overworked horse. And these were Sundanese, by reputation and, indeed, in truth, the gayest of the native races of Java.

At Buitenzorg we stopped for an hour to look at the Botanical Gardens. I am no horticulturist, but I found the gardens disappointing. I had expected a riot of colour. The glory of the gardens is their wealth of rare tropical trees and plants, and to my untutored eye this greenery was monotonous.

I had one pilgrimage to make—to the memorial erected to the memory of Lady Raffles. This monument is a slight Dutch atonement for an insult of over a hundred years' standing. It was in June 1823 that Raffles sailed for the last time from Singapore. He was only forty-two, but his work was done. Like Clive and Hastings he was sailing back to trouble and to Britain's habitual indifference to the work of her servants overseas. But the troubles began long before he reached home. The ship on which he sailed had to call at Batavia, and, as Lady Raffles was far advanced towards childbirth, Raffles, much against his will, had perforce to write to the Dutch Governor-General to ask permission for his wife to land. Baron van der Capellen's reply was couched in stiff terms. It expressed the Governor-General's surprise that a man like Raffles, who had advocated the retention of Java by the British, should come near to Java at all, let alone propose to set foot on Javanese soil.

We had some difficulty in finding the monument, and Miedl, dripping under the scorching sun, failed, with much puffing and panting to understand my zeal. At last an attendant put us on the right track. The monument takes the form of a pedestal with an urn and a plaque. It stands in a little rotunda in an attractive grassy grove not far from the pathway. Unfortunately, it was almost the only thing I saw in Java that was ill-cared-for and untidy. The matter has been mentioned to the Governor-General, and I have no doubt that it has already been put right.

To me the most attractive feature of the gardens was the Governor-General's palace. It stands in the middle of the gardens and is completely shut off in its own grounds. The approach is by a magnificent avenue of lofty kenari trees which form an archway a hundred feet high. There is a huge English park with deer. Before the palace, reflecting its long one-storied outline, is the famous lotus-lake.

The Dutch civil servants are a hard-working and, on the whole, very efficient body of men. Their standard of life is far lower than that of their British prototypes in British Malaya. Their wardrobes and their houses are more modest than ours. But the Governor-General is in a different category. The Governor of Singapore rules over rather less than four millions of people. The Governor-General of the Dutch East Indies is the overlord of nearly seventy millions. In Holland he corresponds to the Viceroy of India, and in the East

Indies he is given the appurtenances and the residences which comport with the dignity of that exalted position.

From Buitenzorg the landscape changed. We were approaching the mountains by the famous road, part of Daendels' great highway, over the 4000 feet high Puntiak. The humid flatness of Batavia had given us no indication of this fairy-land which lay behind it. At first the road seemed to rise and fall in a series of easy switchbacks. Then we began to mount by hairpin bends until the air became cool and finally cold. On the lower slopes there was growing coffee, giving way, as we rose higher, to tea. No wonder that Wallace had said that Java was the best cultivated island in the world. Every inch of soil was put to use.

Indeed, the wealth of the Dutch East Indies is a miracle that never ceases to excite the wonder of the visitor. From them come 92 per cent. of the world's cinchona production, 84 per cent. of the world's cocaine, 79 per cent. of the world's capok, 71 per cent. of the world's pepper, 14 per cent of the world's tea and 6 per cent. of the world's coffee. Add to these the fact that the East Indies take third place in the world's production of sugar, that, after British Malaya, they are the world's largest producers of tin and rubber, and that, in addition to these semi-monopolies, they have such other valuable resources as tobacco, petroleum, palm oil, and copra. Bear in mind that nearly all this wealth comes from the one island of Java and that the sources which produce it were introduced from other countries: rubber from Brazil, sugar-cane from the West Indies, tobacco from Europe, tea from China and Assam, cinchona from the Andes, cocoa from South America, coffee from Arabia, and oil palms from West Africa, and you have some idea both of the enterprise of the Dutch as colonists and of the fabulous richness of the world's most fertile island.

We were fortunate in the morning weather. Looking down on us from the right, majestic and sinister, were the twin peaks of Goenoeng Pangerango and Goenoeng Gedeh.

S

At this time of the year both mountains, nearly 9000 feet high, are usually hidden in the clouds. To-day, they stood out clear in a proximity that was overawing. Like so many of the Java mountains, Gedeh is a volcano which from time to time erupts in a violent and death-dealing manner. The last eruption was in 1899.

Gedeh with its yawning crater, sharp as a jagged razor, looks down on Tjipanas, the highest and most attractive of all the Governor-General's seats. The site is enchantingly beautiful. Dutch flowers were growing in the gardens. Close by was a little mountain lake, its placid waters shining like silver in the sunlight. And here again I marvelled at the material ingenuity and bee-like industry of the Dutch. Even the mountains are put to the use of man. The lower slopes of Pangerango have been turned into a botanical garden for the cultivation of plants and trees which grow only in high altitudes. There is even a laboratory and a guest-house for students of botany.

As we drew near to the top of the pass, an overhanging cliff shut out the sunlight. The air became suddenly colder, affecting the bladders of our Malay chauffeurs and forcing us to stop. My sense of the supernatural, always at its keenest in the mountains, overwhelmed me. There was something uncanny in this grotto with the eeriness of its semi-darkness accentuated by the blue sky above us. I felt suddenly uneasy and slightly afraid. Then in a moment or two we turned the bend, and there far below us, with the rolling line of mountains forming its background, was a vast plain, intersected by rivers, its rich and varied vegetation woven into a waving pattern of every shade of green.

Java is too cultivated and too over-populated to satisfy entirely my standard of grandeur. But this Puntiak view is superb and would gladden and assuredly has gladdened the heart of every picture-postcard photographer. And it is only one of the many similar views which are to be seen in almost every part of Java.

Here there was a small hotel, and we stopped to order the breakfast which our early start had postponed. It seemed an unaesthetic proceeding strangely in contrast with our ethereal surroundings. But we were not alone in our materialism. The hotel verandah was crowded with Dutch families, drinking beer and eating huge slices of bread thickly spread with butter and chunks of cold fish.

The Dutch are a curious race. Their cultural and intellectual standards are far higher than those of the British or the Americans. They have a genuine love and understanding of art in all its forms. This culture is not confined to a small class of intellectuals. Its roots are in the nation. During my stay in Batavia I had my hair cut by a Dutch barber. While he was performing on my locks, the wireless began to play the *Liebestod*. I had to wait in sweating impatience, while the barber, his eyes raised in rapture to the ceiling, beat the time with his scissors until the record was finished. His enthusiasm was genuine, but neither in his case nor in the case of most Dutch men and women is it allowed to interfere with the national capacity for food and drink. Here in this mountain hotel everything that the ingenuity of the proprietor could imagine had been combined to remind his clients of their native Holland. The building was Dutch in design. The cups and plates and glasses were decorated with pictures of Dutch towns and with Dutch proverbs. Prominently displayed on the wooden wall was the Dutch drinking verse:

> "Drink ik te veel, dan sterf ik;
> Drink ik niet, dan bederf ik;
> Beter te viel gedronken en gestorven
> Dan niet gedronken en bedorven."

> "If I drink too much I die,
> If I drink not I decay;
> Better to drink too much and die
> Than not to drink and to decay."

The clients seemed to be doing their best to live up to this aphorism.

The forty miles' run, more or less downhill, to Bandoeng was in the nature of an anti-climax. Not that the route was dull or the scenery unattractive. There were moments when my eyes leapt to meet the challenge of Nature. We crossed several rivers spanned by slender graceful bridges. One river, the Tjitaroem, splashed its way through the greenest of gorges, its waters in contrast to most tropical rivers as clear as a Scottish mountain stream. Again to Miedl's astonishment I bade the chauffeur stop while I got out to look into the depths below. The British in Malaya have recently introduced trout into the mountain rivers of Cameron Highlands. Were there trout here? I should have been thrilled to catch a trout on fly within a few degrees of the Equator. Unfortunately, my Malay vocabulary fell short of the word for trout, and even with the help of signs I was unable to make them understand. Reluctantly I came to the conclusion that trout had not entered into the Dutchman's all-embracing scheme of things.

Bandoeng itself is a mountain city situated more than 2000 feet above sea-level. It is therefore nearly twice as high as the highest village in Scotland. It is also a creation of the energetic Marshal Daendels, but it is only since 1884, when the railway from Batavia was opened, that it has become important. Its population, now over 160,000, has nearly doubled within the last fifteen years. To-day, it is the third largest city in Java and is certainly by far the most attractive to a European. Its climate is magnificent, hot by day but nearly always cool by night, and why the Dutch do not make it their capital is surprising. Probably the Dutch have their own good reasons.

Bandoeng is already the chief military town of the Dutch East Indies and is the seat of the Commander-in-Chief. The army is partly professional and partly conscripted. Every inhabitant of the East Indies is liable to military service between the ages of eighteen and thirty-two. The professional army also includes Dutch soldiers from Holland, but the bulk of the force, approximately 40,000 strong, is composed of native soldiery. Dutch and native soldiers mix more or less together and have quarters in the same barracks. There is a certain number of Javanese officers, especially in the army medical service, and among the white officers a liberal sprinkling of half-castes.

The army is not impressive and looks as if it had been stinted of money. We watched a battalion swinging down the street on its way to new barracks. Both officers and men were poorly turned out, and Miedl, who regarded them with the critical eye of a German, dismissed them, perhaps too rapidly, as "not serious". I discovered that this judgment was not entirely his own. The German colony in Batavia, who are very pro-Dutch and who get on much better with the Dutch residents than do the local British, had told him that everything in Java was first-class except the army and navy. The army, however, has been efficient enough in its local wars. As far as danger from outside is concerned, I suspect that up to now the thrifty Dutch have been content to rely on the belief that in her own interests Britain will never allow an outside Power to lay a hand on the Dutch East Indies.

If the Javanese infantry look slipshod and unmartial, there is good fighting material among the other races of the Dutch East Indies, especially in the outer islands. In the communist revolt of December 1926 and January 1927 it was the Christian Ambonese troops who, when certain Javanese units had wavered, saw red and by a bayonet charge broke the back of the rising in Batavia at a moment when it threatened to assume serious dimensions.

After a leisurely drive round the town, we went into the leading hotel for luncheon. Here we met the two pilots of the Amsterdam airplane which had conveyed us from Singapore to Batavia. They were fine types, placid, friendly, and unassuming. Selefis, a Dutch kilometre millionaire, that is, an airman who has flown more than a million kilometres, impressed me enormously. He neither makes light of nor exaggerates the difficulties and dangers of his strenuous life. He never talks of them. His great hobby is big game shooting, and, as Bandoeng is the headquarters of the K.L.M. pilots during their short stay in Java, he has occasional opportunities of indulging in his favourite sport. I should have thought that his life was strenuous enough without this extra exertion.

These Dutch pilots have only ten days on land between their long flights. During this time they must always be within telephone call, for if, as sometimes happens, the pilot of the previous airplane falls ill, one of the newly-arrived pilots has to take his place. This means twelve days' continuous flying from Europe and back again. And the pay, as in the case of the captains of the great ocean liners, is very inadequate.

Selefis advised us to spend part of the afternoon in driving out to Tangkoeban Prahoe, another crater about twenty miles away towards the north-east. I accepted the suggestion with alacrity. I had no wish to stay longer in Bandoeng. I recognised its claims to be a model city and the last word in Dutch colonial efficiency. But it is a completely modern city, and after a glut of years spent in modern cities I had come East to escape from modernity.

Luncheon had restored our capacity for sight-seeing, and we set out with a refreshed optimism. The optimism was necessary. While we had been indoors, huge black clouds had darkened the horizon. The air had become breathless and unaccountably still. As we began to ascend the steep road, we seemed to be driving straight into the clouds. The view was even finer than our morning view from the Puntiak Pass. The mountains were now black and threatening. On the dark sky-line they looked so near that they seemed to be closing in on us.

At Lembang, a little village about twelve miles from Bandoeng, our chauffeur pulled up and pointed to an extraordinary building at the side of the road. It looked like the bridge of an enormous super-dreadnought. It was the kind of freak palace which a pre-war Moscow millionaire might have built for himself. "Rumah Biretti" (Biretti's house), said the chauffeur with a grin. He had no need to say more. I had not been twelve hours in Batavia without having had the story of Biretti told me by half a dozen people. We had discussed it with the pilots in the Bandoeng hotel less than an hour before.

Biretti was a half-caste genius who had made a fortune as a newspaper and news-agency king. He was a self-made man of inordinate ambition. His fortune, however, seemed to have solid foundations, and his power and his influence were said to extend far beyond his newspaper activities. Then in the late autumn of 1934 he paid a visit to Holland. In well-informed circles it was whispered that the slump, which had ruined so many Dutchmen in the East, had hit him hard. On his way back to Java he was killed in the unexplained disaster of the K.L.M. airplane which crashed in the Syrian desert in January, 1935.

These are the facts. But rumour tells a different story, and after the disaster Biretti's name was bandied from mouth to mouth. This was the first major accident on the Amsterdam-Batavia line, and Dutch pride found an excuse for the mishap in the fable that Biretti, in a dramatic suicide, had shot the pilot through the head. Riotous imagination added lurid details to this fantastic story. Biretti had been in league with the Japanese. He had made away with himself because he was on the verge of exposure. All that was true in these stories was that Biretti was dead and that, whatever his virtues or his faults, Java had lost one of its most remarkable citizens.

His house gave some indication of his character. It would have been fantastic anywhere. Here it was ludicrous and incongruous. No expense had been spared on it. The glass for its windows had been brought from Venice. Its gardens had tiled paths. Goldfish swam in its artificial pond. It was called the "Isola Bella" after the island palace on Lake Maggiore. It looked repellently new. The name had been as fatal to him as it was to be a few weeks later to the reputation of Mr. Ramsay MacDonald and Sir John Simon when they met Mussolini at the Italian "Isola Bella" during the Stresa conference and failed to warn him about his Abyssinian ambitions. But with its wonderful vista of the vast horseshoe-shaped mountain range, the situation of this Javanese Isola Bella was unique. It was a site that only a Napoleon would have chosen.

In spite of the growing and unnatural darkness, we pushed on another four miles to a point where the road bends sharply inwards until it touches the bottom slopes of Tangkoeban Prahoe with its great twin craters. The name means "overturned prahu". It suits the shape of the mountain, but like all Javanese volcanoes there is a myth attached to it. A sultan of bygone days had a son who refused to marry according to his father's wishes. He sailed away with the bride of his own heart and was wrecked. Presumably, in those days Java was under water. Be this as it may, bride and bridegroom are now at the bottom of one of the craters. Is not their upturned boat, which forms the mountain peak, there for all eyes to see!

At that moment the crater was frowning down on us from an ink-black sky. Standing high above the tree line, its stony crest, barren and desolate, seemed like a cap of death on the body of luxuriant life below. The electricity in the air seemed to communicate its evil intent to our souls. One felt that at any moment it would lean forward and crush us. Suddenly a jagged flame rent the sky and fell into the very heart of the crater. It was followed by a roll of thunder that seemed to come from all sides. The clouds emptied their reservoir. The storm had come with one clap.

We had no time to be afraid. The rain was like a waterspout. Before we could fix the hood of the car, our clothes hung to us like bathing-suits. By the time we had reached Bandoeng again, the road was like a Highland burn in spate. I have been in many storms in many countries. But never have I known a storm break with such suddenness or with such volcanic fury.

At Bandoeng, after having had our clothes dried, we decided to return to Batavia by train and to let our Malays bring back the car when the rain stopped. It was a wise and fortunate decision, for the railway stretch between Padalarang and Poerwakarta is unrivalled for its beauty.

As it was a Sunday, the station at Bandoeng was crowded, and, until the train came in, I watched the crowd of natives with a growing fascination. The women, much freer than our Malays, seemed to have smiles for everyone, for the Sundanese are the wantons of Java. Some, obviously the well-to-do, were dressed in European or semi-European clothes and were attended by the usual large family, the boys in sailor-suits and the girls in one-piece dresses with basket hats. Others again were in the native sarong and loose-hanging blouse or "baju". I saw tender scenes of farewell between Dutch soldiers, who were being transferred to Batavia, and their native Sundanese sweethearts. More than one woman had a baby in her arms to remember her departing lover by.

With some difficulty we secured two window seats opposite each other, and I settled down to endure as best I could what I thought would be a steam-bath inferno. But this country of miracles performed another miracle for our benefit. Soon after we left Bandoeng, the great blanket of cloud rose and remained suspended in the heavens, leaving a thin coral strip of clear sky on the horizon. Presently the setting sun dropped slowly from the cloud-blanket, shedding a flood of soft light on the landscape. Below us were deep gorges unlike any that I had ever seen. Their steep slopes were terraced with rice-fields so that each valley looked like a vast amphitheatre with standing rows of green spectators. Rivers, spanned by those graceful bridges which only the Dutch seem to build in the East, ran through them like a silver corridor. Here and there native villages nestled in a grove of slender palms and bamboos.

The effect of this curious sunset, more like moonlight or the lime-lighting of a stage, was unreal and startlingly beautiful. On a tiny lake bordered with willowy reeds I saw a fisherman in a boat—a motionless silhouette of black on a silver surface. I admired the graceful poise of his body, as he leant over his lines or nets. Here was the great enigma of the East. Was this a man—and there were millions like him—who had found in resignation the way of life and in patient waiting the road to the fulfilment of his higher aspirations? Or was he what the Dutch capitalists and the Chinese bourgeois said he was—a willing beast of burden with no other thought than of the four cents a day which now have to suffice for his daily existence? Time which reveals all things would reveal this, too, at the hour of its own choosing. For myself I was content to be grateful to the storm which had enabled me to see this ethereal loveliness.

That night in Batavia I dined with Miedl and two Dutch bankers. As they wished to discuss business, I left them early and went out into the broad main street before the hotel. After the rain the air was cool or less hot, which in Batavia amounts to the same thing, but the street was nearly empty. The traffic had ceased, and there was a pleasant absence of noise. Occasional shadowy figures passed me by: women in pairs leaving a faint aroma of cheap scent in their train and lithe boys with their coloured kerchiefs cunningly fashioned into a becoming headdress and their sarongs falling in a straight line to their ankles. Now and then a woman would smile and whisper "Tuan". Sometimes a boy would make a furtive half-turn and bare his teeth in a significant grin.

Twenty-five years before my curiosity and even my sense of adventure might have been stirred. Now I was merely depressed. I was back in man-made civilisation. Batavia had suffered more severely from the economic depression than Singapore. Its vice had more hungry mouths to feed and was more open.

CHAPTER THREE

I HAVE ALWAYS been an early riser. The habit, developed in my youth in Malaya, has never left me. Yet on the next morning the telephone rang in my room before I had finished dressing. It was the Governor-General's secretary. Jonkheer de Jonge had returned. His Excellency would receive me at eleven o'clock.

Five minutes before the appointed time I was in his palace, a long one-storied white Greek temple with pillars of false doric. With not more than a moment's delay I was ushered into a high-walled room, very cool and comfortably but simply furnished. There was a big table in one corner with a photograph of a girl whom I took to be His Excellency's daughter. A large map of Indonesia hung on the wall. As I entered, a very tall man with iron-grey hair and moustache came forward to meet me. His clear-cut features had a pleasant expression. He had the long-tapered fingers of an artist or an aristocrat. His figure, lank and lean as an Englishman's, astonished me most. He was the only slim Dutchman of over fifty that I had ever seen. His eyes looked tired but were unmistakeably friendly. His English, spoken with an exceptionally pure accent, was excellent. He had been a director of the Royal Dutch oil combine and had lived for nine years in London. He still had a house in Wimbledon. Almost his first question was regarding the present prospects of selling it.

I told him that I was revisiting the East after a long absence and that I should probably write an account of my impressions. He was quite frank about the situation in the Dutch East Indies and made no attempt to minimise the difficulties. The world slump had hit the Dutch Eastern possessions, and especially Java, harder than most countries. Revenue had decreased. Taxation had been raised to its utmost limit. The budget had had to be cut down. The grant for education had been reduced by half. Britain had been partly responsible for some of Java's economic troubles. The once fabulously prosperous Javanese sugar industry had been sorely crippled by the action of British India in shutting the door on Javanese sugar and setting up her own sugar factories. In 1929 there had been over two hundred thriving sugar factories in Java. Now there were not more than thirty.

I learnt that the Dutch followed the political as well as the economic situation in British India very closely. Liberal concessions by the British Government in India always cause repercussions in Java, and there are few Dutch officials and fewer Dutch business men who believe in the policy of yielding too quickly to nationalist aspirations. Jonkheer de Jonge was a great admirer of Lord Willingdon, of whom something in his manner reminded me. I surmised that he was not so enthusiastic about Lord Irwin's policy. The Dutch call de Jonge their Willingdon. His predecessor, Jonkheer de Graeff, had been a governor-general of the Irwin type and his term of office had been marked by similar concessions. It had ended in a communist rising and in the arrest and banishment of the native leaders. As a result he had been blamed both by the natives and by the Dutch residents of the East Indies. Jonkheer de Jonge had taken the precaution not to fall between these two stools. He had concentrated on the economic problem. He believed in a fair deal for the Javanese, but he was not prepared to surrender Dutch security of political tenure to the Javanese nationalists.

"My predecessor made too many promises," he told me frankly. "I always preface my remarks to the nationalists with one sentence: 'We Dutch have been here for three hundred years; we shall remain here for another three hundred. After that we can talk.'"

On the whole the Dutch are rather more reactionary than the British in their attitude to the nationalist problem. But, whether by accident or design, they succeed in alternating liberal governors-general with conservative governors-general with considerable success. This policy of gradualness with a Westinghouse brake has much to recommend it. A too liberal portion of reform would be difficult for the natives to digest. The Dutch East Indies are full of political as well as real volcanoes. An unyielding reaction might cause a second Krakatau. On his own admission Jonkheer de Jonge was one of the brakes.

I turned the conversation to the question of Japan, which invariably crops up in every Anglo-Dutch conversation in the East. Dutch-Japanese trade negotiations were proceeding at that moment in Batavia. The Dutch had been the first Europeans to open direct trade negotiations with Japan. They had established a trading station there as far back as 1800. They had given to Japan her first warship and had taught her to build others. They were the fathers of the Japanese Navy, and to-day certain parts of Japanese ships still have Dutch names. I had heard the Japanese bogey mentioned frequently in British Malaya. The Dutch, more exposed and less able to defend themselves, were likely to be more alarmed. I remembered an opinion of the Japanese, expressed by one of the Dutch traders eighty years ago: "a very resolute folk; lambs in their own land, but almost devils outside." I wanted to know if the Governor-General shared this view.

Once again he was disarmingly frank. There were only 4000 Japanese resident in the Dutch East Indies, but Japanese commercial competition was increasing and had become formidable. It was true that the Japanese were inclined to be aggressive and to demand concessions. They had suggested that, as the Dutch did little to develop their so-called "Outer Possessions", they might be allowed to assist in the work of progress.

The Dutch had taken a firm line in the trade negotiations. Their economic position was very strong. Japan bought little from Holland, but her market in the Dutch East Indies was very valuable to her. Admittedly, the Dutch were weak in the military sense. But the Japanese were ill-adapted for tropical colonisation. They wanted an outlet for their goods and for their surplus population. They would seek it elsewhere. The danger to the Dutch East Indies had been exaggerated.

He rose from his chair and taking a ruler pointed to a place on the map. "That's where Siam will one day cede territory for a canal to Japan or build it herself with Japanese money", he said, "and then goodbye to Singapore." The place to which he pointed was Kra, the isthmus situated in Siamese territory at the narrowest point of the long Malay peninsula, about eight hundred miles north of Singapore. I recalled a conversation with my friend Victor Lowinger, the former Surveyor-General of Malaya and now the very able and active representative of British Malaya on the international tin and rubber restriction committees. Twenty-six years ago he had been surveying the then very vaguely fixed Siamese boundary. The local Malays gave him a great welcome, thinking that he had come to take them over for the British Government. At the time Siam was negotiating for a British loan. Britain could have had the Kra isthmus for the mere chink of her money.

Then nobody cared. Now Japanese influence in Siam was extending rapidly. Japanese imports to the country had doubled within two years. Siamese naval cadets were being trained in Japanese ships. Siam had given the orders for her small navy to Japanese shipbuilding yards.

I asked His Excellency what truth there was in the rumours that I had heard of recent Anglo-Dutch negotiations for the common defence of their Malayan possessions. He turned the question with a laugh.

"I don't need any agreement with Britain," he said. Obviously, like many other Dutchmen, he believed that Britain could not afford to allow Japan to touch a single acre of Dutch East Indian territory. I was not sure. Would Britain fight for New Guinea or the Moluccas? In the present state of Europe it seemed more than doubtful.

There was also the United States to be considered. Because of its repercussions on their own problems, the Dutch followed the situation in the Philippines as closely as they followed the actions and reactions of British policy in India. Their belief in the wealth and potential strength of the American nation was profound and unshakable. They had been disturbed but not unnerved by America's grant of provisional independence to the Philippines and by her promise of complete independence within ten years. Like most Dutchmen and indeed most Englishmen in the East, His Excellency believed that the undertaking would never be carried out. If it were, it would be modified by a comprehensive military alliance between the United States and her former colony.

"And now how can I help you?" We had talked long. His Excellency was a busy and over-worked man. I realised that it was time to go. Hurriedly I asked if he could arrange for me to be received by the Sultan of Djokjakarta, which has always been and is to-day the centre of the Javanese nationalist movement.

He did not refuse, but in his answer I thought I recognised a certain embarrassment. He believed the Sultan was away. The Sultan of Solo would be easier. In any case the interviews would have to be arranged through the local Governor and Resident. There was a rule that no one was allowed to see a native ruler without a Dutch official being present. He would give me a special letter to the Governor at Djokja and to the Resident at Solo and a general letter of recommendation which I could use in Borneo, the Celebes, Bali, Lombok, Timor or anywhere in the whole Archipelago where the Dutch writ ran. He would also instruct the local authorities privately to assist me in every way.

I thanked him from a full heart. He had been more than kind. I formed the opinion that he was a strong man, without the brilliancy and *souplesse* of the politician, but with the assured efficiency of the successful business man, and that what he said he meant. My impression was confirmed. Within half-an-hour of my return to my hotel my letters were on my table.

They were generously worded. They were accompanied by a note that if I were in any difficulty I had only to telephone.

I remained in Batavia for three more days after my interview with the Governor-General. They were something of an anti-climax and rather frivolously spent. With Miedl I indulged in the famous Rijst-tafel at the Hôtel des Indes. It is a ceremony, accompanied by an elaborate ritual, rather than a feast and to the uninitiated an ordeal rather than a pleasure. We took our places at our table. The Dutch head-waiter asked us if we were ready. Then he made a sign. Already I had spotted a train of about twenty Javanese boys, each carrying two dishes, in the offing. Headed by the mandoer, magnificent in his headdress, it now bore down on us.

Before me I had an array of plates including one as large as a soup tureen. Into the soup tureen went first a mountain of rice. The rice-bearer passed on. He was followed by the knight of the curried chicken. He added his pile and withdrew. Fried duck, fried chicken, eggs, sausages, and a varied collection of fish and meat balls, fried bananas, potatoes and other vegetables followed in bewildering succession until my plate looked like a miniature mountain. Another "boy" sprinkled this Ararat with grated coconut. Then came the turn of the smaller plates. In turn they were served with chutney, pickled cucumber, chillies, Bombay duck, and all the other "Sambal" or side-dishes which supply the digestive stimulants to this orgy.

I looked at Miedl with arched eyebrows. He smiled optimistically, and we fell to. We drank beer and more beer. Soon there were great beads of sweat under my eyes. Long before I had made any impression on the pile before me, I was counted out. Even Miedl, twelve years my junior and as bulky and powerful as an ox, was in distress. He sat back in his chair to get his second wind, attacked again, withdrew and finally surrendered. Holland had conquered both Germany and Britain. I have forgotten the chopped onion. It

did not forget me. I spent the afternoon in disturbed and fit-
ful sleep. I had eaten my first and last Rijst-tafel.

I must not be unkind to the Dutch residents of the East
Indies. The Rijst-tafel is their national dish, and they are inordinately proud of it. For this combination of pride and
gourmandise they are prepared to sacrifice their figure and
to tolerate the unseemly fat which hangs in rolls over the
neck of their "tutup", a white drill coat with high collar
worn buttoned to the top like a military tunic. But they can
work twelve hours a day on it, and I take off my hat to them
as a virile and formidable people. Actually, the best part of
this gargantuan concoction is the krupak, a large crisp bis-
cuit made of rice-flour and flavoured with prawns. It would
make an excellent addition to the cocktail bars of London
and New York.

In due course, I presented my letters to the various bankers
and industrialists to whom I had been recommended. Some
of them were not in Batavia. Those whom I saw impressed
me as earnest and serious men, as industrious as ants and very
German in their attention to the Weltpolitik of business. In
spite of the economic depression they stood up bravely to
their troubles. They were, of course, staunch believers in the
capitalist system and were convinced that in time a disor-
dered world would right itself. They reminded me of our
own Scottish business men. They had the same virtues: thrift,
grit, clear-headedness and an immense capacity for work.
But they had also the same Calvinistic worship of wealth and
the same ruthless determination in their pursuit of it. I could
not help feeling that the same short-sighted neglect on the
part of the employing class which has made the slums of
Glasgow a hotbed of discontent was partly responsible for
the impoverished condition of the Javanese coolie.

These Dutch business men believed in restriction. It had
helped already. It would help more. It seems hard to understand how the burning of coffee in Brazil, the use of wheat
for manure in Canada, the ploughing up of cotton in the

T

United States, and the throwing back of herrings into the sea in Britain can help to right things when there are millions of people in the world who lack bread and clothes, not to mention fish and coffee. Doubtless, the economists in their wisdom must be right, for they have succeeded in foisting their policy on nearly all the civilised countries of the old world and the new. But the logic behind it seems to be the same as the excuse of the Chinese merchant who was about to be shot for profiteering. "I kept my grain", he pleaded, "and let it go in small amounts so that it might last longer. I sold it dear. If I had released it at once and given it for nothing, nobody would have realised how precious it was, and the last state of our people would be worse than it is now." History does not say whether he got off, but I feel that he deserved his life.

I met one industrialist, a big cheerful man and a large employer of labour, who was prepared to talk about other things than economics. He began by asking me how I liked my Dutch wife. I was older than he was, and I suggested politely that I had slept with one before he had.

A Dutch wife, I had better explain, is a long bolster which both British and Dutch in the Malay Archipelago sleep with between their legs in order to prevent chafing. The British christened it a Dutch wife, and the amiable Dutch have accepted the name without affront. Then he told me a story on the same theme. An Australian delegation from the town of Albury had recently been visiting Java. The visit had a curious origin. During the great air-race to Melbourne in 1934 the Dutch airplane, piloted by Moll and Parmentier, was well in the lead, when it had to come down on the racecourse at Albury. The mayor and the officials of the racecourse did all they could to help. But the repairs were not finished before dark, and the Dutch chances of a prize seemed to have disappeared.

Then the mayor had a brain-wave. In order to enable the Dutchmen to take off safely, he ordered all the motor-cars in the district to turn out with their full lights on and to make a ring round the course to show where the stands and fences began. Thanks to this lighting the Dutchmen were able to take off successfully by night and to win the second prize.

In gratitude the Dutch in the East Indies gave the mayor and the leading racecourse officials a free trip to Java. At the end of it the mayor, a crippled old Scot, was asked what souvenir he would like to take home with him. He selected a Dutch wife.

From the Dutch wives we passed to the half-caste problem. My new acquaintance, who had done his military service in Java, was strongly in favour of a clear-cut colour line, and told me that the Dutch in the East Indies had now realised the dangers to which their laxity in this matter had exposed them. This laxity, he said, was at its worst in the army. Dutch officers marked down for promotion are required to sign a form declaring that they are not living with a native woman. They send the woman away and sign the form. Then when their promotion is gazetted they take her back.

With the help of this Dutchman I was now able to check the details of a story which for many years had defied my curiosity. Post-war visitors to Lake Geneva will remember Baroness von Klitzing, an attractive little Javanese lady, known to League visitors as Mimosa, who owned a large property on the Vevey side of the lake and who gave charming parties. She had made three marriages, the last to the German baron whose name and title she bore. She was rather a mysterious person, rich in her own right, and there were many romantic stories of her origin. This is the true story. A certain Baron Baud, a relation of the former governor-general of the same name and a very rich man, was living in Batavia some fifty years ago. He had been having difficulties with a nephew whom he regarded as his heir and who wished to marry against his uncle's wishes.

In a last tremendous scene the uncle swore a solemn oath that, if his nephew did not yield, he would leave all his money to the first person whom he met. The nephew defied him. The uncle rushed out of his house and on the steps he met the little daughter of his Javanese gardener. He kept his vow, adopted the girl, sent her to Holland to be educated, and left his money to her. The girl to whom this miracle happened became the future Queen of Lake Geneva. She died two years ago.

This story is a good illustration of the austerity and obstinacy of the Dutch, especially those of the older generation. On the whole, however, the Dutch business man in the East does not differ greatly in his mental outlook on life from the British business man. In the words of one of the Dutch authors, his ambition aims little higher than a Rolls-Royce, a collier of pearls for his wife, and a large or little estate in Holland when he retires. His chief reward is to hear someone say on the boat on his final journey home: "That's old B——. I put his fortune at £500,000."

But he has many virtues. He is always a good father and generally a good husband. He is devoted to his house and garden, and the saying "an Englishman's home is his castle" applies much more to the Dutchman in Batavia than to the Englishman in Singapore. He is, too, much less snobbish and is content with simple pleasures. Above all, he makes no attempt to keep up appearances beyond his means—the most foolish characteristic of social life in Malaya.

He is certainly more of a formalist than the Englishman. If he invites a stranger to his house, the invitation and the occasion itself will be formal. There is none of that "come along and dine" after a few drinks at the club which is such a pleasant feature of life in Malaya. On ceremonial occasions he is a stickler for his rights. When he goes out to a formal dinner, he expects to be seated in the place appropriate to his position.

On the other hand, he is always ready to laugh at his own foibles. The ranking of business men at big official functions is based largely on incomes and salaries, and one of the best stories I heard in Batavia was of a well-known business man, the head of a local shipping line, who was invited to a gala dinner at Buitenzorg by the Governor-General. When he came back, his friends asked him how he had got on and if he had been given his right place. "The champagne was good," he replied drily. "The food was excellent. My place was not so good. That fool of a private secretary forgot to calculate my bonus."

I had planned to have my evenings in Batavia to myself, but fate and weakness of resolution decided otherwise. One morning I went into the local branch of the Hong Kong and Shanghai Bank to cash a cheque. A pleasant young Englishman attended to my wants.

After examining my letter of credit, he said to me: "Are you the author of *Memoirs of a British Agent?*" When I admitted it, he continued: "There are several members of the English colony here who would like to meet you. Would it bore you to come and have a drink with me this evening at the Hôtel des Indes."

They turned up four strong. There was another young banker, intelligent, self-reliant and a good linguist, who had spent three years in Seremban. There was a keen youngster who was an employee of the British American Tobacco Company. The fourth was the head of a printing machinery firm, an older man who had spent ten years in Batavia and who had a remarkable knowledge of local history and an amusing and cynical way of imparting it to others. All four spoke Malay fluently. Two of them had learnt Dutch. I gathered that their business life in Java was not entirely a bed of roses. There were one or two British firms in Java, one over a hundred years old, which, until the depression, had done a wonderful business in the East Indies. The British American Tobacco Company, too, had a privileged position. It had its own factories in the island and, as the whole population smoked, sold millions of cigarettes daily. But the British import firms, the branches of British banks and the local agencies of British merchant houses, had numerous difficulties. The Dutch were hard in business. Their policy was nationalist, and by high taxation and other discriminatory measures they did their best to stamp out foreign competition. They extended this exclusiveness to their social life, and apart from business my new English friends saw little of them. The Dutch were domesticated, resigned to a long stay in Java and anchored to their families. My English friends were bachelors at a loose end; here only for a few years and at any moment likely to be transferred to Singapore or Hong Kong or, indeed, to any port between Colombo and Wei-hai-Wei.

I felt a little sorry for them, but my sympathy was superfluous. They were cheerful young men, and I am confident that at least two of them will take with both hands the chances which, sooner or later, are bound to come to them. I am grateful to them for much valuable information, for their unfailing kindness in showing me the sights of Batavia, and for many curious stories of life in the East Indies.

The Dutch, they told me, were more anxious about the Imperial ambitions of Japan than the Dutch officials had led me to believe. In Singapore I had found the local British more worried by Japanese economic competition than by any scare of conquest, although I had heard a story of a Japanese naval officer who had made a frank indiscretion at a dinner at which he was being entertained by British officers. In replying to the toast of his country he had paid a tribute to the British Navy and had acknowledged the debt that Japan owed to it. Then he added with an enigmatic smile: "But, of course, gentlemen, you realise that in the last war we were on the wrong side." When asked what he meant, he replied: "If we had even flirted with Germany we should now have the colonies that we require so badly."

Here in Batavia stories of this nature could be gathered like plums off a tree. One which my English friends told me was corroborated afterwards by several Dutch officials. Shortly before the war a Japanese applied to the Dutch Government in Batavia for a rubber and fishing concession on two small islands near Singapore. The concession was granted. When after a year had lapsed a Dutch official visited the islands, he found no rubber and no signs of fishing. The Japanese, however, had been busily engaged in sounding and charting the local seas. Two years later the Dutch Consul-General in Singapore gave a dinner to a visiting Japanese warship. The Dutch official who had visited the islands was present. In one of the Japanese officers at the dinner he recognised the rubber and fishing concessionaire.

On my last night in Batavia I dined with my English friends. During dinner a Javanese boy walked round the room with a large blackboard giving the wireless result of the football international between Germany and Holland. The Dutch had been beaten, and there was no enthusiasm. My English friends told me that a few weeks before there had been another European international which the Dutch had won. The news had been carried round the dining-room. The Dutch national anthem had been played, and everyone in the room had stood up and cheered wildly. There had been even greater exultation at the time of the London to Melbourne international air-race, when Anitas, the Biretti news agency, had announced that the Dutch airmen had won. Batavia had gone into the streets, and the outwardly phlegmatic Dutchmen had gone mad. When, later, the news was proved to be false, Biretti had been nearly lynched.

After dinner my English friends took me out in a car for a drive round the town. The local Chinese were celebrating "Chap Gomi", the tail-end of their protracted New Year festivities. As we approached the lower town, progress became impossible. The Oriental population had taken possession of the streets. The crowd was by no means confined to Chinese. There was a generous sprinkling of Malays, and I saw the curious spectacle of Chinese men walking arm in arm with Malay women. Everyone was in tumultuous spirits. Chinese crackers were spitting like machine guns all round us. A Chinese girl in shorts loosed off one almost under our car, and the crowd laughed good-humouredly. An old Malay woman, obviously a former wanton, exchanged a coquettish and ribald badinage with us. The free mingling of Mohammedan and Chinese was remarkable. There is, in fact, considerable intermarriage between the different native races, thus giving to the population of Batavia a nationality of its own, which is summed up in the native expression "anak Batawi", a child of Batavia. In this respect, indeed, Batavia invites comparison with Vienna.

Having feasted our eyes to the full, we turned back and, entering a side street, passed again by the Fish Market and, turning to the left, came home by a country road with the moon casting its pale light on the canals and rice-fields and the low semi-circular stones of a Chinese graveyard. The contrast of this peacefulness with the turbulence which we had just left was eerie, and almost supernatural.

I had an uncontrollable longing to be alone and at the hotel door said goodbye abruptly to my friends on the grounds that I was leaving very early in the morning. I was going to Djokja. I was glad to go. I had exhausted the possibilities of Batavia. I had explored it with an exotic zest until even now I feel that I know it better than Singapore in much the same way as I know the museums of Europe better than those of London. But it has no lasting place in my affections.

The next morning I rose at four-thirty in order to pack. My train for Djokja left at six. On my way to the station in a dawn, opaque and still half-dark, I passed several shadowy figures. They were young Malay girls drifting across the road on their way to the canal to bathe. Dutch Batavia—commercial Batavia—was still asleep.

CHAPTER FOUR

THE JOURNEY FROM Batavia to Djokjakarta lasts seven hours. It has to be made by day, for, unlike the British in Malaya, the Dutch run no night trains. The scenery is pleasant enough and even beautiful, but by their constant recurrence even rice-fields, palms and mountains become commonplace and cloying. Moreover, the density of the population is an irritating distraction, and nowhere in Java could I ever recapture that sense of remoteness and of the power of space which to me is the chief charm of Malaya.

Djokjakarta itself, however, I found enchanting, and after Batavia it gives much the same feeling of satisfied relief as the transition from Singapore to the Malay States. Djokja is the capital of the most important of the four Vorstenlande or Princes' States, which form the southern part of Middle Java. Situated in the heart of the country it is the centre of Javanese native life and of the Javanese nationalist movement. The vast bulk of its 140,000 inhabitants are Javanese. But it is something much more than this. A mixed Hindoo and Buddhist empire flourished here between 500 A.D. and 1400 A.D., giving way later to the great Mohammedan kingdom of Mataram. Thus three great cultures have been blended with the animism of the original inhabitants, and in the neighbourhood of Djokjakarta are to be found the great monuments, the Hindoo temples of Prambanan, the Buddhist temple of Tjandi Mendoet, and Baraboedoer itself, which are the architectural glory of Java.

After the arrival of the Dutch, Djokjakarta was the last stronghold of Javanese independence. It has a national hero, Dipo Negoro, who in 1825 raised all Middle Java against the Dutch. An ascetic imbued with religious fanaticism and xenophobia, he held out for nearly five years. In the end he was forced to capitulate and was banished to Macassar, where he died in 1855. The war cost the Dutch 15,000 lives and 20,000,000 guilders. The Javanese of Djokjakarta have not forgotten the name of Dipo Negoro, nor has their thirst for independence been entirely quenched.

Here was a town which I wished to see, and, as usual, my first task on arriving at my hotel was to hire a car and a Malay-speaking chauffeur. After some trouble I engaged a quiet, rather sad-looking, but neatly-dressed Javanese, and told him to call for me the next morning at six. Then, tired by my journey, I went to my room to have my afternoon siesta.

I had looked forward to being entirely alone in Djokja-karta, but when I rose again at five to go out and inspect the town I ran into General Woodroffe. His wife and daughter had travelled out on the boat with me as far as Singapore, where they had met the General, who was on his way home from China. A brilliant soldier, with a long experience of the East, he had retired from the army and gone into business. He had recently been spending some months in China, where the British company with which he was associated had large interests. He had seen a good deal of Chiang Kai-shek and thought highly of him. He told me that in his life he had met only two men whose eyes could make him feel afraid. One was Chiang; the other was Lord Kitchener. As the General himself has a respect-commanding presence, the compliment is no empty one.

I sat down on the Woodroffes' verandah and talked. The General was much impressed by the peacefulness of Java. In China he had never been able to move out of his house or travel a yard without a guard. Here in Djokjakarta, and, indeed, throughout the East Indies, we slept on the ground floor with doors unlocked and with the verandah open to any intruder.

The Woodroffes were leaving the next day for Bali. The General's talk was engrossing. And that was the end of my walk in the sunset into the town. I went back into the hall of the hotel, ordered myself a "pahit", and had a talk with the manager. Times in Djokja were also bad, and with the high

guilder there was a depression in the tourist traffic. His hotel
figures were down by nearly four times in comparison with
1928. It was not the decline in British visitors which worried
him. The American slump had cut off the supply of rich
Americans. To-day the Englishman no longer impresses the
Oriental by his wealth, and anyone who has money to burn
is promptly labelled an American.

The Dutch manager's complaint was true enough. That
night at dinner only half-a-dozen tables were occupied. But
there was at any rate one American in this excellent and
luxuriously appointed hotel. He was a landmark for even
the most unobservant visitor. He wore a high stiff collar and
a European suit with cloth of winter weight. He was an old
professor of archaeology, who had arrived one day to study
Baraboedoer and the other ancient temples near Djokjakarta. He had stayed on for seven years. He never spoke to
anyone. He always wore his thick European suit. He always
looked cool and composed, and at meals he always read the
New York Times. Had I been an American, I should have
been proud to claim him as a compatriot.

I took my walk after dinner. Although it was after nine
o'clock, the main street was still crowded with Javanese.
Some of the shops were still open, their owners afraid to
miss a chance of selling something to the all-too-rare visitors.
The shops were rather shoddy, with cheap gramophones and
football boots as the chief evidence of European civilisation.
The population looked infinitely sadder, but far more
dignified than that of Batavia. Most of them wore dark blue
Javanese coats and "kains". Unlike the Malay sarong, which
is sewn like a sack without a bottom to it, the Javanese
"kain" is a one-piece cloth which is tied by a series of difficult and attractive folds.

The prevalence of blue is not in itself an expression of the
sadness. The kain industry is a local one—indeed, Djokjakarta is the centre of the famous batik industry—and the blue
is the result of the Sultan's financial interest in indigo dyes.

If the inhabitants of Djokja have a fine dignity, they are also very poor. In the streets were beggars and prostitutes in far greater profusion than in Batavia. Some of the prostitutes were surprisingly bold. One accosted me near the hotel gates in very fair English: "Come home with me, darling." Obviously the English and American tourists have done their bit to spread the cult of the English language.

The next morning I called on the Governor, an efficient, clean-shaven man, without affectation and very simply dressed in a white drill suit with tunic-form coat. He was prepared for my visit. It would not be possible to have a private audience with the Sultan. If I had a dress-suit with me, I could go to the official reception. There would not be one at Djokja until a date far beyond the limits of my stay. There would be an official reception at Solo in a few days. If I wished, the Governor would be pleased to arrange for me to be present. I had no dress-suit. I had left it in Singapore. In any case, I had no particular desire to attend a function which was a fake formality specially staged for Europeans.

His Excellency, however, was helpful in other ways. He would give me a special pass to see the Sultans' graves at Pasar Gedeh. He would arrange for me to see the Kraton or Sultan's palace alone. I tried to draw him on the nationalist question. He laughed and then said quite convincingly: "My dear Mr. Lockhart, except for a few excited intellectuals in the Volksraat (the restricted form of parliament in the Dutch East Indies) there is no nationalist question. It does not exist."

The Governor spoke very fair English. It was not, he said, one of his best languages. His French and German were better. In addition, he had learnt Malay, Javanese, Sundanese and Balinese. He did all his work with the Sultan in Javanese. He was a fine type of civil servant.

Indeed, almost everywhere I went, I formed a high opinion of the Dutch civil servants. Their industry, their knowledge, and their lack of arrogance are impressive. They try to rule as far as possible through native regents, and the substantial control which exists is exercised with a velvet glove. In everything that concerns commerce, agriculture, public health, and vocational training the administration is excellent. Our British colonial officers could learn much from it and, given the geographical juxtaposition of Java and Malaya and the common interest of defence and self-preservation, it is astonishing that no arrangements have been made for an interchange of informative and instructional visits by the civil servants of both countries. I have friends who have spent twenty-five years in Malaya, who have risen to high rank in the Government service, and who have never even set foot in Java. The fault lies with the unimaginative bureaucracy of our Colonial Office. It is impossible to expect a civil servant in Malaya to give up his home leave in order to visit Java. The visits should be part of the official curriculum and should be financed by the local government. The money spent would be well repaid.

My interview over, the Governor passed me on to his Assistant Resident, and in a few minutes I was on my way by car to Pasar Gedeh with an educated Javanese official from the Governor's secretariat as my guide. Pasar Gedeh lies about six miles to the south-east of Djokja. The village, purely Javanese, is still unspoilt. Its chief centre of interest is a long narrow street, where once-rich goldsmiths, silversmiths, coppersmiths and leather-workers ply their various crafts.

The Sultans' cemetery is in a secluded enclosure shut in by high walls, and the approach is by a superb open gateway which leads into the outer courtyard. Here live the members of the bodyguard whose duty it is to guard the entrance to the tombs. As we entered, they were sprawling on a verandah and smoking and playing dice. They sprang to their feet, and a dignified, good-looking young man, magnificently dressed in blue baju trimmed with orange, elegantly folded kain, and batik headdress, came forward to meet us.

Fixed in his belt in the middle of his back was a richly carved kris. He went to fetch his keys—ungainly by contrast with his beautiful hands and large as the giant keys with which the guides at home open the dungeons of some medieval castle.

With proper reverence I entered the cemetery. Here, near the gateway, the tombs were in the open. Some were shut off by small grids with a tiny roof over them. These tombs contained the coffins of minor relatives of the Sultans. Presently we came to a closed temple with a low roof. The body-servant sat down on his haunches, bowed his head, and with his hands stretched out said a long prayer. Then he opened the door, and, feeling like Alice going down the rabbit hole, I crept inside. The interior was semi-dark, the air musty and acrid. It was some time before I could distinguish the graves. Heavily draped with cream-white cloth, they looked like rows of old beds set out in the basement of a primitive store. The graves varied in size according to the rank of their dead incumbents.

The body-servant was determined that I should see everything. In turn he knelt and prayed before each grave. Then gingerly he lifted the bedspread and whispered the name of the dead Sultan. There was something uncanny in this ritual which made me ill at ease and almost frightened, and in my nervousness I nearly giggled. I was glad when we came out into the open again.

Before we left the temple, my eye was suddenly arrested by the sight of a grave which seemed to be built half-inside the temple and half-outside. I asked the guide what it was. He repeated the question to the body-servant. Very gravely he gave his answer. This curious block of stone *was* a grave. It had been built half-outside, half-inside, on purpose. It sheltered the bones of a Sultan's son-in-law, who had rebelled against his father-in-law, and who had therefore been punished in this manner. For the first time I realised that even Mohammedans, like the Christian churches of the Reformation period, could carry their vengeance to the grave.

As we came out of the cemetery, I was taken to another courtyard. In the middle of it was a deep pool closed in by a stone balustrade and covered with a spire-shaped roof. I thought it was a well, but, looking over the wall, I saw fish— huge turtles, fat golden carp, and some species of cat-fish— swimming in the water below. All were glass-case specimens of which an angler might boast for the rest of his life.

My interest leapt to my mouth in a torrent of questions: Could the fish be caught? Did the Sultan fish himself? Were they good to eat? I learnt that in their wisdom these oriental potentates have devised a simpler method of preventing poaching than any European landowner has ever dreamed of. A picturesque old gentleman with a white tuft of beard and the grandiloquent title of Keeper of the Holy Pond explained to me solemnly that the fish were sacred, and that whoever ate one died within an hour.

On my return to Djokja I was taken to inspect the Government Crafts Centre, where young Javanese men and girls of various ages were being taught the method of dyeing called "batik". Some of the craftsmen employed here are the finest in Java, and the whole process is centuries old. The designs are drawn by hand with wax on the cloth itself. The cloth is then dipped in the dye until all except the waxed part is coloured. Then the wax is removed and another pattern is drawn in until as many patterns have been added as the designer wishes.

To-day the cloth for the cheaper sarongs and kains comes from Manchester and now, alas, Japan, but the silk sarongs are still hand-woven, and the dyes are natural dyes extracted mainly from the bark or fruit of trees.

After admiring the skill of the expert craftsmen, I went into a class-room where a young Javanese girl, dressed in European clothes, was teaching design with a piece of chalk on a blackboard. She spoke a halting English. She had learnt it at the secondary school, and regretted that she had not been able to continue her English studies at the high school and university. She explained to me that in the primary schools, attended by children of from seven to twelve, the pupils learn Dutch. At the secondary schools both Dutch and English are taught. At the high schools and universities students can learn Dutch, English, French and German. But the university costs a minimum of 300 guilders a year and the high school eighty guilders, and even eighty guilders is too large a sum for all but the wealthiest Javanese!

I went back to the hotel and lunched in solitary glory. The few visitors like the Woodroffes had left. Even the American professor was away—presumably burrowing under his temples. The Dutch manager came over to me. "Until the next cruise steamer comes in", he said, "we shall be empty. I recommend you to go up to Baraboedoer this evening, stay the night and see it by moonlight and by sunrise. You will be alone, and the visit is worth while." I went off to my afternoon's rest, having decided there and then to take the manager's advice. But before I began to undress, there was a tap on the door, and a tall, young man came into the room. He introduced himself. He was the reporter of the local Dutch newspaper. Could he have an interview?

I am a journalist by necessity rather than by desire, but I had sufficient curiosity to ask by what journalistic miracle he had tracked me down. He produced some cuttings from the *Straits Times* in which my arrival in Singapore had been chronicled with details of my past, present and future activities. That morning he had been to the Governor's secretariat to seek news of arriving tourists. He had been given my name. The deduction that the Lockhart of Djokja was the Lockhart of Singapore was simple.

I gave him the necessary material for his story and then, following the practice which I learnt in the United States, I began to ask him questions about himself. He was a half-caste and proud of his mixed blood. The Dutch, he said, could not get on without the half-castes. They were the nucleus of the whole administration. Some of the best generals in the long series of Dutch colonial wars had been half-castes. To-day they were everywhere, in every government department, even in the Council of India, the small advisory body of seven members nominated by the Crown, who assist the Governor-General.

Incidentally, the Dutch call their Eastern possessions "India". Our India is always referred to as "British India".

My new journalist acquaintance gave me a harrowing account of the effect of the sugar slump on the population of Djokjakarta. The Javanese peasants lived mainly from employment in the sugar factories and from the rent of their land to the European sugar-growers. Now in many districts they were starving.

From local conditions he proceeded to discuss world affairs. When he got on to Russia, in which he was deeply interested, I thought it time to apply the closure. He was an intelligent young man, and I did not regret my lost siesta.

At five I was on my way by car to Baraboedoer with Kamar, my new Javanese chauffeur, a quieter, better educated, but less cheerful edition of Ahmat.

u

CHAPTER FIVE

THE ROAD WAS comparatively empty of vehicles, and there were more native traps than motor-cars. The traps, four-wheeled affairs known as "andong" and more like a doll's carriage than a vehicle for human beings, were drawn by tiny but sturdy Javanese ponies of the same breed as those imported by Napoleon for his European campaigns. To-day their export is forbidden. Our route took us at first through flat country cultivated with rice and tobacco and sugar-cane. A few years before there had been acres and acres of sugar-cane. Now as a result of the slump there were only patches here and there.

From this plain I had my first unimpeded view of Merapi and Merbaboe, the two twin mountains which dominate the whole landscape of Djokjakarta. Each is 10,000 feet high, but while Merbaboe is gentle and innocuous, Merapi is a live volcano with smoke always streaming steadily from its crater.

Merapi has a two-humped peak, and the local natives tell a legend of its origin. Here in olden times lived a giant called Sonostro, whose misdeeds so plagued the local inhabitants that everyone from the sultan to the poorest peasant longed to be rid of him.

In despair sultan and people go to a wise old hermit for advice. The hermit enlists the help of his friends, the monkeys and the rice-birds. The monkeys who understand the giant's language hear him say that he fears neither God nor man, nor even the great mountain spirit who lives at the bottom of Merapi's crater. The hermit sends the rice-birds to tell Sonostro that the mountain spirit accepts his challenge. Sonostro, enraged, ascends the mountain with giant strides, while Merapi hurls a volley of huge stones at him. The giant laughs at the stones and is almost at the top when the spirit exerts himself to the utmost, and by a violent eruption engulfs the giant from head to foot in lava. It is the giant's head which to-day stands out beside Merapi's crown, and, if you do not believe this story, you must give me a better explanation of that second bump.

I saw signs of Merapi's strength myself. We passed what looked like a dried-up river full of vast boulders. It was the gulch made by Merapi in its last terrible eruption in 1930, when 1300 people lost their lives. There was a village then on the slopes below the crater. It disappeared. To-day the villagers have re-built it. I expressed surprise. But my chauffeur shrugged his shoulders. "Where else are they to go?" he said philosophically. "They have their land here, and land is not so easy to come by in this over-populated, over-cultivated land." And, as though to lure man to his fate, the volcano adds an element to the soil which renders it doubly fertile.

In justice to the Dutch, I must admit that they have done their best to persuade the villagers to leave Merapi's slopes, and that to-day they do all that science can do to protect these hostages to the whim of a volcano which, according to popular fancy, is supposed to seek its kill once every ten years. There is now a watch-station near Merapi's summit linked by telephone with the village and with the meteorological department at Djokja to give timely warning of impending danger.

But the villagers still cling to their own methods of self-preservation. At certain times of the year they bring peace-offerings of flowers and fruit, and drop them down the crater to appease the wrath of the spirit which dwells in its depths.

On that afternoon I could feel Merapi's presence as one always can when the thunderclouds gather and the air assumes a deathly stillness. As I drove up the hill plateau on which Baraboedoer stands, I saw the last remains of an angry sunset. I pulled up at the small hotel beside the temple. Two Javanese "boys" came silently forward to take my suitcase. I went up the verandah steps to be greeted in broad American, enriched by a Dutch accent, by the half-caste manager: "Waal, sir, welcome to Baraboedoer." A series of far-off lightning flashes lit up the vast pile of Baraboedoer. There was a low roll of thunder. The storm had begun.

It lasted for over an hour, rising to a crescendo of fury and then dying down into a steady, relentless rain which refused to stop. The effect of the lightning was both awe-inspiring and stimulating. At times the whole temple or rather the monument, for Baraboedoer is, strictly speaking, a monument to Buddha, was lit up for as long as half a minute, while the lightning played on its terraced galleries.

The rain, however, was irksome. I dined alone. I bought a tortoiseshell cigarette case with a Garuda bird design in silver from the Javanese boys, who importuned me to purchase Batik sarongs, head-dresses, and other samples of Javanese craftsmanship. I drank stengahs with the manager and listened to his life-story. He had been everything from a policeman to a prize-fighter, and spoke half-a-dozen languages with amazing fluency. But the rain persisted, and, even when it stopped, the sky refused to clear. My prospects of seeing Baraboedoer by moonlight seemed to have vanished.

The manager, however, was full of optimism. A little patience and all would be well. As a diversion he suggested a drive to Magelang, a garrison town about ten miles away. We could see a Javanese theatre. By the time we returned the moon would be shining.

I woke up Kamar, my chauffeur, and away we went on a crazy drive in the dark. Presently we were racing along an avenue of magnificent kenari trees, which under the glare of our headlights stood out like ghosts. We passed a village where there was not even the glimmer of a candle. The next kampong was very much awake. A Javanese opera troupe was giving a performance, and the whole village had turned out to hear it. I wished to stop, but the manager shook his head. We should see something better in Magelang.

But when we reached the town its streets were deserted, their wet surface like a lake of tears under the rays of the street-lamps. We drove past the barracks and past the courthouse. They, too, were in darkness. A few years before, the half-caste manager told me, the courthouse had been the scene of the degradation of a Dutch officer. His epaulettes had been ripped off, and he had been marched to the railway station in the sight of all the natives, and put in a third-class carriage with a guard to be shipped to Holland to serve his sentence. This was not a Dutch Dreyfus case. It was the usual tragedy of a woman, of extravagant expenditure, and subsequently embezzlement.

We went into the deserted bar of an hotel to seek information about the local wayangs or theatre shows. The bartender was unable to help us. At last Kamar turned into a side street where a crowd of natives was standing before a brightly-lit house. A wayang koelit, the Javanese shadow-play, was in progress. Kamar pulled up with a smile. "Here we are, Tuan," he said.

I hesitated. The house was a Chinese merchant's house. The show was obviously a private one. But Kamar had no qualms. Pushing his way into the courtyard, he asked for the owner. A Chinaman, dressed in a European white-drill suit, came out, and Kamar plunged straight into the heart of the question. The Tuan was an important Englishman. He wanted to see a wayang koelit. There was no other performance in Magelang.

The Chinaman understood at once and bowed me into a long room. It was his birthday or feast day, and about twelve of his friends were there to do him honour. The wayang koelit was proceeding at the far end of the room, but no one was watching it. Some of the Chinese were playing mahjong. Others were engaged in some gambling game with cards. There were two tables laden with sweet cakes and beer. I was offered both, and was then given a seat all by myself in front of the shadow-play. I felt embarrassed, but the Chinese did not seem to mind, and went on with their games in the most natural manner. For some time I watched the "Dalang" or puppet-proprietor as, with the assistance of a boy, he moved his beautifully carved dolls from the side of the stage to the centre and declaimed their parts. The stage itself was merely the soft stem of a banana tree stretched across the room. The puppets had a narrow spike which was easily inserted into the banana stem. They were assembled in rows at the sides of the stage, and were moved into the centre when their turn in the play came. The "Dalang" spoke in Javanese, of which, of course, I understood nothing. The performance, too, seemed interminable. After half-an-hour I had had enough, and with many bows I took my leave.

On our homeward journey to Baraboedoer the manager pointed out to me a loaf-shaped hill just outside Magelang. It has an honoured place in Javanese mythology. It is the nail with which the Creator fastened Java to the world.

As we approached Baraboedoer, the rain began to fall again. The road, however, was now crowded with villagers staggering along patiently with their heavily loaded "pikulans". It was only two a.m., but already they were on their way with their fruit and vegetables to the market in Magelang. The ten miles' walk would take them until the dawn. The sale of their produce would yield them only a few cents.

The moon still defying me, I went to bed as soon as I returned to the hotel. The bedrooms were in an annexe at the side of the hotel. I was the only guest. From my window I could have thrown a stone on the topmost steps of the monument.

Perhaps I was over-excited. Perhaps it was the concert of crickets or the scuttling of the tiny lizards on the ceiling which disturbed me. But I woke at four and thought it was already day. In the bright moonlight Baraboedoer looked like a huge pyramid of bells. The bells had handles. I went out to the monument. I needed all my courage to approach it, pretending to myself that I must not go too far, lest there might be watchdogs which were let loose at night. But in my heart I knew it was the great monument with its bas-reliefs and its gargoyles which over-awed me. A thousand years of time were looking down on me. A thousand years before, Djokjakarta had been the centre of a vast Hindoo temple city stretching as far as Baraboedoer itself. I was exalted and yet afraid, for my exaltation jibbed when I contemplated walking round the monument, each of whose four sides measures two hundred yards. Keeping an open retreat to my room, I gazed my fill until the night air drove me back to bed.

Towards six the manager woke me up to see the sunrise. The moon, just past the full, and its light, already enfeebled by the early dawn, was still in the sky. The plain below me was an undefined mass of dark purple. The lower slopes of Merapi and Merbaboe were still wrapt in mist, but the peaks were clearly visible. Presently the smoke trail from Merapi's crater turned mauve—a mauve which changed gradually to the warmest pink. And then the sun came up from behind the mountain, suffusing the whole plain with rainbow-coloured lights.

Without a thought for its architectural features, I clambered as fast as I could to the top of the monument in order to get a better view. Below me to the left was a tiny plain of rice-fields fringed by a grove of slender palms and ringed in by the mountains.

Some time passed before the garrulous manager could persuade me to inspect the monument itself. There is a Javanese legend about Baraboedoer. A neighbouring prince once sought the hand of the daughter of the local sultan. The sultan gave his consent on condition that the suitor built a temple to the sultan's design in one night. The suitor almost achieved his task. But he forgot one bell-shaped stupa and lost his bride. The temple is the present Baraboedoer.

According to the more prosaic archaeologists Baraboedoer

is a relic of the old Hindoo-Buddhist empire of Mataram. It was built to shelter the ashes of Buddha, for when Buddha died he was cremated, and many cities of the East claim to possess his ashes. The ashes repose under the bell-shaped stupas, of which there are hundreds at Baraboedoer, with an enormous one crowning the peak of the edifice. The bas-reliefs, which, if laid out end to end in a single row, would measure over two miles, illustrate periods from the life of Buddha. There are four hundred separate monuments of Buddha himself, each in a separate niche of its own. The stone of which the monument is built is grey, and of much the same colour as the stone of Westminster Abbey.

With the advent of Islam in the fourteenth century, the Hindoo empire fell on evil days. The fanatical Moham-medans sought to destroy all temples of other religions, and in order to save their sacred monument the Hindoos are sup-posed to have covered it with earth. At any rate Baraboedoer remained buried until 1814, when Sir Stamford Raffles, then Lieutenant-Governor of Java, ordered its excavation, thus setting an example followed by the British Viceroy in India in the case of Taj Mahal. The excavation was completed with remarkable success by the Dutch.

I am not a judge of monuments. There are, I am told, finer Hindoo temples than Baraboedoer in India. There may be architectural edifices, more satisfying to the aesthetic tastes of connoisseurs, in Greece and Italy. But there is, I dare swear, no monument in the world which stands on a more imposing site or which commands a nobler view of the glories of Nature.

Reluctantly I went back to my room to pack my suitcase. At eight-thirty I was on my way to Djokja. The half-caste manager asked if he might come with me, as he had been summoned to the Governor's secretariat to answer a com-plaint by two Americans, who had stayed there two days previously and had objected to being charged three guilders for *hors-d'œuvre*. The charge, then about eight shillings and sixpence in English money, seemed excessive, but doubtless the Americans were paying for their prodigality during the prosperity period, when, according to the manager, tips of fifty dollars were not uncommon and a consumption of two bottles of whisky per night by no means a rarity for a single American male.

I had had enough of the manager. On my way back I wanted to see Tjandi Mendoet alone. But I lacked the moral hardness to refuse his request. Tjandi Mendoet, a pyramid-shaped temple with a colossal statue of Buddha carved from a single stone, is impressive, and at the entrance I saw two wonderful old beggars whom, because of their dignity and venerable white beards, I mistook for priests. Here, from his attitude in approaching the Buddha, I learnt that the half-caste manager was a Buddhist. I wondered if the native blood in him was Chinese. But no. As he had tried many professions, so he had experimented with many religions until in Buddhism he had found the proper haven of peace for his restless mind. His faith had not taught him silence or robbed him of his interest in mundane affairs, for to my boredom he talked all the way home about his financial troubles.

On reaching the hotel I was subjected to another irritation. I had been turned out of my luxurious rooms and relegated to a back-room overlooking the servants' quarters. A world-cruise steamer had come into Semarang, and a hundred tourists from her were coming to Djokja that afternoon. The manager bowed and waved his arms in obsequious apology. I would understand. The rooms had been booked months in advance. To-morrow, I should have the best....

I cut him short. I did not care whether a hundred or a hundred thousand tourists arrived, provided only that I had a bed. I was still under the spell of the previous night and morning. Within twelve hours I had seen Baraboedoer by sunset, by lightning, by moonlight, and by sunrise. That magnificent monument was a lasting testimony to the greatness of a vanished Hindoo empire. When the British and Dutch empires vanished, as one day vanish they must, would they leave behind them as permanent a memorial?

Exhausted but still exalted, I went to my room to make good the lost hours of my sleepless night.

CHAPTER SIX

I HAVE NEVER liked tourists in the mass. This is the confession of an egotist, for throughout my life I have been a sightseer and a traveller. When anyone might so easily say: "Look at the funny little man with the solar topee on his head and the guide-book in his hand," it is not for me to criticise other disciples of the excellent Dr. Baedeker.

And yet, for a moment, I resented the intrusion of that cruising company into the quiet peace of my Djokja life. I had spent an hour before sunset in visiting the Taman Sari or Water Castle in the grounds of the Sultan's palace. Built in baroque style by a Portuguese architect for one of the sultans, it was once a kind of oriental Trianon, standing in its own grounds and enclosed by a high wall. A succession of earthquakes has destroyed its former splendour, and to-day it is in process of decay. Its gardens are a wilderness of long and luxuriant grasses. Tropical flowers sprout from the crevices of its flagstone courtyards and of its outer walls. In its ruined state it has an atmosphere of old-world romance which I found wholly fascinating.

I had come back from the castle in a grateful and generous mood. I had gone up to my room to change for dinner. At eight o'clock I had strolled down to the lounge. The scene which met my eyes was startling. Outside the rain was coming down in a solid stream. Chauffeurs, drenched to the skin, were wrestling with the hoods of a large fleet of cars. Inside, the hall had been re-arranged as if for a concert. Rows of seats had been set out on both sides, leaving a long open space of marble in the middle. I learnt that after dinner we were to have a wayang-wang—a dancing performance by the famous troupe of the Sultan of Djokja.

Standing at the reception counter, sitting on the chairs, leaning against the walls, occupying every inch of space, was the army of tourists. They were of all kinds and conditions: old men, fat women, young girls, quadragenarians wearing

the tie of the Brigade of Guards, and young men in slacks
and open shirts of every hue from Fascist black to the brightest Neapolitan blue.

I watched the confusion with amused interest. Presently
my attention was diverted by a serio-comic tragedy which
was being played with great vigour and effect on the marble
space reserved for the dancers. A Frenchman, accompanied
by his wife and daughter, had arrived by train from Batavia.
He was not a member of the cruise party. He had booked his
rooms months before. He held the manager's letter, acknow-
ledging the reservation, in his hand. The rooms had been
given to the tourists, and in loud and violent language, re-
plete with rare and rich adjectives and accentuated by a
whirlwind of gesticulation, the Frenchman was telling the
manager exactly what he thought of him, of his hotel, of
Djokja, of Java, of the Dutch East Indies, of Holland, and of
the whole Dutch race.

Gradually the storm subsided, the tourists sorted themselves out, and we went into dinner. In the dining-room I
had been relegated to a distant table near the side-door. I did
not blame the Dutch. The world-cruise passengers are the
flesh and bones of the Dutch tourist-traffic. In a materialist
world they very properly come first. Even my table "boy"
was impelled to an unwonted garrulousness by the occasion.
"Tuan," he said to me, "these Americans must be very rich."

"Gold, Thou art not God, but Thou art Almighty," said
the Malay chronicler. Probably it is a variant of the old Arab
aphorism: "The West has the gold, but the East has the
soul." In all certainty both sayings were inspired by contact
with the white man. Without a doubt these tourists were
rich, although ninety-nine per cent. of them were British.
One or two I had already recognised. If they had a soul, it
was covered by a hard exterior. There was a man and his wife
who did not come into dinner until the others had nearly
finished. They had changed into evening dress, and, owing
to their late arrival, they were given a side table near me. I

saw a plump bosom heave with indignation. A pungent odour of some strong scent, overpowering and unpleasant, wafted itself across to me. I felt that there was going to be trouble. There was. The unfortunate manager was sent for. The soup was cold. Could they have something else? If there was nothing fit to eat, was there a decent brand of champagne? My sympathies were now with the Dutch. If I could dislike anyone at first sight, I felt that I could detest these two. Fresh fuel was soon added to the glowing fire of my hate. Owing to their successful intimidation of the manager the wayang performance was held up until they had finished dinner.

In one sense the Javanese, who have a far more ancient culture than that of the Malays of the Peninsula, can be compared with the Russians. Music and dancing are in their blood. To the ordinary European Javanese music is exotic and difficult to understand. The melody is primitive, but the numerous varieties of rhythm are baffling and the tone-scale has different intervals from those of the European scale.

The highest form of native orchestra is the gamelan, composed mainly of percussion instruments in which gongs and various types of zithers, with wooden or metal keys and played with hammers, predominate. There is also a flute and a rebab, a kind of two-stringed violin played by the gamelan leader. A full-sized gamelan has over twenty performers. In Java alone there are 18,000 of these native orchestras. Notation is comparatively modern. Nearly all the musicians still play by ear, and the melodies, partly Hindoo and partly Chinese in origin, have been handed down from player to player for centuries.

The dancing, also Hindoo in origin, dates back to an early form of sacrifice to Shiva, the Hindoo god of the Dance. To-day, the Hindoo religion has long been replaced by Islam, but the dancers remain. The themes are taken from the great Hindoo epics, the Mahabharata and the Ramayana, and the dresses of the dancers have an exotic magnificence which

makes an instant appeal. The best dancers and the best orchestras are, as in Tsarist Russia, the personal servants of the
Sultans of Djokjakarta and Solo. In both Sultanates the dancing girls are held in high honour. Some are princesses of
whose upbringing dancing is a recognised and regular part.
Others are chosen from the people. They are taken into the
Sultan's household and are given an excellent education in
Javanese literature. When their dancing powers decline, they
are married off, at the Sultan's will, to members of the Javanese nobility. Sometimes a girl, who has won the Sultan's
favour or has had a child by him, obtains a permanent place
in the palace as one of the ruler's subsidiary wives.

In Java, at any rate, there is nothing creative about either
the music or the dancing. Both are merely the reproduction
of accepted classical forms. But the technical skill, especially
as regards the movements of the arms and hands, has reached
a perfection which would astonish even those who have
seen the Russian ballet in its greatest days.

Seen in its proper native surroundings, a combined performance of dancing and gamelan is highly impressive. Anything like an intelligent interpretation both of the dancing
and of the music requires years of study by an expert. But the
layman, at any rate, can appreciate a radiance of form which
appeals both to his aesthetic enthusiasm and to his sensuous
emotions. Here, beneath the glaring electric lights of a modern hotel with a European audience chattering restlessly and
trying to take photographs and with native "boys" opening
soda-water bottles for the "whiskies" of sweating sexagen-
arians of both sexes, there was an atmosphere of artificiality
which even I found overpowering.

The dances themselves were alluring enough, but rather
long and slow in movement. The first was a Hindoo varia-
tion of the eternal theme of the love triangle. The girl has a
male friend. Her lover is jealous—of course, without reason—
and wishes to kill her. She defends herself with a "kris".
Afterwards she shoots her lover with a bow and arrow

brought on to the stage by a little trousered boy who reminded me of the page in the *Rosenkavalier*. Then the girl
is heartbroken and mourns over his corpse. The dancing, in
which slow balance plays a predominant part, was techni-
cally perfect, the movement of the arms and, especially, of
the fingers being wonderfully graceful.

Then we were shown a fight between two Javanese dancers armed with clubs, axes, and, finally, bows and arrows.
It was a stately and dignified fight with about as much action
as a scene from a Greek play performed by Sixth Form boys
of a public school on Speech Day. A monkey dance and fight
between two boys with masks and artificial tails aroused the
fidgety European onlookers to a momentary enthusiasm.
This, at least, they could understand. But when it was followed by a long solo dance by the principal girl, in which I
confess the movement seemed to differ not at all from that
of the first dance, their boredom was complete. When one
weather-beaten old lady, bolder than her compatriots, rose
and announced firmly that she was going to bed, the others
followed like sheep, leaving me in embarrassed solitude.

The programme was not nearly ended. The manager came
over and asked if I wished to see more. But my own enthusiasm had now evaporated. As I crossed the courtyard to my
rooms at the back, I passed the troupe of actors and actresses,
magnificent in their old Javanese costumes and squatting
patiently on their haunches and waiting for their turn. Some
of them had not yet appeared. Now their preparations had
been in vain.

I felt ashamed, remembering the atmosphere of hysteria
and frayed nerves behind the scenes of the Big Theatre in
Moscow when anything had gone wrong with a ballet performance. It never occurred to me to doubt that our lack of
appreciation must have pricked that brooding sensitiveness
which lies so close to the surface of the Malayan soul. Yet I
was mistaken. As I passed them, the girls looked up and
smiled. Some were smoking cigarettes. All seemed in the

best of tempers. One male dancer with false moustache and a Homeric helmet was sleeping peacefully with his head leaning on his hand.

This capacity for sleep is perhaps the greatest advantage which the Oriental enjoys over the European. It is his infallible specific against the nervous ailments of our febrile modern world and a sure balm for all the troubles of the soul.

The next morning brought a fresh reaction to the tourist invasion in the form of an eight o'clock telephone message from the Governor's secretary. There would have to be an alteration in the arrangements made for my visit to the Sultan's palace. The tourists were staying for only one day. It would be necessary to show them the palace. He assumed that I should not mind their going with me. If I did, he could make other arrangements for me, but I should have to wait several days. I did not wish to wait so long. I lacked the decision and the courage to say no. In any case I had now begun to see the humour of the tourist racket. Nine o'clock found me at the tail end of the long queue formed up at the gates of the palace.

The Kraton, as the palace is called, is a city in itself. Within its walls live some 30,000 people, all relatives, personal servants, or retainers of the Sultan. The walls, guarded by a moat, are about twelve feet high and as many feet thick. They enclose a rectangle three-quarters of a mile long and a half-mile broad.

Within the precincts of the Kraton the Sultan is supposed to be his own master. But in the throne room there are two thrones. The one on the right is the Sultan's. The other is not for his chief consort. It is for the Dutch governor. Nevertheless, inside this kingdom within a kingdom the Sultan is lord of life and death, and until comparatively recent times deaths were as frequent and as mysterious as in the days of the Borgias. The present Sultan has been on his throne for seventeen years. But before he succeeded three of his brothers died in unexplained circumstances which finally induced the abdication of his father.

The weakness of all oriental sultanates is the number of
royal wives and the number of children who may be regarded as possible successors. The present Sultan has over
forty sons, and, although he is an enlightened ruler compared with his forerunners and has been in Holland, there
must still be many intrigues within the palace which remain
hidden from even the best-informed and most vigilant Dutch
governor.

The Kraton itself was built in the middle of the eighteenth
century, but the palace proper has been frequently renovated
and added to, and the public rooms are an incongruous mix-
ture of oriental magnificence and of the worst examples of
modern vulgarity. To-day, it gives little outward sign of its
sinister and mysterious past.

In spite of the early hour, the heat was already scorching,
and, while we waited under the open sky for the official
army of interpreters and guides to arrive, we received a severe grilling from the sun. At last all was ready, and in a struggling and sweating herd we trooped in behind our bear-
leaders. A hundred and thirteen years before Raffles had
passed through these gates on his first visit to the Sultan after
the British conquest of Java. He had come almost unattended
as a sign of his goodwill, and the Sultan had ordered 10,000
soldiers to line the streets. Raffles' dignity had not flickered
by as much as an eyebrow. I wondered what he would have
thought of his camera-laden compatriots of to-day, as they
stampeded from point to point in breathless haste. They were
the unconscious humourists of what was, in effect, a comic
performance.

We passed through magnificent rooms with priceless treasures, and I noted with some surprise in this stronghold of
Islam a white marble statue of a Christian angel. The long
dining-room, where at official festivities the Sultan can seat
over three hundred guests, would have impressed me by its
dignified spaciousness had my eye not been caught by a
stained-glass window with a florid design of champagne

x

bottles and glasses and the initials H.B.VIII. I surmised that His Highness Hamangkoe Boewono VIII must suffer much from the importunities of European contractors.

In the former Sultan's bedroom, maintained exactly as it was in his lifetime, the chairs were covered with nails with the points upwards as a painful deterrent to *lèse-majesté*. No one is allowed to stand upright on the polished floor. The cleaners who polish it have to do so prostrate. Here again the effect of natural dignity was jeopardised by the prominent display of large modern signed photographs of the Queen of the Netherlands and of her late Consort.

At every place of interest the herd shuffled and stopped, while the interpreters delivered their harangue. The interpreting itself was a laborious performance. A Dutch-speaking Javanese official recited the historical points to the Dutch hotel manager. The manager passed them on in broken English to the cruise entertainment officer, a well-groomed young man who communicated them to the tourists with jocular comments of his own very much in the manner of the approved cabaret conferencier. The tourists added their own asides. Over the entrance to one hall was painted the word "welkom".

"Charles," shouted one married woman to her husband, "come here and see how they spell 'welcome'. Isn't it funny?"

Charles evidently thought it was, for he unhooked his Leica camera and commemorated in photograph the supposed spelling mistake.

To me the big moment of that morning was the changing of the guard—a picturesque ceremony which I was glad to have witnessed. Within the Kraton the Sultan is allowed to maintain a household force of a thousand men. They are not very formidable, but they mount guard like the British guards at St. James's Palace, and every day they have their hour of glory. To the shrill notes of a flute player they parade round the palace. Their uniforms are the queerest in the world. The helmets are like flower-pots turned upside down. The tunics, many of them armless, have as many colours as Joseph's coat. The men themselves are armed, some with old-fashioned muskets, others with enormously long lances and swords and shields, and others again with the native "kris".

These warriors are of all ages. There was one old gentleman, clean-shaven with bushy eyebrows and with the clear-cut features of an aristocrat. He must have been well over sixty. Yet he had the superb carriage of a Red Indian and he wore his flower-pot with a dignity which would have earned him an astronomical salary at Hollywood. I do not think I have ever seen an Oriental with a finer face.

Incidentally, the lances which the soldiers carry are holy and are supposed by the Javanese to have healing properties. Just before the war there was plague in Djokja and in Solo. The Dutch doctors were sorely handicapped in their efforts to fight it because the Javanese had little belief in the white man's medicines and flocked to touch the holy lances—and to infect each other.

The last room which we visited housed the Sultan's state carriages and sedan chairs. Here there was another unrehearsed comedy. A middle-aged and corpulent Englishman, smoking a pipe and dripping at every pore, had climbed on to the platform on which the chairs stood. "How the hell does the Sultan get into this?" he asked loudly, as he tried the handle of a closed-in and rather low chair. The guide showed him. The Englishman shook his head. A great bead of sweat fell from his brow. His pipe emitted a cloud of smoke. "Very undignified," he said. "Very undignified."

I agreed. For some Englishmen an ostrich with its head in the sand would be a better national emblem than the lion and the unicorn.

It was eleven o'clock, and, exhausted by this organised stampede, I took a sudden decision. I should spend the rest of the day in visiting Solo, the capital of the principality of the same name and equal in importance to Djokja. By the evening the tourists would be gone, and I could come back to the hotel. Djokja I was determined not to leave until I had seen something of the nationalist movement at first hand and, although my resolution seemed rather futile, I had not entirely abandoned my belief in a last-minute intervention of providence.

By imposing a severe restraint on Kamar, I took nearly two hours to cover the forty-mile stretch to Solo, which lies east and slightly north of Djokja on the main-line to Soerabaja. The landscape, dominated again by Merapi, is flat. The land is highly cultivated and is covered with tobacco fields and sugar plantations. The only curious feature is the presence of small rivers with streams of liquid sand. They have their source at the foot of Merapi and serve a useful function in carrying away the sand from her smoking crater.

Solo or Soerakarta, as it is officially known, is very like Djokja. It has a slightly larger population. Its Sultan, whose names include the picturesque title of "Nail of the World", is the senior native prince of Java and the titular head of the Mohammedan religion. Like the Sultan of Djokja, he has a Kraton. The city itself is pleasantly laid out with wide avenues planted with trees. There is the same teeming centre of native life as in Djokja, and, like Djokja, Solo is less spoilt, less westernised, than the other cities of Java. If you come to Solo first, you will probably like it better than Djokja. The Dutch do. My own preference is for Djokja, although I admit readily that the few hours which I spent in Solo do not entitle me to make a fair comparison.

Although I made no attempt to seek official help, I was fortunate enough to catch a glimpse of the Sultan during my short stay. As Kamar was pointing out the Kraton to me, the gates opened, and out swung a magnificent yellow car. Two retainers sat by the chauffeur. There was a retainer on each footboard. In the back sat His Highness Pakoe Boewono Soesoehoesan of Soerakarta.

In many respects His Highness is the most remarkable

thing about Solo. In his full ceremonial dress he must be almost the most resplendent figure in the world. He, too, wears a flower-pot hat. His short open coat is bejewelled with the orders of almost every government in the world. He has a fine chest on which to carry them, but if he receives more he will have to use other parts of his anatomy. He wears a jewel in each ear lobe and rings on every finger of his two hands except the thumb and middle finger.

In his private life he has still the privileges of an absolute ruler. He is fond of cards and racing, and like Kemal Ataturk of Turkey he likes to win. When he races, the jockeys of other owners are expected to let the royal horse pass the winning post first. Occasionally this leads to difficulties which on European courses might result in a good thing going wrong. Not so in Solo. At one local race the Sultan's horse jibbed at the start and, in spite of its jockey's efforts, refused to move. When the other jockeys saw what had happened, they pulled up and waited until the Sultan's horse had got into its stride and was able to pass the grand stand a popular and comfortable winner. No one, not even the bookmakers, suffers from this royal idiosyncrasy. The local natives are on the Sultan's horses to a man. Naturally their gains are very small.

The "Nail of the World" has also a royal advantage at cards. He employs a special retainer or one of his sons to go round the table and let him know what is in his opponent's hands. The only time when the royal privilege is suspended is when once or twice a year the Sultan and the Dutch Governor of Solo challenge their counterparts of Djokja to a bridge match.

By these strictly accurate stories I should not like to create the impression that the Sultan of Solo was a kind of comic opera figure. This is far from being the case. He is a shrewd and intelligent ruler, whose foibles are merely different from, and certainly not more harmful than, those of some European monarchs.

He is loyal to the Dutch, by whom he is much liked. He has a slightly anti-British bias, perhaps because the British Government is one of the few governments who have not given him a decoration. He has, too, a proper sense of his own dignity and is quite capable of reproving with true oriental tact any foreigner who tries to take a liberty with him. Not long before my visit, he received an Englishman who spent his time in boasting of the superiority of the British over the Dutch, especially in colonial administration. The "Nail of the World" smiled gently. "Well," he said, "we Javanese are not very well up in European history. But I do know that there was a Dutchman who became King of England. I've never heard of an Englishman who became King of Holland."

Another European who was in Solo at the same time as myself was Dr. Voronoff, the Russian monkey-gland rejuvenation expert and now a man of over sixty. The local newspapers said that he was touring the East Indies in order to find new types of monkeys, including the man-like orangoutan, for his gland-grafting experiments. Actually he was on his honeymoon.

I left Solo at five in the afternoon. As my car turned out of the main street, I passed three elegant Javanese walking sedately along the road. Their dress was of beautiful silk batik. Each was accompanied by a retainer who carried an umbrella over his master's head. Kamar told me that they were relatives of the Sultan and perhaps even his sons. The sun was hardly high enough to warrant the need of an umbrella, but Kamar told me that its use is *de rigueur* whenever members of the Sultan's suite go abroad on foot.

On my way back to Djokja I tried to summarise my impressions of a hectic and confused day. I wished to get a proper perspective of this tourist business. I felt a little ashamed. In my egocentric conceit I had allowed myself to be irritated and even to become downright sulky. Yet here was I with a Leica camera strung on my back and an armful of guide books, the complete caricature of the very type of tourist to whom I most objected.

I was not even a good tourist. In the Kraton I had let my attention be diverted by childish things. I was certainly a very bad photographer. I had spent hundreds of guilders on gadgets for my camera. Up to date I had taken nearly five hundred photographs, and not one in twenty had come out at all.

On the other hand, I was genuinely alarmed by the levity of the huge army of rich tourists. In my day tourists had been rare even in the big ports. They never went inland. Now they spread themselves over every square inch of the East. I was slightly shocked by the advertisements of fashionable dressmakers which I saw displayed in the travel literature: "Ideas for Lighter Moments on the Cruise. Coolie jackets, coolie trousers, etc." and by the attempts of some of the tourists to put these ideas into practice. It seemed to me that this aping of native dress must earn the contempt of the native himself.

In theory it was a good thing that English people should see something of their empire. But I wondered if Kipling, when he wrote his "what do they know of England who only England know", ever calculated the effect of a cruise-load of travelling Britons on the Eastern subjects of that empire.

Remembering Sir Ernest Birch's dictum about the importance of finding out what the Oriental thought of us, I turned to Kamar:

"What do you Javanese think of the tourists?" I asked.

He smiled wanly. "Tuan," he said, "times are not what they were six years ago. If there were more ships and more tourists like you, we should live better."

I fear that there are more capitalists and more sycophants in this world than Lenin ever dreamt of.

CHAPTER SEVEN

THE NEXT DAY luck broke my way, but not until the late
afternoon, when I had abandoned all hope and had resigned
myself to leaving Djokja the next morning. Earlier in the
day I had called on the Governor to pay my respects and to
thank him for his courtesy. He was away, but I was received
by the Assistant Resident. He expressed his regret that it had
not been possible for me to be received by the Sultan of
Djokja, but added to my knowledge of that potentate by
telling me that in the past the Sultans of Djokjakarta had not
encouraged their relatives to learn Dutch. The present
Sultan's father had forbidden it. In consequence, it had been
very difficult for the Dutch to find a minister of sufficient
experience and standing to act as a link between them and
the sultan. The present Sultan's minister was a man who
had learnt Dutch surreptitiously. In the future, however,
this would never be necessary again. To-day all the young
Javanese nobility were learning Dutch. The Sultan's sons
were in Holland. The change was not altogether to the
good. The young men, especially those who went to Holland, learnt far too many things which they could not digest.
The Javanese of the older generation were much wiser.

As I left the Governor's office, a violent thunderstorm had
darkened and drenched the town. Before the rain had ceased,
it was late in the afternoon. I had already packed and had
gone to the bookshop in order to send home by parcel post
the collection of Dutch books that I had bought. I had already made friends with the Dutch bookseller, an exceptionally intelligent and well-read young man. But I did not
know his name and he did not know mine. When I wrote
out the label for my books, he read it and smiled. "You are
the author of *British Agent?*" he said. I pleaded guilty. His
interest was stimulated. Was I going to write a book about
the Dutch East Indies? How had I liked Djokja?

I told him that I had wanted to see something of the

320

nationalist movement and, if possible, to meet some of the nationalist leaders. "I'll soon fix that for you," he said. He went to the telephone, and within a few minutes I was on my way to the house of a Dutchman who was in sympathy with the nationalist movement. He was a slip of a man with pale complexion and an enormous forehead. He was clean-shaven and rather bald. He wore glasses and looked like a student. I guessed that he was about forty. He was a student. Every room in his small house was stacked with books in half a dozen languages. He was a socialist and an anti-imperialist.

We sat down on the verandah and drank iced lemonade and talked Marx in German. At first he was reserved. But I drew him out by references to my Russian experiences and to my meetings with Lenin and Trotsky, and soon he was giving me first-hand information about the various nationalist parties with whom he was obviously in close touch. Organised nationalism had begun only a few years before the war. The first nationalist society, Boedi Oetomo, which means "Beautiful Endeavour", had been confined mainly to Javanese intellectuals. It had been followed by Sarekat Islam, a wider and more popular society, which was formed in Djokja in 1910. Started at first by the disgruntled members of the Javanese batik industry, who saw their home-made products being ousted by Chinese competition, it soon developed political ambitions. Under the banner of Islam it sought to extend its activities so as to embrace all the native peoples of the Dutch East Indies. Other parties, including trade union and co-operative societies, sprang up like mushrooms. Of these the most significant and in the long run probably the most dangerous is the Insulinde party, formed in 1912 and composed of Eurasians and Javanese.

As in other countries the nationalist movement in Java received a great stimulus from the Great War, and in 1916, yielding to the pressure, the Dutch introduced the Volks-raat, a kind of local native parliament with severely limited powers. Within two years of its creation a Dutch socialist had succeeded in uniting the various nationalist parties into a concentrated opposition.

At first the nationalist parties had no higher ambition than a self-governing autonomy within the Dutch Empire. But as so often happens in countries unripe for constitutional reform, the extremists took the upper hand, and by the end of the war a fully-fledged communist party, affiliated to Moscow, was competing with the other parties for popular support. In 1926 and 1927 there had been a serious communist revolt, which had ended in the arrest and exile of the communist leaders. They had been sent with their families to a settlement in New Guinea, at Tanah Merah, a place which, curiously enough, means "Red Land". Originally about 1200 people were deported there, but a combination of blackwater fever and recantation of communist principles has now reduced that number to approximately 700.

The Dutch Government, my Marxist friend told me, had now turned right wheel, and for the moment all was quiet. He himself, however, was convinced that the days of Dutch imperialism were drawing to their inevitable end. The Dutch were the greatest colonists that the world had ever seen. But they were also the greatest exploiters. He was not a communist, but he foresaw already the eventual triumph of the Russian economic system in the East. He drew a striking parallel between Russia and Java. Here in Java were the same pre-conditions of bolshevism: a small nobility, no middle class worth speaking of, and a teeming proletariat, underfed and underpaid. Emancipation had already begun. In the case of the men it had been started by the educated intellectuals; in the case of the women by the Javanese Princess Kartini, whose letters, first published in 1911 and now translated into half a dozen European languages, have become a classic. The emancipation could not be stopped. The Javanese were now education conscious. The poor half-castes, of whom there were many, would side with the natives in the struggle for independence. The native rulers and regents had no power. They could do nothing without the Dutch. When the dam burst, the Javanese princes and their feudal system would be swept away.

Our conversation was purely academic, but I felt slightly guilty. It was long since dark. The house itself was in an isolated position overlooking a park, and the shadowy outline of the trees, faintly revealed by the single electric hand-lamp on the verandah table, helped to create a conspiratory atmosphere which reminded me of my secret conversations with the revolutionary leaders in Russia during the Tsarist regime.

After many pipes my host asked me if I would like to meet a Javanese prince. Of course I said yes, and he went into the inside room to telephone. Although I tried to appear indifferent, I was full of anxiety. Having already booked my steamer passage for a tour of the Outer Islands, I dared not postpone my departure even for a day. It was already ten o'clock. It seemed unlikely that the Prince would receive me so late at night. The telephone conversation in Dutch seemed interminable. Then my host came back. For the first time there was a faint smile on his face. All was well. The Prince would receive us at once.

Fortunately I had kept my car, and soon we were at the Kraton gates. A word from my Dutch companion, and we had passed the bodyguard. We were inside the city within a city. Here all was silent. The palace itself was in darkness. The night air, pungent with the scent of flowers, was still and warm. Slowly we passed the groups of separate houses, turned into a drive, and pulled up outside the fenced-in garden of a well-built bungalow. The soft notes of a gamelan orchestra floated across to us. By the light of a lamp I could distinguish a group of Javanese squatting silently on the steps of the verandah. As we entered the gate, they slipped away in Indian file and vanished in the darkness.

We walked forward to the steps, and the Prince came down to meet us. He was dressed in a Javanese "kain", a high-necked blue "baju" with long-flowing sleeves, and a magnificent Javanese kerchief headdress. His silky moustache and rather plump figure gave him a slightly Pooh-Bah appearance. But his smile was pleasant, and he had beautifully kept hands with tapering fingers of which even a Habsburg might have been proud. The only incongruous thing about him was his pince-nez.

His verandah was elegantly but unostentatiously furnished. There was a fine teak table and half a dozen Dutch chairs with semi-rocking legs. He was expecting us. Tea, cigars and cigarettes were laid out with symmetrical neatness on the table. The teacups had lids in order to keep the tea warm. He poured me out some tea, and then carefully replaced the lid on my cup. This ceremony was repeated every time we drank.

The Prince had no English, but he spoke fluent Dutch. He had been educated in Holland, and in his knowledge of economics and political history could have held his own with almost any European. He would have made a first-class diplomatist, for his natural dignity was supplemented by reserves of tact and discretion. He said nothing that could be considered even remotely seditious. But, unless I do him wrong, I surmised that he was a nationalist to the tips of his long, delicately-shaped fingers.

I was careful not to embarrass him with indiscreet questions, and confined my opening remarks to a desire for knowledge about the system of education. He expanded at once, enlarging eloquently on the Javanese thirst for knowledge. Very few Javanese, he said, could afford to go to a university. Recently the Dutch had cut down the number of schools, but in order to maintain the rate of progress the Javanese had started their own schools. Every Javanese made sacrifices to support them. Many of the teachers took no salary. Many of the poorest parents sacrificed as much as seventy per cent. of their income in order to send their children to school.

From education I ventured gladly into the field of nationalism. I told him that I had been amazed by the large number of nationalist parties and nationalist leaders. Did he not think that this dissipation of forces was a weakness of the movement? He explained to me that owing to the diversity of interests represented and to the number of different races in the Dutch East Indies many leaders were inevitable and even necessary. He insisted that the nationalist feeling was strong even among the poorest Javanese and, as far as driving out the Dutch was concerned, stronger among the proletariat than among the nobility and the intelligentsia. The poorer Javanese were now poverty-conscious. They had come to realise that the Dutch gave them enough to eat and no more.

I asked the Prince if he did not think that education in Holland had a deleterious effect on those Javanese who went there. I quoted cases of young Malayan princelings who had been educated in England, and who had come back with a taste for white women, alcohol, racing, extravagance and other European habits. He saw no danger of Javanese princes being contaminated by Western civilisation. His view was that they went to Holland to learn all that the white man had to teach them, that they worked harder than at home, and that they came back to Java with stronger national feelings and with more pride in their own civilisation than ever. It had been true in his own case. But I doubt if there are many Javanese like him.

Unlike my new Dutch socialist friend, he was convinced that there were no communist tendencies among the Javanese, and that communism was ill-suited to the national character. It was true that the Dutch called everyone who aspired to independence a communist. But the vast bulk of Java was peasantry. The peasant wanted land and more of it.

I tried to make him say how long he thought the Dutch

rule would last. But he was not to be drawn. He quoted to me a three-hundred-years-old Javanese proverb to the effect that another foreign rule would succeed the Dutch. The Japanese perhaps, I suggested. He shook his head. He was not afraid of the Japanese. I do not think that he took the proverb very seriously. Unlike most Malays he had long since shed all trace of superstitious belief.

I felt instinctively that he still believed in the divine right of sultans, but did not like to ask him on so delicate a subject. Instead, I asked him if the sultans still had any power. He smiled rather sourly. "Only the shadow," he said. "Look at my relative, the Sultan of Djokja. He is a songless canary in a golden cage."

He was, however, convinced that the prestige of the white man in the East had gone for ever. Many events had helped to shatter it: first, the Russo-Japanese war, then the Great War, and, finally, the Chinese revolution and the triumph of Kemal Ataturk. But, most of all, the Great War. The eyes of the East had been opened by the spectacle of the white men's civil war.

I asked him if he did not think the white man's cinema had also been a contributory cause. He reflected before giving his answer. "With the intellectuals, yes," he said, "but not with the people. The charge for admission to a cinema is ten cents. The peasantry here cannot afford ten cents for a cinema."

He asked me a few pertinent questions about India, which in my ignorance I was unable to answer with any completeness. He told me that the Javanese nationalists followed the political situation in India very closely. Dutch Java was a hundred years behind India in the development of political self-government, but since the war progress in Java had been relatively more rapid. The East would move more rapidly still during the next twenty-five years.

It was now long after midnight. We had drunk innumerable cups of tea, and I, at least, had smoked half-a-dozen cigars. My Dutch friend had warned me in advance that I must make the first move to leave. The Javanese nobility were so polite that the Prince would wait until dawn rather than hint that it was time to go to bed. Twice I had risen to go and twice I had been forced to drink another cup of tea. At last I rose firmly and finally. We shook hands and bowed. Then the Prince produced a great book in which were entered the minutes of the meetings of the agricultural co-operative society which he had founded and which he ran himself. I scrawled my name with the date, in the same way as one signs the visitors' book in an English country house. We bowed again, and then we went out into the night.

After dropping my Dutch friend at his house, I drove home through the silent town. The teeming millions of Java were asleep. They had been sleeping for three hundred years. How far ahead was the day of awakening? Within a few days I had heard a Dutch governor declare that there was no nationalist question and a Dutch socialist maintain that Dutch imperialism was doomed.

The next morning I left at dawn for Soerabaja. The train, much faster but less comfortable than the trains in Malaya, was uncomfortably hot. Fortunately, what would have been a tedious journey was made enjoyable through a chance acquaintanceship with a Dutch official, who was the only other occupant of our miniature Pullman carriage. He was full of that encyclopaedic knowledge which one soon learns to expect from the Dutch, and very proud of his country and insistent that I should miss none of the virtues of Dutch colonisation. The virtues were there before my eyes in rolling fields of sugar-cane, tobacco, rice, and a hundred other tropical products, and in wonderful schemes of irrigation which had put every inch of the soil except the craters of the volcanoes to profitable use.

I expressed my admiration in suitably flattering terms. But I could not help remembering that, as doubtless had been the case in most British colonies, these virtues had been achieved at the expense of needless abuses. It was Raffles who, during the Napoleonic wars, had freed the slaves of Java. But not many years afterwards slavery or something akin to it had been restored by the introduction of the forced cultivation system. Holland had been ruined financially by a succession of wars, and to make good these losses the Governor-General of the East Indies had forced the Javanese to plant up a part of their land with products which were in great demand in Europe. The Javanese had no say in the matter. The selection of the product was left to special Government officials, who received a special remuneration in the form of a percentage of the yield. In this way were built up the great Dutch East Indian industries of sugar, indigo, tobacco, tea and coffee. The profits of the Government were enormous and were sent back to Holland for the reduction of the public debt and of taxation, and for the construction of railways and military defences. But the abuses were cruel. The Javanese had to give up their best land for this forced cultivation, and were miserably paid for what they produced. Natives who had no land had to work for the Government without pay for sixty-six days in the year. Corruption was rife among the Dutch officials entrusted with the supervision of the system.

It was left to a retired Dutch official, called Dekker, to expose the iniquities of forced cultivation. Under the name of Multatuli he wrote a book called *Max Havelaar*. Published in 1860, it stirred the sleeping conscience of the Dutch in much the same manner as Mrs. Beecher Stowe's *Uncle Tom's Cabin* roused the apathy of the American public towards the slavery in the American cotton fields. The worst features of the system were removed, and gradually forced cultivation was given up. It was not, however, until 1915 that with the abandonment of the forced cultivation of coffee the system was finally abolished.

Naturally I kept these thoughts to myself, and presently the sight of numerous idle sugar factories set my companion on a new train of thought—a lament for the good days of the post-war boom. Seven years after the war Javanese sugar was selling at 100 florins per 100 kilos. To-day the price was five florins. I should have been in Soerabaja in those days, he told me. Then it was the gayest place in the East, and the Dutch sugar factory managers, some of whom made as much as 300,000 guilders in bonus in a single year, were the gayest, the most generous, and the most reckless spenders in the world. Now times had changed. Soerabaja was full of unemployed whites. They gave more trouble to the Dutch officials than all the 400,000 unemployed Javanese put together. The natives could go back to their kampongs, where the fertile soil would yield them enough at any rate to provide life.

He sighed and, opening his despatch case, began to turn over a sheaf of Government papers. He did not speak again until he saw me staring out of the window at a curiously-shaped mountain standing out like a sugar-loaf hat in the distance. "That's Kloet," he said, "the most active volcano in Java. She's wicked. After the war she killed many people."

The name awoke memories in my mind of Antony Fokker, the great Dutch airplane constructor. I remembered how he had told me at Lord Beaverbrook's country place near Leatherhead shortly before my departure for the East that he had been born within the shadow of Kloet in 1890. His father had a plantation there. He sold it in 1896 and went home with his family to Europe. While they were on the sea, Kloet belched again, and the former Fokker home was totally destroyed. It was on this occasion, too, that Fokker told me how at the beginning of the war he had wanted to help England. He had come to London and had offered to sell his patents to Britain. No one had shown any interest in them, and in the end he had sold his machines to Germany. Volcanoes in Java inspire a deep respect. If Kloet had belched a few days sooner, Germany might have been deprived of her best flying machines in the war.

Y

I arrived in Soerabaja, which means Crocodile Town, in time for a late luncheon, and after my meal I went out to have a look at the town. It was the first place at which Captain Bligh of *Bounty* fame landed on his way home from Timor. He described it in his log as "one of the most pleasant places I ever saw". In the circumstances I understand his enthusiasm, but do not share it.

The town itself is admirably built, has fine business offices, wide streets and excellent bookshops, and as the nearest approach to a European city in Java is much liked by the local Dutch. It is, however, very flat, and the heat there is stifling. Like the other cities in Java it has enchanting hill stations within comparatively easy distance. Of these Tosari, with its Bromo Hotel, situated at a height of over 6000 feet, is world-famous. The name of the hotel always makes English and American people laugh. It is called after the volcano of the same name which is in the immediate vicinity.

Sheltered and protected by the island of Madura, Soerabaja is the chief naval port of the Dutch East Indies. It is also the main harbour for the export of sugar. Since the mutiny of the cruiser *De Seben Provinzien* in 1933, the Dutch in Java have not been very happy about their navy. The mutiny itself makes rather a sordid story. The mixed crew of Dutch and Maduranese revolted for better conditions of pay and service. They overpowered their officers and, taking possession of the ship, began to steam along the coast. A lucky hit by an airplane brought them to their senses, and the revolt was quickly quelled.

It has left a sting with the brave but hot-tempered Maduranese, a fisher-folk, who with the Buginese make the best sailors in the East Indies. They were induced to join the revolt by the Dutch sailors, who after the surrender tried to put the blame on their native colleagues. The Maduranese, who like most Malays have long memories, have not forgotten their experience.

The trouble, I imagine, had its roots in something deeper than economic discontent. While the Dutch army in the East Indies is a local force, the navy is imperial. The officers are sent out from home and serve a term of only three years on the East Indies station. Just when they are beginning to learn something of the language and to establish contact with their ratings they go home. I was told recently by Dr. Colijn, the Dutch prime minister, that this absurd system is being altered.

Although Soerabaja has fallen on hard times, it is gayer than Batavia. The capital has no proper night-club. Soerabaja still has two. Being at a loose end after dinner, I went to one, which appropriately enough was called the "Tutti Frutti". It was like the usual continental cabaret: supper tables and dancing and a few professional turns. Outwardly it was ultra-respectable. The "spate" of champagne had ceased with the end of prosperity. The Europeans were drinking whisky and soda or Bols gin. I was, however, more interested in the sellers than in the buyers of vice.

In these East Indian cabarets the artistes are mostly Hungarians and Russians. They are devoid of all sentiment. They are heavily made up in order to hide the ravages of a life which is harder than the lot of European cabaret artistes. Indeed, the heat and drink—for hard drinking is a necessary adjunct to their work—soon plays havoc with the remains of their beauty. If they are a genuine troupe of performers, they are often stranded, and have to be given a steerage passage to another port. Many of the women, however, are members of Mrs. Warren's profession. In the years of the sugar boom one or two with harder heads than their colleagues made big money, and returned in triumph to Budapest to be interviewed as "stars" by the local newspapers and to encourage other young girls to follow their example. But most of them fall by the way, and their end does not even get into the births and deaths column.

Here in the Soerabaja "Tutti Frutti" there was a certain

imitation of European elegance. But the atmosphere was even more depressing than that of London night-life. When the dancing began, I sent for one of the dancing girls and ordered a bottle of champagne. She had a smile as set as her peroxided hair. She drank quickly and in a business-like manner. She was Hungarian-born, the daughter of a German father and a Hungarian mother. Her German had the sing-song intonation of Budapest. She danced well. But she was not there to waste her time.

"Also", she said, "wie werden wir unsere Sache regeln?"
I led her on. "What do you mean?" I asked.
"Well, what are you going to pay?"

The price was 200 guilders—£30 for the night. It was the tariff. In the boom days the Dutch sugar planters paid it when they came to Soerabaja for a "jolly". Since the slump they can no longer afford it. The girls, however, have not reduced their price. They have merely changed their clientele. To-day they sleep with the Arabs and Chinese, who, slump or no slump, are always rich.

That night I slept late. The next afternoon I embarked on the *Merah*, and steamed down the Straits of Madura past the dirty-grey outline of a Dutch destroyer flotilla on my way to the Outer Islands.

BOOK V

WHITE MAN'S TWILIGHT

"ALAS! CAN we ring the bells backward? Can we unlearn the arts that pretend to civilise, and then burn the world? There is a march of science; but who shall beat the drums for its retreat?"

CHAPTER ONE

IN THE DAYS of my youth, when I was the only white man in Pantai, I had one dream which haunted me in my hours of depression. I saw myself in a sea-prahu, manned only by Malays, heading for an uninhabited island in the Malay Archipelago. I never reached the island, but the vision of it was very clear to me. Everything on it was perfect. The sun was always shining. Yet everything was green. There was always a cooling breeze to temper the tropical heat. There was the soothing music of the surf. To perfect the modern idea of "going native" there was a comfortable bungalow complete with hot and cold water. There was no cocktail bar. In those days dreams had not included cocktails in their scheme of things. But there was an English grass lawn past which flowed a tropical river strangely like the Spey. It teemed with fish. Of course, they took a fly, although on my island there were neither mosquitoes nor other winged pests.

In those days I had neither the money nor the leisure to put my dream to the test of reality. But, like many other people, I have dreamed it often since the war. Now, after at least the partial realisation of my dream, I am bound to confess that one tropical island is very like another. Those islands which are uninhabited are uninhabitable. Those which are inhabited have already become tainted by civilisation and are no longer dream islands.

And yet on sober reflection I think that, if I were given the choice and the opportunity to do what I liked with the next three years of my life, I could spend them most happily touring the islands of the Archipelago in the packet steamers of the Royal Dutch Packet Navigation Company, known throughout the East by its three Dutch initials of K.P.M. The boats are small, but comfortable. The food is good. There are few first-class passengers. The captains are men of power and parts. And they know the life of the islands as no one else knows it.

In the *Merah* I had a cabin to myself fitted with an electric fan. After Bali we carried only one other European passenger, a young Englishman employed in the service of a Singapore trading company. I had my first view of that vaunted paradise at six in the morning, when we anchored at Boeleleng, the port of the island. It was an angry sunrise: a single fiery patch of orange in a bank of dark clouds. I did not go ashore, but stood on deck and watched the freight being loaded from open boats with side supports like a catamaran. It was a curious freight: mostly capons and pigs, for the Balinese are pig-eaters, pig-breeders and pig-exporters. Pigs and capons were packed alive in tight-fitting palm-leaf coops. The packing seemed incredibly cruel. Yet, strangely enough, both animals and poultry survive a longish journey in these suffocating strait-jackets. At Macassar they would be transhipped and despatched to Portuguese Timor, to Christian Ambon, and perhaps even to Hong Kong.

All that morning we steamed along the north coast of Bali on our way to Ampenan, which was our next port of call. The coast, palm-fringed and very narrow, has a background of green hills. As we passed the east corner, I had a wonderful view of Goenoeng Agoeng, the ten-thousand-feet-high peak which dominates the whole island.

Ampenan, which we reached at two in the afternoon, is the port of Lombok, the neighbouring island to Bali. Although it is separated from Bali by only a narrow strait, its flora and fauna are totally different. It has numerous kinds of parrot and perroquets which are unknown west of the Straits of Lombok, but lacks tigers and other wild animals. Outwardly, the island is very like Bali and nearly as beautiful. Ampenan itself has nothing to recommend it and, as we stayed there for two hours, I hired a car and set out for Mataram, the capital of the island.

This tiny town, only a few miles distant from the sea, has an interesting history. The inhabitants of Lombok are Sassaks, who for two hundred years were ruled and brutally oppressed by the Balinese. In 1894 they appealed to the Dutch for assistance. When the Balinese ruler of Mataram refused to carry out the proposed reforms, the Dutch sent a military expedition. While the Dutch general was still negotiating with the Sultan, the Balinese troops made a treacherous attack by night, slaughtered many of the Dutch officers and men, and forced the others to beat a hasty retreat. Reinforcements were sent as quickly as possible, and the Dutch took a fierce revenge, many Balinese being shot down more or less in cold blood, and many fine buildings being destroyed. As a further punishment the Dutch drove out the Balinese and placed Lombok under their own administration.

The Poeri or palace of the Balinese sultan was in Mataram itself. But to-day there is no trace of it. The Dutch razed it to the ground, together with many temples and other examples of Hindoo architecture. Where the palace once stood is now a pleasant park with a monument to the memory of the Dutch who fell in the expedition. The Sassaks are docile and good-natured, and the Dutch keep a natural peace with a handful of native police.

On my chauffeur's advice I drove a mile or two farther on to Tjakra Negara, where the last Balinese ruler had a second palace. Opposite the palace is a temple which for a few hours gave shelter to the Dutch on that fatal night when they were treacherously attacked in open bivouac. On the way back I stopped at a little shrine by the roadside. It is known as the Pera Dalem. Here every year come pilgrims from Bali to pray to Doerga, the Goddess of Death. Close by is a plain obelisk to the memory of General van Ham, the most important Dutch victim of the war.

Curiously enough, both Dutch and British acquired their Malayan possessions by playing off one sultan against another. But whereas the British succeeded in establishing their suzerainty with comparatively little bloodshed, the Dutch had to fight their way in nearly all the islands. Nearly everywhere, too, one finds monuments and obelisks similar to those to the Dutch officers and men who fell at Mataram.

These wars, which lasted until the beginning of the twentieth century, were very different from the British war in New Zealand, in which a Maori chief sent a herald to inquire why the British had ceased fire. On being told that it was because the British had run short of ammunition, he promptly offered to supply some from his own store. Here in the Dutch East Indies there were no knightly courtesies, but only savage cruelty on both sides.

Indeed, the war in Acheh, which lasted for thirty years, has as black a record as any war in modern history. The Dutch, frequently ambushed and stabbed in the back, were driven to adopt harsh measures. Their Achinese enemies were always hiding in the jungle. In order to track them down the Dutch finally had to resort to moral persuasion. It took the form of taking the children from the mothers' breasts and threatening to throw them into the sea to the sharks or into the rivers to the crocodiles if the women did not tell where their husbands were hiding. If the information was refused, the threat was carried out.

The chief exponent of this policy was a Swiss major. I was informed by a former Dutch minister of the Crown that he is still alive. He now regrets his military past, and has become a confirmed theosophist and a whole-hearted admirer of the late Annie Besant.

From a Frenchman, who is a great authority on the East, I acquired a curious piece of information about the war in Acheh. In the early years of the war the Dutch employed a contingent of French Communards, who had been banished after the suppression of the Paris Commune in 1871. These first bolsheviks were known by the Malays as the "orang didong" or "didong men", because of their frequent use of the French expression "dis, donc". When I dined with Dr. Colijn, the present Dutch prime minister, in the Hague, I told him this story and asked if he could confirm it. He won his own spurs in the Acheh war, for like many well-known Dutchmen he began his career in Java. He was full of anecdotes about Acheh, but he had never heard of the "orang didong". They were, of course, long before his time. And as the war started in 1873 and was not ended until 1904 the story may well be true.

From Mataram we went to Labuan Haji, the east coast port of the island, where we arrived the next morning at dawn. I did not go ashore, but stayed on deck to watch the cargo being loaded. It was an exciting performance, for there was a heavy swell, and at any moment it seemed as if the native loaders must lose their footing. They were, however, as nimble as monkeys, and had need to be, for if they had fallen into the water their chances would have been small. Here the cargo was mostly small onions, which I was told were in great demand for flavouring soups. For the next twenty-four hours they flavoured everything.

The heaviest item was an unexpected addition to our freight. I had noticed a Chinese kitchen hand fishing from a lower porthole with a line like a rope and a huge hook baited with raw meat, but had paid little attention to him. Suddenly I heard a yell. The Chinese "koki" was into something big. Two heads were now protruding from the porthole and four skinny hands were holding on to the line. There was a violent commotion in the water. Down came the crane with a rattle, while officers and crew rushed to the side. The loaders quickly manœuvred their boats to the spot and, grinning and grunting simultaneously, began to lash out fiercely with their broad-shaped paddles. In less time than a fly-fisher would take to land a trout of a pound they had the shark on board one of the boats and had finished it off with their knives. With the aid of the crane it was soon on board our steamer.

As sharks go, it was only a small one, but it looked ugly and savage enough to have frightened any bather. I think that the shark itself had been terrified out of its resistance by the fierce onslaught of the paddles. At any rate it provided me with a thrill and the Chinaman with a day's glory and, I expect, a succulent meal.

The rest of that day I spent in making friends with the Dutch officers. At first I found them rather stolid and heavy, but at "pahit" time they expanded, and, although I found the Bols gin hard to stomach, I struggled nobly in my pursuit of knowledge. On further acquaintance I found them very good fellows, and much better-read than their British prototypes. Both the chief engineer and the captain had seen twenty-five years' service in these seas and looked fit enough for another fifteen. Both were big, powerful men. Both spoke English and German and, of course, fluent Malay.

With the chief engineer I talked sex. Women seemed to have seared his soul. At any rate, in his view, they were out of place in the East. They had cast their spell on the post-war youth. Nearly all the white man's troubles in the East came from young men forming attachments to girls too early in their career. Their only thought was to get married, and then they wanted a soft job near a city. To-day you could not find young men to stay in the outlandish places where the best chances were. In a service like his, early marriage without sufficient money was hell. It was true that his service had been affected by the slump like every other service in the East. But to a man who could cool his ardour for marriage it brought its rewards. In good times a captain of these packet steamers made as much as £100 a month in bonus in addition to his salary, and this was more than the income of the captains of the great Atlantic liners.

Curiously enough, on my return home, I heard one of our greatest colonial administrators expound this same theory of early attachments and early marriage as one of the chief drawbacks to the efficiency of the present-day British colonial service.

The captain was a family man with his feet firmly planted

on the ground. He cared for, and knew more about, freight than passengers. In the course of his career he had visited all the islands, and had been living in Macassar for fourteen years. If he was a philosopher, he kept his philosophy to himself. But he impressed me more than anyone else I met during my Eastern journey by his self-reliance and his stolid concentration on his job. As long as Holland can produce sufficient men of his type, she will have little cause for anxiety about her Eastern possessions.

I told him that I wanted to visit Timor. He produced his time-tables. There was no boat for over a fortnight, and I could not afford the time. My face fell.

"You won't miss anything," he said. "There's nothing to see. Some years ago I was on that route. I'm glad I've left it."

I told him that I had a whimsical desire to see the last remaining outpost of Portugal's former vast Malayan empire. Then he proceeded to tell me his own experiences with the Portuguese in Timor. The Portuguese held the Eastern portion of the island, and a fine time the Dutch officials had in trying to check the cattle and horse-thieving which flourished on this artificial frontier. The Portuguese administration, he said, was comic. The governor and his handful of officials were paid no salary from Portugal, but took it from the proceeds of the coffee sales. When coffee was bad, times were bad. The coffee plantations were on the other side of the island from the official headquarters. Sometimes the weather was bad, and the steamers could not take the coffee on board. Then the officials had to go without their salary!

In the captain's time the real boss of the island was the local Portuguese banker. He fixed the exchange price of coffee and had his own estate. He was an ex-naval man. The governor had his own official launch, which carried a gun. He used the launch for collecting his coffee. When the launch commander was on leave, the governor had to beg the banker to navigate the launch for him.

These occasions were jam for the banker, who not only dictated his own terms but also arranged for the free transport of his own coffee. Once my captain had accompanied the Dutch governor on a visit to the Portuguese over one of the usual horse-smuggling cases. They found the governor living in his adjutant's house. His own residence, too old to stand, had collapsed during a minor earthquake!

I am bound to admit that this state of affairs refers to the period of the Great War. Since the Salazar dictatorship came into power, Portuguese colonial administration has been put on a very different footing.

Timor, nevertheless, is a tragic example of the decline of a great empire and a warning to Britain. The Portuguese were once the best and the bravest sailors in the world. Of all the reasons adduced for their decline luxury is the first and the foremost.

Timor to-day has a strategic importance to Britain as a flying station on the Empire route to Australia, and to Japan as a naval base. From time to time fears are expressed even in well-informed British circles lest Portugal may one day sell part of the island to Japan. The fears are unfounded. In the event of her wishing to sell her rights, Portugal is bound by treaty to give first refusal to the Netherlands.

At eight o'clock the next morning we entered Macassar harbour. I do not think that I have ever seen a more peaceful or more enchanting sight. A coral reef studded with little islands guarded the entrance like a sheltering arm. The sea was as smooth as a billiard-table, and I could follow every wave of our wash until it rolled itself gently against the breakwater. Tiny fishing boats, their sails slack for want of wind, lay motionless between the islands. Away to the right, as far as the eye could see, stretched a mountainous panorama of green loveliness.

Macassar, although somewhat exposed to the north-east monsoon, is one of nature's harbours, and her work has been done without the ugliness of man's inventive genius.

True, there were huge godowns and modern wharves splendidly equipped to take the largest ships. But behind, nestled together like a flock of birds, were scores of sea-prahus with graceful masts and high raised stern exactly as they had been in the days when the Buginese were the great sailors and pirates of the archipelago.

I admit that I was prepared to be sentimental. Macassar was the capital of the Celebes. The name itself had an old-world ring. Vaguely I remembered the antimacassars which covered the black horse-hair chairs in my great-grandmother's house at Nairn in Scotland. They were the Victorian safeguard against stains from the sleek, Macassar-oiled hair of the Victorian male. But, above all, Macassar meant to me Conrad. It was the fount and origin of his two great Malayan novels, *Almayer's Folly* and *An Outcast of the Islands*. Here Almayer had come as a young man, ambitious, full of hope, ready to conquer the world. Here Williams, the strong outcast, had married old Hudig's half-caste daughter and had taken the first step towards his descent. Here had come that great Conrad hero, Tom Lingard. Rajah Laut the Malays had called him—the King of the Seas. He, too, had been one of the heroes of my youth, and whatever the literary critics may say, I still maintain that these two early novels with *Lord Jim* and *The Nigger of the Narcissus* are Conrad's best books, and are the works by which his name will live.

It has always struck me as peculiar manifestation of genius that neither Conrad nor Mr. Somerset Maugham, who in their respective spheres are the outstanding interpreters of this part of the world, were ever residents of the East. Mr. Maugham was a casual visitor. I do not think that he ever picked up more than a few words of Malay. Conrad's six trips as a mate in the merchant service covered a period of eight years, but most of them were spent on the sea, and between cruises there were long gaps. His Malay was "bazaar" Malay and poor at that. He had no first-hand knowledge of the up-country life which he described so well. Yet both of these men have given to the world a picture of the East which no local expert is ever likely to excel.

It was because of Conrad that I had chosen to visit the Celebes in preference to the other islands. In his time Macassar had been teeming with life and commerce. It was, as he wrote, "the point in the islands where tended all those bold spirits who, fitting out schooners on the Australian coast, invaded the Malay Archipelago in search of money and adventure. Bold, reckless, keen in business, not disinclined for a brush with the pirates that were to be found on many a coast as yet, making money fast, they used to have a general 'rendezvous' in the bay for purposes of trade and dissipation."

The period coincided with my own birth, that is, nearly fifty years ago. Williams, Almayer and Tom Lingard himself had been drawn from real men. Fifty years were an eternity anywhere and especially in the East. But vaguely I hoped that somehow, somewhere, I might find the flotsam of a life which had always made an irresistible appeal to my sense of the romantic and adventurous. Above all, I was attracted by the possible opportunity of discovering new material about Conrad himself.

CHAPTER TWO

WITH THESE THOUGHTS in my mind I went ashore and drove to the Oranje Hotel, the same hotel, but now modernised by a new building, as the Sunda Hotel of Conrad's novels. After engaging a room, I went through my usual performance of selecting a likely chauffeur and, fortune aiding me, I tumbled almost immediately on a sturdy Buginese who in his younger days had been part-owner of a "prahu" sailing between Macassar and Singapore. Now the sailor had become a chauffeur. He looked very smart in his short white coat and gaily coloured Buginese trousers. I did not regret my choice. He was the best and most intelligent of all the chauffeurs I engaged.

My first visit was to the Governor to whom I had a special letter. Because of his grand manner, his predecessor had been called the "Kaiser of the Celebes". The Governor whom I met was a rather stout, good-looking man with silver hair. He had no frills. Like most of the Dutch officials, he was full of friendliness and very willing to impart information. Macassar, he told me, had fallen on hard times. It was still the centre of a large *entrepôt* trade with the islands which brought their spices, their copra, and their fruits to the port to be transhipped there into freighters. But the slump had hit the town badly. There were no more adventurers and no more pirates. Those old days had gone for ever. Even macassar oil was no longer produced except in insignificant quantities.

The Celebes, or rather Macassar itself, had been conquered by Speelman, another great Dutch colonial captain, nearly three hundred years ago. But the warlike Buginese of Boni had continued to give trouble up to 1905. In 1860 there had been a great revolt under an Amazon sultana who had put up a fierce resistance. There had been further fighting in 1905, and the Sultan of Goa had been deposed. The rest of the Celebes was governed through native chiefs with an "elder brother", as the Dutch wisely call their residents, to guide them. Goa, however, which includes Macassar, is under direct administration. The Governor hoped that in Goa, too, the Sultan's nominal control would soon be restored. This system was the most practical way of administering the country.

His Excellency was an admirer of the Buginese, and, more especially, of their prowess as sailors. They still sailed their prahus by the stars and by an old book written by a Buginese three hundred years ago. With a following wind they could make Singapore in five days. They were strong competitors of the Dutch K.P.M. boats, for their freight rates were much cheaper. They took most of the rice-trade.

They still retained their war-like character and their reputation for quick temper. They were forbidden to carry knives, but no one had ever been able to enforce the law. Hardly a day passed without one or two stabbing cases coming before the court. Nearly every case had something to do with a woman or with the share-out after a prahu cruise, for the prahus are run on a co-operative basis, profits being shared out equally among the crew. Macassar still justifies Wallace's description of it as the most celebrated place in the East for "running amuck".

I asked His Excellency about Conrad, but he could tell me nothing. I doubt if he had ever heard of him. I returned to the subject of the Buginese. Could he tell me what happened to the old sultana who gave the Dutch so much trouble in 1860? As I put my question, a car drove up to the front entrance. The Governor took out his watch and smiled. He led me to the window. In a ramshackle car outside sat a small wizen-faced Buginese. At his side was a middle-aged woman dressed in a brilliant coloured sarong and jacket. Her lips were red from betel-chewing. She was far from beautiful, but there was character in her face. "That's the ex-sultan", said the Governor, "and the woman is his sultana. She comes to see me about politics every week. She wears the trousers and leaves him in the car. She's a relation of the old Amazon who fought us seventy years ago."

Before I took my leave I had one request to make. Might I have a permit to see the grave of Dipo Negoro, the great Sultan of Djokja, who had been banished to Macassar and had died there? The Governor cocked his eyebrows. He sent for his Assistant Resident. Neither of them knew that Dipo Negoro was buried in Macassar.

The arrival of the Assistant Resident was a stroke of luck for me, for, as I said goodbye to the Governor, this excellent man suggested that his assistant should show me over Fort Rotterdam and the other landmarks of the town.

We went first to Fort Rotterdam, which lies close to the sea on the eastern side of the town and dates back to the time of the Portuguese occupation. The Assistant Resident, a slim, well-built man of about forty and very English-looking, was proud of the fort, which is a little Kremlin complete with its old church and barracks and office-buildings. In olden times it was the centre of the Dutch administration and the refuge of all Europeans in time of trouble. To-day, its low walls do not look as if they would defy the assault of a toy cannon or, indeed, the jumping prowess of an American athlete. But as recently as 1905, when the Sultan of Goa made his revolt, all the Europeans of Macassar were ordered to take shelter within the fort. Among them was the Assistant Resident's father-in-law who was then a judge in the Dutch colonial service.

The Assistant Resident ordered the church to be opened for me. The entrance was by high steps, and I had the impression that I was going into a loft. Inside, the quaint old wooden pews and austere white-washed walls seemed to breathe the spirit of Calvinism. The church itself, not much bigger than a barn, was dominated by a small pulpit, whose wooden edges had been worn by frequent hammerings. In the two hundred and fifty years of its existence how many Dutch John Knoxes had banged it with their fists; how many Dutch congregations had listened to their exhortations to spurn the flesh and to prepare for the day of wrath!

With the single exception of Malacca, Macassar has more old-world atmosphere than any other town in the whole Archipelago.

From the fort we made a rapid drive through the town; the European residential part with wide and shady streets, Dutch villas, and numerous parks; the business centre narrow with rows of Chinese shops intersected by temples. Then, turning into a splendid highway, we went out to see the sultans' graves beyond Goa, the former seat of the Sultan.

The Assistant Resident told me that the road ran through the spot on which the former palace of the Sultan had stood. As a consequence of the 1905 revolt the palace had been removed and the road had been planned purposely in this manner in order to show the power of the Dutch and the insignicance of the Sultan.

We had to walk some way to the graves. Architecturally, they were not impressive, being rather like those low, semicircular-shaped cement mounds which one finds close to reservoirs at home. But their isolated position, far from any road and habitation, gave them a dignity which is lacking in the crowded city cemeteries of Europe and America.

The Assistant Resident was a highly intelligent and self-reliant man who I feel sure will have a brilliant career. Like most colonial officials who knew their job he would prefer less uninformed interference from home. He told me something of the multiple and varied examinations which the Dutch had to pass in order to qualify for the colonial service. Their standards are far higher than our own. I felt glad that I was a citizen of a rich and easy-going nation. Had I and, indeed, most of our colonial officials been Dutchmen, we should have had to earn our living by manual labour.

After dropping the Assistant Resident at his office, I returned to the hotel to lunch and to continue my Conrad researches. In the lounge I found the assistant manager and over a "pahit" I repeated my question. He was the most nervous and most garrulous Dutchman I have ever met. But though he, too, had never heard of Conrad, he was not defeated. The hotel proprietor had been a lifetime in the Celebes and had met everyone who had ever been in Macassar. We sought him out in his office. He was a splendid type of vigorous old man who was ready enough to talk about his own troubles: how like everybody else he had put all his money into real estate during the prosperous post-war years and how nobody came to Macassar. But my trouble he could not solve. He, too, had a suggestion. There was only one man in Macassar who could have known Conrad. This was an old Swiss gentleman named Jenni. He was over eighty, had spent sixty years in the Celebes and had not been home since 1900.

I determined to look up Mr. Jenni. Meanwhile, I went back with the assistant manager to our "pahits" at which we were joined by the young Englishman who had been my only fellow-traveller in the *Merah*, and a young Dutchman, the son of a very rich merchant in Holland.

For half-an-hour we listened to the local gossip of the twitching manager. It was a tale of woe. Macassar was nearly moribund—and quite dead as far as the hotel business was concerned. Occasionally mysterious Germans and Americans and Japanese arrived to buy rattan. It was required for shell baskets for the fleets. But there had been no excitement for some years—none, in fact, since the visit of the American squadron. That had been a real "how-de-do", but the hotel profits had been swallowed up by the breakages. The American ratings had gone wild, and for a time things had looked ugly. Now business was almost at a standstill. The Japanese had driven the Europeans off the market. Yet their cheap goods were a godsend, for how else could a Dutch employee live on his miserable salary. Here in Macassar a Dutchman could fit himself out from head to foot for four years for the price of one English suit.

I challenged him to produce the figures, and, taking a pencil, he gave me the following list:

20 white drill suits	@ 5 guilders	= 100 guilders
20 singlets	@ 50 cents	= 10 guilders
50 pairs of socks	@ 20 cents	= 10 guilders
20 shirts	@ 1.50 guilders	= 30 guilders
1 raincoat	@ 10 guilders	= 10 guilders
10 pairs of shoes	@ 1 guilder	= 10 guilders
10 pairs of pyjamas	@ 2 guilders	= 20 guilders
Handkerchiefs, ties, etc.	@ 5-6 cents	= 10 guilders

Total 200 guilders.

One Saville Row English suit £16 16s.
£16 16s. at par of exchange = 200 guilders.

To prove his figures the manager pointed to his own clothes. Everything he had on was Japanese. Except perhaps for the five-cent tie his clothes did not seem to be very different from ours. Being an incredulous Scot, I made my chauffeur take me to a Japanese store the next morning, where at the expense of a cheap pair of socks and a six-cent handkerchief I checked the figures. They were substantially correct.

Shedding the manager, we went into luncheon, where I heard more first-hand information about the Japanese. Macassar, I gathered, was Japanese-conscious and Japanese-afraid. I heard a strange story, doubtless untrue but symptomatic of the atmosphere of uncertainty, about a Japanese mission which had come to investigate the Dutch system of education. They had gone into one school where there was a map of the East Indies on the wall. When they left, the word Dutch across the Celebes had been crossed out and "Japanese" scrawled in its place!

There were now, I was told, no English in Macassar, and in the Celebes altogether there are only a few thousand Europeans, including the garrison, out of a total population of over two-and-a-half millions. Large tracts of the island were still unexplored, and life in the outlying districts was still as lonely as it had been two hundred years before.

I heard of one young man who had been sent to an outlandish post in the northern part of the island. He was a man of refinement and high ideals. But in his loneliness he had taken a Malay woman into his house, had had children by her, had come to love her, and had then fallen desperately ill with fever. After weeks of illness a doctor had been sent to bring him down to the coast. He had been shipped home to recuperate, had gone into business, and was now head of a big office and was married. Yet he was unhappy and obsessed by only one wish: to return to his former Celebes home in the jungle. Was it the spur of conscience or nostalgia for the East which urged him? I should have liked to know. My friends could not tell me.

The story reminded me of the first short story I ever wrote. That was twenty-five years ago. My story, too, was founded on fact, but it had a different ending. A young British official was living miles away from civilisation. In his loneliness he, too, had taken unto himself a native woman. And then on Christmas Eve he shot himself. His Malays rowed down the river to fetch his nearest white colleague—a journey of twelve hours. The colleague came back and found the would-be-suicide lying on the verandah floor but still alive. He had blown one side of his face away, and the ants were feeding on the raw flesh. The colleague took him down the river—a fourteen hours' row—and put him into hospital. Six weeks later the young man came out, looked at himself in the mirror, went down to the nearest Chinese store, bought himself a revolver, and this time did the job properly.

After luncheon I took no siesta but went out again with my Malay-speaking Buginese chauffeur. I did not feel tired. There was a fresh breeze from the sea. I liked Macassar. I liked its old houses and its colourful picturesqueness. There

was no depressing Djokja blue here. The sarongs of the women and the trousers of the men were bright splashes of red,
green and yellow, and reminded me of Scottish tartans. I
liked, too, these Buginese. They were not so good-looking as
the Javanese, but they were men and not beasts of burden.
They carried no "pikulan". I felt that the Celebes were all
the better for the Pax Batavica. Otherwise these cheerful rascals would have been at each other's throats.

I found my chauffeur playing dice with his colleagues. He
rose with a grin. "Can you show me Dipo Negoro's grave?"
I asked.

"Of course, Tuan," he said without a moment's hesitation.

He turned into a little *cul-de-sac* within a minute's run from
the governor's house, and there it was—a queer little hut
with a corrugated tin roof built at the side of a gate into a
small disused yard. But for its open barred bamboo walls it
might have passed for a Scottish golf-caddies' shelter. There
was a small native laundry at right angles to it, and on a
rope strung across the *cul-de-sac* the week's washing was
hanging out to dry. Neglected and cage-like, it was, indeed,
a prisoner's grave. But obviously it was not forgotten. My
Buginese chauffeur was impressed. "The Tuan knows the
story of Dipo Negoro?" he asked incredulously. I nodded. I
felt that I had gone up in his estimation. Straightway he took
me to a large block of empty buildings. "The school for native sailors for the Dutch Navy" said my chauffeur. "Mostly
for Maduranese. There were Maduranese in the mutiny of
De Seben Provinzien. Since then the school has been
closed."

The Maduranese come from the island which abuts on the
north-east coast of Java. Like the Buginese they are a great
seafaring people and equally quick with their knives.

"Tuan like see Bantimoeroeng waterfall?" he asked again.
His energy was rare enough to be amusing. I realised that I
must have been his best client for many months. Although
the trip there and back was over fifty miles, I was glad that I

made it. The waterfall, so foaming as to give the impression of a solid mass of white against the background of thick jungle, was worth seeing.

Even more impressive than the waterfall were the small birds which from time to time swooped down on the heaviest part of the torrent until they seemed to be lost in the foam. They looked like swifts. Presumably they were picking up the flies and insects that were being washed down from above.

Incidentally, the best birds' nests for Chinese soups come from the Celebes and from Borneo. There is a considerable export to China, and the nests yield an appreciable sum in export duty, for they are heavily taxed at a rate of something like sixty shillings a pound. The best nests are made by a species of swift and have a whitish colour. The natives believe that the gelatinous substance, so attractive to the Chinese gourmet, is dried sea-foam which the birds bring from the sea. Actually, it is a tough transparent substance which the swift exudes from its bill as it builds its nest.

Pleasing as the river was, what attracted me most was the countryside itself. There were no European houses, no European estates; above all, no signs of industry. There were no Chinese. The cultivation was confined to rice and coconuts. In the plain the green "sawahs" looked like ruffled velvet. Buginese villages nestled in graceful palm-groves. By the river bank I saw Buginese fishing, not with nets, but with rods. In the background the mountains had that same blue-green tint as the hills at Pantai. I was enchanted. I found myself in danger of forgetting my first landscape love, and landscapes are more reliable friends than human beings, for, while their moods are always changing, they are always constant.

On my way back to town we passed a huge field which had recently been levelled. "What's that?" I asked. "Flying ship port," replied the chauffeur. "Not ready yet, but soon will be. English flying men come here not long ago." What was an aerodrome doing in this spot, twenty miles from Macassar? Was there after all some truth in these rumours of Anglo-Dutch co-operation? Later, I was informed officially that the field was to be the new civil aerodrome of the Celebes.

It was nearly sunset when we reached Macassar. "What about Tuan Jenni?" I said firmly, remembering my Conrad quest.

"No good see Tuan Jenni now, Tuan," was the answer. "Tuan Jenni very wise man. Get up with the sun, go to bed with the sun. Tuan must see my village."

He drove me rapidly through the town until we emerged on the northern side. He stopped for a moment to show me a Chinese garden with a large pond—very beautiful but too artificial to fit in with the *laissez-faire* haphazardness of Macassar. Then, turning into a bumpy apology for a road and crossing a ramshackle bridge, he pulled up beside a narrow river-mouth and waved his hand. "That's my village," he said proudly.

It was a kind of Malayan Venice. Before a background of tall palms and flowering trees stood a row of slender houses built on poles on the water's edge and with little "prahus" attached to their front doors. They were probably rat-infested and certainly insalubrious, but in the fading sunlight they made a picture of exquisite loveliness. I hope that, when the white medical officers have cleared away all these old Malayan water-villages, the Venice of Macassar will be one of the last to go. For here—and in my eyes it was the chief attraction of Macassar—time, for the moment at any rate, has stood still.

From the little headland there was a glorious view of the bay, its lagoons saffron-coloured by the setting sun and the horizon a desert of rose brick relieved by patches of cloud which wove themselves into a strange pageant of far-off cities and illusory islands. Lying at anchor by itself in a little bay shut off from the main harbour was a tiny motor-yacht. It was flying the British flag. It belonged to a retired naval commander. He had sailed his fragile boat from Australia. He had come to Macassar for pleasure and not for gain, but in my mood of the moment I pictured him as the last of the Conrad adventurers. His boat, at any rate, was the only British vessel in Macassar. To-day, the Dutch have a virtual monopoly of the inter-island shipping.

I went back to the hotel. It had been a strenuous day, but my Buginese was still indefatigable. "After dinner, Tuan, I show you the town by night." Rather against my better judgment, for I was tired, I went out again with my English companion. It was only ten o'clock. But Macassar was already asleep. Even the Harmonie, the Dutch club, was in darkness. Somewhere in the narrow streets there should have been the red lights which shine in every port, but they, too, were dimmed. In the brilliant moonlight even the sea was almost silent, its wash against the shore the faintest of lullabies.

The next morning I was up, packed, and dressed and on my way to Mr. Jenni's by seven o'clock. I found him already walking outside his house at the corner of a shady boulevard just opposite the hotel. The veriest idiot could not have failed to recognise him. He carried a stick, but his tall, slim figure was still erect. He was wearing a brown, soft, cone-shaped Javanese straw hat, a short white coat, and brightly coloured Buginese trousers. Sixty years ago it was the standard costume of the local Dutch, and Mr. Jenni had stayed with his own times. But it was his face which endeared me to him. In spite of his eighty years his cheeks were as pink as a boy's. His keen, blue eyes twinkled merrily. His beard, white with a faint flaxen tint, was well-trimmed. He was so like Mr. Bernard Shaw that for a moment I wondered if I had stumbled on that great man masquerading in Macassar.

I gave him my note from the hotel proprietor. He read it gravely and then addressed me in excellent English: "Conrad, he was a writer, was he not? I'm afraid I never knew him.

I don't think he could have stayed in Macassar. Jack London, yes. He came here before the war—after the war. I cannot remember. But I met him. He was a good writer. But of course he knew nothing about the East."

This last sentence was pronounced with the slightly contemptuous authority of all local experts who are only too prone to measure knowledge by the number of years spent in the East. And with his sixty years of residence Mr. Jenni could look down on them all.

My hopes vanished. Poor Conrad! How well I remembered that letter of his written at the height of his fame. "Excuse this discordant note, but I have just received my account from my publishers. I read that all my 'immortal' works brought me in last year less than five pounds in royalties."

If Mr. Jenni was vague about authors, his memory of other matters was remarkably clear. He had spent all his life in an import and export house in Macassar itself. The place had changed. The old camaraderie between Buginese and Dutch had gone. There was too much bureaucracy. Why, in the troubles of 1905 the military commander had gone so far as to order—yes, order—all the Dutch to leave their houses and come into the fort. He had, of course, refused. He was a friend of the Sultan.

"Did no one molest you?" I asked.

"Of course. Some foolish young men with guns and krises came along one night. I said to them: 'Mr. Jenni's compliments to the Sultan. Tell him I don't want my sleep disturbed. And now—go to hell quick!' They went and did not come back."

"The Sultan", he continued, "used to make the Dutch officials take out permits for shooting on his land. He never made me take out one. He was a fine old chap. We understood each other very well."

Mr. Jenni was a fine old chap himself. Nor did he exaggerate. My chauffeur told me afterwards that he was held in great respect by all the Buginese. He certainly had a very high regard for the dignity of the white man's position in the East, and I do not think that in his whole life he had ever put a foot wrong.

I would gladly have listened longer to this great old gentleman. But we were sailing at ten. When I arrived at the docks, half the population of Macassar was on the quay. An officer of the local garrison was being transferred to Java, and his brother officers were giving him an official send-off. The officers were a curious lot. They ranged from pure white through every shade of colour to pure Javanese.

I could not help noting that, whereas the purely Dutch officers looked heavy and corpulent, the half-castes were vigorous and athletic. There was one swarthy young man whose well-cut white uniform, flashing eyes, and conscious swagger would have qualified him for any hero's role in Hollywood.

The officer who was being seen off was the regimental doctor. He was a pure-bred Javanese and as fat and as plump as the pure-Dutch major. There was a guard of honour. A Javanese military band with tubas nearly as big as themselves was playing military marches of the kind so dear to the sentimental Teuton. I confess that I have a similar weakness for these musical honours, and the scene in Chekoff's "Three Sisters", when the regiment leaves with the music growing fainter and fainter, never fails to stir my emotions to their most watery depths. It is true that on this occasion it was not the band which was marching away from us, but we who were sailing away from the music. Almost I persuaded myself that this brass-band farewell had been arranged for my special benefit and my own parting with my Buginese chauffeur threatened to become sentimental. On both sides it was marked by two genuine emotions: gratitude on his part for the unexpected windfall which my sight-seeing mania had brought him; regret on mine to be leaving a place which had afforded such a pleasant contrast to the physical and spiritual suffocation of my London life.

At the last minute the assistant manager rushed up to say good-bye. His hand was clammy. He seemed more down-in-his-luck than ever. With a nervous smile he informed me that he had just been sacked. For the first time I felt sorry for him and ashamed of my own egotism. To me, the transient visitor, the departed glory of Macassar was its greatest charm. To him it meant unemployment and perhaps starvation. Departed glory brings no compensations to those whom it has left behind.

CHAPTER THREE

ON THE VOYAGE back we carried more passengers. They were mostly minor Dutch officials going on leave or being transferred. The centre of interest was the Javanese regimental doctor. His wife and family were also on board, but they did not come into the saloon for meals. He himself sat with me at the captain's table and ate the same heavy food which the Dutch eat. He was both dignified and reserved, taking little part in the conversation.

I should have liked to discuss politics with him, but was restrained by my over-sensitive self-consciousness. In any case the language difficulty would have been a bar. I had been warned not to address Javanese, who had been educated in Holland, in Malay. They were apt to regard it as an insult. The doctor knew no English and very little German. As far as reading was concerned, my Dutch had made good progress but had not reached the stage of coherent speech.

With the ship's officers, however, I discussed him at great length. Opinion was divided regarding the advisability of admitting Javanese officers to equal rank with the Dutch. Some were in favour; others were doubtful. One officer, who had been in the army himself and who was travelling as a passenger in order to join another ship, had a poor opinion of the Javanese as soldiers and would have scrapped the lot. Contrary to the opinion which I had formed, he ranked the Dutch army officers far higher in ability than the Dutch civil servants.

He gave me a first-hand account of the communist rising in Batavia in 1926. The communists, having first blocked the roads to Batavia with barricades, had seized the telegraph and telephone office. A company of Javanese refused to fire on their compatriots. Then Ambonese troops, who were Christians and not Mohammedans, had been rushed forward, and the end had been quick. What happened to the communists no one quite knew. The Ambonese were

359

very good soldiers. But once started they did not stop. They saw red. Like the Ghurkas they preferred the bayonet to the bullet.

My Dutch informant had also been in New Guinea and had spent several weeks in Tanah Merah, the communist settlement to which the mutineers had been banished. It was, he said, a grim spot nearly three days' journey up river. At first the supervision had been carried out by civilian guards. There had been trouble. Then, of course, the Government had to send a soldier, and at once the disaffection ceased. The communists were divided into two camps: one for the well-behaved and the other for the recalcitrants. Escape was almost impossible. If a communist tried to make his way through the interior, the Papuans got him and probably ate him.

The shark-infested sea did not invite any attempts by swimming. Only four men had made a successful breakaway. With knives they had fashioned a boat, had rigged up a sail of sarongs, and after an extraordinary Odyssey had succeeded in reaching Thursday Island. Here they had given themselves up to the English, and the English had sent them back. I thought, but did not say so, that it was an un-English thing to do. There are some Moscow-and-Canton infested Marxists among the Javanese. But the Dutch, like the British in India, use the word communist very loosely, and among the prisoners of Tanah Merah there are probably more nationalists than real communists.

That evening I gave a farewell "pahit" party to the ship's officers, and by dint of repetition succeeded in overcoming my nausea for their Bols. I cannot say that I liked it. But they had been very kind and hospitable to me, and there are times when politeness must be maintained even at the cost of discomfort. I admired their quiet efficiency and their dignity. They seemed a very happy family, and their relations with their native crew were an excellent combination of firmness and friendliness. During the five days that I was with them, I never heard a cross word. If ever they got on each other's nerves, I saw no sign of it.

The next morning we anchored off Boeleleng, and after more farewells I went ashore in the K.P.M. motor-boat. I was on Balinese soil. I had little time to analyse my emotions. Such as I was conscious of were in my stomach. A crowd of Chinese guides, chauffeurs, native porters, and idle on-lookers surged forward to meet me. The company's agent brushed them aside, and before I knew where I was, I found myself in the hall of the K.P.M. tourist office.

"Mr. Lockhart, I think," said an energetic young Dutch-man in excellent English. "We've received instructions about you from Batavia. Everything is in order. Here is your ticket for your hotel accommodation. I have an excellent car and chauffeur for you and an English-speaking guide. You are in luck. There's a cremation to-day, and if you wish to see it you must leave at once."

When this whirlwind of efficiency had ceased, I inter-vened. "I don't want a guide," I said firmly. "I want a reli-able Malay-speaking chauffeur."

He smiled and shook his head. "You will waste money by saving money," he said. "The chauffeurs know nothing about the history of the temples or the dances."

I explained that it was not a question of expense, but of my stupid, but deep-rooted aversion, born of long experi-ence in foreign countries, to English-speaking guides.

When he saw that I meant what I said, he was crestfallen; but only for a minute. He was not going to be beaten by any tourist. "I've got it," he said delightedly. "We've a young Balinese prince here who wants a trial. He speaks a little English, but he knows the island, and, if you speak Malay, you will get on splendidly."

More out of physical exhaustion than inclination, I agreed to see him. A good-looking young man, very neatly dressed in clean white coat and sarong, came forward to meet me. He was not a prince, but a member of the priest caste, which

2 A

is higher than the princely caste. There was a delicate refinement about his features, and a sad, remote expression in his eyes which appealed to me. I engaged him without further ado.

"What am I to call you?" I asked. He told me his name: Ida Bagoes Mahadewa. It had an attractive ring, but it was too long. "If you've no objection, I'll christen you 'Bagoes' for our trip," I said. In Malay the word means "handsome".

We set out immediately to call on the Dutch resident at Singaradja, the capital, which is close to Bouleleng. He was out—much to my Prince Handsome's delight, for he was intent on getting me to the cremation. He had time, however, to point out a temple to me with an image of Shiva mounted on a bicycle. I had read that Balinese art was a living force. There was certainly no stagnant classicism about this cycling Shiva.

In a few minutes we were racing along at sixty miles an hour on the eighty-miles' journey to Den Pasar on the south side of the island. The chauffeur, a North Balinese and a Mohammedan, obviously shared the Indonesian passion for speed. Bagoes seemed more highly-strung.

"You must be in time for the cremation. All tourists want to see cremations," he informed me gravely.

"To hell with the cremation," I said, clutching my topee with both hands as the swaying of the car threw me violently out of my seat on to the floor. Seeing my ridiculous position, Bagoes grinned broadly. He had a sense of humour. I felt that we should get on together.

The country through which we passed was pleasing to the eye. Detail was lost in the speed at which we travelled, but I formed a general impression of deep canyons, cultivated to the top by means of attractive rice terraces, of green rice-fields, and of apple-green hills. Certain features made themselves immediately obvious. Bali was greener than any other part of the Archipelago that I had seen. The villages were totally unlike the kampongs of the Mohammedan Malays.

They were laid out rectangularly, intersected by roads, and
closed in by high clay walls. The island—and I noted the
fact with some feeling of regret—was not only densely cultivated, but densely populated. Java, long reputed the most
densely populated island in the world, has three hundred
inhabitants to the square mile. Bali has four hundred and
fifty; the Celebes have only forty-four. The figures in themselves are a sufficient indication of the island's fertility.

I did not need to observe the scores of temples with their
open carved entrances to know that I was in a Hindoo
country. I passed two men with their sarongs tucked up
under their fork—like a loin cloth. They were carrying a live
pig packed tight in an oblong open bamboo basket and
slung on a long bamboo pole. Pigs, cattle, and water-
buffaloes abound in Bali. As good Hindoos the Balinese regard the cow as sacred. But they eat buffalo meat, and pork,
which is anathema to the Mohammedan, is their culinary
joy.

Farther on, we came across scores of natives also in loin
cloths. They were busily engaged in road-mending. Obvi-
ously they were working for the Government. I asked
Bagoes what rate of pay they received. He told me none.
These were the Balinese who cannot pay their taxes. The
Government takes it out of them in forced labour.

The Dutch told me afterwards that the Balinese ryot prefers this work to paying taxes. I can well believe it. There
are many Englishmen and more Scots who would willingly
work a day in each week breaking stones in order to be released from the persecution of the income-tax inspector.

I saw a cloud on Bagoes's face. "You do not like it?" I
asked.

"No," he replied. "It is undignified."

Road-mending, Bagoes informed me, was being carried
out with special energy at that moment, because the Governor-General was to pay an official visit to the island in
April. Everything had to be spick-and-span before his

arrival, and among the local Dutch there had been quite a boom in top-hats.

Not far from Tabanan I made the chauffeur stop at some cross-roads. A plot of grass with a stone border had attracted my attention. In the middle of it was a large carved image sitting on a throne. "What's that?" I asked.

"That is Gana," said Bagoes. "He is the remover of obstacles. He keeps away the spirits from the roads. We put his image at all the danger points."

I understood. He was the Balinese St. Christopher of Catholic motorists. Doubtless, as a Belisha beacon Gana was in his proper element, but to my untrained eyes St. Christopher, although no Adonis, had the advantage in looks. No European motorist, driving alone at night, would like to meet Gana's huge cavernous mouth for the first time.

We now were well inside the southern half of the island. This is the most fertile and densely-populated part and the centre of attraction for tourists. The villages became more numerous and closer together. Soon we were in the main street of Den Pasar and had pulled up at the K.P.M. Hotel, a new modern building stamped with the hallmark of Dutch cleanliness and Dutch efficiency. My accommodation had been booked previously from Batavia. It was a wise precaution, for every room was occupied.

At the moment, however, the hotel was empty. Everyone was at the cremation. It was now two o'clock. The heat was stifling, for Den Pasar is one of the hottest spots not only in Bali, but in the whole Archipelago. I wanted luncheon and a cool drink more than anything in the world. But Bagoes was hopping round in nervous impatience, and in a weak moment I allowed him to carry me off.

We drove a little way beyond the town, turned into a side road and left our car at the entrance to a grove. We walked along a shaded path until we reached three gaudy, garlanded wooden bulls mounted on bamboo trestles. Farther down the road was the high funeral tower bedecked with ornaments and mounted on a platform. There was a large concourse of people, including many Balinese. But the chief points of vantage were held by the European tourists. I saw several Balinese women with naked breasts, but they looked modest beside an English girl in an almost transparent dress with no back to it. From time to time a tourist would unfold his Leica and take a snapshot of the images. Otherwise there was a long lull of inactivity. We had arrived too soon. The heat was stifling.

After what seemed an interminable wait a priest appeared and, after shooting off four arrows towards the four points of the compass, took his place in a kind of throne before the funeral tower. Beside him was a huge dragon-head with a long tail. It was fastened to the chair by a rope. Gradually the mourners or rather the joy-makers, for a cremation is properly an occasion for joy and not for sorrow, sorted themselves into a procession. First came women bearing offerings of rice and flowers and little vessels filled with holy water; men with lances and banners, and the relatives of the deceased. The relatives held the rope attached to the dragon-head. After someone had fastened a pair of white chickens to the funeral tower as an encouragement to the souls which were to fly to heaven after the cremation, a score or so of men crawled under the platform and, raising it on their shoulders, carried it gently to a meadow just beyond the grove. A full gamelan orchestra provided a musical accompaniment. With Bagoes I brought up the rear behind the sweating Europeans.

In the meadow, twenty-five yards from the tower, was the funeral pyre on which the wooden bulls had now been mounted. The corpses were taken from their coffins in the tower and placed inside the hollow stomachs of the bulls.

Before the burning started, there were further elaborate ceremonies, including a dance by a number of old gentlemen dressed in square-checked trousers and carrying lances and eggs. On both sides the tourists, their cameras clicking with the regularity of a taximeter, closed in on the dance until they formed a narrow lane. Suddenly the old gentlemen, now rather frenzied, began to throw their eggs on the ground. They were raw, and my white coat was splashed with yolk. For a moment I thought they were starting an attack on us, as we richly deserved for our unmannerly curiosity. But no! the eggs were for more dangerous interlopers. They were intended, so Bagoes told me, for the evil spirits who, having been fed, would then do no harm.

When the dance is over, there is a sudden rush for the tower. Stormed by the local youth, it is stripped of its decorations and then set in flames. The crowd turns and makes a dash for the pyre. The tourists turn with them, and one old English lady, not to be outdone, gathers up her skirts and charges across the grass like a bull that has been stung by a hornet. Girls and women place their offerings on the pyre. The men pile logs round the feet of the effigies. Handfuls of coins are then thrown to the crowd, and men and women, girls and boys, pushing and shouting raucously like a Yale football crowd urging on its heroes against Harvard, dive and scramble for this largesse. The battery of cameras is turned on the scrimmage. Natives and tourists draw back, while young men set fire to the logs with torches. The fire licks its way round the bodies of the wooden effigies. Soon the whole pyre is a blazing mass of flames, which add a new fierceness to the stifling heat.

The Balinese will wait beside the pyre until nightfall. On the morrow they will carefully gather up the ashes and consign them to the sea, for only by the double purification of fire and water can the soul be freed from its terrestrial bondage.

But I have had enough. I am, I think, not insensitive to the decencies and solemnities of all ceremonial. I admit that I should have been impressed by those rites, and that my thoughts should have been concentrated on comparative religion. I should have asked myself what the Balinese would think of our own lugubrious funeral services with their processions of top-hats and black crêpe. But try as I might, I could not attune my mind to the occasion. If, from some hidden point of vantage, I could have watched a Balinese cremation at which no Europeans were present, my emotions might have been different. But, as it was, the whole scene reminded me of a film being shot in exotic surroundings. I felt—quite erroneously, of course—that the efficient organisers of the K.P.M. had arranged the show for the tourists' special benefit.

I turned to my high-caste guide, who was an expert on these rites. "Bagoes", I said, "let us go. I have seen my first and my last cremation." He made no protest.

"It wasn't much of a show," he said. "You should see a prince's cremation. That *is* something."

It was true. Cremations are very expensive, and the richer Balinese spend on them thousands of guilders and in some cases thousands of pounds. The poor, on the other hand, may have to wait for months and even years before they can afford to cremate their dead, and thus release the soul to one of the eleven Hindoo heavens, where it can rest in peace until its re-incarnation in another terrestrial body.

We went back to the hotel. I was exhausted. I had stood for three hours under a fierce sun. Never before had I succumbed so completely to the heat of the tropics. I threw off my clothes and lay down on my bed, thanking providence and the Dutch who had provided me with a modern electric fan. I turned it on. Nothing happened. Dutch zeal for economy during difficult times had decreed that the electricity, and therefore the fans, should not operate between the hours of 6 a.m. and 6 p.m.!

After a sleep and a bath, I felt better. I was in a quandary what to put on. The tourists were exclusively English and Americans. Doubtless, they would dress for dinner. I compromised with a white drill dinner jacket and walked across to the grass terrace in front of the hotel. It was empty. I found a pleasant seat under a shady tree and ordered myself a drink. The terrace was separated from the main street only by a low hedge. I had not been there for more than a few seconds when I heard a rustle. Looking down, I found a Balinese boy kneeling by my chair and offering post-cards. I shook my head. He was followed by another and yet an-another. Finally, one came who had some English: "Like visit pretty Balinese dancer, sir? Very nice—I show you."

I do not know who first discovered Bali to the English-speaking world. The Dutch have known it ever since 1601, when the Prince of Karangasam presented a beautiful girl to van Heemskerck, the great Dutch explorer. Alfred Wallace was here in 1856, and was delighted by its natural beauty. Conrad, too, must have visited the island, for he mentions it more than once in *Almayer's Folly*, and he makes the proud and warlike Dain, with whom Nina, Almayer's half-caste daughter, throws in her lot, a Brahmin and a son of a Balinese rajah. When Mr. Somerset Maugham was in Bali after the war, the island was still unspoilt and there was no European hotel.

The visits of these great men struck no travel-compelling chord in the hearts of their countrymen. Since then, how-ever, an English peeress, finding in its romantic surroundings a pleasant relief from the rigours of the London season, has made the charms of Bali known to her compatriots. Mr. André Roosevelt, a cousin of the president, who lived here and who made the first film of Bali, has done the same for the Americans. They have been followed by the journalists and the writers, and during the last three or four years a score of books have sung the praises of "the last paradise." The Dutch genius for tourism and the lurid advertisements of the shipping companies have completed the work of popularisation. Those who seek a resort where an old-world civilisation remains intact must come quickly. The conver-sion of "the last paradise" into the newest hell is proceeding apace, and all too soon Bali may become a second Port Said.

After dinner, a six-course affair with hot and heavy European foods, I made friends with the Dutch representative of the American Express Company and with Mr. Minas, an Armenian tourist agent. Both spoke fluent English. Both were amusing cynics with very definite views on the "cussedness" of the Balinese, and on the real nature of the attractions which brought the tourists or, at any rate, the male tourists to Bali. They had a grudging admiration for the K.P.M., who had acquired almost a monopoly of the tourist traffic. The K.P.M. boys were smart. They had made a good business of it. There was not much left for the others. The Armenian claimed to have supplied most of the material to the writers of the dozen or so English books on Bali which have appeared during the last five years. Doubtless, he had, for there was little about the island that he did not know.

From tourists the conversation changed to missionaries, a subject on which I had been well primed by Dutch officials both in Holland and in the East Indies. Actually, most of the Dutch colonial officials would prefer the missionaries to be debarred from all proselytising activities in the Archipelago. But politics in Holland are strongly influenced by the various religious parties, and the officials are forced to make a compromise. They do it in a curious manner. In New Guinea the northern part of the Dutch territory is a reservation of the Catholics, while the southern part is given to the Protestants. In Sumatra no missionaries are allowed in Acheh, but between the Achinese and the warlike Menangkabaus there is a wedge of Bataks who are Christians. Not very long ago they were cannibals and chess players with a few geniuses who were a match for the world's greatest champions. They still play chess, but they no longer eat "long pork". They are now fathered by the famous Rhineland Mission. In Bali, missionaries are encouraged neither by the Dutch nor by the Balinese, and the only missionaries who have visited the island soon retired for lack of converts.

My new acquaintances, however, had their own theories. In Bali, they said, the Dutch attitude towards missionaries was influenced entirely by commercial considerations. The K.P.M. "bosses" feared that the missionaries would introduce bust-bodices and that the tourist traffic would suffer.

CHAPTER FOUR

I HAD ORDERED Bagoes and the chauffeur to come round with the car at seven the next morning. Long before this hour I was awake. My sleep had been disturbed by the yelping of the Balinese dogs. Miserable mongrels, they are the curse of the island. Every Balinese family keeps at least one, and, although tens of thousands have been killed off by the Dutch for fear of rabies, they are still a plague.

In my case their howling was a godsend, for it compelled me to read an old Dutch book, which had been given to me by a Dutch friend in the Hague. Its author was a Dr. van Weede, a member of the expedition of 1906, and I had come to the chapter dealing with the Dutch advance on Den Pasar. By the aid of the plan I had realised that the street in which my hotel stood had been the scene of the greatest immolation in modern history. It was a thrilling story. The war had broken out because a year-and-a-half before, the Balinese had plundered a Chinese schooner. When the Prince of Badoeng, in whose territory the outrage had taken place and whose palace was in Den Pasar, refused to pay the 3000 guilders which the Dutch demanded as compensation, the Dutch decided to send a military expedition against him. There were other reasons for the war which followed, but these I shall refer to later.

Three other South Bali princes, including the Dewa Agoeng of Kloeng-Koeng, joined forces with their colleague of Badoeng. Part of the Dutch forces landed at Pabean Sanoer, the nearest point on the coast to Den Pasar and the actual scene of the plundering of the schooner. Within a few days they had quelled all resistance and had encompassed Den Pasar.

It was then that the obstinate prince decided to die fighting in the traditional national manner known in Balinese as "poepoetan". On the night of the 20th September, 1906, he burnt his poeri or palace. The next morning he assembled his household before the ruins. They were mostly relations and nobles and included men, women, and children. They had dressed themselves in their best. The men were in red and black. They wore ornaments of gold and carried bejewelled krises. Their hair was combed and scented with perfumed oils. The women, too, had put on all their finery. Draped in white, they wore their hair loose. They carried a kris or a lance. Children, capable of lifting a knife, were likewise armed. Young babies were carried at their mothers' breasts.

At nine o'clock, when the first news of the Dutch advance was received, the little band, barely 250 strong, moved forward along what is now the main road. According to custom the prince went first, carried on the shoulders of one of his household. Not even the Persians advancing on Leonidas's seven hundred at Thermopylæ could have been more astonished than was the Dutch infantry company when on that September morning it caught its glimpse of this glittering array moving slowly forward to a certain death. Only three hundred paces separated the two forces, and the Dutch had a machine-gun. To do him justice, the Dutch captain did all he could by signs and shouting to persuade the Balinese to surrender. But they had already committed their souls to heaven.

Unheeding, they advanced until they were so close that the captain dared no longer endanger the lives of his own men. At seventy yards the Balinese charged, and the Dutch captain gave the order to fire. Many fell. Those who survived pressed forward until they, too, were shot down. Women, afraid lest they might be spared, bared their breasts and pointed to their heart in order that they might die a warrior's death. The wounded committed suicide or begged their companions to finish them off. One old man, jumping nimbly over the heap of corpses, krissed all who remained alive until he himself was shot dead.

While the slaughter was at its height, a second force of

Balinese approached. It was headed by the prince's half-brother, a youth of twelve scarcely able to carry his lance. The captain summoned him to surrender. For a moment he hesitated. Then, urged on by his followers, he gave the order to charge. All met the same fate. When the firing ceased, a few children were seen crawling away from the heaps of corpses. They were the only survivors of the "poepoetan". The body of the prince was found at the very bottom of the highest heap. He had led the way and had fallen first. His dead followers had made a human cairn over him.

Only one Dutch soldier was killed—a sergeant called Bakker. He, too, died a hero's death. Unwilling to make war on the women, the Dutch, in many cases, had refused to fire and had tried to ward off the Amazons' krises with their rifle butts. Some were wounded in this manner, and these were the only other casualties. Bakker paid for his humaneness with his life.

When Bagoes arrived, I was still under the emotional impression of this stirring story and I plied him with questions. A well-informed young man, who had been educated at the high school in Djokjakarta, he knew the history of the expedition thoroughly, for his grandfather, a North Balinese, had supported the Dutch during the war. We got into the car, and he showed me the remaining landmarks of the battle. Where the poeri once stood is now a museum and a football field. The K.P.M. hotel is on the site of the former palace temple.

Turning away from this now peaceful scene, we took the road to Kloeng-Koeng. Bagoes had mapped out a strenuous day for me, which, fortunately, was to take me far from Den Pasar. Our way lay through thickly-populated country with villages so close to one another that they seemed like one vast agricultural metropolis. Yet each village had its own wall to keep out the evil spirits, its own temple, and its temple bell. Each house had its own shrine and its fighting cocks kept in bamboo baskets. Dogs and pigs disputed the playground of the road with children walking on bamboo stilts or chasing dragon flies with long wands smeared with lime.

Many people were at work, but they were mostly women. For the Balinese man will undertake only work which a woman is incapable of doing, and in the Balinese philosophy work of this kind is rare. In consequence the Balinese man has the necessary leisure, not only for cock-fighting, which is his chief sport, but also for dancing and sculpture, the two primary and essential arts which have made him so attractive in the eyes of the European. As in the poultry world the male is definitely the finer animal, and with the exception of the young girls of thirteen and fourteen the much-vaunted women are disappointing.

I soon discovered from Bagoes that only the "soedra" or lowest-caste women go about with their breasts uncovered. Toil in the fields leaves its inevitable mark on their figures, and for the same reason they are darker than Malays of the Mohammedan faith, who regard nakedness as a sin and therefore wear more clothes. Swaying along with baskets of fruit and rice and even coconuts on their heads, they make an attractive picture. But this pleasing effect is diminished when one sees them dump their baskets and sit down by the roadside and begin to pick the lice from each other's hair. The high-caste women have not the same liberty of movement as their low-caste sisters and rarely appear in public.

Kloeng-Koeng itself, with its attractive market-place and its teeming native life, was a delightful contrast to Den Pasar. Here, too, the local prince, known as the Dewa Agoeng, committed the same national suicide or "poepoetan" as his colleague of Badoeng. His palace was destroyed, and its site is now an open square dominated by the Dutch comptroller's residence. There are, however, a few remains, including some fine gateways and a couple of quaint Balinese statues. One shows a Dutchman counting guilders; the other a Dutchman drinking beer. The statues are an accurate reflection of the white man's life in the East in the days before an enlightened policy towards the native put some check on commercial rapacity.

I stated previously that there were other reasons for the Balinese war of 1906 than the piratical plundering of the Chinese schooner. The practice of "suttee" was one. The attitude of the Dewa Agoeng of Kloeng-Koeng was another.

In another Dutch history book I found his story. Two of his daughters had erred from the path of virtue in company with two young men. The Dewa Agoeng took a terrible revenge. With their hands tied behind their backs his two daughters were thrown to the sharks. One of the young men was tortured to death. The other succeeded in escaping to the Dutch in North Bali. The Dewa Agoeng demanded that he should be given up. When the Dutch refused he replied graciously that his honour would be satisfied if they would behead the culprit immediately. The second Dutch refusal angered him and was one of the causes of the war.

I asked Bagoes if the story was true. His answer was that the Dutch taught history in their own way, but that the Dewa Agoeng had the reputation of being a stern as well as a brave warrior. Looking at Bagoes with his gentle, Musset-like, *fin-de-siècle* expression, I found it hard to believe that he came of a race of fighters. I could not see him committing hara-kiri in a last desperate charge against a Dutch machine-gun. Yet thirty years ago there was not a high-caste Balinese who would have hesitated to follow his prince. To-day, there are no Dutch troops in Bali, and the whole island of over a million inhabitants is administered by a Dutch Resident, two Dutch assistants, seven Dutch controllers and a handful of police!

Very wisely the Dutch rule through the native regents, who, in most cases, are the lawful heirs of the former princes. When they are not the legitimate heirs, they are less popular with their own people, for in spite of the speed of modern life the Balinese still retain much of their former feudal loyalty. Regents are chosen by the Government, but the native form of administration is retained throughout, and in the lower branches such as the headsmanship of a village the office is elective. On the whole, the system works well, and, whether it be permanent or not, the *Pax Batavica* is in some ways a more remarkable achievement than even the *Pax Britannica*.

In Kloeng-Koeng we had the good fortune to run into Bagoes's uncle, who is an official of the local administration. He took us over to a high-roofed but otherwise open hall, built on an old part of the former palace and approached by a splendid staircase. Here the native court was sitting. The presiding judge was a priest. Beside him sat the Regent, a son of the Dewa Agoeng who had perished in the "poepoetan". The Regent, a pleasant, good-tempered man, had been a child of ten then, but he, too, had taken part in the "poepoetan". He still limps from the Dutch bullet which hit him in the knee. He is now a grandfather, is very popular with both the Dutch and his own Balinese, and has no vices except gambling on his fighting cocks.

The roof of the court was decorated with weird friezes illustrating the heavenly punishments which await the evildoers. They were intended to intimidate and were far sterner than those prescribed by law for this temporary world. They were mostly to the address of women, whose two chief crimes in Balinese eyes are indolence and sterility. There was one picture of a woman who had been unwilling or unable to learn weaving. She was being prodded with a fork by a Satanic monster. A dog had his teeth deeply fixed in her posterior. Another picture showed a huge two-headed caterpillar sucking the breasts of a woman. The caterpillar was held in position by an evil spirit. The woman's crime on earth had been that she was unable to bear children. In Bali sterility is treated in various ways. A Balinese woman who bears male-and-female twins is turned out of her village for one Balinese month, that is, for forty-two days, and must remain in a cemetery until she is purified. The reason for this ostracism is the belief, apparently justified by modern science, that male-and-female twins are non-productive.

From Kloeng-Koeng we set out for Besakih, the largest, the highest and most sacred temple of Bali. This is the finest drive in the island. The road is mountainous and twists and turns across hills and canyons cultivated with superb terraces of rice-fields. The last part of the road is only a grass track and was not properly open to motor traffic. Twice our wheels stuck in the soft ruts. Then after much straining and pushing we crested the steepest corner and came to a grassy plateau with cattle and ponies scampering across our path. There was a welcome absence of habitation. Before us was the vast panorama of the 10,000-feet-high Goenoeng Agoeng and to the left its servant, Goenoeng Batoer, smaller in size, but infinitely more dangerous because of its volcanic activities. A mile ahead, partly concealed by a grove of trees, was the many-roofed temple, its approach guarded by a double hedge of Indian laburnum.

The Balinese are supposed to have come to the island from Java at the time when the Hindoo empire there was crumbling before the onslaught of Islam. For seven centuries they have been an isolated outpost of Brahminism and Buddhism in an Archipelago which is predominantly Mohammedan. Their religion, however, is still largely influenced by the primitive animism of a pre-Hindoo civilisation, and only an expert who has spent a lifetime in the study of it can venture to describe its intricacies. Indeed, most Europeans make little attempt to unravel the maze of superstitions and mixed beliefs which are woven around it.

Besakih is one of the seven wonders of the East and, by reason of its situation alone, there is no human being, no matter what his race or faith, who can fail to be impressed by it. It stands over 3000 feet above sea-level, and from its terraces there is a majestic view over land and sea.

The temple itself, or rather the temples, for there are three, is built on a series of terraced courts. The lowest part is or-

2 B

nate and new with brick walls. The numerous towers which guard the temple like sentinels have attractive black roofs made of sugar-cane bark. Every Balinese is supposed to visit Besakih once a year. Every district of the island has its own tower there.

We were shown over part of the building by a priest. The Balinese New Year, which begins on March 6, was only a few days ahead. It is heralded by a day of complete silence. For twenty-four hours no Balinese opens his door. Traffic and trade stop, and even Europeans may use their motor-cars on that day only by paying a heavy fine. It is the day on which Heaven is swept for evil spirits. After the silence there are feasts followed by an orgy of cock-fighting.

During my visit the temple was already being prepared for the feast, and at intervals women climbed the steps and deposited their offerings of fruit and flowers. Several of them brought a kind of fruit which, after it has been blessed, is supposed to have special powers of fecundity. While we were talking to the priest, a car drove up. A middle-aged Englishman and a young English girl got out. I could not tell whether they were father and daughter or husband and wife. They were attended by a Chinese guide. The girl was carrying some yellow fruit in her hat. She explained to the guide that she wanted it blessed for fecundity. There was an awkward pause. The guide whispered something which the girl did not understand. She walked forward towards the priest. This time the Chinese guide raised his voice: "No, no, Missie, these are the wrong fruits. This kind make you pass water six or seven times."

Balinese religious customs take a lot of knowing. After this episode I was not surprised when, on leaving, Bagoes took me aside and informed me tactfully that the priest ex-pected to be tipped. I produced the Dutch equivalent of five shillings. The priest showed less embarrassment in taking this offering than I did in giving it.

On our way home we made a long detour by Karangasem

and the coast. Before we came down to the more densely populated part, we passed a group of Balinese carrying fighting cocks. They were taking the birds into Kloeng-Koeng or Gjanjar for the coming feast-day. I wanted badly to see a cock-fight, but in order to prevent the natives from ruining themselves, the Dutch allow cock-fighting only on feast days. I could not wait until the next feast-day. The road was more or less deserted.

"Bagoes," I said, "if I put up a purse, will these fellows stage a fight?" Bagoes seemed frightened, but I made him translate my message to the men. They grinned, and in a few minutes they had made a ring on a flat piece of ground behind a hill and out of sight of the road.

The fight itself was not very exciting. The cocks were fierce enough but rather small. They wore no spurs. Long before any serious damage was done my better feelings reasserted themselves, and I gave the signal to stop. Not understanding my motives, the men looked disappointed until I handed them their reward. Then they grinned again. They had earned it, for they themselves had put up an excellent performance, dancing around their animals like professional boxers and urging them on with the same vigour and, doubtless, the same expletives as a cockney brings to bear on a donkey race. I expect that after we left there was a dispute over the decision of the prize money. Almost certainly the fight was continued to a finish, for Bagoes told me that all the men had been making side bets, and without a proper finish the bets could not be settled.

The Balinese, indeed, are great gamblers, and more than one regent has nearly ruined himself through his betting losses. The gambling instinct is strong in every class and caste of the population. Any form of competition is an excuse for a bet. The fighting cocks, who are given a special diet of maize and rice, are hung up opposite each other in baskets in order to stimulate hatred. But when no feast is near the Balinese use them for another form of gamble. They take one down and let him loose among the village hens. They then sit round and bet on which hen the lord of the kampong poultry will bestow his affection. The fellow who picks the first hen favoured collects the stakes.

Even the children bet on insect races and on a particularly cruel form of duelling between crickets, whose gladiatorial arena is an ordinary European match-box. Here they are enclosed until one has killed the other. Indeed, cricket duels and dragon-fly catching are the chief amusements of the Balinese children. The dragon-fly catching, however, is utilitarian. The dragon-flies are toasted and eaten, generally with shrimps. They are considered a great delicacy.

Balinese boys, I noticed, did more work than the men. Throughout the day I had been impressed by the glorious panorama of the rice-fields. Every sawah has its shrine to Dewi Sir, the guardian goddess of rice, who brings the slender green shoots to fruition. More mundanely effective are the shelter huts for the Balinese boys whose task it is to chase away the rice-birds from the ripe ears. They employ an ingenious labour-saving device. They stretch a long string, with tin cans attached to it, across the sawah. When the birds fly down to the ears, the boy pulls the string and the tins rattle. According to Bagoes the birds never grow accustomed to the din, but I expect that they reap a good harvest, for Nature, in her bountiful provision for all the world's creatures, ensures that during the heat of the day nine out of ten of the little watchers go to sleep.

To me a rice-field is man's most beautiful handiwork, and in the picturesqueness of their setting the sawahs of Bali surpass all other rice-fields in the world. The soil and climate are so favourable and the system of irrigation, learnt from the Hindoos a thousand years ago, is so perfect that every field yields two harvests in every year with an "in-between" crop of maize or pea-nuts. In consequence rice ripe for harvest, half-ripe rice, green rice, and rice newly planted are to be seen all the year round, and the colours of the sawahs range from a golden yellow to the most vivid shade of green.

The manner of cultivation is elaborate. First, the old harvest is burnt off. The ground is then softened and ploughed and harrowed. The water is let in and the sawah is harrowed wet. The rice is grown from seed in a special nursery. After forty days each shoot is taken out and is planted separately in rows in the sawah. Everything is done by the eye alone. The system is so good that the Dutch with all their efficiency have been able to add to it only very minor improvements.

At Koesambe, a small village on the coast to the south of Kloeng-Koeng, we stopped to inspect the Goa Lawah or Bats' Cave. It is a holy place and belongs to the category of cave temples. Here in 1906 the Balinese princes met to swear common cause against the Dutch. Stimulated by this historic association I advanced to the mouth of the huge cavern. Thousands of large bats clung to its walls, emitting a stench more overpowering, more nauseating, than a shipload of rotten durians. Bagoes told me that there was a big god and a big snake inside. I did not see either. The big smell was more than enough for me.

That evening, after dinner, I went out on to the hotel terrace to watch the dancing performance which had been specially arranged for the tourists. It was my first experience of Balinese dancing, but I had been prepared for disappointment. I had seen the hotel dancing at Djokja. I had learnt that a hotel front is not the ideal setting for Eastern dances. I knew, too, that for all my love of the Russian ballet Javanese and Balinese music and dancing were an exotic taste to be acquired only after years of study. On the whole I was agreeably surprised. It is true that the setting, with half the native population of Den Pasar watching from the street and the tourists teed up on chairs in front of the hotel, was grotesque. But the dancing itself was much less stereotyped than that which I had seen in Java. The music, too, was more modern and at times the rhythmic effects bore a strong resemblance to modern American music.

Two girls, so young that they seemed to belong to the nursery rather than to the stage, danced a legong dance with a grace of technical perfection which was marred only by the set vacant expression on their faces. There was a comedian who frightened the children and drew roars of laughter from the native audience by a patter comment which was full of references to Arab moneylenders, who spoke bad Malay, and to other similar subjects which delight the man in the street of every nation. Then Goesti Ngura Raka, one of the best male dancers of Bali, danced a long fan dance, in which he moved across the stage without ever releasing his legs from their crossed sitting position. The arm movements and the swaying of the lithe body were very attractive, and even to the uninitiated it was a remarkable performance.

The dances, however, were long, and before the end I found myself yawning. And without a genuine expert to explain things I believe that most Europeans will find it hard to sit through a whole evening's performance, especially in the artificial surroundings of a European hotel.

Whatever the limitations of my knowledge, I felt that Bali was growing on me. As I went to bed, I was already prepared to include the island among the delectable corners of the earth to which I should retire in order to farm as soon as I could escape from Fleet Street. Scotland, Slovenia, Dalmatia and Negri Sembilan, of course, offered a severe competition, and musing over a final selection prevented me from sleeping for some time. Finally I decided that if Scotland could grow rice my choice would be a farm in the Highlands. It was not, I felt, a very satisfactory solution. But by inducing sleep it served its purpose.

CHAPTER FIVE

FROM NOVEMBER TO April Bali is unpleasantly hot during the middle of the day. The monsoon brings moist clouds, and on most afternoons the air is charged with thunder. But the mornings are cool, and for some hours after dawn the sky is cloudless. It is a time which wise men seek to turn to profit. During each day of my stay in Bali I had Bagoes and the chauffeur on my mat at six-thirty.

The next morning I spent in visiting the various villages near Den Pasar and in talking, with Bagoes's aid, to the local inhabitants. In one village we found a djanger dance in full progress at eight o'clock in the morning. Here the setting was almost perfect. The dancers were seated in a square formation, with the men and women facing each other, on a level piece of ground before a temple. Lofty coconut palms and heavily scented champaka trees formed a natural stage, and through the leafy branches the sun threw glints of light upon the jewelled dresses. Here I could have lingered long, but once again my view was impeded by the stampede of tourists who rushed forward at every movement of the dance with Kodak or Leica to perpetuate the memory of their visit with a photograph. It was their show. They were leaving at midday and had ordered it specially.

With stoical patience I turned to Bagoes and began to question him about the life of the dancers. Both dancers and musicians, I learnt, are organised in guilds. All the money earned by each individual is paid into the guild. It is then used to buy properties: dresses and costumes for the dancing-guilds and instruments for the gamelan-guilds. Unlike the dancing girls of Djokja and Solo, the Balinese girls do not make brilliant marriages. They themselves are of all castes. If they marry a regent, they are only number three or number four wife, and never number one. Usually they marry in their own villages. Most of them retire from dancing when they are about fifteen.

The guild system, which is a form of natural communism, prevails throughout Bali. There are guilds for sculptors, carvers, decorators and builders. There is little or no attempt to evade the rules of the guild. When Baron von Plessen was making his Bali film, "Black Magic", he engaged a handsome young cement worker to play a leading native role. The young man was offered what to a Balinese must have been a fabulous salary. He refused to take it until the film was finished. Then he gave his money to the guild.

In another village I spent some time in watching and talking to a group of sculptors who were engaged in making a new temple gate. They seemed to take a genuine pleasure in their work. Indeed, in their love of architecture, dancing, and the drama, the Balinese afford a striking comparison with the ancient Greeks in the time of Pericles. Here in Bali every man is an artist to whom dancing and sculpture are the natural means of expressing himself and the harmonious symbols of his spiritual life. Both, of course, are intimately entwined with his religion. When I thought of the low level of entertainment provided in the great cities of Britain and the United States, the so-called march of civilisation seemed a poor and shoddy thing. If mass happiness is the test of human progress, then the Balinese are centuries ahead of both the British and the Americans. And Balinese art is no stereotyped tradition which has been handed down from some remote classical period. It is a living force, constantly progressing, continuously experimenting. Natural conditions have favoured this progress as far as sculpture is concerned. Balinese stone crumbles quickly. That is why there are so many new temples in Bali, and why the island is the sculptor's paradise.

I tried to question Bagoes about the sexual life of his compatriots. One of the Dutch business men on the island had told me that the islanders were rotten with venereal disease. On this subject Bagoes, as a married man, was inclined to be reticent. Wooing, he told me, was still conducted on a

basis of tolerated abduction. There was considerable freedom and promiscuity before marriage. After marriage there
was little infidelity. I remembered how Catherine the
Great's liaison with Count Poniatowski had been revealed
by her fierce little lap-dog jumping up and fawning on the
Polish nobleman before the rest of her courtiers. Dogs were
the worst betrayers of illicit lovers, and in Bali dogs were
legion. Doubtless, Bagoes's testimonial to the sanctity of
Balinese marriages was correct.

There is one other Balinese trait which is to their credit.
Although they have certain rather cruel superstitions, they
are tolerant towards other religions. In one respect the
island bears some resemblance to Ireland. The north side,
which has been exposed to contact with the outside world,
has a considerable number of Mohammedans. The southern
part is entirely Hindoo. I asked Bagoes what happened when
a Balinese Hindoo girl married a Mohammedan. He gave a
typically Balinese answer. At first the family outlaw her.
Then they feel a little sorry. Perhaps, they say, there may be
something in this God Allah after all. Then they put up a
shrine to Allah as a kind of insurance policy.

In the afternoon I drove out with Bagoes to Tampaksiring to see the royal tombs. On the way we stopped near
Oeboed, and Bagoes made me crawl down a slope below
the road to see the rock temple of Poera Gowa, which dates
back to the twelfth century. It is another of the cave temples,
and the entrance is guarded by the head of a giant forcing,
as it were, his head through the wall. Being no archaeologist,
I was glad to escape quickly.

At Oeboed itself I saw something more to my fancy—a
charming modern Balinese house, which would have made
an admirable home for a European. I guessed that it must
have been built by one of the various European artists who
have made Bali their temporary home. But I was wrong.
The house belonged to the Balinese deputy of the Dutch
East Indies Parliament. It was this progressive Balinese who

took the first troupe of Balinese dancers to Europe. They appeared at the French Colonial Exhibition at Vincennes in 1931, and took all Paris by storm. The dancers themselves resisted all the blandishments of gilded European youth. But the deputy lost his heart to a Frenchwoman. Their marriage must have been almost the first mixed marriage in Bali. Now they live in semi-European state in Oeboed.

With Bersakih the royal tombs near Tampaksiring are the most impressive monument in Bali. They are difficult to approach. I had to leave my car and scramble down a steep path which leads to a canyon with a swift stream running through it. An attempted short cut through the long lalang grass ended in disaster, for the ground was soft from the constant rains. But the ruin to my suit was richly rewarded when eventually we reached the riverside. Facing us were five tombs, hewn in the virgin rock on the side of a steep hill. To the right was a monastery, grey-stoned, majestic and as old as time itself. The monastery dates from the ninth century and is now deserted. To-day tombs and monastery stand in a deserted glory, to which solitude and landscape have combined to give a solemnity unrivalled by any other sepulchre in the New World or the Old.

That evening I had a stroke of fortune. While I was inspecting the visitors' book in the hotel lounge before dinner, Victor Cunard came up to me. Victor, a former correspondent of *The Times* in Paris and a member of the family which has given its name to the famous shipping line, had travelled with me as far as Singapore. I had known him slightly in London and better on board ship, and was glad to see him again.

"Come and dine with me," he said. "You must meet Spiess."

I went over to their table and was introduced to a tall, fair man with attractive blue eyes and the long, tapered fingers of an artist. I had seen him on the night before at the dance performance on the hotel terrace. But he had gone away early as though bored by the whole proceedings. I did not know his name then, but I had heard of him as a German who had lived in Bali for some years. Actually, I had a letter of introduction to him. But its terms were vague and told me nothing about the man himself, and with my usual reluctance to make new acquaintances I had not bothered to use it.

My surprise was great when after a few minutes' conversation I discovered that he was Spiess of Moscow. I had known his family well in my Moscow days. They were one of the numerous Russo-German concerns in Russia, and had been established there since the Napoleonic wars. Before his father made a fortune in oil, the firm had done considerable business with England. I had dined in their Moscow house several times. I had visited them even after the war, for they were not immediately interned, and I had always looked on them more as Russians than Germans. Vaguely I tried to recognise in this good-looking expert the young boy whom I had seen in Moscow in 1914.

He told me his story in a few words. His parents had been ruined by the Russian revolution. Art ran in his family. His grandfather had been a famous architect, and had built the memorial church erected on the spot where the Emperor Alexander II was murdered. He had an aunt who was making her living in Russia now by teaching singing. He himself had studied both painting and music. After the war he had found Europe distasteful, and had come out to the East Indies. For five years he was employed as Director of Music by the Sultan of Djokja. For the last seven years he had been living in Bali painting and studying music. He had learnt Javanese, Malay and Balinese.

At dinner we were joined by Miss Waterman, an American lady, who has also made Bali her temporary home. She told me that there were several Europeans who claimed to be authorities on Balinese life and Balinese art, but that Walter Spiess stood in a class by himself. I needed no telling. The man spoke with the modesty and diffidence which mark the real expert. Between them, Miss Waterman and Spiess arranged a programme for us for the next evening. It included a Balinese dinner and a real dancing performance in a little village temple, where there would be no other Europeans but ourselves.

That night, when I went to bed, I said a special prayer for Victor, to whose kindness I owed this lucky chance. I contrasted his unselfishness with my own egotism. Had I been given the opportunity of spending a Balinese evening with Walter Spiess as cicerone, I should not have voluntarily suggested sharing it with anyone else.

The next morning I told Bagoes of my chance meeting. I saw at once from his expression that Spiess was a popular hero to the Balinese. He was, Bagoes told me, the great champion of the people, respected by everybody, including the Dutch officials, and fearless in his outspokenness when he thought Balinese rights were being infringed.

As we drove out to the sacred forest of Boekit Sari, Bagoes told me the tragedy of Spiess's life. His brother came out to join him some years ago. He was taken by a shark while bathing in the sea.

Bali is not a bathing paradise, although there is one strip of beach at Koota near Den Pasar which is safe from sharks. Nor, strangely enough, are the Balinese great fishermen. Unlike Lombok, however, the island has its complement of wild animals. They are not found in Central and Eastern Bali, because these parts are too well cultivated. But there are tigers and wild buffalo in the west. Occasionally a hunt is organised for Anglo-Saxon tourists with big-game hunting ambitions.

In this connection Bagoes told me a good story. A party of American men came to Bali. Inspired by an ardent wish to bring back the first Balinese wild buffalo head to the United States, they determined to organise a hunt. They sought the services of a local English-speaking agent, and were well pleased when he promised to arrange everything and to take payment by results only. The charge was fixed at a hundred dollars a head.

With a great show of efficiency the Americans were brought to their destination. They took up their places in platforms built in the trees, and there they waited until the buffalo came down to drink close by. The agent had a brother in Western Bali, who kept a large herd of tame buffaloes. At nightfall he drove his animals towards the platforms. The Americans did a valiant execution. The agent and his brother netted a handsome profit. Thus both parties were satisfied. Would that all big-game expeditions ended so happily.

Our visit to the Sacred Forest was a complete success. At the village of Sangeh, about eleven miles due north of Den Pasar, we left our car and, after providing ourselves with a store of bananas and pea-nuts, we walked down a grassy path alongside a forest of tall and stately trees. Almost at once a troupe of monkeys came out to meet us. Their friendliness, explained by frequent processions of pea-nut-armed tourists, was amazing. They fed from my hand. They followed us along the path until we came to the temple in the grove itself. I felt like a young schoolmaster in a private school taking the boys out for their Sunday walk.

I noticed that many of the monkeys bore scars. Several had raw wounds. Bagoes explained to me that two tribes of sacred monkeys inhabited the grove. Their territories were delimitated with the precision of a League of Nations plebiscite commission. Occasionally a band of monkeys, intent on rape or plunder, would make a sally into their neighbours' territory. Then a battle royal ensued, in which both tribes took part until one side had enough and retired, leaving its wounded and its dead behind. When I thought of the present state of Europe, the monkeys seemed more human than ever. Between the tribal law of the forest and the racial law of the European nationalists there is, in fact, little difference.

I made friends with a grey-whiskered old gentleman, whose grave mien and dignified gait would have entitled him to a seat of honour in any assembly of politicians. He was the leader of the tribe. I soon saw that, like the wolf law in Kipling's *Jungle Book*, the tribal law of monkeys is the law of the strong. The leader is leader only so long as he can beat the others. I had observed that our *Fuehrer* took the necessary precautions to keep his subjects at some distance from himself. His was therefore the major share of the pea-nuts.

My sympathy with the under-dog asserted itself. I began to throw my pea-nuts to a smaller monkey who was trailing far behind. His wistful and woe-begone expression revealed both his hunger and his fear. For a moment or two the leader watched this performance with growing anger. The next pea-nut provoked him to action. Two bounds, and his teeth were fixed in the posterior of his offending subject, who took this forceful hint at its proper value, and with a reproachful glance at me scampered away into the grove.

Followed by the leader and one or two female monkeys, who presumably belonged to his harem, we went into the court of the temple, a kind of roofless rectangle with low brick walls. The morning air was cool and sweet, and the shadows cast through the trees by a sun not yet high in the heavens made curious interlaced patterns of black and white on the earthen floor. The place, marvellously peaceful, engendered a deeper feeling of holiness than many a European cathedral or New York church. Even the monkey leader seemed to acquire an appropriate solemnity, for he took his place beside us and sat placidly on the low wall, while I took in the beauty of the scene. True, when the pea-nuts were finished, he made a descent from dignity, for he ambled across the courtyard and, taking to himself one of the females, gently made love to her. Perhaps the act was a natural sacrifice to Arjuno, who is the Don Juan of the Balinese gods. At any rate, when it was finished, he came back to us, waited until we had gazed our fill, and conscious perhaps of his obligations as guardian of this sacred grove, escorted us back to the path. Then, slowly and solemnly, he withdrew into the forest. In his own world he was a great king. I trust that he still reigns in Boekit Sari.

From the sacred grove we went to the neighbouring village of Bongkasa, where I saw a banyan tree whose drooping spread of branches must have covered over an acre. Like the grove and the monkeys the tree was sacred and had its little temple, for in this tolerant island the worship of mountain, wood and lake spirits still exists as a relic of the primitive animism on which Shivaism and Buddhism have long since been superimposed.

I went back to the hotel and spent a lazy afternoon with my history books. Then, towards sunset, I set out with Victor Cunard to visit Miss Waterman and Spiess. Miss Waterman was living in a house, only half an hour by car from Den Pasar, yet right in the country and shut off by trees from the outside world and overlooking a charming vista of rice-fields. It had been built for an American musician, who had been studying Balinese music for some years, and who had gone back temporarily to New York. On our way to pick up Spiess we stopped at a hollow where there was a cave-temple known as "The Elephant's Cave". Here in a natural amphitheatre half enclosed by champaka and palm-trees another djanger dance was being performed. No Europeans were present and only a few natives, and I was able to admire the beauty of the costumes without hindrance. The most striking was that of the Garuda, the sun-bird of Vishnu, and a magnificent apparition with a plumage which would have put all the costumes in M. Rostand's *Chantecler* to shame. Here, too, we picked up Limba, the Balinese dancer, who was to be our master of ceremonies for the evening.

If Miss Waterman's villa was attractive, Spiess's was enchanting. It was perched on the side of a small canyon with a mountain stream splashing merrily below. Over the stream itself was a slender bamboo bridge. For once I had found the illusory cottage of my dreams. For the first time since I had been in the Dutch East Indies I was able to rid myself of the feeling that I was surrounded by people.

We found Spiess at his piano, and at our request he gave us a short interpretation of Balinese music. It was difficult to understand but not unattractive, and the rhythm effects were amazingly varied. He stopped soon with an apology for the inadequacy of his interpretation, pointing out that seven pianos were necessary in order to score Balinese music.

By the time we reached the temple where Limba had staged the dance for us it was quite dark. We went down some steps, and then in an open court lit by coconut-oil braziers placed on the tops of long posts I saw some two hundred men seated in a circle. They were of all ages. They represented the entire male population of the neighbouring village. All were to take part in the dance. We took our places on a little wooden bench under a thatched roof. Limba gave the signal to start, and the two hundred men, naked except for a loin cloth, formed themselves into a squatting human circle full of bronzed bodies from the centre to the circumference. We were seeing the famous "kechak".

At first the men leaned forward until their heads touched their feet. Then they lay right back. The movements, made in perfect unison, were like the opening and shutting of a flower. They were repeated frequently. They were accompanied by intonations which at times swelled to an angry chorus. The story, taken from the Hindoo sagas, was a battle between a prince and a tribe of monkeys. Limba himself was the prince. At intervals he entered the circle and danced standing up—a human stamen in the centre of the mass of bronze petals. And while the circle swayed to and fro, now swiftly in passion, now slowly in a languorous ecstasy, the flickering light of the lanterns cast weird shadows on the trees, on the temple walls, and on the brown bodies.

The dance must have lasted an hour or more, but to me it seemed like a few minutes. No Western dance has ever

captivated me in the same manner or held my attention so
completely. I am a ballet enthusiast. During the last twenty-
five years I have seen every Russian dancer of note from
Pavlova and Nijinsky to Danilova and Lifar. They are already confused though pleasant figures in the shadows of
my mind. But, even if I never see the East again, that
"kechak" in the scented warmth of a Bali night will remain
distinctly with me as long as memory lasts.

During the intervals when he was not performing Limba
brought us bananas and sweet rice wine and explained the
dance to us. He spoke fluent Malay. The "kechak", he said,
ought strictly to be danced in times of sickness. Originally it
was a kind of cleansing dance, which drove away the evil
spirits of disease. Only a few years ago, when South Bali
was being swept by an epidemic, "kechaks" were danced in
the villages every night for weeks on end. On these occasions
all kinds of side-dances were introduced. The dancing reached
such a pitch of ecstasy that girls in a trance could dance all
night and show no signs of tiredness the following day. Others
could dance on fire, and their feet remained unmarked.

When the dance was over, we went back to Miss Waterman's to dinner. The food was Balinese, and included
young bamboo shoots and other exotic dishes more attractive on the menu than in the stomach. It was served by two
magnificent Balinese boys naked down to the waist.

After dinner we listened to Spiess, who talks as well as he
paints and plays. He had a genuine affection for the Balinese.
He admired their happy philosophy of life, their devotion to
dancing and music, their natural good taste, and the plasti-
city of their minds, always receptive of new ideas. But he,
too, was filled with forebodings regarding their future and
with fears of their decay from the corroding rust of tourism
and modern civilisation. Already many of the leading Balinese dancers had received extravagant offers from American
impresarios and Hollywood agents. So far they had refused,
but one day the temptation would be too strong.

2 C

I could well believe it. One had only to look at Limba, good-looking, intelligent, and an artist to his finger-tips, to realise that New York and London, who acclaimed Russian and negro dancers with the same extravagant exuberance which the over-civilised always manifest for anything exotic and new, would go into similar raptures, for one season at any rate, over the Balinese. And that would be the beginning of the end.

Spiess gave me one significant example of the effect of European civilisation. He had a Balinese friend, formerly a brilliant gamelan leader, who had been sent to Java to receive a higher education. He had become a schoolmaster, proud of the scraps of Dutch grammar he had learnt, but very lonely. He had no one to talk to now that he was an "educated" man. "But what about your gamelan orchestra?" asked Spiess. The Balinese gave a superior smile. "Oh, now I play the mandoline."

I learnt, too, that the economic development, stimulated by the Dutch, had not been wholly beneficial. Bali, once a prosperous entity, was suffering like other countries from the world economic depression. Copra was doing badly. The price of beef had fallen from twenty-six cents a kilo to six cents. Pig prices had declined on the same scale. Government wages had been reduced. The Balinese made little out of the tourist traffic. They were the magnet that attracted it. But the Dutch took the profits.

I went back to my hotel with an empty feeling in my heart. Spiess's calm, dispassionate remarks had robbed the evening of some of its previous rapture. My mind went back to the words of Babalatchi, the old Malay minister in Conrad's novel: "You are strange, you white men. You think it is only your wisdom and your virtue and your happiness that are true. You are stronger than the wild beasts, but not so wise. A black tiger knows when he is not hungry. You do not."

CHAPTER SIX

ON MY RETURN journey from Den Pasar to Boeleleng to catch
my boat back to Java I took a different route and travelled
via Kintamani by the east trunk road. Twenty miles or so
from Den Pasar the road rises steeply into mountainous and
less cultivated country. The morning sky was clear, and, as
my steamer did not leave until four o'clock, I travelled
slowly with many halts. The solitude was very pleasant.

At Koeboepenelokan, over four thousand feet above sea-
level, there is a view which in the extent of mountain scenery
that it unfolds is unrivalled in the tropics. To the right of
Goenoeng Agoeng and behind it, across the narrow straits, is
the cone-shaped peak of Lombok. Straight in front of one,
with a wide valley intervening, is a semi-circular range of
mountains with Goenoeng Batoer in the centre. Deep down
at its base the placid waters of Lake Batoer glisten in the sun.
The whole scene reminded me of the Cairngorms, and the
resemblance between Lake Batoer and Loch Avon was remarkable. There were, however, two differences. From no
point in Scotland is there such an unimpeded view of the
mountains. From no Scottish peak does there issue the sinister smoke which rises always from Goenoeng Batoer.

This peak is less than six thousand feet high, but one of its
slopes is a barren waste of sooty-coloured lava. Ten years
ago there was a village and a temple here. The villagers had
no qualms. Their faith in the temple was sublime. Twice before, in 1905 and in 1917, a previous stream of lava had
stopped just before the temple gate. The holiness of the place
became magnified in the eyes of the villagers. The evil spirit
of the volcano had been afraid to touch the god. Who once
is afraid fears three times. When, therefore, in August, 1926,
Batoer began to hurl his thunderbolts of rock and stone, the
villagers paid little heed. On this occasion their confidence
was misplaced. To-day, there is no trace of the village or the
temple, but only a black field of lava. With Bagoes I walked

395

down the slope and across the valley until we reached the lava border. The surface was like a black crust through which our feet sunk as in loose sand.

From Penelokan we drove slowly to the Dutch rest-house at Kintamani, passing on the way the new village of Batoer which has been rebuilt on the hill overlooking the valley. Kintamani itself is the highest village in Bali and stands nearly five thousand feet above sea-level.

Even in the midday sunshine the air was comparatively cool and the temperature more like that of a summer day in Scotland than tropical. In the garden of the rest-house I found European flowers growing: nasturtium, rosemary, and violets.

I went into the hotel for luncheon, and when I came out again the sky was overcast with heavy clouds. "We must hurry," said Bagoes. We did, but long before we had come down from the mountains the rain began to fall. Huge claps of thunder brought it down in torrents, and soon it began to drip through the hood of our open car. I had no coat, and the air cut like a lancet. The rain lasted until we descended to the narrow strip of low-lying coast. By the time we reached Boeleleng the sun was shining again.

Here I had an hour to wait for my steamer. I spent it talking to Bagoes who, although he had not been home for five days, insisted on seeing me off. In front of the K.P.M. office he introduced me to Ma Patimah, a well-preserved, middle-aged Balinese woman, about whom many·legends are told. The stock one is that·she is a princess and one of the widows of the Dewa Agoeng of Kloeng-Koeng who fell at the head of his household in the "poepoetan" of 1908. Ma Patimah is said to have taken part in this death charge and to have escaped. In this case fiction is more romantically strange than fact. True it is that Ma Patimah was in the household of the Dewa Agoeng but not in the role of wife. She should have been in the "poepoetan", but had gone over previously to the Dutch. Nor is she a princess, for she belongs to the soedra or lowest caste and, in addition, has been converted to Islam.

She is, nevertheless, the most remarkable woman in Bali and has justified her refusal to immolate herself on the bayonets of the Dutch by her subsequent success in life. To-day, she runs a fleet of motor-cars and does a lively trade with the tourists in the products of Balinese arts and crafts. I talked to her for a few minutes and took a photograph of her. When she saw me raise my Leica, she begged me to wait. Then, summoning four of her chauffeurs, she posed for me sitting between them. In this she showed the instinctive sense of power which has made her the only woman capitalist in Bali. She talked shrewdly and with much humour. Her high forehead would have stamped her anywhere as a woman of natural intelligence.

My farewell with Bagoes was emotional. I had taken a genuine liking for him. I judged him slightly embittered and, like Spiess's gamelan leader, another victim of over-education. He ought to have been doing something better than running round with tourists. I asked him why he did not try to obtain a post in the Government Service. He had tried, but there had been no vacancy. I expect that, like most Orientals, one effort had exhausted his energy. Learning languages, for which he had a natural aptitude, appealed to him most, and his face lit up when I told him that I would send him some English books and an English newspaper as soon as I reached England. We parted with many promises to write to each other. I sent him the books. I wrote to him twice and for the last year I have taken out a subscription for him for the *Weekly Times*. Perhaps its contents were too heavy. At any rate I have never heard from him.

My steamer was much larger than the one in which I had travelled to the islands. There was an army of tourists on board, and it was from a deck crowded with European children shrieking over deck games that I took my farewell of the "last paradise". My feelings were mixed. In a house like

Spiess's I could have been happy. Already in Boeleleng with its mongrel population of Arabs, Chinese, Javanese, Buginese and Indians that part of Bali seemed remote. Here on board the *Treub* I was back with a vengeance in European civilisation.

Subconsciously I saw myself again in New York dining at a friend's house in order to meet Mr. H. M. Warner, the head of the great film company which bears his name. The company had bought the film rights of my first book, *British Agent*, and, as I had come to New York, Messrs. Warner's literary adviser, who had put through the deal, thought it right that his chief should make my acquaintance.

I soon realised that Mr. Warner, a quiet, modest man who had been born in Manchester and been taken as a child to the States, knew nothing about *British Agent* except its name and perhaps the price that his company had paid for it. I am not sure that he even realised that I was the author. In the circumstances conversation languished.

At intervals his literary adviser whispered something to him in an obvious effort to prompt him. Then at last we found a point of contact.

"I understand you're a Scot," Mr. Warner said pleasantly. "Well, I'm going over to Europe this summer for a week. I've got to put in two days in Italy, two in France, and two in London, but I'm keeping one day for your little country. There's a place there I've got to see. But I can't remember the name."

I suggested in turn Edinburgh, Glasgow, Inverness, Perth, Loch Lomond, and even Aberdeen. He shook his head. "That don't sound like the name to me," he said. "I tell you what it is. I'm taking golf lessons from a Scottish professional and it was he who told me I had to go there."

"Carnoustie!" I said triumphantly.

"That's it," he said, and I felt that I had laid my approach nearly dead.

But no. Again there was a long silence, broken at last by

the butler coming in to call the great man to the telephone. A smile, human, tender, and full of love, lit up his whole face, giving to it the kindliest expression. "Mr. Lockhart," he said, "you'll excuse me. That's my little daughter calling up all the way from Bali."

At the time that incident struck a chord in my own heart. It had given me a new insight into the character of film magnates. It had strengthened my belief in human nature. Now, as it suddenly flashed across my mind in this crowded tourist steamer, it seemed to illustrate with a startling clearness the extent to which our so-called superior civilisation threatened Bali. It was not a cheering thought.

I must not be ungrateful to the *Treub*. It provided me with one of the most thrilling episodes in my long life as a traveller. Owing to my chance meeting with Spiess I had cut my time-table rather fine. In order to keep important appointments I had to be in Batavia the next day. The journey could be accomplished only by a combination of steamer and airplane. My steamer was not due in Soerabaja until seven a.m. The airplane to Batavia left at the same hour. It was used mainly by Dutch business men travelling between Soerabaja and Batavia. It never waited for the steamer. My only hope of making the connection depended on the steamer's beating its time schedule.

The Dutch authorities, to whose kindness and efficiency I have frequently referred with profound gratitude, had requested the captain to push the *Treub* along so that I might make the connection. He pushed to such effect that we arrived at the entrance to the harbour at five-thirty a.m. And then Fate played a cruel jest. The tide was so low that there was no hope of our tying up before seven-thirty. As the minutes passed, my heart sank. If I missed the airplane, I should lose twenty-four hours.

The captain, however, refused to take defeat lying down. He signalled to the shore, and presently a fast motor-boat came speeding out to take me off. I was rushed to the dock and bundled into a powerful car driven by a Maduranese chauffeur. It was already seven o'clock. The harbour-master told me that the air authorities had promised to hold the 'plane back for fifteen minutes. The aerodrome was ten miles distant from the dock. The normal time for the drive through the crowded city was forty-five minutes.

Then began a terrifying experience. The Maduranese are reputed for their courage. My man was not only a Maduranese. He was a madman. Stepping on the gas, he drove at breakneck speed through the streets already thronged with natives going to work. He turned corners on one wheel. He shaved other cars and cut in between carts with a coat of paint to spare between safety and perdition. He raced through a level crossing as the gates were closing. Policemen stood in his track to stop him. He bore down on them ruthlessly and grinned as they leaped aside. And all the while he blew his horn with a fierce persistence which reminded me of the last trump.

In Malay, Soerabaja means the Crocodile City. During every second of that drive I felt the saurian's teeth piercing their way into my flesh. I longed to cry out: "Stop for God's sake. I'll stay in Soerabaja all my life rather than face another mile of this death-ride."

When, after fourteen breathless minutes, my madman deposited me beside the waiting 'plane, I was a wreck.

I pushed ten guilders into his hands.

"It is too much, Tuan," he said. "That was nothing. If we had been really pressed, I could have knocked off another two minutes."

Against a strong wind we had a bumpy flight. Visibility was good, but as always from the air the scenic effect was more curious than alluring. The richly cultivated land looked like a jig-saw puzzle with strange Assyrian figures. Where the rice was ripe, the fields formed a vast chess-board on which the little huts of the watchers stood out like chessmen. The plain near Cheribon was flooded, and I saw a train

ploughing its way through the water like a toy train crossing
a miniature Tay Bridge. Apart from the mountains the clear-
est landmarks were the semi-circular white-stoned Chinese
graves. They gave no impression of a burial-place, but
looked like stones placed there purposely to guide the pilot
on his way.

We were two hours late in reaching Batavia. Nevertheless, thanks to the Dutch air and steamship officials, who
charged me not an extra cent for the trouble I had given
them, I had done the trip from Bali to Batavia in twenty-one
hours. The tourists who were making the journey by sea
would take four days.

The first person I met on entering the compound of the
Hôtel des Indes was Ahmat, my former chauffeur. I had not
expected to see him again. But he had discovered from the
reception clerk that I had booked a room, and there he was
waiting to greet me.

The heat was appalling, the worst, in fact, that Batavia
had experienced for many years. Nevertheless, my nerves
still exhilarated by my air flight, I went off with Ahmat to
pay the visit which had been the chief reason for my hurrying back to Batavia. This was to Thamrin, the Javanese
nationalist leader, to whom my socialist friend in Djokja had
given me letters.

Fortunately, I found him at home. He received me at
once. He was dressed in European clothes. Clean-shaven,
sturdily built, with Mongolian eyes and an attractive smile,
he reminded me at once of Kerensky. He had begun his life
as a shipping clerk in the Dutch line which had taken me to
Bali and the islands. Now he was living in a comfortable
villa with a car and a "boy" to wait on him.

Although he had never been out of Java, he spoke English
tolerably well. For nearly two hours we discussed the nationalist question in all its aspects. He was strongly anti-com-
munist and maintained that there was no real communism
in Java and never would be. His great theme was that the

Dutch East Indian Government should stimulate Javanese nationalism as a bulwark against the danger of Japanese encroachment. He was very cautious in his references to the Dutch. But he had no illusions about Europe, was fully conscious that the East had awakened, and prophesied that events in the Pacific would move swiftly.

As we said good-bye, he gave me a collection of his speeches in the Volksraat. They were printed both in Dutch and in Malay. They dealt with economic and political problems and revealed considerable erudition. They might have been delivered with success by any of the callow politicians who have sprung up like mushrooms in the new states of post-war Europe. Thamrin himself was the epitome of the new type of politician which to-day is emerging from the white man's system of education in the East. I guessed that, like all nationalists, he was in favour of Javanese independence, but that a natural caution had converted him to the policy of gradualness.

Unable to sleep because of the heat, I spent the evening and the best part of the night in reading a French book that I had picked up in one of the excellent book-shops of Batavia. It was called *Pacifique '39*. It predicts a war in the Pacific in 1939. In this war the Japanese fleet destroys the naval might of the United States. Britain, engaged elsewhere, makes discretion the better part of valour, remains neutral, and contents herself with India as her most valuable Eastern possession. France, who is friendly with Japan, keeps out of trouble and retains Indo-China. At the conference after the war France and Japan become the controllers of peace in the East. The Dutch and British possessions east of Singapore become independent.

The book is interesting only because its author, M. de Pouvourville, is a recognised authority on the East and because it shows to what lengths anxiety for the security of France's possessions can drive a Frenchman.

The next day I spent in arranging my passage home, in

packing my books, and in paying calls on the Dutchmen who had helped me so efficiently in my travels. To my deep re-regret one Dutchman to whom I had letters of introduction was not in Batavia. This was Dr. Callenfels, the great archae-ologist and pre-historian, whose fame extends over the world. In pursuit of his studies he has travelled the whole of the Malay Archipelago. He is much liked by the British in the Malay States. A giant in intellect and body, he weighs over twenty stone. Neither late hours nor alcohol have any effect on his massive frame and active brain, and, if patriotism demands it, he can drink any Englishman or, for that matter, any Scot under the table. The stories told of him and by him are legion. Here is one of his own, for the truth of which I can vouch.

Callenfels, like most great scholars, likes to think of him-self as the laziest man in the world. Some years ago he was told that there was a jungle tribe in Sumatra whose men were even lazier than himself. He at once organised an expedition in order to test the truth of this report.

On his way back he stopped at Singapore and went to see some English friends in our Government Service.

"I have zeen this tribe of which they talk zo much," said Callenfels. "It is true that the men are a little lazy. I saw one old gentleman being driven slowly away in a cart from the market-place. His wife walked behind, a pikulan across her shoulder, weighed down with oil, hens in baskets, rice and everyzing that they had bought in ze market. The man was lying back on cushions. He looked very comfortable, but I saw that in his right hand he carried a small cage with a dove. And zen I knew that I had nozzing to learn from zat man or from zat tribe. If I had been zere, I should have had a second wife to carry ze dove."

In the evening I dined with Miedl, my German friend, who was still in Batavia and still engaged in wrangling with the Dutch over his mining claims. The heat was stifling. For three days a low blanket of heavy cloud had hung over the town. The slightest movement made the sweat run down one's face. Even breathing was an effort. It was a salutary reminder that, even with all the modern comforts of ice and electric fans, the tropics can still reduce the strongest man to the mental and physical equivalent of a wet rag.

Sleep being out of the question, we decided to go round the town. It was a dismal night. The streets were empty, and even the rain was disagreeably tepid. The cabaret that had been recommended to us was closed. We went on to a place called Maxim's. It was open but empty except for the waiters and the orchestra of three. We went in, ordered drinks, and sent for the pianist. He was a Viennese. Both his colleagues were Austrians. All three were obviously men of education. Indeed, the pianist had taken a doctor's degree at Vienna University.

We asked him to play some old Viennese Schlager for us. To the fierce patter of the tropical rain, with the sweat dripping in beads from his brow, he hammered out "Servus Du" and "In der kleinen Amerikan Bar". I hope that he was a better doctor than he was a pianist. False notes and a piano sadly out of tune were too much for us. We paid him lavishly and went out again into the rain.

After many futile peregrinations our chauffeur pulled up outside a small villa in the "down town" area. A Javanese "boy" ushered us into a large living-room with easy chairs and a gramophone, brought a row of beer bottles, and went to fetch his mistress, a Batavian Malay past her early youth, but not without allure. She clapped her hands, and presently in came three young girls dressed in sarongs and rubbing their eyes.

The mistress opened negotiations at once. When I explained to her that we were not interested in "business", but had come for a talk and a drink and were prepared to pay for both, she was full of suspicion. Doubtless, she took us for police agents. Finally, the beer was opened, and one of the girls started up an American one-step on the gramophone.

Very solemnly two of the girls came up to us. Obviously we were expected to dance, but not even the exotic curiosity of dancing with a Malay girl could tempt me to move in that stifling atmosphere. Miedl, however, took the floor, and for a few minutes ambled round with his partner like a bear dancing with a small monkey. The sight of this German giant dancing with a slip of a girl whose head barely came up to his chest should have been funny. But there was no laughter in my heart. I felt suddenly old beyond my years. My zest for night life had been prompted by a youthful curiosity. It had been prolonged unduly by the restlessness of the post-war period. Now it seemed that it had gone for ever. Then I remembered how, a few weeks before I set out on my Eastern trip, I had gone with some Russian friends to a tiny restaurant in Paris. We had had the place to ourselves, and until the early hours of the morning I had listened to the old gipsy songs of my Russian days. There had been only one singer, an elderly woman, very dignified in her simple black dress and with the beautiful deep voice of the real gipsy. Then, to the accompaniment of the guitar, she had sung an *émigré* song which was new to me. The tune was old, but the words, although they made no direct reference to politics, had an unmistakable significance. It was an exile's song with the same appeal as the songs of the Liberal exiles in the days of Tsardom:

> "Molis, Kunak, v stranye chujoi;
> Molis, kunak, za krai rodnoi;
> Molis za tyekh kto serdtsu mil,
> Shtoby Gospod yikh sokhranil."

> "Pray, cavalier, now on a foreign strand;
> Pray, cavalier, for our dear fatherland;
> Pray now for those who in our hearts are sleeping
> That God may hold them always in His keeping."

I had been profoundly moved. I had begged the singer to repeat the three verses again and again. Now, in this tawdry

Batavian villa, I realised that age had very little to do with the emotional follies of man and that my lack of zest was due to other reasons. I was a European. Between the East and the West there was a gulf which all the international sentiment in the world would never bridge in our time.

I turned to Miedl. He nodded, and we went out into the grey mist of the pre-dawn, carrying away with us the cloying smell of patchouli and cheap scent.

When I reached my hotel, it was too late to go to bed. The air was still and stifling, and the damp heat weighed like a load of hot bricks on my head. I sat down on my verandah. On the table were two copies of the Bible: one in Dutch and the other in English. They had been placed there by the "Gideonites", an American Bible society started in the 'nineties by two commercial travellers for other commercial travellers. I was tired and angry with myself. I had arrived from Bali bronzed and well. These last two days in Batavia had been expensive and unprofitable.

I sailed the next day at noon. There was an enormous crowd on board to speed the parting Dutchmen going home on holiday or leaving the East for ever. It was with motorboats dashing across our bows and to the accompaniment of jazz and sirens and the popping of champagne corks that I took my last leave of Batavia.

CHAPTER SEVEN

DURING THE THIRTY-FOUR hours' journey from Batavia to Singapore I kept myself aloof from the other passengers. I wanted to capture all I could from these last few hours in the East. True, there would be the pleasant voyage home. I should meet my friends again. The Pembrokes were already on board. The Rosslyns I should pick up in Singapore.

There would be two days in Sumatra with an enchanting visit to the Batak country with the glorious mountain drive to Brast'agi, and beyond to the point where one looks down on the huge expanse of Lake Toba, twice as big as Lake Geneva and surrounded by mountains more imposing than the Alps. There would be thoughts of cannibals, for it is not so long ago since the Bataks abandoned the joys of human flesh, and at Toba itself there is an old Batak chief still living who has eaten his missionary "long pork". His son is now studying at Leyden University, and what he learns will probably be more dangerous to the Dutch than his father's teeth have ever been. There would be entertaining and instructive conversations with the brilliant van Karnebeek, the former Dutch Foreign Minister, to whom I am indebted for so much valuable information about the Dutch. But, as far as I was concerned, Singapore would be the end of my journey.

It was sunset of the next day before we reached the entrance to the harbour. On this occasion I was approaching the port from a new angle, and the groups of islands which studded the sea filled me with delight. I was glad that they had not yet been turned into golf-courses and oil-stations.

It was too late for our steamer to berth at the dock, and Freddie came aboard in a launch to take me off to spend my last night on Malayan soil. We went to Raffles to find it crowded with men and women in evening dress. At a table I saw the Sultan of Johore. To-morrow his white sultana would join us on the boat as a passenger to England. But for the Chinese "boys" the scene might be duplicated on any Saturday night at one of the big hotels of an English south coast resort.

Avoiding the dancing-hall and the dining-room Freddie and I went out into the garden and dined alone. We sat long, discussing the future.

Freddie took a packet from his pocket and untied it carefully. It contained the photographs he had taken of my Pantai visit. There was a marvellous picture of the survivors of my old football team, seated in chairs like Cup Final winners. As I was not coming back, they wanted a written message. I scribbled a few words in Malay on a copy for each.

There was also a picture of Amai standing by the golden rice before a background of jungle and mountains. It made her look younger. My memory jumped across the years, and I saw her again, dressed in all her finery and setting off in a gharry for Seremban to have her first photograph taken by the local Japanese photographer. The photograph had been successful, and I remembered her childish delight when it arrived. She was a young girl then, fearless, lissom, and beautiful even according to European standards. My copy of that photograph had perished with the rest of my belongings in the Bolshevik revolution.

Amai, too, wanted a message. But I handed back the fountain-pen to Freddie. He shook his head.

"You must write something," he said. "Her pride will be hurt if you don't, and in any case you'll let her down with her friends."

Pride is the undying flame that continues to burn long after love and passion are dead. I took the pen again and wrote out an old Malay pantun that I had learnt from her, years before, when she took the place of my Malay teacher:

"Permata jatoh di-dalam rumput,
Jatoh di-rumput bĕrgilang-gilang;

Kaseh umpama ĕmbun di-ujong rumput,
Datang mata-hari nĕschaya hilang."

.　.　.　.　.

"A pearl may fall within the grass,
But still undimmed will shine its ray;
Love is like the dew, alas!
With sunrise both soon fade away."

.　.　.　.　.

From Amai we turned to the future. During these last
few days I had begun to crystallise the impressions I had
formed during my trip. I wanted to try them out on Freddie
before I went home.

The changes since my time had been immense. In the
Dutch East Indies and even in Malaya I had found most
thinking Europeans obsessed with the danger of Japan.
Their fears were inspired, partly, by the commercial successes of the Japanese exporters and, partly, by the military
might of the Japanese nation. There was the incontrovertible
fact that Japan is to-day the most powerful nation in Asia,
and that her word, and not the word of the League of
Nations or any other combination of powers, is law to half
the world.

As for Japanese trade, Japan had more than doubled her
population during my lifetime. She had to import increasingly, and to pay for her imports she had to export increasingly. To express surprise and indignation at the growth of
Japan's export trade was merely to shut one's eyes to the
acutest population problem of our times. If Japanese goods
were to be shut out, Japan must either starve or fight. For
climatic reasons she would probably find her main outlet
elsewhere than in the Malay Archipelago.

Karnebeek, the former Dutch Foreign Minister and my
fellow-passenger, was strong on this point. He had represented his country at the Washington conference after the
Great War, when the four Powers, Britain, France, the

2 D

United States and Japan, had signed a declaration to respect each other's colonial possessions. The Netherlands had not been included in this declaration, and Karnebeek had gone in a state of perturbation to the Japanese delegate to see if he could obtain a special declaration for the Dutch East Indies. The Japanese delegate had acquiesced at once. "Why not?" he said. "We would rather that you were there than anyone else."

Then, too, there was America. It was the habit of the British to speak lightly of the Americans as colonial administrators. They lacked experience. As a race they were not distinguished for their knowledge of foreign languages or of foreign peoples. But during my tour nearly every responsible British and Dutch official that I met went out of his way to praise the American administration in the Philippines.

It had done a wonderful work in promoting health services, education and general welfare—a work so beneficial that now that the High Commissioner was being withdrawn the Filipinos themselves had formed an association whose sole object was to plead for the maintenance of American protection. There was no American who knew the East who believed that this withdrawal was inspired by altruistic motives. It was dictated by American big business interests, which wanted to exclude the Philippines sugar from the benefit of free entry into the United States. There was no Englishman or Dutchman in the East who thought for one moment that the withdrawal would ever be put into full effect or that in the face of an outside threat the United States would withhold its protection.

It would be foolish to ignore the Japanese problem, but to my mind the real danger to colonial empires in the East would come in the long run from the inside. I had been astounded by the vast strides in education made since my time by the various native races under European rule. It seemed to me that Europeans in the East were too inclined to regard the supremacy of the European races as something inviolate and eternal. Yet viewed through the telescope of life on this planet that supremacy was of comparatively recent origin. The Europeans of to-day possessed the inventive genius of the world, but some of their discoveries were only re-discoveries. Even the lipstick which had now conquered Singapore dated back to the early Egyptians. Empires were like flowers, trees, animals, human beings and everything else that had life. They had their birth, their childhood, their youth, their manhood, their middle age, their decline, and then their death.

How long could Europe keep these Asiatic races, now fertile with new ideas and new ambitions, under subjection? Estimates differed about the length of time. I had heard one high official at home, a man who knew the East as few men know it, asked if he were in favour of giving Germany her colonies. "I don't think it matters", he had said. "Self-determination is moving so fast that in twenty-five years time it will make no difference who owns colonies". Even if the final period of withdrawal were represented by X, there was obviously a limit.

Most experts, including many British, held the view that the French would go from Asia first, the British second, and the Dutch last. I could not speak of the French. But my own firm impression was that, as far as the Malay Archipelago was concerned, the Dutch were in a weaker position than the British if only because of their efficiency. Their colonial empire had reached a very high degree of development. It contained a far higher percentage of educated natives than did British Malaya, and education was the threshold to nationalism. It had a population more than fifteen times as large, and, although it comprised many races, these races had a common Malay origin and, in the main, a common religious faith in Islam. And that same population furnished the coolie class. There was, too, the complicated half-caste problem. To-day, there were fewer Dutchmen who boasted that they had no colour prejudice.

With a Malay population and a Chinese population almost equal in size, the British in Malaya were in a stronger
position. There were no Malay coolies. The Malay had been
well cared for, perhaps too well for his chances of survival.
Nationalism had barely reached the embryo stage. And there
was no half-caste problem. In spite of the intellectual globe-
trotters who travelled through in two days and wrote cheap
sneers about the old school tie spirit and the snobbishness of
the British, the absence of half-castes was not in itself a
proof of colour prejudice. In this respect, as places like the
New World showed, there had been a transformation since
my days, and my most vivid impression of Malaya is the
picture of a whole hotch-potch of oriental races, living
happily together and working side by side, under British
protection. The British were neither better nor worse than
other Europeans in the East, but, as a high official put it
bluntly, they did not believe in breeding bastards, and the
fact remained that to-day the number of children of white
men and native women in the peninsula is insignificant.

But there was no reason why either the British or the
Dutch should be ousted quickly. In this part of the world
the *Pax Britannica* and the *Pax Batavica* still meant order instead of chaos, health instead of sickness, and even in bad
times comparative plenty instead of starvation. And whatever the sins of colonial exploitation might have been in the
past, to-day there was honest administration and a genuine
regard for native interests.

The Dutch Civil Service had impressed me by its efficiency.
If the British Civil Service showed some falling away from its
former high standard, it still had picked men of outstanding
ability. And their task was comparably more difficult than
that of their predecessors.

The weaknesses of the British Service in Malaya leapt
readily to the eye. They were those which are common to
all services restricted to one small area: parochialism of outlook and an inevitable staleness. To eradicate these defects I

should make the British Colonial Service interchangeable or
partly interchangeable, with the British Consular Service in
Siam and in the Dutch East Indies. I should certainly see to
it that some of the picked men in Malaya could acquire a
first-hand knowledge of those two neighbouring countries.

The experience would be invaluable to high officials and
to future governors. But Whitehall would raise its hands in
pious horror at the mere suggestion. There would be opposition from both the Foreign Office and the Colonial Office,
and the Treasury would put forward a frigid and well-
reasoned objection.

A Treasury, however, should be the handmaid and not
the master of a great Empire. Yet since the war the British
Treasury had acquired a dominating position, and had
assumed for its chief the new and dangerous title of Head of
the Civil Service. Policy at home had no definite objectives
and was complicated by contradictory aims of uninspired
opportunism. The administrative machine was too big.

Rome had given to the world the greatest free trade empire and the longest period of peace that it has ever known.
But in the end the efficiency of the Roman colonial administration had been destroyed by the over-centralisation and
over-bureaucratisation of the civil service at headquarters.
The same fate now threatened the British colonial administration in the East. Already this centralisation was expressing
itself in a certain lack of initiative on the part of the colonial
servant abroad. I remembered the bitter words of Sir Frank
Swettenham, as I sat with him in his London flat shortly
before my voyage: "A masterly inactivity is to-day a better
road to a successful official career than all the enterprise,
resolution and drive in the world." Inertia was the first sign
of that moral decadence which always precedes zoological
extinction.

One thing seemed to me clear. It was useless to blame the
Civil Servants for their education policy. However good or
bad it might be, the real educationalist in the East was the

international trader. Here in Singapore, in Batavia, in every port of the Archipelago, were representatives of every nation trying to sell films, silk stockings, lipstick, gramophones, bicycles and even cars to the natives and trying to educate them up to their use. It might be dangerous to go too fast. But there could be no putting the clock back. There were only two ways to treat native subject races: to hold them back by restricting medical and education services, or to admit them gradually, according to their development, to a greater share in the administration of their own affairs. It was too late for the first method. The secret of successful colonial government lay in choosing the right men and in allowing them a free hand to maintain a proper balance between concessions and the necessities of ordered progress.

Freddie listened to me very patiently. He made a good point. The changes to-day were so rapid that the most dangerous advisers at home were the men who had spent their lives in the East and who had retired twenty years ago.

It was midnight when I went to bed, in one of the old high bedrooms where I had spent my first night in Singapore twenty-eight years ago. For some time I looked out of my balcony window across the harbour. The lights of a hundred ships lit up the water like street lamps on a wet night. But there was no sound. The Lion city was asleep. Symbolic of the storms which perhaps lay ahead, great clouds raced across the sky.

In spite of a wonderful battery of electric fans I slept fitfully.

The next morning I rose at dawn and packed my suitcase. The hotel still slumbered. A tired Indian clerk at the reception office handed me my receipted bill, and I went out into the city. The European quarter was almost deserted. I drove out to the Botanical Gardens and to Sepoy Lines. The trees and plants in the gardens were heavy with scented dew. I passed a few early riders. On the Sepoy Lines golf-course an officer in shorts was practising mashie shots with a couple of Malay "caddies".

I turned back into the native quarter. In North Bridge Road all was already bustle. Malay and Sikh policemen directed the traffic almost automatically with outstretched arms lengthened by a white flail. Tamils, Bengalis, Arabs, Malays and Chinese jostled each other in the streets. Scores of Government clerks, among them several Chinese girls, were cycling to their offices. Unlike Shanghai, Singapore has not yet its women police, but when they come they will cause no surprise. Chinese rickisha pullers, mostly old men, stood at their stand waiting for jobs, their red-lacquered vehicles glistening in the sun.

I went into a Japanese store to buy some films for my Leica camera. A young Japanese, speaking better English than any Japanese diplomat that I have heard, tried earnestly to make me buy various Leica accessories at a price thirty per cent. cheaper than I could buy them in England. For a moment I was tempted. Never again should I be able to buy anything so cheap. But sterner resolutions prevailed. For the last two years I have tried to impress on my son that the secret of modern life is to be mobile, to rid one's self of all but essential possessions. These camera accessories were so much junk which I should never look at again. I should never be a camera fiend. After Singapore my Leica, a present from a friend, would be a present again.

Forlorn in a city where once I had been without a care in the world, I made my way to the docks. It was nine o'clock when I went on board. We were not due to sail until ten, but Freddie had promised to meet me. I was almost relieved not to find him. These Singapore steamer farewells mean early morning drinks, and I was in no mood for alcohol.

Just as we were leaving, Freddie appeared on the quay to wave me goodbye. A great sadness filled me. The last time I had left Singapore, I had sailed East. The direction seemed symbolic of youth and of adventure. Now I was returning West, to the long hours of the hardest and most precarious routine job in the world. There would be no more roaming.

I hated the huge liner, in which one was on the sea and yet remote from it. I dreaded the common-place remarks of the passengers and even the sympathetic comments of my friends. One can feel more lonely in the Waldorf-Astoria in New York or in a flat in London than in the Sahara. But there is no place in the world where solitude is at a higher premium or where acquaintanceship is more difficult to avoid than on an ocean liner. And in these last few hours of farewell the desire to be alone was overwhelming in its physical pain.

The conversation I had had with Freddie on the previous evening went round and round in my head. I thought of Byron and his passion for the rather unattractive modern Greeks. My own sentimental attachment to the Malays was strong. Almost I could understand a European taking up their cause, especially in Java where the lot of the Javanese was worse than that of the Malays of the Peninsula.

A European had opened the gates of Spain to the Moors. A European deserter had supplied Sultan Mohammed with the engine of artillery which facilitated his capture of Constantinople. Among the Dutch and, doubtless, even among the British there were men and women who for their socialist ideals and in their detestation of Imperialism might one day play a similar role in the East. But that way I could not go. I was no die-hard, but, after all, there was such a thing as a dividing line between sedition and a natural sympathy with freedom. I could see the illogicality of the European position. Nationalism was a virtue in Britain, in France, in Germany, in Italy, in all the homes of the colonial powers. But it was a vice in India, in Malaya, and in the Dutch East Indies. Moscow was the great supporter of national independence in the East. Yet nationalism was a virtue in Moscow and a vice in Turkestan and the other Central Asiatic possessions of Soviet Russia. And in spite of all the chatter about Federated Socialist Republics the fact remained that, in order to suppress native nationalism, Moscow kept more troops and more police agents in Central Asia than did the British and the Dutch together in the Malay Archipelago.

It was easy to attack Imperialism. But what did the Geneva idealists, the socialists, the foreign journalists who came, saw, and formed their judgment in the space of a few days, propose to put in its place? There was no answer. If we went out prematurely, some other Power would step in and take our place. Common sense and the benefit of all the races concerned dictated that our rule should continue until such time as we could withdraw, leaving behind us some assurance of ordered government and permanent stability. The period might be shorter than the three hundred years prophesied by the Dutch governor-general, but it was not yet within the range of profitable calculation.

One doubt obsessed my mind: the effect on the East of the spectacle of a Europe apparently intent on self-destruction. The last war had done more to undermine the prestige of the white man in the East than a hundred years of education. Another European war within the next few years would probably mean the end not only of Europe's possessions in the East, but also of the benefits of her ordered rule to millions of people.

There was not very much that was wrong with the British in the East. If trouble came, they would do their duty like the "lost legion" in the days of Rome's decline. But civilisation destroyed itself from within. The future of our Eastern Empire would be decided not in India, not in Malaya, nor in Hong Kong or in Ceylon, but by the will-power and survival fitness of the British at home. When I thought of our huge urban population and of the rows and rows of uniform dreary houses now spreading their ugliness across the face of the English countryside, I remembered Lord Beaverbrook's favourite Biblical quotation: "Where there is no vision, the people perish."

The history of the Pacific was opening at a new chapter. It began with astronomical figures: 400,000,000 Chinese, 300,000,000 Indians, and 100,000,000 various Malay races of the Malay Archipelago, awake, rapidly assimilating the white man's education, and stimulated in their nationalist aspirations by the example of Japan. How petty the wrangles of Europe seemed in the face of this immense problem.

After luncheon I went down to my cabin to write up my diaries. It was after five o'clock when I came on deck again. We were close to the shore. Tommy Rosslyn had told the captain of our steamer that I wished to see the last of Port Dickson, and with the usual Dutch courtesy towards British passengers he had promised to take us in as near as he dared. Away to the left was Cape Rachado, its white lighthouse standing out like a Rhenish castle on a wooded cliff. It was the beginning of that haunting stretch of semi-circular coast which ends with Pulau Arang and the harbour of Port Dickson itself. We were going to pass it closer than any liner that I had ever watched in my youth from my old bungalow at the third mile. The sea was like a sheet of unruffled ice. The evening sky was clear but for a few threads of cloud which caught the rays of the sun and turned them into fire.

In my mind I had planned this farewell, even to the hour of sunset. And now, as though by a miracle, it had come true. As we drew still closer in, I could distinguish all the old landmarks: the dark outline of coast with a faint streak of white where the sea met the sandy beach, Freddie's bungalow, and the little islands near Magnolia Bay. Behind, lit by the sunlight, were the purple hills of Negri Sembilan, turning slowly to mauve and then grey until they were blotted out in the descending gloom. The last light came from a small white cloud above the mountains, its reflection shining like a searchlight on the white sail of a tiny Malay "prahu" making for home. Somewhere beneath that cloud was Amai whom

I was now leaving again. Twenty-eight years ago I thought
this strip of coast the fairest sight that Nature has to offer to
the eyes of men. I think the same to-day.

Passionately I desired to prolong the scene, but the great
motor-ship moved silently and relentlessly on her course.

As we passed the point at Port Dickson, only a few lights
twinkled from the shore.

INDEX

PRINTED IN GREAT BRITAIN
BY ROBERT MACLEHOSE AND CO. LTD.
THE UNIVERSITY PRESS, GLASGOW

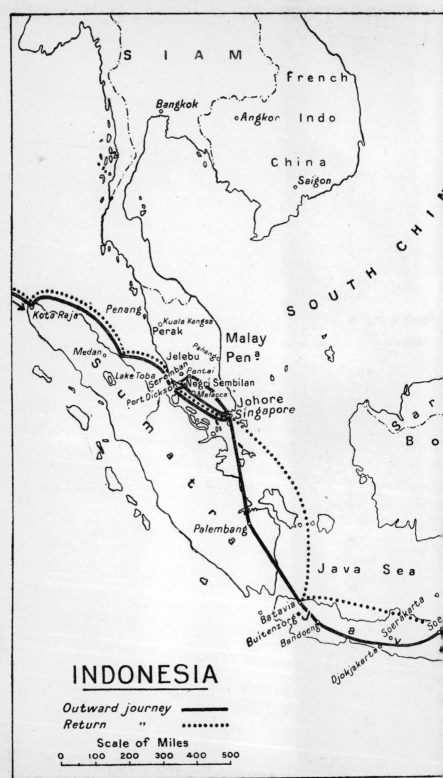

S I A M

French

Bangkok

o *Angkor* Indo

C h i n a

o *Saigon*

S O U T H   C H I

• • • • • •
Kota Raja

Penang

o *Kuala Kangsa*

Perak

Medan o

Pahang

Malay

Pen^a

Jelebu

Lake Toba

Seremban *Pantai*

Port Dickson *Negri Sembilan*

o *Malacca*

Johore

Singapore

ar

Bo

S

U

M

A

T

R

A

Palembang

Java Sea

Batavia

Buitenzorg *Bandoeng* a *Soerakarta* *Soe*

Djokjakarta

INDONESIA

Outward journey ──────

Return   "   • • • • • •

Scale of Miles

0   100   200   300   400   500

Sifton, Praed & Co. Ltd., St. James's St., London, S.W.I.